Programming Windows Presentation Foundation

Chris Sells and Ian Griffiths

Beijing · Cambridge · Farnham · Köln · Paris · Sebastopol · Taipei · Tokyo

Programming Windows Presentation Foundation
by Chris Sells and Ian Griffiths

Copyright © 2005 O'Reilly Media, Inc. All rights reserved.
Printed in the United States of America.

Published by O'Reilly Media, Inc., 1005 Gravenstein Highway North, Sebastopol, CA 95472.

O'Reilly books may be purchased for educational, business, or sales promotional use. Online editions are also available for most titles (*safari.oreilly.com*). For more information, contact our corporate/institutional sales department: (800) 998-9938 or *corporate@oreilly.com*.

Editor:	John Osborn
Development Editor:	Michael Weinhardt
Production Editor:	Sanders Kleinfeld
Cover Designer:	Ellie Volckhausen
Interior Designer:	David Futato

Printing History:

September 2005:	First Edition.

Nutshell Handbook, the Nutshell Handbook logo, and the O'Reilly logo are registered trademarks of O'Reilly Media, Inc. *Programming Windows Presentation Foundation*, the image of a kudu, and related trade dress are trademarks of O'Reilly Media, Inc.

Microsoft, the .NET logo, Visual Basic .NET, Visual Studio .NET, ADO.NET, Windows, and Windows 2000 are registered trademarks of Microsoft Corporation.

Many of the designations used by manufacturers and sellers to distinguish their products are claimed as trademarks. Where those designations appear in this book, and O'Reilly Media, Inc. was aware of a trademark claim, the designations have been printed in caps or initial caps.

While every precaution has been taken in the preparation of this book, the publisher and authors assume no responsibility for errors or omissions, or for damages resulting from the use of the information contained herein.

 This book uses RepKover,™ a durable and flexible lay-flat binding.

ISBN: 0-596-10113-9
[C]

Table of Contents

Preface

It's been a long road to Windows Presentation Foundation, better known to many as *Avalon*, the in-house Microsoft code name for the new Windows Vista presentation framework.

I learned to program Windows from *Programming Windows 3.1* by Charles Petzold (Microsoft Press). In those days, programming for Windows was about windows, menus, dialogs and child controls. To make it all work, we had WndProcs (windows procedure functions) and messages. We dealt with the keyboard and the mouse. If we got fancy, we would do some nonclient work. Oh, and there was the stuff in the big blank space in the middle that I could fill however I wanted with the graphics device interface (GDI), but my 2-D geometry had better be strong to get it to look right, let alone perform adequately.

Later, I moved to MFC (the Microsoft Foundation Classes), where we had this thing called a "document" which was separate from the "view." The document could be any old data I wanted it to be, and the view, well, the view was the big blank space in the middle that I could fill however I wanted with the MFC wrappers around GDI.

Later still, there was this thing called DirectX, which was finally about providing tools for filling in the space with hardware-accelerated 3-D polygons, but DirectX was built for writing full-screen games, so building content visualization and management applications just made my head hurt.

Windows Forms, on the other hand, was such a huge productivity boost and I loved it so much that I wrote a book about it (as did my co-author). Windows Forms was built on top of .NET, a managed environment that took a lot of programming minutiae off my hands so that I could concentrate on the content. Plus, Windows Forms itself gave me all kinds of great tools for laying out my windows, menus, dialogs and child controls. And the inside of the windows where I showed my content? Well, if the controls weren't already there to do what I wanted, I could draw the content however I wanted using the GDI+ wrappers in System.Drawing, which was essentially the same drawing model Windows programmers had been using for the last 20 years, before even hardware graphics acceleration in 2-D, let alone 3-D.

In the meantime, a whole other way of interacting with content came along: HTML was great at letting me arrange my content, both text and graphics, and it would flow it and reflow it according to the preferences of the user. Further, with the recent emergence of AJAX (Asynchronous Java And XML), this environment got even more capable. Still, HTML isn't great if you want to control more of the user experience than just the content or if you want to do anything Windows-specific—both things that even Windows 3.1 programmers took for granted.

More recently, Windows Presentation Foundation (WPF) happened. Initially it felt like another way to create my windows, menus, dialogs and child controls. However, WPF shares a much deeper love for content than has yet been provided by any other Windows programming framework.

To support content at the lowest levels, WPF merges controls and graphics into one programming model; both are placed into the same element tree in the same way. And while these primitives are built on top of DirectX to leverage the 3-D hardware acceleration that's dormant when you're not running the latest twitch game, they're also built in .NET, providing the same productivity boost to WPF programmers that Windows Forms programmers enjoy.

One level up, WPF provides its "content model," which allows any control to host any group of other controls. You don't have to build special `BitmapButton` or `IconComboBox` classes; you put as many images, shapes, videos, 3-D models or whatever into a `Button` or a `ComboBox` as suit your fancy.

To arrange the content, whether in fixed or flow layout, WPF provides container elements that implement various layout algorithms in a way that is completely independent of the content they're holding.

To visualize the content, WPF provides data binding, styles and animation. Data binding produces and synchronizes visual elements on the fly based on your content. Styles allows you to replace the complete look of a control while maintaining its behavior. Animation brings your application to life, giving your users immediate feedback as they interact with it. These features give you the power to produce data visualizations so far beyond the capabilities of the data grid, the pinnacle most applications aspire to, that even Edward Tufte would be proud.

Combine these features with ClickOnce for the deployment and update of your WPF applications, both as standalone clients and as applications blended with your web site inside the browser, and you've got the foundation of the next generation of Windows applications.

The next generation of applications is going to blaze a trail into the unknown. WPF represents the best of the control-based Windows and content-based web worlds, combined with the performance of DirectX and the deployment capabilities of

ClickOnce, building for us a vehicle just itching to be taken for a spin. And, like the introduction of fonts to the PC, which produced "ransom note" office memos, and the invention of HTML, which produced blinking online brochures, WPF is going to produce its own accidents along the road. Before we learn just what we've got in WPF, we're going to see a lot of strange and wonderful sights. I can't tell you where we're going to end up, but, with this book, I hope to fill your luggage rack so that you can make the journey.

Who This Book Is For

As much as I love the designers of the world, who are going to go gaga over WPF, this book is aimed squarely at my people: developers. We're not teaching programming here, so experience with some programming environment is a must before reading this book. Programming in .NET and C# are pretty much required; Windows Forms, XML and HTML are all recommended.

How This Book Is Organized

Here's what each chapter of this book will cover:

Chapter 1, *Hello, WPF*
> This chapter introduces the basics of WPF. It then provides a whirlwind tour of all the features that will be covered in the following chapters, so you can see how everything fits together before we delve into the details.

Chapter 2, *Layout*
> WPF provides a powerful set of tools for managing the visual layout of your applications. This chapter shows how to use this toolkit, and how to extend it.

Chapter 3, *Controls*
> Controls are the building blocks of a user interface. This chapter describes the controls built into the WPF framework and shows how to make your application respond when the user interacts with controls.

Chapter 4, *Data Binding*
> All applications need to present information to the user. This chapter shows how to use WPF's data-binding features to connect the user interface to your underlying data.

Chapter 5, *Styles and Control Templates*
> WPF provides an astonishing level of flexibility in how you can customize the appearance of your user interface and the controls it contains. Chapter 5 examines the customization facilities and shows how the styling and template mechanisms allow you to wield this power without compromising the consistency of your application's appearance.

Chapter 6, *Resources*

This chapter describes WPF's resource-handling mechanisms, which are used for managing styles, themes, and binary resources such as graphics.

Chapter 7, *Graphics*

WPF offers a powerful set of drawing primitives. It also offers an object model for manipulating drawings once you have created them.

Chapter 8, *Animation*

This chapter describes WPF's animation facilities, which allow most visible aspects of a user interface—such as size, shape, color, and position—to be animated.

Chapter 9, *Custom Controls*

This chapter shows how to write custom controls and other custom element types. It shows how to take full advantage of the WPF framework to build controls as powerful and flexible as the built-in controls.

Chapter 10, *ClickOnce Deployment*

ClickOnce allows applications to take full advantage of WPF's rich visual and interactive functionality while enjoying the benefits of web deployment.

Appendix A, *XAML*

The eXtensible Application Markup Language, XAML, is an XML-based language that can be used to represent the structure of n WPF user interface. This appendix describes how XAML is used to create trees of objects.

Appendix B, *Interoperability*

WPF is able to coexist with old user-interface technologies, enabling developers to take advantage of WPF without rewriting their existing applications. This appendix describes the interoperability features that make this possible.

Appendix C, *Asynchronous and Multithreaded Programming in WPF Applications*

Multithreaded code and asynchronous programming are important techniques for making sure your application remains responsive to user input at all times. This appendix explains WPF's threading model and shows how to make sure your threads coexist peacefully with a WPF UI.

That's not to say that we've covered everything there is to know about WPF in this book. As of this writing, WPF is still pre-beta, so not everything is working as well as we'd like, some things are just plain missing, and still other things would require entire other books to get their just due. In this book, you will find little or no coverage of the following topics, among others: printing, "Metro," 3-D, video, UI automation, binding to relational data, and "eDocs."

What You Need to Use This Book

This book was produced with WinFX Beta 1, which includes WPF and WCF, and Visual Studio 2005 Beta 2. WPF is supported on Windows XP, Windows Server 2003, and, eventually, Longhorn.

By the time you read these words, Microsoft will have moved beyond these versions and provided new community technology previews of one or more of both of these technologies. However, I can say with certainty that the vast majority of the ideas and implementation details will be the same. For those that aren't, you should look at this book's web site for errata information, which we'll try to keep updated at major releases of WPF, right up until we release a new edition of this book at the release of WPF 1.0.

Conventions Used in This Book

The following typographical conventions are used in this book:

Italic
> Indicates new terms and filenames.

`Constant width`
> Indicates code, commands, options, switches, variables, attributes, keys, functions, types, classes, namespaces, methods, modules, properties, parameters, values, objects, events, event handlers, XML tags, HTML tags, macros, the contents of files, and the output from commands.

`Constant width bold`
> Shows code or other text that should be noted by the reader.

`Constant width elipses (...)`
> Shows code or other text not relevant to the current discussion.

> This icon indicates a tip, suggestion, or general note.

> This icon indicates a warning or caution.

Using Code Examples

This book is here to help you get your job done. In general, you may use the code in this book in your programs and documentation. You do not need to contact us for permission unless you're reproducing a significant portion of the code. For example, writing a program that uses several chunks of code from this book does not require permission. Selling or distributing a CD-ROM of examples from O'Reilly books *does* require permission. Answering a question by citing this book and quoting example code does not require permission. Incorporating a significant amount of example code from this book into your product's documentation *does* require permission.

We appreciate, but do not require, attribution. An attribution usually includes the title, author, publisher, and ISBN. For example: "*Programming Windows Presentation Foundation*, by Chris Sells and Ian Griffiths. Copyright 2005 O'Reilly Media, Inc., 0-596-10113-9."

If you feel your use of code examples falls outside fair use or the permission given above, feel free to contact us at *permissions@oreilly.com*.

Safari® Enabled

 When you see a Safari® Enabled icon on the cover of your favorite technology book, it means the book is available online through the O'Reilly Network Safari Bookshelf.

Safari offers a solution that's better than e-books. It's a virtual library that lets you easily search thousands of top technology books, cut and paste code samples, download chapters, and find quick answers when you need the most accurate, current information. Try it for free at *http://safari.oreilly.com*.

How to Contact Us

For the code samples associated with this book and errata—especially as WPF changes between the Beta 1 against which this book was written and major milestones before the release of WPF 1.0—visit the web site maintained by the authors at *http://www.sellsbrothers.com/writing/avbook*.

O'Reilly also maintains a web page for this book, where we list errata, examples, and any additional information. You can access this page at:

>   *http://www.oreilly.com/catalog/avalon*

To comment or ask technical questions about this book, send email to:

>   *bookquestions@oreilly.com*

For more information about our books, conferences, Resource Centers, and the O'Reilly Network, see our web site at:

http://www.oreilly.com

Ian Griffiths:

http://www.interact-sw.co.uk/iangblog/

Chris Sells:

http://sellsbrothers.com

Ian's Acknowledgments

Writing this book wouldn't have been possible without the support and feedback generously provided by a great many people. I would like to thank the following:

The readers, without whom this book would have a rather sad, lonely, and pointless existence.

My coauthor, Chris Sells, both for getting me involved in writing about WPF in the first place, and for his superb feedback and assistance.

Tim Sneath, both for his feedback and for providing me with the opportunity to meet and work with many members of the WPF team.

Microsoft employees and contractors, for producing a technology I like so much that I just had to write a book about it. And in particular, thank you to those people at Microsoft who gave their time to answer my questions or review draft chapters, including Chris Anderson, Marjan Badiei, Jeff Bogdan, Mark Boulter, Ben Carter, Dennis Cheng, Karen Corby, Beatriz de Oliveira Costa, Vivek Dalvi, Nathan Dunlap Ifeanyi Echeruo, Pablo Fernicola, Filipe Fortes, Aaron Goldfeder, John Gossman, Mark Grinols, Namita Gupta, Henry Hahn, Robert Ingebretson, Kurt Jacob, Karsten Januszewski, David Jenni, Michael Kallay, Amir Khella, Nick Kramer, Lauren Lavoie, Daniel Lehenbauer, Kevin Moore, Elizabeth Nelson, Seema Ramchandani, Rob Relyea, Chris Sano, Eli Schleifer, Adam Smith, Eric Stollnitz, Zhanbo Sun, David Teitlebaum, Stephen Turner, and Dawn Wood.

John Osborn and Caitrin McCullough at O'Reilly for their support throughout the writing process.

The technical review team: Matthew Adams, Craig Andera, Ryan Dawson, Glyn Griffiths, Adam Kinney, Drew Marsh, Dave Minter, and Brian Noyes. And particular thanks to Mike Weinhardt for his extensive and thoughtful feedback.

Finally, I especially want to thank Abi Sawyer for all her support, and for putting up with me while I wrote this book—thank you!

Chris's Acknowledgments

I'd like to thank the following people, without whom I wouldn't have been able to write this book:

First and foremost, the readers. When you've got something to say, you've got to have someone to say it to. I've been writing about WPF in various forums for more than 18 months, and you guys have always pushed and encouraged me further.

My coauthor, Ian Griffiths. Ian's extensive background in all things graphical and video-related, including technologies so deep I can't understand him half the time, plus his wonderful writing style, made him the perfect co-author on this book. I couldn't have asked for better.

Microsoft employees and contractors (in order that I found them in my WPF email folder): Lauren Lavoie, Lars Bergstrom, Amir Khella, Kevin Kennedy, David Jenni, Elizabeth Nelson, Beatriz de Oliveira Costa, Nick Kramer, Allen Wagner, Chris Sano, Tim Sneath, Steve White, Matthew Adams, Eli Schleifer, Karsten Januszewski, Rob Relyea, Mark Boulter, Namita Gupta, John Gossman, Kiran Kumar, Filipe Fortes, Guy Smith, Zhanbo Sun, Ben Carter, Joe Marini, Dwayne Need, Brad Abrams, Feng Yuan, Dawn Wood, Vivek Dalvi, Jeff Bogdan, Steve Makofsky, Kenny Lim, Dmitry Titov, Joe Laughlin, Arik Cohen, Eric Stollnitz, Pablo Fernicola, Henry Hahn, Jamie Cool, Sameer Bhangar, and Brent Rector. I regularly spammed a wide range of my Microsoft brethren, and instead of snubbing me, they answered my email questions, helped me make things work, gave me feedback on the chapters, sent me additional information without an explicit request, and, in the case of John Gossman, forwarded the chapters along to folks with special knowledge so that they could give me feedback. This is the first book I've written "inside," and with the wealth of information and conscientious people available, it'd be very, very hard to go back to writing "outside."

The external reviewers, who provide an extremely important mainstream point of view that Microsoft insiders can't: Craig Andera, Ryan Dawson, Glyn Griffiths (Ian's dad was an excellent reviewer!), Adam Kinney, Drew Marsh, Dave Minter and Brian Noyes.

Christine Morin for her work on the shared source Windows Forms version of solitaire and James Kovacs for his work extracting a UI independent engine from it so that I could build WPF Solitaire on top of it; this is the app that opened my eyes to the wonder and power of WPF. Also, to Peter Stern and Chris Mowrer who produced the faces and backs of the WPF Solitaire cards long before the technology was ready to support such a thing.

Caitrin McCullough and John Osborn from O'Reilly for supporting me in breaking a bunch of the normal ORA procedures and guidelines to publish the book I wanted to write.

Shawn Morrissey for letting me make writing a part of my first two years at Microsoft and even giving me permission to use some of that material to seed this book. Shawn put up with me, trusting me to do my job remotely when very few Microsoft managers would. Also, Sara Williams for hiring me from my home in Oregon in spite of the overwhelming pressure to move all new employees to Washington.

Don Box for setting my initial writing quality bar and hitting me squarely between the eyes until I could clear it. Of course, thank you for the cover quote and for acting as my soundboard on this preface. You're an invaluable resource and dear friend.

Barbara Box for putting me up in the Chez Box clubhouse while I balance work and family in a way that wouldn't be possible without you.

Tim Ewald for that critical eye at the most important spots.

Michael Weinhardt as the primary developmental editor on this book. His feedback is probably the single biggest factor in whatever quality we've been able to cram into this book. As if that weren't enough, he produced many of the figures in my chapters.

Chris Anderson, architect on WPF, for a ton of illuminating conversations even after he started a competing book (although I'm convinced he'd be willing to talk to almost anyone once he'd entered the deadly "writer avoidance mode").

My family. This was the first book I've ever written while holding a full-time job and, worse than that, while I was learning a completely new job. Frankly, I neglected my family pretty thoroughly for about three solid months, but they understood and supported me, like they have all of my endeavors over the years. I am very much looking forward to getting back to them.

CHAPTER 1

Hello, WPF

Windows Presentation Foundation (or WPF, as we will refer to it throughout this book) is a completely new presentation framework, integrating the capabilities of those frameworks that preceded it, including User, GDI, GDI+, and HTML, and heavily influenced by toolkits targeted at the Web, such as Macromedia Flash, and popular Windows applications such as Microsoft Word. This chapter is meant to give you the basics of WPF from scratch and then take you on a whirlwind tour of the things you'll read about in detail in the chapters that follow.

I know that "Avalon" is now officially the "Windows Presentation Foundation," but that's quite a mouthful and "WPF" is something I'm still getting used to, so during this difficult transition, please don't think less of me when I use the term "Avalon."

WPF from Scratch

Example 1-1 is pretty much the smallest WPF application you can write in C#.

Example 1-1. Minimal C# WPF application

```
// MyApp.cs
using System;
using System.Windows; // the root WPF namespace

namespace MyFirstAvalonApp {
  class MyApp {
    [STAThread]
    static void Main() {
      // the WPF message box
      MessageBox.Show("Hello, Avalon");
    }
  }
}
```

If you're not familiar with the STAThread attribute, it's a signal to .NET that when COM is initialized on the application's main thread, to make sure it's initialized to be compatible with single-threaded UI work, as required by WPF applications.

Building Applications

Building this application is a matter of firing off the C# compiler from a command shell with the appropriate environment variables,* as in Example 1-2.

Example 1-2. Building a WPF application manually

```
C:\1st>csc /target:winexe /out:.\1st.exe
  /r:System.dll
  /r:c:\WINDOWS\Microsoft.NET\Windows\v6.0.4030\WindowsBase.dll
  /r:c:\WINDOWS\Microsoft.NET\Windows\v6.0.4030\PresentationCore.dll
  /r:c:\WINDOWS\Microsoft.NET\Windows\v6.0.4030\PresentationFramework.dll
  MyApp.cs

Microsoft (R) Visual C# 2005 Compiler version 8.00.50215.44
for Microsoft (R) Windows (R) 2005 Framework version 2.0.50215
Copyright (C) Microsoft Corporation 2001-2005. All rights reserved.
```

Here, we're telling the C# compiler that we'd like to create a Windows application (instead of a Console application, which we get by default), putting the result, *1st.exe*, into the current folder, bringing in the three main WPF assemblies (WindowsBase, PresentationCore and PresentationFramework), along with the core .NET System assembly, and compiling the *MyApp.cs* source file.

Running the resulting *1st.exe* produces the world's lamest WPF application, as shown in Figure 1-1.

Figure 1-1. A lame WPF application

In anticipation of less lame WPF applications, refactoring the compilation command line into an *msbuild* project file is recommended, as in Example 1-3.

Example 1-3. A minimal msbuild project file

```
<!-- 1st.csproj -->
<Project
```

---

* Start → Programs → Microsoft WinFX SDK → Debug Build Environment or Release Build Environment.

Example 1-3. A minimal msbuild project file (continued)

```
    DefaultTargets="Build"
    xmlns="http://schemas.microsoft.com/developer/msbuild/2003">
    <PropertyGroup>
      <OutputType>winexe</OutputType>
      <OutputPath>.\</OutputPath>
      <Assembly>1st.exe</Assembly>
    </PropertyGroup>
    <ItemGroup>
      <Compile Include="MyApp.cs" />
      <Reference Include="System" />
      <Reference Include="WindowsBase" />
      <Reference Include="PresentationCore" />
      <Reference Include="PresentationFramework" />
    </ItemGroup>
    <Import Project="$(MsbuildBinPath)\Microsoft.CSharp.targets" />
</Project>
```

Msbuild is a .NET 2.0 command-line tool that understands XML files in the form shown in Example 1-3. The file format is shared between msbuild and Visual Studio 2005 so that you can use the same project files for both command-line and IDE builds. In this *.csproj* file (which stands for "C# Project"), we're saying the same things that we said to the C# compiler—i.e., that we'd like a Windows application, that we'd like the output to be *1st.exe* in the current folder, and that we'd like to reference the main WPF assemblies while compiling the *MyApp.cs* file. The actual smarts of how to turn these minimal settings into a compiled WPF application are contained in the .NET 2.0 *Microsoft.CSharp.targets* file that imported at the bottom of the file.

Executing *msbuild.exe* on the *1st.csproj* file looks like Example 1-4.

Example 1-4. Building using msbuild

```
C:\1st>msbuild 1st.csproj
Microsoft (R) Build Engine Version 2.0.50215.44
[Microsoft .NET Framework, Version 2.0.50215.44]
Copyright (C) Microsoft Corporation 2005. All rights reserved.

Build started 7/6/2005 8:20:39 PM.
_____ _ _

Project "C:\1st\1st.csproj" (default targets):

Target PrepareForBuild:
    Creating directory "obj\Release\".
Target CompileRdlFiles:
    Skipping target "CompileRdlFiles" because it has no inputs.
Target CoreCompile:
    Csc.exe /noconfig /nowarn:"1701;1702" /reference:C:\WINDOWS\Microsoft.net\Wi
ndows\v6.0.4030\PresentationCore.dll /reference:C:\WINDOWS\Microsoft.net\Windows
\v6.0.4030\PresentationFramework.dll /reference:C:\WINDOWS\Microsoft.NET\Framewo
rk\v2.0.50215\System.dll /reference:C:\WINDOWS\Microsoft.net\Windows\v6.0.4030\W
```

Example 1-4. Building using msbuild (continued)

```
indowsBase.dll /out:obj\Release\1st.exe /target:winexe MyApp.cs
Target CopyAppConfigFile:
    Skipping target "CopyAppConfigFile" because it has no outputs.
Target CopyFilesToOutputDirectory:
    Copying file from "obj\Release\1st.exe" to ".\1st.exe".
    1st -> C:\1st\1st.exe

Build succeeded.
    0 Warning(s)
    0 Error(s)

Time Elapsed 00:00:00.98
```

As I mentioned, msbuild and Visual Studio 2005 share a project file format, so loading the project file into VS is as easy as double-clicking on *1st.csproj*, which provides us all of the rights and privileges thereof (as shown in Figure 1-2).

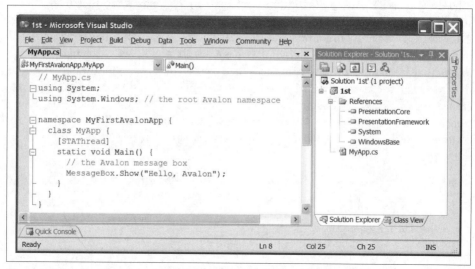

Figure 1-2. Loading the minimal msbuild project file into Visual Studio

Unfortunately, as nice as the project file makes building our WPF application, the application itself is still lame.

The Application Object

A real WPF application is going to need more than a message box. WPF applications have an instance of the Application class from the System.Windows namespace. The Application class provides events like StartingUp and ShuttingDown for tracking lifetime; methods like Run for starting the application; and properties like Current,

ShutdownMode, and MainWindow for finding the global application object, choosing when it shuts down, and getting the application's main window. Typically, the Application class serves as a base for custom application-wide behavior, as in Example 1-5.

Example 1-5. A less minimal WPF application

```
// MyApp.cs
using System;
using System.Windows;

namespace MyFirstAvalonApp {
  class MyApp : Application {
    [STAThread]
    static void Main(string[] args) {
      MyApp app = new MyApp();
      app.StartingUp += app.AppStartingUp;
      app.Run(args);
    }

    void AppStartingUp(object sender, StartingUpCancelEventArgs e) {
      // By default, when all top level windows
      // are closed, the app shuts down
      Window window = new Window();
      window.Text = "Hello, Avalon";
      window.Show();
    }
  }
}
```

Here, our MyApp class derives from the Application base class. In Main, we create an instance of the MyApp class, add a handler to the StartingUp event, and kick things off with a call to the Run method, passing the command-line arguments passed to Main. Those same command-line arguments are available in the StartingUpCancelEventArgs passed to the StartingUp event handler. (The StartingUp event handler will show its value as we move responsibility for the application's entry point to WPF later in this chapter.)

Our StartingUp handler creates our sample's top-level window, which is an instance of the built-in WPF Window class, making our sample WPF application more interesting from a developer point of view, although visually less so, as shown in Figure 1-3.

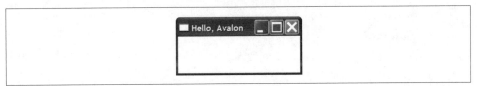

Figure 1-3. A less lame WPF application

While we can create instances of the built-in classes of WPF like Window, populating them and wiring them up from the application, it's much more encapsulating (not to mention abstracting) to create custom classes for such things, like the Window1 class in Example 1-6.

Example 1-6. Window class declaring its own controls

```
// Window1.cs
using System;
using System.Windows;
using System.Windows.Controls; // Button et al

namespace MyFirstAvalonApp {
  class Window1 : Window {
    public Window1() {
      this.Text = "Hello, Avalon";

      // Do something interesting (sorta...)
      Button button = new Button();
      button.Content = "Click me, baby, one more time!";
      button.Width = 200;
      button.Height = 25;
      button.Click += button_Click;

      this.AddChild(button);
    }

    void button_Click(object sender, RoutedEventArgs e) {
      MessageBox.Show(
        "You've done that before, haven't you...",
        "Nice!");
    }
  }
}
```

In addition to setting its caption text, an instance of our Window1 class will include a button with its Content, Width, and Height properties set and its Click event handled. With this initialization handled in the Window1 class itself, our app's startup code looks a bit simpler (even though the application itself has gotten "richer"), as in Example 1-7.

Example 1-7. Simplified Application instance

```
// MyApp.cs
using System;
using System.Windows;

namespace MyFirstAvalonApp {
  class MyApp : Application {
    [STAThread]
    static void Main(string[] args) {
      MyApp app = new MyApp();
```

Example 1-7. Simplified Application instance (continued)

```
        app.StartingUp += app.AppStartingUp;
        app.Run(args);
    }

    void AppStartingUp(object sender, StartingUpCancelEventArgs e) {
        // Let the Window1 initialize itself
        Window window = new Window1();
        window.Show();
    }
  }
}
```

The results, shown in Figure 1-4, are unlikely to surprise you much.

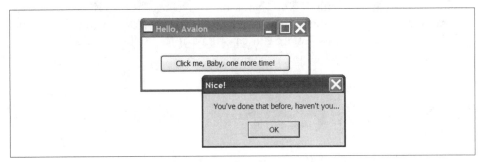

Figure 1-4. A slightly more interesting WPF application

As the Window1 class gets more interesting, we're mixing two very separate kinds of code: the "look," represented by the initialization code that sets the window and child window properties, and the "behavior," represented by the event-handling code. As the look is something that you're likely to want handled by someone with artistic sensibilities (a.k.a. "turtleneck-wearing designer types"), whereas the behavior is something you'll want to leave to the coders (a.k.a. "pocket-protector-wearing engineer types"), separating the former from the latter would be a good idea. Ideally, we'd like to move the imperative "look" code into a declarative format suitable for tools to create with some drag 'n' drop magic. For WPF, that format is XAML.

XAML

XAML is an XML-based language for creating and initializing .NET objects. It's used in WPF as a serialization format for objects from the WPF presentation stack, although it can be used for a much larger range of objects than that. Example 1-8 shows how our Window-derived class is declared using XAML.

Example 1-8. Declaring a Window in XAML

```
<!-- Window1.xaml -->
<Window
```

Example 1-8. Declaring a Window in XAML (continued)

```
  x:Class="MyFirstAvalonApp.Window1"
  xmlns="http://schemas.microsoft.com/winfx/avalon/2005"
  xmlns:x="http://schemas.microsoft.com/winfx/xaml/2005"
  Text="Hello, Avalon">
    <Button
      x:Name="button"
      Width="200"
      Height="25"
      Click="button_Click">Click me, baby, one more time!</Button>
</Window>
```

The root element, Window, is used to declare a portion of a class, the name of which is contained in the Class attribute from the XAML XML namespace (declared with a prefix of "x" using the "xmlns" XML namespace syntax). The two XML namespace declarations pull in two commonly used namespaces for XAML work, the one for XAML itself and the one for WPF. You can think of the XAML in Example 1-8 as creating the *partial class* definition* in Example 1-9.

Example 1-9. C# equivalent of XAML from Example 1-8

```
namespace MyFirstAvalonApp {
  partial class Window1 : Window {
    Button button;

    void InitializeComponent() {
      // Initialize Window1
      this.Text = "Hello, Avalon";

      // Initialize button
      button = new Button();
      button.Width = 200;
      button.Height = 25;
      button.Click += button_Click;

      this.AddChild(button);
    }
  }
}
```

XAML was built to be as direct a mapping from XML to .NET as possible. Generally, every XAML element is a .NET class name and every XAML attribute is the name of a property or an event on that class. This makes XAML useful for more than just WPF classes; pretty much any old .NET class that exposes a default constructor can be initialized in a XAML file.

Notice that we don't have the definition of the click event handler in this generated class. For event handlers and other initialization and helpers, a XAML file is meant to

---

* Partial classes are a new feature in C# 2.0 that allow you to split class definitions between multiple files.

be matched with a corresponding *code-behind* file, which is a .NET language code file that implements behavior "behind" the look defined in the XAML. Traditionally, this file is named with a *.xaml.cs* extension and contains only the things not defined in the XAML. With the XAML from Example 1-9 in place, our single-buttoned main window code-behind file can be reduced to the code in Example 1-10.

Example 1-10. C# code-behind file

```
// Window1.xaml.cs
using System;
using System.Windows;
using System.Windows.Controls;

namespace MyFirstAvalonApp {
  public partial class Window1 : Window {
    public Window1() {
      InitializeComponent();
    }

    void button_Click(object sender, RoutedEventArgs e) {
      MessageBox.Show(...);
    }
  }
}
```

Notice the partial keyword modifying the Window1 class, which signals to the compiler that the XAML-generated class is to be paired with this human-generated class to form one complete class, each depending on the other. The partial Window1 class defined in XAML depends on the code-behind partial class to call the InitializeComponent method and to handle the click event. The code-behind class depends on the partial Window1 class defined in XAML to implement InitializeComponent, thereby providing the look of the main window (and related child controls).

Further, as I mentioned, XAML is not just for visuals. For example, there's nothing stopping us from moving most of the definition of our custom MyApp class into a XAML file, as in Example 1-11.

Example 1-11. Declaring an Application in XAML

```
<!-- MyApp.xaml -->
<Application
  x:Class="MyFirstAvalonApp.MyApp"
    xmlns="http://schemas.microsoft.com/winfx/avalon/2005"
    xmlns:x="http://schemas.microsoft.com/winfx/xaml/2005"
    StartingUp="AppStartingUp">
</Application>
```

This reduces the MyApp code-behind file to the event handler in Example 1-12.

Example 1-12. Application code-behind file

```
// MyApp.xaml.cs
using System;
using System.Windows;

namespace MyFirstAvalonApp {
  public partial class MyApp : Application {
    void AppStartingUp(object sender, StartingUpCancelEventArgs e) {
      Window window = new Window1();
      window.Show();
    }
  }
}
```

You may have noticed that we no longer have a Main entry point to create the instance of the application-derived class and call its Run method. That's because WPF has a special project setting to specify the XAML file that defines the application class, which appears in the msbuild project file, as in Example 1-13.

Example 1-13. Specifying the application's XAML in the project file

```
<!-- MyFirstAvalonApp.csproj -->
<Project ...>
  <PropertyGroup>
    <OutputType>winexe</OutputType>
    <OutputPath>.\</OutputPath>
    <Assembly>1st.exe</Assembly>
  </PropertyGroup>
  <ItemGroup>
    <ApplicationDefinition Include="MyApp.xaml" />
    <Compile Include="Window1.xaml.cs" />
    <Compile Include="MyApp.xaml.cs" />
    <Reference Include="System" />
    <Reference Include="WindowsBase" />
    <Reference Include="PresentationCore" />
    <Reference Include="PresentationFramework" />
    <Page Include="Window1.xaml" />
    <Page Include="MyApp.xaml" />
  </ItemGroup>
  <Import Project="$(MsbuildBinPath)\Microsoft.CSharp.targets" />
  <Import Project="$(MSBuildBinPath)\Microsoft.WinFX.targets" />
</Project>
```

The combination of the ApplicationDefinition element and the WinFX-specific *Microsoft.WinFX.targets* file produces an application entry point that will create our application for us. Also notice in Example 1-13 that we've replaced the *MyApp.cs* file with the *MyApp.xaml.cs* file, added the *Window1.xaml.c* file, and included the two corresponding XAML files as Page elements. The XAML files will be compiled into partial class definitions using the instructions in the *Microsoft.WinFX.targets* file.

This basic arrangement of artifacts—i.e., application and main window each split into a XAML and a code-behind file—is such a desirable starting point for a WPF application that creating a new project using the Avalon Application project template from within Visual Studio 2005 gives you just that initial configuration, as shown in Figure 1-5.

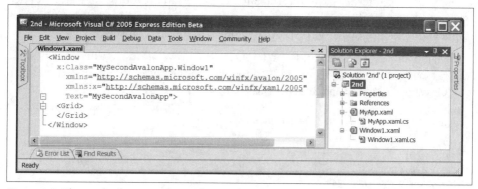

Figure 1-5. The result of running the Avalon Application project template

Navigation Applications

If you create a new WPF application using Visual Studio, you may notice that a few icons down from the Avalon Application icon is another project template called Avalon Navigation Application, as shown in Figure 1-6.

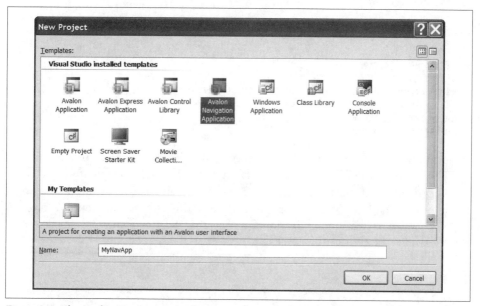

Figure 1-6. The Avalon Navigation Application project template in Visual Studio

WPF itself was created as a unified presentation framework, meant to enable build-ing Windows applications with the best features from existing Windows application practice and existing web application practice. One of the nice things that web appli-cations generally provide is a single window showing the user one page of content/functionality at a time, allowing for navigation between the pages. For some applica-tions, including Internet Explorer, the Shell Explorer, Microsoft Money and a bunch of Control Panels, this is thought to be preferable to the more common Windows application practice of showing more than one window at a time.

To enable more of these kinds of applications in Windows, WPF provides the NavigationApplication in Example 1-14 to serve as the base of your custom applica-tion class instead of the Application class.

Example 1-14. The C# portion of a navigation application

```
// MyApp.xaml.cs
using System;
using System.Windows;
using System.Windows.Navigation;

namespace MyNavApp {
  public partial class MyApp : NavigationApplication {}
}
```

The NavigationApplication itself derives from the Application class and provides additional services such as navigation, history, and tracking the initial page to show when the application first starts, which is specified in the application's XAML file, as in Example 1-15.

Example 1-15. The XAML portion of a navigation application

```
<!-- MyApp.xaml.cs -->
<NavigationApplication
  x:Class="MyNavApp.MyApp"
  xmlns="http://schemas.microsoft.com/winfx/avalon/2005"
  xmlns:x="http://schemas.microsoft.com/winfx/xaml/2005"
  StartupUri="Page1.xaml">
</NavigationApplication>
```

In addition to the StartupUri, which specifies the first XAML page to show in our navigation application, notice that the NavigationApplication element doesn't have a Text property. In fact, if you were to set one, that would cause a compilation error, because a navigation application's main window title is set by the current *page*. A page in a WPF navigation application is a class that derives from the Page class, e.g., the XAML in Example 1-16.

Example 1-16. A sample navigation page

```xml
<!-- Page1.xaml -->
<Page
  x:Class="MyNavApp.Page1"
  xmlns="http://schemas.microsoft.com/winfx/avalon/2005"
  xmlns:x="http://schemas.microsoft.com/winfx/xaml/2005"
  Text="Page 1">
  <TextBlock FontSize="72" TextWrap="Wrap">
    Check out
    <Hyperlink NavigateUri="page2.xaml">page 2</Hyperlink>,
    too.
  </TextBlock>
</Page>
```

Remember that the root element of a XAML file defines the base class, so this Page root element defines a class (MyNavApp.Page1) that derives from the WPF Page class. The Text property of the page will be the thing that shows in the caption as the user navigates from page to page.

Navigation

The primary way to allow the user to navigate is via the Hyperlink element, setting the NavigateUri to a relative URL of another page XAML in the project. The first page of our sample navigation application looks like Figure 1-7.

Figure 1-7. A sample navigation page in action

In Figure 1-7, the hyperlinked text is underlined in blue, and if you were to move your mouse cursor over the hyperlink, it would show up as red. Further, the page's Text property is set as the window caption, as well as on the toolbar across the top. This toolbar is provided for navigation applications for the sole purpose of providing the back and forward buttons. The act of navigation through the application will selectively enable and disable these buttons, as well as fill in the history drop-down maintained by each button.

Let's define *page2.xaml*, as shown in Example 1-17.

Example 1-17. Another sample navigation page

```
<!-- Page2.xaml -->
<Page
  x:Class="MyNavApp.Page2"
  xmlns="http://schemas.microsoft.com/winfx/avalon/2005"
  xmlns:x="http://schemas.microsoft.com/winfx/xaml/2005"
  Text="Page 2">
    <TextBlock FontSize="72" TextWrap="Wrap">
    Hello, and welcome to page 2.
    <Button FontSize="72" Click="page1Button_Click">Page 1</Button>
    <Button FontSize="72" Click="backButton_Click">Back</Button>
    <Button FontSize="72" Click="forwardButton_Click">Forward</Button>
  </TextBlock>
</Page>
```

Clicking on the hyperlink on page 1 navigates to page 2, as shown in Figure 1-8.

Figure 1-8. Navigation history and custom navigation controls

Notice in Figure 1-8 that the history for the back button shows page 1, which is where we were just before going to page 2. Also notice the three buttons, which are implemented in Example 1-18 to demonstrate navigating to a specific page, navigating backward, and navigating forward.

Example 1-18. Custom navigation code

```
// Page2.xaml.cs
using System;
using System.Windows;
using System.Windows.Navigation;

namespace MyNavApp {
  public partial class Page2 : Page {
    void page1Button_Click(object sender, RoutedEventArgs e) {
      NavigationService.GetNavigationService(this).
        Navigate(new Uri("page1.xaml", UriKind.Relative));
    }
```

Example 1-18. Custom navigation code (continued)

```
    void backButton_Click(object sender, RoutedEventArgs e) {
      NavigationService.GetNavigationService(this).GoBack();
    }

    void forwardButton_Click(object sender, RoutedEventArgs e) {
      NavigationService.GetNavigationService(this).GoForward();
    }
  }
}
```

Example 1-18 shows the use of static methods on the NavigationService class to navigate manually just as the hyperlink, back and forward buttons do automatically.

Content Model

While the different kinds of WPF application styles are interesting, the core of any presentation framework is in the presentation elements themselves. Fundamentally, we have "bits of content and behavior" and "containers of bits of content and behavior." We've already seen both kinds; e.g., a Button is a control, providing content and behavior and a Window is a container. There are two things that may surprise you about content containment in WPF, however.

The first is that you don't need to put a string as the content of a Button; it will take any .NET object. For example, you've already seen a string as a button's content, which looks like Figure 1-9, created with the code in Example 1-19.

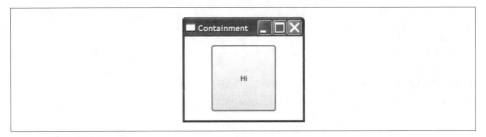

Figure 1-9. A button with string content

Example 1-19. A button with string content
```
<Window ...>
  <Button Width="100" Height="100">Hi</Button>
</Window>
```

However, you can also use an image, as in Figure 1-10 and implemented in Example 1-20.

Figure 1-10. A button with image content

Example 1-20. A button with image content

```
<Window ...>
  <Button Width="100" Height="100">
    <Image Source="tom.png" />
  </Button>
</Window>
```

You can even use an arbitrary control, like a TextBox, as shown in Figure 1-11 and implemented in Example 1-21.

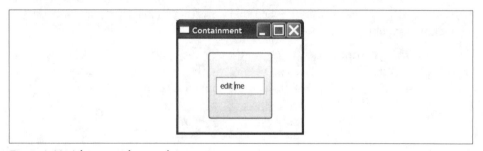

Figure 1-11. A button with control content

Example 1-21. A button with control content

```
<Window ...>
  <Button Width="100" Height="100">
    <TextBox Width="75">edit me</TextBox>
  </Button>
</Window>
```

Further, as you'll see in Chapters 2 and 5, you can get fancy and show a collection of nested elements in a Button or even use nonvisual objects as the content of a Button. The reason that the Button can take any object as content is because it's derived ultimately from a class called ContentControl, as are many other WPF classes—e.g., Label, ListBoxItem, ToolTip, CheckBox, RadioButton and, in fact, Window itself.

A ContentControl knows how to hold anything that's able to be rendered, not just a string. A ContentControl gets its content from the Content property, so you could specify a Button's content like so (this is the longhand version of Example 1-19):

```
<Button Width="100" Height="100" Content="Hi" />
```

ContentControls are especially useful, because you get all of the behavior of the "thing,"—e.g., Button, Window, or ListBoxItem—but you can display whatever you like in it without having to build yourself a special class—e.g., ImageButton, TextBoxListBoxItem, etc.

XAML Property-Element Syntax

Still, while setting the Content property as a string attribute in XAML works just fine for specifying a string as content, it doesn't work at all well for specifying an object as content, such as in the image example. For this reason, XAML defines the *property-element* syntax, which uses nested Element.Property elements for specifying objects as property values. Example 1-22 shows the property-element syntax to set a string as a button's content.

Example 1-22. Property element syntax with a string

```
<Button Width="100" Height="100">
  <Button.Content>Hi</Button.Content>
</Button>
```

Example 1-23 is another example using an image:

Example 1-23. Property element syntax with an Image

```
<Button Width="100" Height="100">
  <Button.Content>
    <Image Source="tom.png" />
  </Button.Content>
</Button>
```

Since XML attributes can only contain one thing, property-element syntax is especially useful when you've got more than one thing to specify. For example, you might imagine a button with a string and an image, defined in Example 1-24.

Example 1-24. Can't have multiple things in a ContentControl

```
<Button Width="100" Height="100">
  <!-- WARNING: doesn't work! -->
  <Button.Content>
    <TextBlock>Tom: </TextBlock>
    <Image Source="tom.png" />
  </Button.Content>
</Button>
```

While normally the property-element syntax would be useful for this kind of thing, in this particular case, it doesn't work at all. This brings us to the second thing that may surprise you about content containment in WPF: while Button can take any old thing as content, as can a Window, both of them can only take a single thing which, without additional instructions, WPF will center and fill up the element's entire client area. For more than one content element or a richer layout policy, you'll need a panel.

Layout

Taking another look at Example 1-24 with the TextBlock and the Image as content for the Button, we don't really have enough information to place them inside the area of the button. Should they be stacked left-to-right or top-to-bottom? Should one be docked on one edge and one docked to the other? How are things stretched or arranged if the button resizes? These are questions best answered with a *panel*.

A panel is a control that knows how to arrange its content. WPF comes with the general-purpose panel controls listed in Table 1-1.

Table 1-1. Main panel types

Panel type	Usage
DockPanel	Allocates an entire edge of the panel area to each child; useful for defining the rough layout of simple applications at a coarse scale.
StackPanel	Lays out children in a vertical or horizontal stack; extremely simple, useful for managing small scale aspects of layout.
Grid	Arranges children within a grid; useful for aligning items without resorting to fixed sizes and positions. The most powerful of the built-in panels.
Canvas	Performs no layout logic—puts children where you tell it to; allows you to take complete control of the layout process.

Grid Layout

The most flexible panel by far is the *grid*, which arranges content elements in rows and columns and includes the ability to span multiple rows and columns, as shown in Example 1-25.

Example 1-25. A sample usage of the Grid panel

```
<Window ...>
  <Grid>
    <Grid.RowDefinitions>
      <RowDefinition />
      <RowDefinition />
      <RowDefinition />
```

Example 1-25. A sample usage of the Grid panel (continued)

```
      </Grid.RowDefinitions>
      <Grid.ColumnDefinitions>
        <ColumnDefinition />
        <ColumnDefinition />
        <ColumnDefinition />
      </Grid.ColumnDefinitions>
      <Button Grid.Row="0" Grid.Column="0" Grid.ColumnSpan="2">A</Button>
      <Button Grid.Row="0" Grid.Column="2">C</Button>
      <Button Grid.Row="1" Grid.Column="0" Grid.RowSpan="2">D</Button>
      <Button Grid.Row="1" Grid.Column="1">E</Button>
      <Button Grid.Row="1" Grid.Column="2">F</Button>
      <Button Grid.Row="2" Grid.Column="1">H</Button>
      <Button Grid.Row="2" Grid.Column="2">I</Button>
    </Grid>
  </Window>
```

Example 1-25 used the XAML property-element syntax to define a grid with three rows and three columns inside the RowDefinition and ColumnDefinition elements. In each element, we've specified the Grid.Row and Grid.Column properties so that the grid knows which elements go where (the grid can have multiple elements in the same cell). One of the elements spans two rows, and one spans two columns, as shown in Figure 1-12.

Figure 1-12. A sample Grid panel in action

Using the grid, we can be explicit about how we want to arrange an image with a text caption, as in Example 1-26.

Example 1-26. Arranging an image and text in a grid

```
<Button Width="100" Height="100">
  <Button.Content>
    <Grid>
      <Grid.RowDefinitions>
        <RowDefinition />
        <RowDefinition />
      </Grid.RowDefinitions>
      <Image Grid.Row="0" Source="tom.png" />
      <TextBlock
        Grid.Row="1"
```

Example 1-26. Arranging an image and text in a grid (continued)

```
        HorizontalAlignment="Center">Tom</TextBlock>
    </Grid>
  </Button.Content>
</Button>
```

Figure 1-13 shows how the grid arranges the image and text for us.

Figure 1-13. A grid arranging an image and a text block

Since we're just stacking one element on top of another, we could've used the stack panel, but the grid is so general-purpose that many WPF programmers find themselves using it for most layout configurations.

XAML Attached Property Syntax

You may have noticed that in setting up the Grid.Row and Grid.Panel attributes of the Button elements, we used another dotted syntax, similar to the property-element syntax, but this time on the attribute instead of on the element. This is the *attached-property* syntax and is used to set a property as associated with a particular element— e.g., a Button—but as defined by another element—e.g., a Grid.

The attached-property syntax is used in WPF as an extensibility mechanism. We don't want the Button class to have to know that it's being arranged in a Grid, but we do want to specify Grid-specific attributes on it. If the Button were being hosted in a Canvas, the Grid properties wouldn't make any sense, so building Row and Column properties into the Button class isn't such a great idea. Further, when we define our own custom panel that the WPF team never considered—e.g., HandOfCards—we want to be able to apply the HandOfCards attached properties to arbitrary elements it contains.

This kind of extensibility is what the attached-property syntax was designed for, and it is common when arranging content on a panel.

For the nitty-gritty of layout, including the other panels and text composition that I didn't show, you'll want to read Chapter 2.

Controls

While the layout panels provide the container, the controls are the important things you'll be arranging. So far, you've already seen examples of creating instances of controls, setting properties, and handling events. You've also seen the basics of the content model that makes controls in WPF special. However, for the details of event routing, command handling, mouse/keyboard input and an enumeration of the controls in WPF, you'll want to check out Chapter 3. Further, for information about packaging up custom UI and behavior, as well as the techniques discussed in the rest of this chapter and the rest of this book, you'll want to read Chapter 9.

Data Binding

Once we've got a set of controls and a way to lay them out, we still need to fill them with data and keep that data in sync with wherever the data actually lives. (Controls are a great way to show data but a poor place to keep it.)

For example, imagine that we'd like to build an actual WPF application for keeping track of people's nicknames. Something like Figure 1-14 would do the trick.

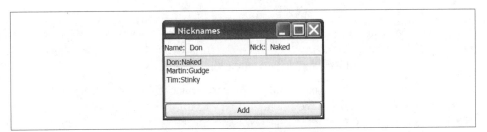

Figure 1-14. Data binding to a collection of custom types

In Figure 1-14, we've got two TextBox controls, one for the name and one for the nickname; the actual nickname entries in a ListBox in the middle; and a Button to add new entries. The core data of such an application could easily be built with a class, as shown in Example 1-27.

Example 1-27. A custom type with data binding support

```
public class Nickname : INotifyPropertyChanged {
  // INotifyPropertyChanged Member
  public event PropertyChangedEventHandler PropertyChanged;
  protected void OnPropertyChanged(string propName) {
    if( PropertyChanged != null ) {
      PropertyChanged(this, new PropertyChangedEventArgs(propName));
    }
  }
}

  string name;
```

Example 1-27. A custom type with data binding support (continued)

```csharp
  public string Name {
    get { return name; }
    set {
      name = value;
      OnPropertyChanged("Name"); // notify consumers
    }
  }

  private string nick;
  public string Nick {
    get { return nick; }
    set {
      nick = value;
      OnPropertyChanged("Nick"); // notify consumers
    }
  }

  public Nickname( ) : this("name", "nick") { }
  public Nickname(string name, string nick) {
    this.name = name;
    this.nick = nick;
  }
}
```

This class knows nothing about data binding, but it does have two public properties that expose the data, and it implements the standard INotifyPropertyChanged interface to let consumers of this data know when it has changed.

In the same way that we have a standard interface for notifying consumers of objects when they change, we also have a standard way to notify consumers of collections of changes called INotifyCollectionChanged. WPF provides an implementation of this interface called ObservableCollection, which we'll use to fire the appropriate event when Nickname objects are added or removed, as in Example 1-28.

Example 1-28. A custom collection type with data binding support

```csharp
// Notify consumers
public class Nicknames : ObservableCollection<Nickname> { }
```

Around these classes, we could build nickname-management logic that looks like Example 1-29.

Example 1-29. Making ready for data binding

```csharp
// Window1.xaml.cs
...
namespace DataBindingDemo {
  public class Nickname : INotifyPropertyChanged {...}
  public class Nicknames : ObservableCollection<Nickname> { }

  public partial class Window1 : Window {
```

Example 1-29. Making ready for data binding (continued)

```
  Nicknames names;

  public Window1( ) {
    InitializeComponent( );
    this.addButton.Click += addButton_Click;

    // create a nickname collection
    this.names = new Nicknames( );

    // make data available for binding
    dockPanel.DataContext = this.names;
  }

  void addButton_Click(object sender, RoutedEventArgs e) {
    this.names.Add(new Nickname( ));
  }
 }
}
```

Notice the window's class constructor provides a click event handler to add a new nickname and creates the initial collection of nicknames. However, the most useful thing that the Window1 constructor does is set its DataContext property so as to make the nickname data available for data binding.

Data binding is about keeping object properties and collections of objects synchronized with one or more controls' view of the data. The goal of data binding is to save you the pain and suffering associated with writing the code to update the controls when the data in the objects change and with writing the code to update the data when the user edits the data in the controls. The synchronization of the data to the controls depends on the INotifyPropertyChanged and INotifyCollectionChanged interfaces that we've been careful to use in our data and data-collection implementations.

For example, because the collection of our sample nickname data and the nickname data itself both notify consumers when there are changes, we can hook up controls using WPF data binding, as in Example 1-30.

Example 1-30. An example of data binding

```
<!-- Window1.xaml -->
<Window x:Class="DataBindingDemo.Window1"
    xmlns="http://schemas.microsoft.com/winfx/avalon/2005"
    xmlns:x="http://schemas.microsoft.com/winfx/xaml/2005"
    Text="Nicknames">
  <DockPanel x:Name="dockPanel">
    <StackPanel DockPanel.Dock="Top" Orientation="Horizontal">
      <TextBlock VerticalAlignment="Center">Name: </TextBlock>
      <TextBox Text="{Binding Path=Name}" />
      <TextBlock VerticalAlignment="Center">Nick: </TextBlock>
      <TextBox Text="{Binding Path=Nick}" />
    </StackPanel>
```

Example 1-30. An example of data binding

```
      <Button DockPanel.Dock="Bottom" x:Name="addButton">Add</Button>
      <ListBox
        ItemsSource="{Binding}"
        IsSynchronizedWithCurrentItem="True" />
    </DockPanel>
  </Window>
```

This XAML lays out the controls as shown in Figure 1-14, using a dock panel to arrange things top-to-bottom and a stack panel to arrange the editing controls. The secret sauce that takes advantage of data binding is the {Binding} values in the control attributes instead of hardcoded values. By setting the Text property of the TextBox to {Binding Path=Name}, we're telling the TextBox to use data binding to peek at the Name property out of the current Nickname object. Further, if the data changes in the Name TextBox, the Path is used to poke the new value back in.

The current Nickname object is determined by the ListBox because of the IsSynchronizedWithCurrentItem property, which keeps the TextBox controls showing the same Nickname object as the one that's currently selected in the ListBox. The ListBox is bound to its data by setting the ItemsSource attribute to {Binding} without a Path statement. In the ListBox, we're not interested in showing a single property on a single object, but rather all of the objects at once.

But how do we know that both the ListBox and the TextBox controls are sharing the same data? That's where setting the dock panel's DataContext comes in. In the absence of other instructions, when a control's property is set using data binding, it looks at its own DataContext property for data. If it doesn't find any, it looks at its parent and then that parent's parent, and so on, all the way up the tree. Because the ListBox and the TextBox controls have a common parent that has a DataContext property set (the DockPanel), all of the data-bound controls will share the same data.

XAML Markup-Extension Syntax

Before we take a look at the results of our data binding, let's take a moment to discuss the XAML *markup-extension syntax*, which is what you're using when you set an attribute to something inside of curly braces—e.g., Text="{Binding Path=Name}". The markup-extension syntax adds special processing to XAML attribute values. For example, the BindingExtension class creates an instance of the Binding class, populating its properties with the parsed string that comes afterward. Logically, the following:

```
      <TextBox Text="{Binding Path=Name}" />
```

turns into the following:

```
      Binding binding = new Binding();
      binding.Path = "Name";
      textbox1.Text =
        binding.ProvideValue(textbox1, TextBox.TextProperty);
```

In fact, the binding-extension syntax is just a shortcut for the following (which you'll recognize as the property-element syntax):

```
<TextBox.Text>
  <Binding Path="Name" />
</TextBox.Text>
```

For a complete discussion of markup extensions, as well as the rest of the XAML syntax, you'll want to read Appendix A.

Data Templates

With the data-binding markup syntax explained, let's turn back to our sample data-binding application, which so far doesn't look quite like what we had in mind, as seen in Figure 1-15.

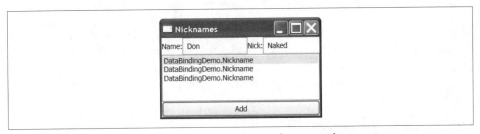

Figure 1-15. ListBox showing objects of a custom type without special instructions

It's clear that the data is making its way into the application, since the currently selected name and nickname are shown for editing. The problem is that, unlike the TextBox controls which were each given a specific field of the Nickname object to show, the ListBox is expected to show the whole thing. Lacking special instructions, the ListBox calling the ToString method of each object, which only results in the name of the type. To show the data, we need to compose a data template, as shown in Example 1-31.

Example 1-31. Using a data template

```
<ListBox
  ItemsSource="{Binding}"
  IsSynchronizedWithCurrentItem="True">

  <ListBox.ItemTemplate>
    <DataTemplate>
      <TextBlock>
        <TextBlock TextContent="{Binding Path=Name}" />:
        <TextBlock TextContent="{Binding Path=Nick}" />
      </TextBlock>
    </DataTemplate>
  </ListBox.ItemTemplate>

</ListBox>
```

The ListBox control has an ItemTemplate property that expects a *data template*: a template of elements that should be inserted for each listbox item, instead of the results of the call to ToString. In Example 1-31, we've composed a data template from a text block that flows together two other text blocks, each bound to a property on a Nickname object separated by a colon, as shown in Figure 1-16.

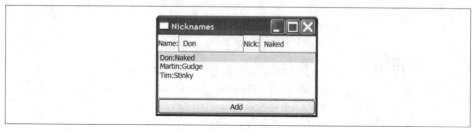

Figure 1-16. How a ListBox shows objects of a custom type with a data template

At this point, we've got a completely data-bound application. As data in the collection or the individual objects changes, the UI will be updated and vice versa. However, there is a great deal more to say on this topic, not least of which is pulling in XML as well as object data, which are covered in Chapter 4.

Dependency Properties

While our data-source Nickname object made its data available via standard .NET properties, we need something special to support data binding on the target element. While the TextContent property of the TextBlock element is exposed with a standard property wrapper, for it to integrate with WPF services such as data binding, styling and animation, it also needs to be a *dependency property*. A dependency property provides several features not present in .NET properties, including the ability to inherit its value from a container element, support externally set defaults, provide for object-independent storage (providing a potentially huge memory savings), and change tracking.

Most of the time, you won't have to worry about dependency properties versus .NET properties, but when you need the details, you can read about them in the Chapter 9.

Resources

Resources are named chunks of data defined separately from code and bundled with your application or component. .NET provides a great deal of support for resources, a bit of which we already used when we referenced *tom.png* from our XAML button earlier in this chapter. WPF also provides special support for resources scoped to elements defined in the tree.

As an example, let's declare some default instances of our custom `Nickname` objects in XAML in Example 1-32.

Example 1-32. Declaring objects in XAML

```
<!-- Window1.xaml -->
<?Mapping XmlNamespace="local" ClrNamespace="DataBindingDemo" ?>
<Window
    x:Class="DataBindingDemo.Window1"
    xmlns="http://schemas.microsoft.com/winfx/avalon/2005"
    xmlns:x="http://schemas.microsoft.com/winfx/xaml/2005"
    xmlns:local="local"
    Text="Nicknames">
  <Window.Resources>
    <local:Nicknames x:Key="names">
      <local:Nickname Name="Don" Nick="Naked" />
      <local:Nickname Name="Martin" Nick="Gudge" />
      <local:Nickname Name="Tim" Nick="Stinky" />
    </local:Nicknames>
  </Window.Resources>
  <DockPanel DataContext="{StaticResource names}">
    <StackPanel DockPanel.Dock="Top" Orientation="Horizontal">
      <TextBlock VerticalAlignment="Center">Name: </TextBlock>
      <TextBox Text="{Binding Path=Name}" />
      <TextBlock VerticalAlignment="Center">Nick: </TextBlock>
      <TextBox Text="{Binding Path=Nick}" />
    </StackPanel>
    ...
  </DockPanel>
</Window>
```

Notice the `Window.Resources`, which is property-element syntax to set the `Resources` property of the `Window1` class. Here, we can add as many named objects as we like, with the name coming from the `Key` attribute and the object coming from the XAML elements (remember that XAML elements are just a mapping to .NET class names). In this example, we're creating a Nicknames collection named `names` to hold three `Nickname` objects, each constructed with the default constructor, and then setting each of the `Name` and `Nick` properties.

Also notice the use of the `StaticResource` markup extension to reference the `names` resource as the collection to use for data binding. With this XAML in place, our window construction reduces to the code in Example 1-33.

Example 1-33. Finding a resource in code

```
public partial class Window1 : Window {
  Nicknames names;

  public Window1() {
    InitializeComponent();
    this.addButton.Click += addButton_Click;
```

Example 1-33. Finding a resource in code (continued)

```
    // get names collection from resources
    this.names = (Nicknames)this.FindResource("names");

    // no need to make data available for binding here
    //dockPanel.DataContext = this.names;
  }

  void addButton_Click(object sender, RoutedEventArgs e) {
    this.names.Add(new Nickname());
  }
}
```

Now instead of creating the collection of names, we can pull it from the resources with the FindResource method. Just because this collection was created in XAML doesn't mean that we need to treat it any differently than we treated it before, which is why the Add button event handler is the exact same code. Also, there's no need to set the data context on the dock panel, because that property was set in the XAML.

XAML Mapping Syntax

Before we go on with resources, we need to discuss a new XAML syntax that's come up, the *mapping syntax*. The XAML mapping syntax provides the ability to bring in types not already known by the XAML compiler. Our use of the mapping syntax looks like Example 1-34.

Example 1-34. XAML mapping syntax

```
<?Mapping XmlNamespace="local" ClrNamespace="DataBindingDemo" ?>
<Window
    x:Class="DataBindingDemo.Window1"
    xmlns="http://schemas.microsoft.com/winfx/avalon/2005"
    xmlns:x="http://schemas.microsoft.com/winfx/xaml/2005"
    xmlns:local="local"
    Text="Nicknames">
  <Window.Resources>
    <local:Nicknames x:Key="names">
    ...
  </Window.Resources>
  ...
</Window>
```

When bringing in a new type in XAML, we have to do a two-step mapping. The first step is to map a CLR namespace to an XML namespace. That's what the <?Mapping ... ?> line does. The second step is to map the XML namespace to a namespace prefix, which is what the xmlns:local attribute establishes. I've used local for both the XML namespace and prefix. I've chosen local because the CLR namespace to which I'm referring must be part of the assembly being compiled along with the XAML in question. You can import CLR namespaces for another assembly by specifying the optional `Assembly` attribute as part of the mapping, as Figure 1-17 shows.

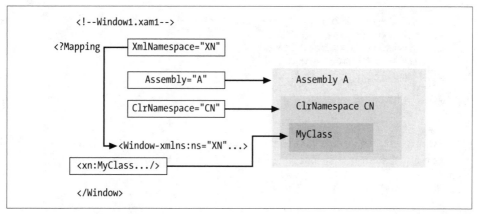

Figure 1-17. XAML mapping syntax summary

 As of the current build at the time of writing, when you're using a mapping directive in a XAML file, you must also specify a UI culture in the *.csproj* file, which you can do by adding a `UICulture` property to a `PropertyGroup` element, e.g.:

```
<!-- DataBindingDemo.csproj -->
<Project ...>
  <PropertyGroup>
    <UICulture>en-US</UICulture>
    ...
  </PropertyGroup>
  ...
</Project>
```

With the mapping completed, you're able to use the XML namespace prefix in front of any class with a default constructor to create an instance of it in a XAML file.

For the full scoop on resources, including resource scoping and lookup, as well as using them for theming and skinning, read Chapter 6.

Styles and Control Templates

One of the major uses for Resources is for styles. A style is a set of property/value pairs to be applied to one or more elements. For example, recall the two `TextBlock` controls from our `Nickname` sample, each of which was set to the same `VerticalAlignment` (see Example 1-35).

Example 1-35. Multiple TextBlock controls with the same settings

```
<!-- Window1.xaml -->
<Window ...>
  <DockPanel ...>
    <StackPanel ...>
      <TextBlock VerticalAlignment="Center">Name: </TextBlock>
      <TextBox Text="{Binding Path=Name}" />
      <TextBlock VerticalAlignment="Center">Nick: </TextBlock>
      <TextBox Text="{Binding Path=Nick}" />
    </StackPanel>
    ...
  </DockPanel>
</Window>
```

If we wanted to bundle the VerticalAlignment setting into a style, we could do this with a Style element in a Resources block, as shown in Example 1-36.

Example 1-36. An example TextBlock style

```
<Window ...>
  <Window.Resources>
    <Style x:Key="myStyle" TargetType="{x:Type TextBlock}">
      <Setter Property="VerticalAlignment" Value="Center" />
      <Setter Property="FontWeight" Value="Bold" />
      <Setter Property="FontStyle" Value="Italic" />
    </Style>
  </Window.Resources>
  <DockPanel ...>
    <StackPanel ...>
      <TextBlock Style="{StaticResource myStyle}">Name: </TextBlock>
      <TextBox Text="{Binding Path=Name}" />
      <TextBlock Style="{StaticResource myStyle}">Nick: </TextBlock>
      <TextBox Text="{Binding Path=Nick}" />
    </StackPanel>
    ...
  </DockPanel>
</Window>
```

The style element is really just a named collection of Setter elements for a specific class (specified with the Type markup extension). The TextBlock myStyle style centers the vertical alignment property and, just for fun, sets the text to bold italic as well. With the style in place, it can be used to set the Style property of any TextBlock that references the style resource. Applying this style as in Example 1-36 yields Figure 1-18.

Notice that only two of the TextBlock controls we used in this example use our style, because we only applied it to two TextBlock controls. If we want to take the next step and apply this style to all TextBlock controls defined in the scope of the style definition, we can do so by specifying the target type without specifying a key, as in Example 1-37.

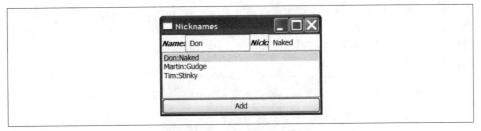

Figure 1-18. Named style in action on two TextBlock controls

Example 1-37. Styles assigned based on type

```
<Window ...>
  <Window.Resources>
    <Style TargetType="{x:Type TextBlock}">
      <Setter Property="VerticalAlignment" Value="Center" />
      <Setter Property="FontWeight" Value="Bold" />
      <Setter Property="FontStyle" Value="Italic" />
    </Style>
  </Window.Resources>
  <DockPanel ...>
    <StackPanel ...>
      <TextBlock>Name: </TextBlock>
      <TextBox Text="{Binding Path=Name}" />
      <TextBlock>Nick: </TextBlock>
      <TextBox Text="{Binding Path=Nick}" />
    </StackPanel>
    ...
  </DockPanel>
</Window>
```

In Example 1-37, we've dropped the x:Key attribute while leaving the TargetType property set. The use of just TargetType applies the style to all elements of that type, which means that we can also drop any mention of style on the individual TextBlock elements. Figure 1-19 shows the results.

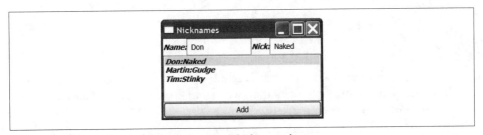

Figure 1-19. A type-based style applied to TextBlock controls

In addition to setting styles on controls, you can set them on arbitrary types (like the Nickname object we defined earlier) or replace a control's entire look, both of which you can read about in Chapter 5.

Further, if you'd like to apply property changes over time, you can do so with styles that include animation information, which is discussed in Chapter 8 (although Figure 1-20 is a small taste of what WPF animations can produce).

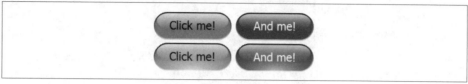

Figure 1-20. Buttons with animated glow (Color Plate 1)

Graphics

If no element or set of elements provides you with the look you want in your application, you can build it up from the set of graphics primitives that WPF provides, including rectangles, polygons, lines, ellipses, etc. WPF also lets you affect the way it renders graphics in any element, offering facilities that include bordering, rotating, or scaling another shape or control. WPF's support for graphics is engineered to fit right into the content model we're already familiar with, as shown in Example 1-38. from Chapter 7.

Example 1-38. Adding graphics to a Button

```
<Button LayoutTransform="scale 3 3">
  <StackPanel Orientation="Horizontal">
    <Canvas Width="20" Height="18" VerticalAlignment="Center">
      <Ellipse Canvas.Left="1" Canvas.Top="1" Width="16" Height="16"
        Fill="Yellow" Stroke="Black" />
      <Ellipse Canvas.Left="4.5" Canvas.Top="5" Width="2.5" Height="3"
        Fill="Black" />
      <Ellipse Canvas.Left="11" Canvas.Top="5" Width="2.5" Height="3"
        Fill="Black" />
      <Path Data="M 5,10 A 3,3 0 0 0 13,10" Stroke="Black" />
    </Canvas>
    <TextBlock VerticalAlignment="Center">Click!</TextBlock>
  </StackPanel>
</Button>
```

Here we've got three ellipses and a path composed inside a canvas, which is hosted inside a stack panel with a text block that, when scaled via the LayoutTransform property on the button, produces Figure 1-21.

Figure 1-21. A scaled button with a collection of graphic primitives

Notice that there's nothing special about the graphic primitives in XAML; they're declared and integrated as content just like any of the other WPF elements we've discussed. The graphics and the transformation are integrated into the same presentation stack as the rest of WPF, which is a bit of a difference for User/GDI programmers of old.

Further, graphics in WPF are not limited to 2-D; Figure 1-22 shows an example of a simple 3-D figure that was defined declaratively just like a 2-D graphic.

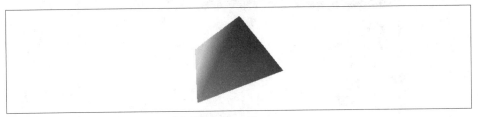

Figure 1-22. A very simple 3-D model (Color Plate 2)

For a complete discussion of how graphics primitives, retained drawings, color, lines, brushes, and transformations happen in WPF, both declaratively and in code, as well as an introduction to 3-D and video, you'll want to read Chapter 7.

Application Deployment

Once you've packed all of the features that WPF supports into your application, you still have the challenge of getting it to your users. As part of its effort to merge the best of Windows and the Web, WPF leverages the ClickOnce application-deployment support built into .NET 2.0 to enable WPF applications to be deployed over the Web.

You can deploy your WPF application to a web server for their enjoyment by right-clicking on the project in the Solution Explorer and choosing the Publish option, which brings up the Publish Wizard, which asks you where and how you would like to publish the output of your project.

If you choose the defaults, you'll have chosen to publish a ClickOnce "local install" application to the local machine's web server. A successful publication will bring up a Visual Studio–generated HTML file for you to test your application, as shown in Figure 1-23.

This version of *publish.htm* uses the default settings, including the name of the company of the author who built this sample (which is only coincidently the name of the company that developed WPF), the project name of the application, and the version number for the initial publication of this application.

Clicking on this link deploys the application. The first step is downloading the files that make up the application, as shown in Figure 1-24.

Once the files are downloaded, they're checked for a certificate signature from a known publisher. Since this requires nondefault settings, what you'll see is Figure 1-25.

Figure 1-23. Visual Studio–generated publish.htm

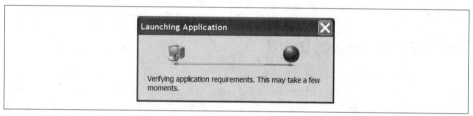

Figure 1-24. Launching a ClickOnce application

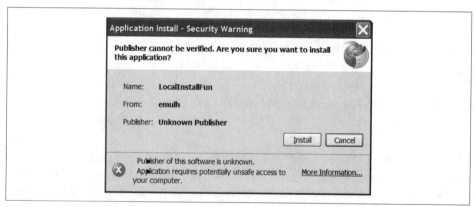

Figure 1-25. Launching a ClickOnce application from an unknown publisher

The Security Warning dialog is shown when the user hasn't already awarded a publisher the permissions to take certain liberties on their computer or when the publisher isn't known at all. If the user presses the Cancel button at this point, no potentially "evil" code has been downloaded or executed. If the user presses the Install button, the application's files are put into the right place, a Start menu folder is established and the application itself is executed, just like a normal WPF application.

If the user can establish a connection to the web server, subsequent runs will detect application updates and offer to upgrade the user's copy of the application, providing them a way to roll back to previous versions (or even uninstall completely) using the Add or Remove Control Panel. Also, even if there is no network connection, since the application is locally installed, no connection is needed to launch the application from the Start menu.

Those of you with trusting souls will now be thinking to yourself, "Wow! What an easy way to get bits out to my users and keep them up to date with the latest features and bug fixes!" and you'd be absolutely right; that's exactly what ClickOnce was designed for and why WPF was specially engineered to work with it.

Those of you with suspicion in your hearts will now be thinking, "Wow! What a great way for naughty men to format my hard drive, send incriminating email to my boss in my name, or reset my Minesweeper high scores!" and you'd be right, too—except that ClickOnce applications run in the .NET Code Access Security sandbox.

 As of this writing, WPF locally installed ClickOnce applications require "full trust" (which is .NET-speak for "I have always depended on the kindness of strangers"), but this will not be the case for the release of WPF 1.0.

This has been the quickest possible overview of ClickOnce deployment of WPF applications. For much more detail on WPF application deployment, including express applications that are deployed over the Web and hosted in the browser, please read Chapter 10.

Where Are We?

The Application object forms the initial piece on which to build your WPF applications. The Application definition, along with any Window or Page objects you may have, are most often split between a declarative XAML file for the look and an imperative code file for the behavior. Your applications can be normal, like a standard Windows application, or navigation-based, like the browser. In fact, the latter can be integrated into the browser, and both can be deployed and kept up to date over the Web using ClickOnce.

Building your application is a matter of grouping controls in containers: either single content containers, such as windows or buttons, or multiple content containers that provide layout capabilities, such as the canvas and the grid.

When bringing your controls together, you'll want to populate them with data that's synchronized with the in-memory home of the data, which is what data binding is for, and keep them pretty, which is what styles are for. If you want to declare data or styles in your XAML, you can do so using resources, which are just arbitrary named objects that aren't used to render WPF UI directly.

If no amount of data or style property settings makes you satisfied with the look of your control, you can replace it completely with control templates, which can be made up of other controls or graphics primitives. In addition, you can apply graphic operations—such as rotating, scaling, or animation—to graphic primitives or controls in WPF's integrated way.

CHAPTER 2

Layout

All applications need to present information to users. For this information to be conveyed effectively, it should be arranged onscreen in a clear and logical way. WPF provides a powerful and flexible array of tools for controlling the layout of the user interface.

There is a fine line between giving the developer or designer enough control over the user interface's layout, and leaving them to do all the work. A good layout system should be able to automate common scenarios such as resizing, scaling, and adaptation to localization but should allow manual intervention where necessary.

WPF provides a set of *panels*: elements that handle layout. Each individual panel type offers a straightforward and easily understood layout mechanism. As with all WPF elements, layout objects can be composed in any number of different ways, so while each individual element type is fairly simple, the flexible way in which they can be combined makes for a very powerful layout system. And you can even create your own layout element types should the built-in ones not meet your needs.

In this chapter, we will look at where each of the basic layout panels fits into a typical UI design. We will also examine some of the text-layout features of WPF.

Layout Basics

Layout in WPF is managed by panels. A panel is a special-purpose user-interface element whose job is to arrange the elements it contains. The type of panel you choose determines the style of UI layout within that panel. Table 2-1 describes the main panel types built into WPF. Whichever panel you use, the same basic rule always applies: an element's position is always determined by the containing panel. Some panels also manage the size of their children.

Table 2-1. Main panel types

Panel type	Usage
DockPanel	Allocates an entire edge of the panel area to each child; useful for defining the rough layout of simple applications at a coarse scale.
StackPanel	Lays out children in a vertical or horizontal stack; extremely simple, useful for managing small scale aspects of layout.
Grid	Arranges children within a grid; useful for aligning items without resorting to fixed sizes and positions. The most powerful of the built-in panels.
Canvas	Performs no layout logic—puts children where you tell it to; allows you to take complete control of the layout process.

Using a panel is simple: just put the children you need to lay out inside it. Example 2-1 shows several elements inside a StackPanel.

Example 2-1. Simple StackPanel layout

```
<StackPanel Orientation="Vertical">
    <TextBlock>This is some text</TextBlock>
    <Button>Button</Button>
    <Button>Button (different one)</Button>
    <CheckBox>Check it out</CheckBox>
    <TextBlock>More text</TextBlock>
</StackPanel>
```

This StackPanel arranges the children into a column, or *stack*, as Figure 2-1 shows.

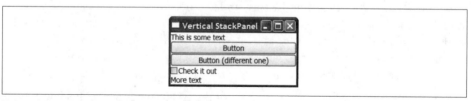

Figure 2-1. Vertical StackPanel layout

In this example, the child elements inside the panel are oblivious to the way in which they are being arranged. We could flip from a vertical to a horizontal layout without changing any of the children by changing the StackPanel's Orientation attribute from Vertical to Horizontal:

```
<StackPanel Orientation="Horizontal">
...as before
```

The elements will now be arranged in a horizontal line, as shown in Figure 2-2.

Figure 2-2. Horizontal StackPanel layout

The child elements are not always completely passive—they will often want to influence the way in which the parent arranges them. For example, setting a child's Width or Height properties overrides the size that the parent would have chosen. Also, most of the built-in panel types offer a range of ways in which child elements can indicate to the panel what their requirements are. For example, if you set the DockPanel.Dock property to Left on a child of a DockPanel, the panel will put that child on the left. Nonetheless, it is always ultimately the panel that decides the children's positions. Let's look at the built-in panels.

DockPanel

DockPanel is useful for describing the overall layout of a simple user interface. You can carve up the basic structure of your window using a DockPanel and then use the other panels to manage the details.

A DockPanel arranges each child element so that it fills a particular edge of the panel. If multiple children are docked to the same edge, they simply stack up against that edge in order. You may also optionally specify that the final child fills any remaining space not occupied by controls docked to the panel's edges. Although this may sound like a small feature set, the DockPanel provides a surprisingly flexible way of laying out elements, particularly as DockPanels can be nested.

Example 2-2 shows a simple DockPanel-based layout. Five buttons have been added to illustrate each of the options. Notice that four of them have a DockPanel.Dock attribute applied. This attached property is defined by DockPanel to allow elements inside a DockPanel to specify their position.

Example 2-2. Simple DockPanel layout

```
<DockPanel LastChildFill="True">
    <Button DockPanel.Dock="Top">Top</Button>
    <Button DockPanel.Dock="Bottom">Bottom</Button>
    <Button DockPanel.Dock="Left">Left</Button>
    <Button DockPanel.Dock="Right">Right</Button>
    <Button>Fill</Button>
</DockPanel>
```

Figure 2-3 shows how the UI built in Example 2-2 looks onscreen. Notice how the Top and Bottom buttons have filled the entire top and bottom edges of the window, and yet the Left and Right buttons do not fill their edges—the Top and Bottom buttons have taken control of the corners. This is because Top and Bottom were added to the panel first.

If you swapped these over so the Left and Right buttons came first in the markup, as shown in Example 2-3, they would fill their whole edges, including the corners, leaving the Top and Bottom buttons with just the remaining space. Figure 2-4 shows the results.

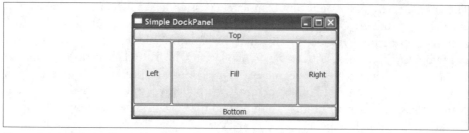

Figure 2-3. Simple DockPanel layout

Example 2-3. Docking left and right before top and bottom

```
<DockPanel LastChildFill="True">
    <Button DockPanel.Dock="Left">Left</Button>
    <Button DockPanel.Dock="Right">Right</Button>
    <Button DockPanel.Dock="Top">Top</Button>
    <Button DockPanel.Dock="Bottom">Bottom</Button>
    <Button>Fill</Button>
</DockPanel>
```

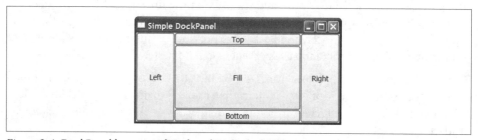

Figure 2-4. DockPanel layout, with Left and Right docked first

Elements never overlap in a DockPanel, so each successive child only gets to use space not already used by the previous children. You can get the final child to take all of the remaining space by setting the LastChildFill attribute of the DockPanel to True, and not specifying a DockPanel.Dock attribute on the last child.

You may be wondering how the DockPanel decides how tall to make an item docked to the top or bottom. It sets the width to fill the space available, but how does it pick a height? And how does it choose the width for items docked to the left or right?

The short answer is the child element gets to decide. When docking to the top or bottom the DockPanel stretches the item horizontally to fill the space, but lets it choose its own height. In Figures 2-3 and 2-4, the buttons at the top and bottom are the normal height for a button. What is less obvious is that the buttons docked to the left and right are the default width for a button—this is harder to see because they have been stretched vertically. However, it becomes clearer if we put a lot more text into one of the buttons. If the amount of text is wider than the default width for the button, the button will try to expand in order to make the text fit. We can see in Figure 2-5 that the DockPanel is letting the button be exactly as wide as it wants to be.

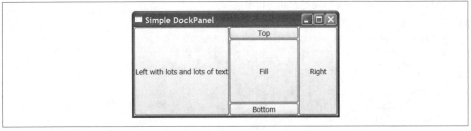

Figure 2-5. DockPanel layout, again with Left and Right docked first

The general rule with layout in WPF is that elements will tend to be as large as they need to be, unless you force them to do something else. This is a slight oversimplification, as we shall see when we start nesting panels, but it is true most of the time. This behavior is sometimes called *size to content* and it's what makes building flexible user-interface layouts in WPF particularly easy. The way this works is that panels ask their children how much space they require before deciding how to arrange them. (This process is described in more detail in the "Custom Layout" section, later in this chapter.)

We've used buttons in these examples because they make it easy to see where the elements have been placed and how large they are. Now let's look at a more realistic example.

Figure 2-6 shows the user interface for a documentation viewer, similar to the MSDN Library viewer. This has a number of typical user-interface features. It has a menu and a toolbar at the top, a search panel at the side, search results and a status bar at the bottom, and a main area containing a document. The DockPanel is perfect for constructing this overall layout. Example 2-4 shows the use of a DockPanel to provide the basic layout.

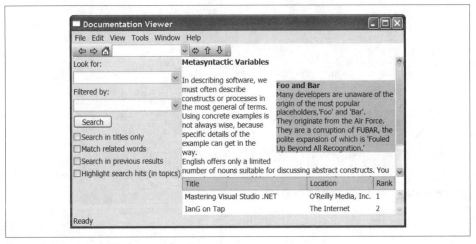

Figure 2-6. A typical Windows application

Example 2-4. Documentation viewer basic layout

```
<Window xmlns="http://schemas.microsoft.com/winfx/avalon/2005"
    xmlns:x="http://schemas.microsoft.com/winfx/xaml/2005"
    Text="Documentation Viewer"
    Width="350" Height="250"
    >
    <Window.Resources>
        ...omitted for clarity - full code available from book web site...
    </Window.Resources>

    <DockPanel LastChildFill="True">
        <Menu DockPanel.Dock="Top">
            <MenuItem Header="File"/>
            <MenuItem Header="Edit"/>
            <MenuItem Header="View"/>
            <MenuItem Header="Tools"/>
            <MenuItem Header="Window"/>
            <MenuItem Header="Help"/>
        </Menu>

        <ToolBarTray DockPanel.Dock="Top">
            <ToolBar>
                <ToolBar.Items>
                    <Button Content="{StaticResource back}" />
                    <Button Content="{StaticResource forward}" />
                    <Button Content="{StaticResource home}" />
                    <ComboBox />
                    <Button Content="{StaticResource sync}" />
                    <Button Content="{StaticResource prev}" />
                    <Button Content="{StaticResource next}" />
                </ToolBar.Items>
            </ToolBar>
        </ToolBarTray>

        <StatusBar DockPanel.Dock="Bottom">Ready</StatusBar>

        <TextBlock DockPanel.Dock="Left" Background="White">
            Search panel goes here
        </TextBlock>

        <TextBlock DockPanel.Dock="Bottom" Background="White">
            Search results panel goes here
        </TextBlock>

        <TextBlock Background="Gray">
            Content panel goes here
        </TextBlock>
    </DockPanel>
</Window>
```

So far we've only done the top-level layout, which you can see in Figure 2-7. We will be using other layout techniques inside the search, results, and content panels, so Example 2-4 uses TextBlock placeholders for these parts of the UI.

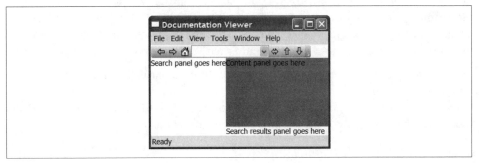

Figure 2-7. Basic viewer layout using DockPanel

 Note that the buttons in the ToolBar all have their Content properties set to StaticResource references. These are references to the graphics for the buttons. They have not been shown here because they take up quite a lot of space, and are not relevant to the basic layout. However, they can be found in the full source code, available for download from the book's web site. Resource references are discussed in detail in Chapter 6.

This example shows how multiple elements can be docked to the same edge. Both the Menu and the ToolBarTray have been docked to the top, and they have simply been stacked on top of one another. Likewise, the StatusBar and search results are docked to the bottom. The content does not have a DockPanel.Dock property, but we have set the LastChildFill property on the DockPanel itself to True, so the content fills the remaining space.

The status bar and search results are both docked to the bottom, and they seem to appear in the opposite order from the source code. The StatusBar appears first in the markup, above the search results, but onscreen they have appeared the other way up. This is a slightly counterintuitive feature of the DockPanel. Elements are docked to their chosen edge in the order in which they appear. This means that for elements docked to the bottom, whichever appears first in the markup will be nearest to the bottom, hence the apparent reverse ordering. Likewise, if multiple elements are docked to the right, they will be in right-to-left order in the markup.

The DockPanel has enabled us to create the basic structure of the user interface, but it is less well suited to arranging the contents of these elements. For example, the search panel will consist of a set of controls arranged in a vertical list. We could do this with a DockPanel, but there is a more convenient panel available: StackPanel.

StackPanel

StackPanel is a very simple panel. It simply arranges its children in a row or a column. We've seen it once already in Example 2-1, but that was a somewhat unrealistic example. You will rarely use StackPanel to lay out your whole user interface. It is at its most useful for small-scale layout—you use DockPanel or Grid to define the overall structure of your user interface, and then StackPanel to manage the details.

For example, we used DockPanel in Example 2-4 for the basic layout of our documentation viewer. We will now use StackPanel to arrange the contents of the search panel on the left-hand side. The markup in Example 2-5 replaces the placeholder TextBlock that contained the text "Search panel goes here."

Example 2-5. StackPanel search layout

```
<StackPanel DockPanel.Dock="Left" Orientation="Vertical"
            Background="#ECE9D8">
    <TextBlock>Look for:</TextBlock>
    <ComboBox />
    <TextBlock>Filtered by:</TextBlock>
    <ComboBox />
    <Button>Search</Button>
    <CheckBox>Search in titles only</CheckBox>
    <CheckBox>Match related words</CheckBox>
    <CheckBox>Search in previous results</CheckBox>
    <CheckBox>Highlight search hits (in topics)</CheckBox>
</StackPanel>
```

This first attempt is a particularly straightforward layout—we have simply provided a list of the controls. Figure 2-8 shows the results.

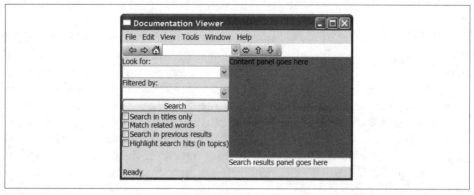

Figure 2-8. Documentation viewer with search panel

This is approximately what we require, but there are a few rough edges to the layout. The controls are all rather close to the edge of the panel, and to each other. This makes the user interface feel rather cramped, and it would look better with some breathing space.

This problem can be solved using the Margin property, which is present on all WPF elements. It indicates the amount of space that should be left around the edges of the element when it is laid out. The Margin property is described in more detail in the "Common Layout Properties" section, later in this chapter. Example 2-6 shows the search StackPanel again, this time with Margin specified for each of the elements.

Example 2-6. Adding space with Margin

```
<StackPanel DockPanel.Dock="Left" Orientation="Vertical"
            Background="#ECE9D8">
    <TextBlock Margin="3">Look for:</TextBlock>
    <ComboBox  Margin="3"/>
    <TextBlock Margin="3">Filtered by:</TextBlock>
    <ComboBox  Margin="3"/>
    <Button    Margin="3,5">Search</Button>
    <CheckBox  Margin="3">Search in titles only</CheckBox>
    <CheckBox  Margin="3">Match related words</CheckBox>
    <CheckBox  Margin="3">Search in previous results</CheckBox>
    <CheckBox  Margin="3">Highlight search hits (in topics)</CheckBox>
</StackPanel>
```

Most of the controls have a uniform margin of 3. (Since only one number has been specified, this applies to all sides.) The Button has a horizontal margin of 3 and a vertical margin of 5. This leaves little more space above and below the Button than the other elements in order to make the UI look less cramped.

With these margins specified, the panel looks a lot less crowded, as Figure 2-9 shows. While this is an improvement, there is still one problem with this layout. The Search button looks a little odd—it is much wider than you would normally expect a button to look.

Figure 2-9. Search StackPanel with Margin

The default behavior of a vertical StackPanel is to make all of the controls the same width as the panel. (Likewise, a horizontal StackPanel will make all of the controls the same height.) For the ComboBox controls, this is exactly what we want. For the TextBlock and CheckBox controls, it doesn't show that the controls have been stretched to be as wide as the panel, because they only look as wide as their text makes them look. However, a Button's visuals always fill its entire logical width, which is why the button in Figure 2-9 is unusually wide.

We would like the button to have a normal width, rather than being stretched across the panel's whole width. This is done by setting the button's HorizontalAlignment property to Left:

```
<Button Margin="3,5" HorizontalAlignment="Left">Search</Button>
```

HorizontalAlignment determines an element's horizontal position and width in situations where the containing panel gives it more space than it needs. The default is Stretch, meaning that if there is more space available than the child requires, it will be stretched to fill that space. The alternatives, Left, Right, and Center, do not attempt to stretch the element—these determine where the element will be placed within the excess space, allowing the element to use its natural width. Here we are using Left, meaning that the control will have its preferred width and will be aligned to the left of the available space (Figure 2-10).

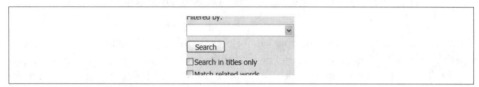

Figure 2-10. Search panel with unstretched Button

Note that HorizontalAlignment is only significant when the chosen layout style means more space is available than is needed. This happens with a vertical StackPanel, because the panel will typically make sure it is wide enough for the widest element. If the elements have different widths, this means that all but the widest will have more space than they require, at which point HorizontalAlignment comes into play. This does not occur in a horizontal StackPanel, because that will let each control be exactly as wide as it wants to. However, in that case, it usually sets the panel height to be large enough to accommodate the tallest control, at which point the VerticalAlignment property becomes significant for all the others.

Margin, HorizontalAlignment, and VerticalAlignment are all examples of layout properties present on all elements, which are honored by the built-in panel types where possible. (In certain cases, these properties have no meaning and are therefore ignored. For example, the Canvas always uses absolute positioning and allows its children to use their preferred size, so the alignment properties do nothing.) A complete list of these panel-independent layout properties is given in the "Common Layout Properties" section later in this chapter.

The search panel is a relatively simple user interface, so the StackPanel was able to meet all of its requirements. However, it is common to encounter layout problems which are hard to address with either the StackPanel or DockPanel. These are particularly common with dialog design, so we will now create a Properties dialog for our documentation viewer using the Grid panel.

Grid

Consider the document properties dialog shown in Figure 2-11. This is from the Microsoft SDK help viewer application, and we are going to add a similar dialog to our document viewer. Notice how the main area of the form is arranged as two columns. The column on the left contains labels, and the column in the middle contains information.

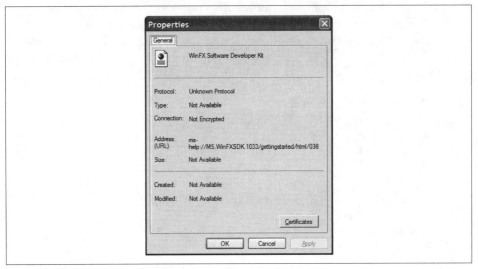

Figure 2-11. Document properties dialog

Achieving this kind of layout with a StackPanel is difficult, because it is not designed with two-dimensional alignment in mind. We could try to use nesting: Example 2-7 shows a vertical StackPanel with three rows, each with a horizontal StackPanel.

Example 2-7. Ineffective use of StackPanel

```
<StackPanel Orientation="Vertical">
    <StackPanel Orientation="Horizontal">
        <TextBlock>Protocol:</TextBlock>
        <TextBlock>Unknown Protocol</TextBlock>
    </StackPanel>
    <StackPanel Orientation="Horizontal">
        <TextBlock>Type:</TextBlock>
        <TextBlock>Not available</TextBlock>
    </StackPanel>
    <StackPanel Orientation="Horizontal">
        <TextBlock>Connection:</TextBlock>
        <TextBlock>Not encrypted</TextBlock>
    </StackPanel>
</StackPanel>
```

The result, shown in Figure 2-12, is not what we want at all. Each row has been arranged independently, and there is no consistency.

```
Protocol:Unknown Protocol
Type:Not available
Connection:Not encrypted
```

Figure 2-12. Inappropriate use of StackPanel

The Grid panel solves this problem. Rather than working a single row or a single column at a time, it aligns all elements into a grid that covers the whole area of the panel. This allows consistent positioning from one row to the next. Example 2-8 shows the same elements as Example 2-7, but arranged with a Grid rather than StackPanels.

Example 2-8. Grid Layout

```xml
<Grid ShowGridLines="True">
    <Grid.ColumnDefinitions>
        <ColumnDefinition />
        <ColumnDefinition />
    </Grid.ColumnDefinitions>
    <Grid.RowDefinitions>
        <RowDefinition />
        <RowDefinition />
        <RowDefinition />
    </Grid.RowDefinitions>

    <TextBlock Grid.Column="0" Grid.Row="0">Protocol:</TextBlock>
    <TextBlock Grid.Column="1" Grid.Row="0">Unknown Protocol</TextBlock>
    <TextBlock Grid.Column="0" Grid.Row="1">Type:</TextBlock>
    <TextBlock Grid.Column="1" Grid.Row="1">Not available</TextBlock>
    <TextBlock Grid.Column="0" Grid.Row="2">Connection:</TextBlock>
    <TextBlock Grid.Column="1" Grid.Row="2">Not encrypted</TextBlock>

</Grid>
```

The Grid needs to know how many columns and rows we require, and we indicate this by specifying a series of ColumnDefinition and RowDefinition elements at the start. This may seem rather verbose—a simple pair of properties on the Grid itself might seem like a simpler solution. However, you will typically want to control the characteristics of each column and row independently, so in practice, it makes sense to have elements representing them.

Notice that each element in the grid has its column and row specified explicitly using attached properties. This is mandatory: without these, everything ends up in column 0, row 0. (Grid uses a zero-based numbering scheme, so these correspond to the top-left corner.)

Figure 2-13 shows the result of Example 2-8. This example has lines showing the grid outline, because we enabled the ShowGridLines property. You would not

Grid, Element Order, and Z Order

You might be wondering why the Grid doesn't simply put items into the grid in the order in which they appear—this would remove the need for the Grid.Row and Grid.Column attached properties. There are a couple of reasons why it doesn't work this way.

Grid cells can be empty. If the grid's children simply filled the cells in order, you would need to put placeholders of some kind to indicate blank cells. But since elements indicate their grid position, you can leave cells empty simply by providing no content for that cell.

Cells can also contain multiple elements. In this case, the order in which the relevant elements are listed in the markup determines which appears "on top." Elements that appear later in the document are drawn over those that appear earlier. The order in which overlapping elements are drawn is usually referred to as the *Z order*. This is because the x- and y-axes are traditionally the ones used for drawing onscreen, so the z-axis would logically be used to determine how overlapping elements are ordered.

In general, panels that allow their children to overlap (e.g., Grid and Canvas) rely on the order in which elements appear in the XAML to determine the Z order.

normally do this on a finalized design—this feature is intended to make it easy to see how the Grid has divided up the available space. With grid lines displayed, it is clear that the Grid has made all the columns the same width and all the rows the same height.

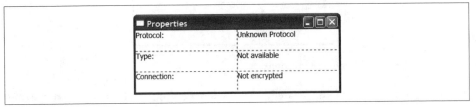

Figure 2-13. Grid layout

This default "one size fits all" behavior is useful when you want all the items in the grid to be the same size, but it's not what we want here. It would make more sense for the column on the left to be wide enough to contain the labels and for the column on the right to be allocated the remaining space. Fortunately, the Grid provides a variety of options for managing column width and row height.

Grid Column Widths and Row Heights

The column widths and row heights in a Grid are configured using the ColumnDefinition and RowDefinition elements. There are three options: fixed size, automatic size, and proportional sizing.

Fixed sizing is the simplest to understand, but often the most effort to use, as you end up having to do all of the work yourself. You can specify the Width of a column or the Height of a row in logical pixels. (A logical pixel is $\frac{1}{96}$th of an inch. WPF's coordinate system is described in Chapter 7.) Example 2-9 shows a modified version of the column definitions in Example 2-8, specifying a fixed width for the first column.

Example 2-9. Fixed column width

```
...
<Grid.ColumnDefinitions>
    <ColumnDefinition Width="50" />
    <ColumnDefinition />
</Grid.ColumnDefinitions>
...
```

Figure 2-14 illustrates the main problem with using fixed column widths. If you make the column too narrow, the contents will simply be cropped. Fixed widths and heights may seem an attractive idea because they give you complete control, but in practice they tend to be inconvenient. If you change the text or the font, you will need to modify the sizes to match. Localization of strings will also require the sizes to be changed. (See Chapter 6 for more information about localization.) So, in practice, fixed widths and heights are not what you will normally want to use.

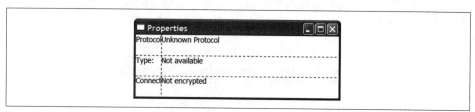

Figure 2-14. Fixed-width column truncation

The most appropriate sizing strategy for our label column will be automatic sizing. This tells the Grid to make the column wide enough to contain the widest element. Example 2-10 shows a modified version of the column and row definitions from Example 2-8, specifying automatic width for the first column and automatic heights for all of the rows.

Example 2-10. Automatic width and height

```
...
<Grid.ColumnDefinitions>
    <ColumnDefinition Width="Auto" />
    <ColumnDefinition />
</Grid.ColumnDefinitions>

<Grid.RowDefinitions>
    <RowDefinition Height="Auto" />
```

Example 2-10. Automatic width and height (continued)

```
    <RowDefinition Height="Auto" />
    <RowDefinition Height="Auto" />
</Grid.RowDefinitions>
...
```

This is not quite right yet—as you can see from Figure 2-15, the Grid has not left any space around the text, so the results seem rather cramped. The solution is exactly the same as it was for the StackPanel: we simply use the Margin property on the TextBlock elements in the Grid to indicate that we want some breathing room around the text. The Grid will honor this, giving us the layout we require.

Figure 2-15. Automatic width and height

If the idea of adding a Margin attribute to every single element sounds tedious, don't worry. We can give all of the TextBlock elements the same margin by defining a *style*, as Example 2-11 shows.

Example 2-11. Applying a consistent margin with a style

```
<Grid ShowGridLines="True">
    <Grid.Resources>
        <Style TargetType="{x:Type TextBlock}">
            <Setter Property="Margin" Value="5,3" />
        </Style>
    </Grid.Resources>
    <Grid.ColumnDefinitions>
        <ColumnDefinition Width="Auto" />
... as before
```

As Figure 2-16 shows, this provides the better-spaced layout we require. (Styles are described in detail in Chapter 5.)

Figure 2-16. Using margins

The final mechanism for specifying width and height in a Grid is the proportional method. This is sometimes called "star" sizing because of the syntax used to represent it in XAML. If you set the width or height of a column or row to be "*", this tells the Grid that it should fill all the leftover space after any fixed and automatic items have taken their share. If you have multiple items set to "*", the space is shared evenly between them.

The default value for column width and row height is "*", so you have already seen the effect of this. As Figure 2-13 shows, when we don't specify column widths or row heights, each cell ends up with exactly the same amount of space.

The star syntax is a little more flexible than this. Rather than dividing up space evenly between all the rows or columns marked with a star, we can choose a proportional distribution. Consider this set of row definitions:

```
<Grid.RowDefinitions>
    <RowDefinition Height="Auto" />
    <RowDefinition Height="2*" />
    <RowDefinition Height="*" />
</Grid.RowDefinitions>
```

Here, the first row has been set to size automatically, and the other two rows both use proportional sizing. However, the middle row has been marked as "2*". This indicates that it wants to be given twice as much of the available space as the row marked with "*". For example, if the grid's total height was 350, and the first row's automatic height came out as 50, this would leave 300 for the other rows. The second row's height would be 200, and the third row's height would be 100. The results are shown in Figure 2-17.

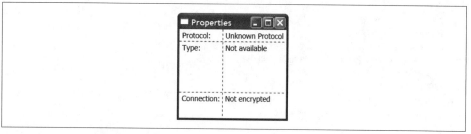

Figure 2-17. Proportional Grid sizing

The numbers before the "*" specify relative sizes, not absolute sizes. If the example above were modified to use "6*" and "3*" instead of "2*" and "*", the net result would be exactly the same. It's equivalent to saying that you want the rows to use six ninths and three ninths of the available space, instead of saying that you want them to use two thirds and one third—it's just two ways of expressing the same ratio.

 If you are familiar with HTML, you may have been wondering whether you can use percentage sizes. You can't, but this * mechanism lets you achieve the same effects.

You may have noticed that regardless of which of the three grid sizing strategies we choose, we end up using the same Width and Height properties. Each of these properties contains both a number and the sizing system. `Width` and `Height` are both of type `GridLength`. The `GridLength` type holds a number and a unit type. The number is stored as a `Double`, and the unit type is represented by the `GridUnitType` enumeration.

For a fixed size, the unit type is `Pixel`.[*] In XAML, this is indicated by providing just a number. For automatic sizing, the unit type is `Auto` and no number is required. In XAML, this is indicated by the string `"Auto"`. For proportional sizing, the unit type is `Star`. In XAML this is indicated either by just `"*"` or a number and a star—e.g., `"3.5*"`. If you use a mixture of unit types in a single grid, the grid will allocate space to fixed-size and auto-sized columns or rows first, and then divide the remaining space up amongst any star-sized items.

Spanning Multiple Rows and Columns

Looking at the Properties dialog shown earlier in Figure 2-11, there is a feature we have left out. The dialog has two horizontal lines dividing the UI into three sections. However, the aligned columns span the whole window, straddling these dividing lines.

It would be inconvenient to try to achieve a layout like this with multiple grids. If you used one for each section of the window, you could keep the columns aligned in all the grids by using fixed column widths. As discussed earlier, use of fixed widths is inconvenient because it tends to require manual adjustment of the widths whenever anything changes. With this layout, it becomes triply inconvenient: you would have to change all three grids every time anything changed.

Fortunately, it is possible to add these dividing lines without splitting the UI up into separate grids. The way to do this is to put the dividing lines into cells that span all of the columns in the grid. An element indicates to its parent `Grid` that it would like to span multiple columns by using the attached `Grid.ColumnSpan` property. Example 2-12 illustrates this approach.

Example 2-12. Using Grid.ColumnSpan

```
<Grid>
    <Grid.Resources>
        <Style TargetType="{x:Type TextBlock}">
            <Setter Property="Margin" Value="5,3" />
        </Style>
    </Grid.Resources>

    <Grid.ColumnDefinitions>
        <ColumnDefinition Width="Auto" />
```

---

[*] WPF's resolution independence means that this isn't necessarily a real physical pixel. This issue is discussed in Chapter 7.

Example 2-12. Using Grid.ColumnSpan (continued)

```
        <ColumnDefinition />
    </Grid.ColumnDefinitions>
    <Grid.RowDefinitions>
        <RowDefinition Height="Auto" />
        <RowDefinition Height="Auto" />
        <RowDefinition Height="Auto" />
        <RowDefinition Height="Auto" />
        <RowDefinition Height="Auto" />
        <RowDefinition Height="Auto" />
        <RowDefinition Height="Auto" />
        <RowDefinition Height="Auto" />
    </Grid.RowDefinitions>


    <TextBlock Grid.Column="0" Grid.Row="0">Title:</TextBlock>
    <TextBlock Grid.Column="1" Grid.Row="0">Information Overload</TextBlock>

    <Rectangle Grid.Row="1" Grid.ColumnSpan="2" Margin="5"
               Height="1" Fill="Black" />

    <TextBlock Grid.Column="0" Grid.Row="2">Protocol:</TextBlock>
    <TextBlock Grid.Column="1" Grid.Row="2">Unknown Protocol</TextBlock>
    <TextBlock Grid.Column="0" Grid.Row="3">Type:</TextBlock>
    <TextBlock Grid.Column="1" Grid.Row="3">Not available</TextBlock>
    <TextBlock Grid.Column="0" Grid.Row="4">Connection:</TextBlock>
    <TextBlock Grid.Column="1" Grid.Row="4">Not encrypted</TextBlock>

    <Rectangle Grid.Row="5" Grid.ColumnSpan="2" Margin="5"
               Height="1" Fill="Black" />

    <TextBlock Grid.Column="0" Grid.Row="6">Created:</TextBlock>
    <TextBlock Grid.Column="1" Grid.Row="6">Not available</TextBlock>
    <TextBlock Grid.Column="0" Grid.Row="7">Modified:</TextBlock>
    <TextBlock Grid.Column="1" Grid.Row="7">Not available</TextBlock>

</Grid>
```

Example 2-12 uses a single Grid to show three sets of properties. These sets are separated by thin Rectangle elements, using Grid.ColumnSpan to fill the whole width of the Grid. Because a single Grid is used for all three sections, the columns remain aligned across all three sections, as you can see in Figure 2-18. If we had used three separate grids with the left-most column set to use automatic width, each would have chosen its own width, causing the right-hand columns to be misaligned.

The Grid class also defines a Grid.RowSpan attached property. This works in exactly the same way as Grid.ColumnSpan, but vertically.

You are free to use both Grid.RowSpan and Grid.ColumnSpan on the same element—any element may occupy as many grid cells as it likes. Also, note that you are free to put multiple overlapping items into each cell.

Figure 2-18. Dividing lines spanning multiple columns

Example 2-13 illustrates both of these techniques. It adds two Rectangle elements to color in areas of the grid. The first spans multiple rows, and the second spans both multiple rows and multiple columns. Both Rectangle elements occupy cells in the Grid that are also occupied by text.

Example 2-13. Multiple Items in a Grid Cell

```
<Rectangle Grid.Column="1" Grid.Row="2" Grid.RowSpan="3"
        Margin="5,3" Fill="Cyan" />
<Rectangle Grid.Column="0" Grid.Row="6" Grid.ColumnSpan="2"  Grid.RowSpan="2"
        Margin="5,3" Fill="Khaki" />

<TextBlock Grid.Column="0" Grid.Row="0">Title:</TextBlock>
...as before
```

Figure 2-19 shows the results. Note that the order in which the elements appear in the markup is crucial, as it determines the Z order for overlapping elements. In Example 2-13, the Rectangle elements were added before the TextBlock items whose cells they share. This means that the colored rectangles appear behind the text, rather than obscuring them. If the rectangles had been added at the end of the Grid after the text, they would have been drawn over the text.

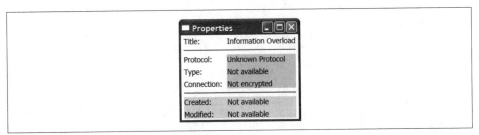

Figure 2-19. Overlapping Grid items (Color Plate 3)

This example illustrates why the Grid requires the row and column of each item to be specified explicitly, rather than being implied by the order of the elements. Cells can be shared by multiple elements. Elements can span multiple cells. This makes it impossible for the Grid to guess which element goes in which cell.

Consistency Across Multiple Grids

Although the row and column spanning features described in the previous section often make it possible to arrange your UI as you need, it will not always be possible to put all of the information you wish to present into a single Grid element. For example, consider a scrollable Grid with headings. You could just put headings and contents into a single Grid, and then place that Grid in a ScrollViewer to make it scrollable, but this suffers from a problem, which Example 2-14 illustrates.

Example 2-14. Grid in ScrollViewer

```
<ScrollViewer>
    <Grid>
        <Grid.Resources>
            <Style TargetType="{x:Type TextBlock}">
                <Setter Property="Margin" Value="5,3" />
            </Style>
        </Grid.Resources>

        <Grid.ColumnDefinitions>
            <ColumnDefinition Width="*" />
            <ColumnDefinition Width="Auto" />
            <ColumnDefinition Width="Auto" />
        </Grid.ColumnDefinitions>
        <Grid.RowDefinitions>
            <RowDefinition Height="Auto" />
            <RowDefinition Height="Auto" />
            <RowDefinition Height="Auto" />
        </Grid.RowDefinitions>

        <Border Grid.Column="0" Grid.Row="0"
                Background="LightGray" BorderBrush="Gray"
                BorderThickness="1">
            <TextBlock>Title</TextBlock>
        </Border>
        <Border Grid.Column="1" Grid.Row="0"
                Background="LightGray" BorderBrush="Gray"
                BorderThickness="1">
            <TextBlock>Location</TextBlock>
        </Border>
        <Border Grid.Column="2" Grid.Row="0" Background="LightGray"
                BorderBrush="Gray" BorderThickness="1">
            <TextBlock>Rank</TextBlock>
        </Border>

        <TextBlock Grid.Column="0" Grid.Row="1">
            Mastering Visual Studio .NET
        </TextBlock>
        <TextBlock Grid.Column="1" Grid.Row="1">O'Reilly Media, Inc.</TextBlock>
        <TextBlock Grid.Column="2" Grid.Row="1">1</TextBlock>

        <TextBlock Grid.Column="0" Grid.Row="2">IanG on Tap</TextBlock>
```

Example 2-14. Grid in ScrollViewer (continued)

```
        <TextBlock Grid.Column="1" Grid.Row="2">The Internet</TextBlock>
        <TextBlock Grid.Column="2" Grid.Row="2">2</TextBlock>
    </Grid>
</ScrollViewer>
```

Figure 2-20 shows the results. If you look at the right-hand side you can see that the scrollbar runs the entire height of the Grid, including the header line with the titles. This means that as soon as you scroll down, the headings will disappear. This is not particularly helpful.

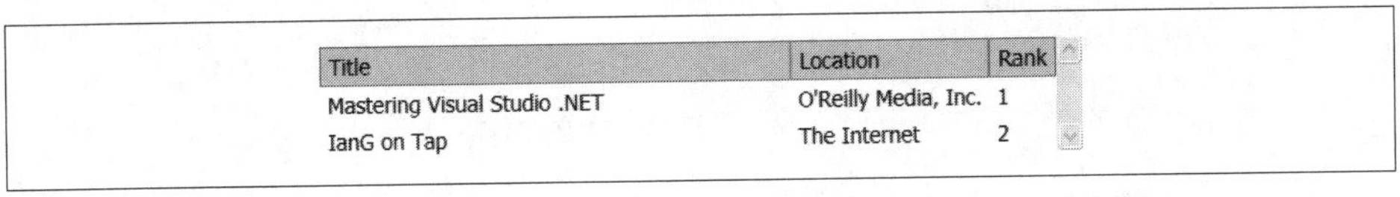

Title	Location	Rank
Mastering Visual Studio .NET	O'Reilly Media, Inc.	1
IanG on Tap	The Internet	2

Figure 2-20. Grid in ScrollViewer

We could solve this by using two grids, one for the header, and one for the main results area. Only the second grid would be placed inside a ScrollViewer. Figure 2-21 shows the results.

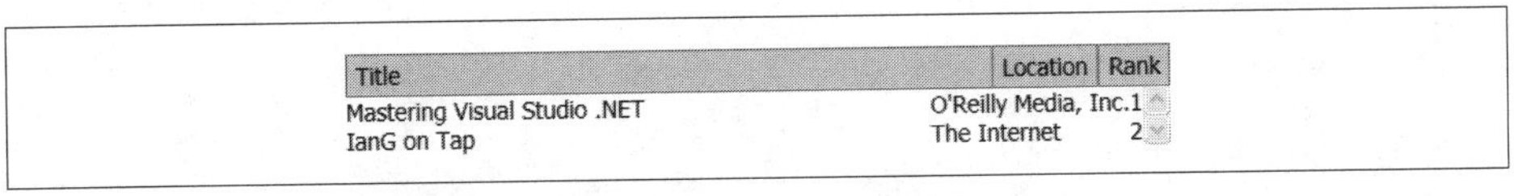

Title	Location	Rank
Mastering Visual Studio .NET	O'Reilly Media, Inc.	1
IanG on Tap	The Internet	2

Figure 2-21. Separate grid in ScrollViewer

The scrollbar is now applied just to the part that needs to be scrollable, but the alignment is all wrong. Each Grid has arranged its columns independently, so the headings no longer line up with the main contents.

The Grid supports shared-size groups to solve this problem. A *shared-size group* is simply a named group of columns that will all have the same width, even though they are in different grids. We can use this approach to keep the headings Grid consistent with the scrollable contents Grid, as shown in Example 2-15.

Example 2-15. Shared-size groups

```
<DockPanel Grid.IsSharedSizeScope="True">
    <DockPanel.Resources>
        <Style TargetType="{x:Type TextBlock}">
            <Setter Property="Margin" Value="5,3" />
        </Style>
    </DockPanel.Resources>
    <Grid DockPanel.Dock="Top">
        <Grid.ColumnDefinitions>
            <ColumnDefinition Width="*" />
            <ColumnDefinition Width="Auto" SharedSizeGroup="Location" />
            <ColumnDefinition Width="Auto" SharedSizeGroup="Rank" />
            <ColumnDefinition Width="Auto" />
```

Example 2-15. Shared-size groups (continued)

```
        </Grid.ColumnDefinitions>
        <Grid.RowDefinitions>
            <RowDefinition Height="Auto" />
        </Grid.RowDefinitions>

        <Border Grid.Column="0" Grid.Row="0" BorderThickness="1"
                Background="LightGray" BorderBrush="Gray">
            <TextBlock>Title</TextBlock>
        </Border>
        <Border Grid.Column="1" Grid.Row="0" BorderThickness="1"
                Background="LightGray" BorderBrush="Gray">
            <TextBlock>Location</TextBlock>
        </Border>
        <Border Grid.Column="2" Grid.Row="0" BorderThickness="1"
                Grid.ColumnSpan="2"
                Background="LightGray" BorderBrush="Gray">
            <TextBlock>Rank</TextBlock>
        </Border>

        <FrameworkElement Grid.Column="3"
            Width="{DynamicResource {x:Static SystemParameters.ScrollWidthKey}}" />

    </Grid>
    <ScrollViewer>
        <Grid>
            <Grid.ColumnDefinitions>
                <ColumnDefinition Width="*" />
                <ColumnDefinition Width="Auto" SharedSizeGroup="Location" />
                <ColumnDefinition Width="Auto" SharedSizeGroup="Rank" />
            </Grid.ColumnDefinitions>
            <Grid.RowDefinitions>
                <RowDefinition Height="Auto" />
                <RowDefinition Height="Auto" />
            </Grid.RowDefinitions>

            <TextBlock Grid.Column="0" Grid.Row="0">
                Mastering Visual Studio .NET
            </TextBlock>
            <TextBlock Grid.Column="1" Grid.Row="0">
                O'Reilly Media, Inc.
            </TextBlock>
            <TextBlock Grid.Column="2" Grid.Row="0">1</TextBlock>

            <TextBlock Grid.Column="0" Grid.Row="1">IanG on Tap</TextBlock>
            <TextBlock Grid.Column="1" Grid.Row="1">The Internet</TextBlock>
            <TextBlock Grid.Column="2" Grid.Row="1">2</TextBlock>
        </Grid>
    </ScrollViewer>
</DockPanel>
```

Example 2-15 illustrates the use of shared-size groups. The overall layout is defined by a DockPanel, using the attached Dock.Top property to position the header Grid at the top, and allowing the ScrollViewer to fill the remaining space.

Shared-size groups are identified by strings. Strings are prone to name collisions—it's quite possible that two developers independently working on different parts of the user interface might end up choosing the same name for their shared-size groups, inadvertently causing unrelated columns to have the same size. To avoid this problem, WPF requires that we indicate the scope within which we wish to use a particular shared-size group. This is the purpose of the Grid.IsSharedSizeScope attached property on the DockPanel—it indicates that the DockPanel is the common ancestor, and prevents the groups defined inside the DockPanel from being associated with any groups defined elsewhere in the UI.

Having defined the scope of the names, using shared-size groups is very straightforward. We just apply the SharedSizeGroup attribute to the "Location" and "Rank" ColumnDefinition, ensuring that the columns are sized consistently across the two grids. Figure 2-22 shows the results.

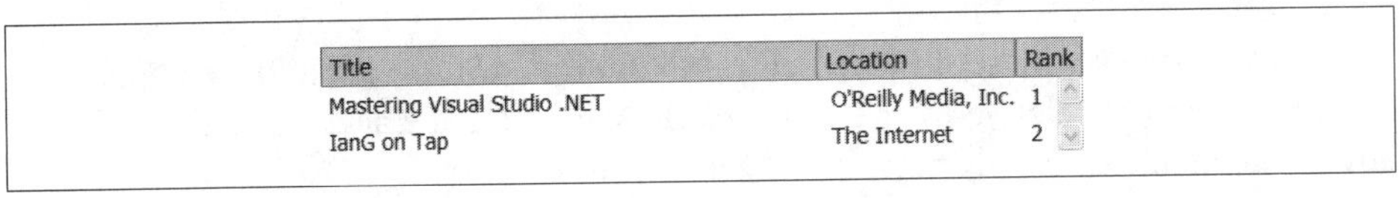

Title	Location	Rank
Mastering Visual Studio .NET	O'Reilly Media, Inc.	1
IanG on Tap	The Internet	2

Figure 2-22. Shared-size groups

The ScrollViewer adds a scrollbar to the display, and this meant that a small hack was required to get this working on the pre-release build of WPF that was current at the time of writing. This scrollbar takes away some space from the main Grid, making it slightly narrower than the header Grid. Remember that the "Title" column's size is set to "*" meaning that it should fill all available space. The ScrollViewer's scrollbar eats into this space, making the "Title" column in the main Grid slightly narrower than the one in the header Grid, destroying the alignment.

You might think that we could fix this by adding a shared-size group for the title column. Unfortunately, specifying a shared-size group seems to disable the "*" behavior—the column reverts to automatic sizing.

The fix for this is to add an extra column to the header row. This row needs to be exactly the same width as the scrollbar added by the ScrollViewer. So we have added a fourth column, containing a FrameworkElement, with its Width set to the system scroll-width metric in order to make sure that it is exactly the same width as a scrollbar. (We are using a DynamicResource reference to retrieve this system parameter. This technique is described in Chapter 6.) It's unusual to use a FrameworkElement directly, but since we just need something that takes up space but has no appearance, it makes a good lightweight filler. Its presence keeps all of the columns perfectly aligned across the two grids. (A more elegant solution will no doubt be possible in the final release of WPF.)

 The Grid is the most powerful of the built-in panels. You can get the Grid to do anything that DockPanel and StackPanel can do—those simpler elements are provided for convenience. For nontrivial user interfaces, the Grid is likely to be the best choice for your top-level GUI layout, as well as being useful for detailed internal layout.

Canvas

Occasionally, the automatic layout offered by DockPanel, StackPanel, or Grid will not enable the look you require, and it will be necessary to take complete control of the precise positioning of every element. For example, when you want to build an image out of graphical elements the positioning of the elements is dictated by the picture you are creating, not by any set of automated layout rules. For these scenarios, you will want to use the Canvas.

The Canvas is the simplest of the panels. It allows the location of child elements to be specified precisely relative to the edges of the canvas. The Canvas doesn't really do any layout at all—it simply puts things where you tell it to.

 If you are accustomed to working with fixed layout systems such as those offered by Visual Basic 6, MFC, and the most basic way of using Windows Forms, then the Canvas will seem familiar and natural. However, it is strongly recommended that you avoid it unless you really need this absolute control. The automatic layout provided by the other panels will make your life very much easier, because they can adapt to changes in text and font. They also make it far simpler to produce resizable user interfaces. Moreover, localization tends to be much easier with resizable user interfaces, because different languages tend to produce strings with substantially different lengths. Don't opt for the Canvas simply because it seems familiar.

When using a Canvas, you must specify the location of each child element. If you don't, all of your elements will end up at the top left-hand corner. Canvas defines four attached properties for setting the position of child elements. Vertical position is set with either the Top or Bottom property, and horizontal position is determined by either the Left or Right property, an approach that is illustrated in Example 2-16.

Example 2-16. Positioning on a Canvas

```
<Canvas Background="Yellow">
  <TextBlock Canvas.Left="10" Canvas.Top="20">Hello</TextBlock>
  <TextBlock Canvas.Right="10" Canvas.Bottom="20">world!</TextBlock>
</Canvas>
```

Example 2-16 shows a Canvas containing two TextBlock elements. The first has been positioned relative to the top-left corner of the Canvas: the text will always appear ten pixels in from the left and twenty pixels down from the top. (As always, these are logical pixels—nominally 1/96th of an inch, and not necessarily a single screen pixel.) Figure 2-23 shows the result.

Figure 2-23. Simple Canvas layout

The second text element is more interesting. It has been positioned relative to the bottom right of the form, which means that if the canvas gets resized, the element will move with that corner of the canvas. For example, if the Canvas were the main element of a window, the second TextBlock element would move with the bottom right corner of the window if the user resized it.

> If you have used Windows Forms, you may be wondering whether setting both the Top and Bottom properties (or both Left and Right properties) will cause the element to resize automatically when the containing canvas is resized. Sadly, unlike with anchoring in Windows Forms, this technique does not work. If you specify both Left and Right, or both Top and Bottom, one of the properties will simply be ignored. (Top takes precedence over Bottom, and Left takes precedence over Right.)
>
> Fortunately, it is easy to get this kind of behavior with a single-cell Grid and the Margin property. If you put an element into a grid with a margin of, say, "10,10,30,40" its top-left corner will be at (10,10) relative to the top left of the grid, its right-hand side will always be 30 pixels from the right edge of the grid, and its bottom edge will always be 40 pixels from the bottom of the grid. So this is another reason to prefer Grid over Canvas.

The main use for Canvas is to arrange drawings. If you employ graphical elements such as Ellipse and Path, which are discussed in Chapter 7, you will typically need precise control over their location, in which case the Canvas is ideal.

When child elements are larger than their parent panel, most panels crop them, but the Canvas does not by default. This is sometimes useful because it means you do not need to specify the size of the canvas—a zero-sized canvas works perfectly well. However, if you want to clip the content, set ClipToBounds to True.

The price you pay for the precise control offered by the Canvas is inflexibility. However, there is one common scenario in which you can mitigate this rigidity. If you've used a Canvas to arrange a drawing, and would like that drawing to be automatically resizable, you can use a Viewbox in conjunction with the Canvas.

Viewbox

The Viewbox element automatically scales its content to fill the space available. Viewbox is not strictly speaking a panel—it derives from Decorator. This means that, unlike most panels, it can only have one child. However, its ability to adjust the size of its content in order to adapt to its surroundings make it a useful layout tool.

Figure 2-24 shows a window that doesn't use a Viewbox but probably should. The window's content is a Canvas containing a rather small drawing. The markup is shown in Example 2-17.

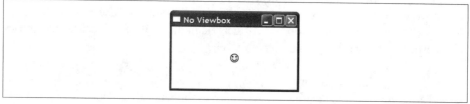

Figure 2-24. Canvas without Viewbox

Example 2-17. Canvas without Viewbox

```
<Window xmlns="http://schemas.microsoft.com/winfx/avalon/2005">

    <Canvas Width="18" Height="18" VerticalAlignment="Center">
        <Ellipse Canvas.Left="1" Canvas.Top="1" Width="16" Height="16"
                 Fill="Yellow" Stroke="Black" />
        <Ellipse Canvas.Left="4.5" Canvas.Top="5" Width="2.5" Height="3"
                          Fill="Black" />
        <Ellipse Canvas.Left="11" Canvas.Top="5" Width="2.5" Height="3"
                          Fill="Black" />
        <Path Data="M 5,10 A 3,3 90 0 0 13,10" Stroke="Black" />
    </Canvas>

</Window>
```

We can use a Viewbox to resize the content automatically. The Viewbox will expand it to be large enough to fill the space, as shown in Figure 2-25. (If you're wondering why the drawing doesn't touch the edges of the window, it's because the Canvas is slightly larger than the drawing it contains.)

All we had to do to get this automatic resizing was to wrap the Canvas element in a Viewbox element, as is done in Example 2-18.

Figure 2-25. Canvas with Viewbox

Example 2-18. Using Viewbox

```
<Window xmlns="http://schemas.microsoft.com/winfx/avalon/2005">

    <Viewbox>
        <Canvas Width="20" Height="18" VerticalAlignment="Center">

            ...as before

        </Canvas>
    </Viewbox>

</Window>
```

Notice how in Figure 2-25 the Canvas has been made tall enough to fill the window, but not wide enough. This is because by default, the Viewbox preserves the aspect ratio of its child. If you want, you can disable this so that it fills all the space, as Figure 2-26 shows.

Figure 2-26. Viewbox with Stretch

To enable this behavior we set the Stretch property. Its default value is Uniform. We can make the Viewbox stretch the Canvas to fill the whole space by setting the property to to Fill, as Example 2-19 shows.

Example 2-19. Specifying a Stretch

```
...
    <Viewbox Stretch="Fill">
...
```

The `Stretch` property can also be set to `None` to disable stretching—you might do this from code to flip between scaled and normal-sized views of a drawing. There is also a `UniformToFill` setting, which preserves the aspect ratio, but fills the space, clipping the source in one dimension if necessary (see Figure 2-27).

Figure 2-27. UniformToFill

 The `Viewbox` can scale any child element—it's not just for `Canvas`. However, you would rarely use it to size anything other than a drawing. If you were to use a `Viewbox` to resize some non-graphical part of your UI, it would resize any text in there as well, making it look inconsistent with the rest of your UI. For a resizable user interface, you are best off relying on the resizable panels shown in this chapter.

It's time to return to our example. The document viewer's overall layout is complete, as is the layout for the panels around the edge of the window. The one remaining piece is the main document view. For this, we will use WPF's text-layout services.

Text Layout

The simplest element for presenting text is `TextBlock`, which is efficient but has limited functionality. `TextFlow` offers more advanced typography and layout functionality but with slightly more overhead.

TextBlock

`TextBlock` is useful for putting short blocks of text into a user interface. If you don't require any special formatting of the text, you can simply wrap your text in a `TextBlock`:

```
<TextBlock>Hello, world!</TextBlock>
```

However, even though `TextBlock` is the simplest text-handling element, it is capable of a little more than this example shows. For example, it has a set of properties for controlling the font, shown in Table 2-2.

Table 2-2. TextBlock font properties

Property	Usage
FontFamily	Typeface name; e.g., "Times New Roman" or "Lucida Console"
FontSize	Size of the font
FontStretch	Used to indicate condensed or expanded versions of a typeface, where available
FontStyle	Normal, Oblique, or Italic
FontWeight	Weight; e.g., "Bold," "Light" or "Black"

Text wrapping

The TextBlock is capable of wrapping text across multiple lines where necessary. This is enabled with the TextWrap property, as shown in Example 2-20.

Example 2-20. Text wrapping

```
<TextBlock FontSize="24" TextWrap="Wrap">
    Split across multiple lines
</TextBlock>
```

The result is shown in Figure 2-28. (If you try this, note that you will only see wrapping if the TextBlock is in a sufficiently narrow space to need it. Even with wrapping enabled, the TextBlock prefers to put everything on one line when it can.)

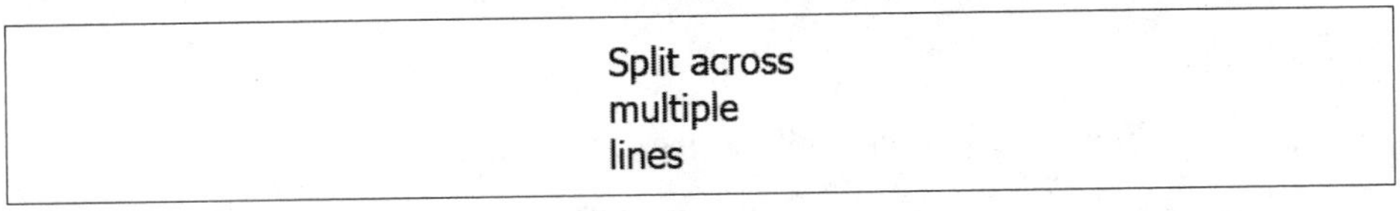

Split across
multiple
lines

Figure 2-28. Text wrapping

This wrapping facility can also be used to flow other elements across multiple lines. The TextBlock can have a mixture of text and arbitrary elements, as you can see in Example 2-21.

Example 2-21. Flowing non-text elements

```
<TextBlock TextWrap="Wrap">
    <Button>Split</Button>
    <CheckBox>across</CheckBox>
    <TextBox>multiple</TextBox>
    lines
</TextBlock>
```

The results are shown in Figure 2-29. Elements are treated in exactly the same way as words—if they are too wide to fit on the current line, they will be moved onto the next line.

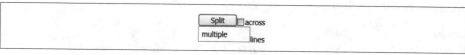

Figure 2-29. Element wrapping

Text styles

As well as supporting a mixture of text and other elements, the TextBlock is also able to support a mixture of text styles. If you would like a word to be in italic, bold, or a different typeface, this is easily achieved. WPF defines a number of so-called "inline" elements for modifying the appearance of text within a single control. These are shown in Table 2-3.

Table 2-3. Inline text elements

Element name	Usage
AccessKey	Underlines the section in the style of an accelerator key.
Bold	Makes the text bold.
Hyperlink	Displays the text as a hyperlink.
Italic	Makes the text italic.
Subscript	Shows the text raised, and in a smaller typeface.
Superscript	Shows the text lowered, and in a smaller typeface.
Underline	Underlines the text.

Example 2-22 shows a few of these inline elements in use.

Example 2-22. Inline elements

```
<TextBlock FontSize="18">
    <AccessKey>T</AccessKey>his <Italic>is</Italic> <Bold>rather</Bold>
    <Underline>messy</Underline>. <Hyperlink>www.example.com</Hyperlink>
</TextBlock>
```

Text and Whitespace

As Figure 2-30 shows, there's a trap for the unwary when using inline elements. XML parsing does not necessarily preserve whitespace, because many XML documents use whitespace for formatting. For example, most of the XAML in this book uses indentation to make the structure of the markup easier to follow. When there is nothing but whitespace between two elements, the XAML compiler strips out this space by default. Unfortunately, this is undesirable in this particular example—it has removed the space we wanted between the words. (Notice that it has only affected adjacent inline elements. We can still see a space between "This" and "is," and between the "." and "www.example.com" because in those cases, there was more than just whitespace between the inline elements.)

> This *is*rather**messy**. **www.example.com**

Figure 2-30. Inline elements with lost spaces

The solution to this is a standard XML feature. You can mark elements with the xml:
space="preserve" attribute to indicate that the whitespace it contains is significant.
Example 2-23 shows a modified version that fixes the problem.

Example 2-23. preserve attribute

```
<TextBlock FontSize="18" xml:space="preserve"><AccessKey>T</AccessKey>his
<Italic>is</Italic> <Bold>rather</Bold> <Underline>messy</Underline>.
<Hyperlink>www.example.com</Hyperlink></TextBlock>
```

 Note that the code in Example 2-23 has been split across multiple
lines in order to fit into the book. If you try this, type it in on a single
line.

This solves the problem, as Figure 2-31 shows. However, it has come at the cost of
making the markup much more untidy. We cannot add any spaces, tabs, or line
breaks in order to make the markup easier to read, as these will now be faithfully
represented onscreen.

> This *is***rather** messy. **www.example.com**

Figure 2-31. Inline elements with preserved space

As a compromise, you could use the xml:space attribute more selectively. Rather
than applying it to the top level, you could apply it to just those elements that are
causing you problems. This might make the markup a little more verbose, but it does
give you more freedom to format it however you like. Example 2-24 uses this technique, and produces the same output as Example 2-23.

Example 2-24. space attribute

```
<TextBlock FontSize="18">
    <AccessKey>T</AccessKey>his <Italic>is</Italic>
    <Bold xml:space="preserve"> rather </Bold>
    <Underline>messy</Underline>. <Hyperlink>www.example.com</Hyperlink>
</TextBlock>
```

If you place a line break in a section of text marked with xml:space="preserve", that
line break will be honored on the display. If you would like to add a line break without using xml:space="preserve", you can add a LineBreak element.

Text alignment

The TextBlock offers a TextAlignment property that allows you to choose whether text is left-aligned, right-aligned, centered, or justified. Example 2-25 shows all of these styles. Figure 2-32 shows the results.

Example 2-25. Text alignment

```
<StackPanel Orientation="Horizontal">
  <TextBlock Width="80" TextAlignment="Left" TextWrap="Wrap" Margin="15">
    This text is left-aligned. Its right edge is ragged.
  </TextBlock>
  <TextBlock Width="80" TextAlignment="Right" TextWrap="Wrap" Margin="15">
    This text is right-aligned. Its left edge is ragged.
  </TextBlock>
  <TextBlock Width="110" TextAlignment="Center" TextWrap="Wrap" Margin="15">
    This text is centered. Both edges are ragged, in a symmetrical way.
  </TextBlock>
  <TextBlock Width="120" TextAlignment="Justify" TextWrap="Wrap" Margin="15">
    This text is justified. Both edges  are straight. Words are spaced out
    in order to achieve this
  </TextBlock>
</StackPanel>
```

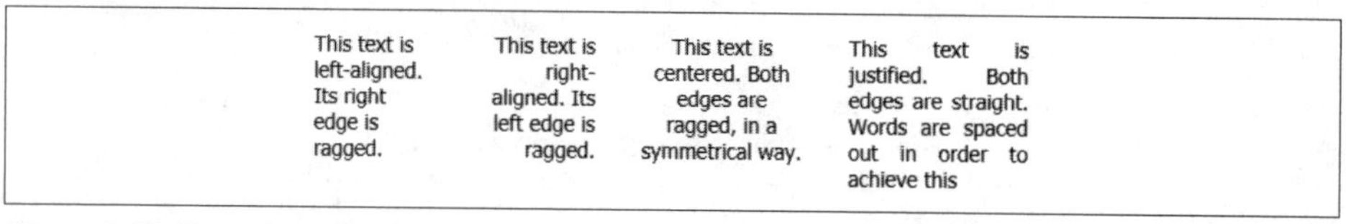

This text is left-aligned. Its right edge is ragged.	This text is right-aligned. Its left edge is ragged.	This text is centered. Both edges are ragged, in a symmetrical way.	This text is justified. Both edges are straight. Words are spaced out in order to achieve this

Figure 2-32. Text alignment

The ability of the TextBlock to support wrapping, arbitrary inline UI elements, line breaking, and a mixture of text styles makes it useful for a wide variety of simple text scenarios. However, its layout capabilities are somewhat limited compared to the TextFlow element.

TextFlow

TextFlow can perform all of the same duties as TextBlock, but provides much more sophisticated layout support. As well as supporting all of the inline elements described in the previous section, TextFlow adds support for so-called "block" elements. These are listed in Table 2-4.

Table 2-4. Block element types

Element name	Usage
Paragraph	A paragraph
List	Numbered or bulleted list
Table	A table of information

Table 2-4. Block element types (continued)

Element name	Usage
Floater	An element arranged outside of the main flow, and which everything else can flow around
Figure	Similar to a Floater, but with a caption, and with extra control over exactly where the element is placed

Paragraph

The Paragraph element doesn't strictly enable anything that couldn't be achieved with the LineBreak element in a TextBlock. However, it is often more convenient, as paragraphs are part of the logical structure of the text. It usually makes more sense to deal with paragraphs rather than the gaps between them.

For example, if a particular paragraph represents a heading, you can apply a font or style to the Paragraph element containing the heading. (Paragraph supports all of the same font properties as TextBlock.) Choosing a font for a LineBreak, on the other hand, would not be useful.

List

The List element allows numbered or bullet lists to be added to the text. The same syntax is used whether you require numbers or bullets. The style is selected with the MarkerStyle property, as shown in Example 2-26.

Example 2-26. List marker styles

```
<TextFlow FontSize="18">
    <List MarkerStyle="Decimal">
        <ListItem><Paragraph>First item</Paragraph></ListItem>
        <ListItem><Paragraph>Second item</Paragraph></ListItem>
    </List>
</TextFlow>
```

The MarkerStyle property supports several styles, both numeric and bulleted. Figure 2-33 shows all of them in use.

Decimal:	UpperRoman:	LowerRoman:	UpperLatin:	LowerLatin:
1. First item	I. First item	i. First item	A. First item	a. First item
2. Second item	II. Second item	ii. Second item	B. Second item	b. Second item

	Circle:	Disc:	Square:	Box:
	O item	• item	❑ item	▪ item

Figure 2-33. List styles

Table

The Table element presents information in tabular form. It may seem curious for WPF to offer both a Table and a Grid element, but they address slightly different problems. Although there is some overlap in functionality, neither offers a complete subset of the other's functionality. The Grid is designed entirely for laying out elements and can be used to arrange user interfaces that don't look obviously tabular (e.g., it is useful for a wide range of dialog layouts). The Table is designed exclusively for presenting tables of information.

Table is less flexible than Grid when it comes to layout. Each cell in a Table must be occupied by exactly one item. (Items can still span cells.) However, it does provide some features not offered by Grid. It has support for header and footer information. And if a table is viewed in a context that supports pagination, such as printing or the DocumentViewer control, Table has special support for being split across multiple pages.

Example 2-27 shows a Table with headers. The result is shown in Figure 2-34.

Example 2-27. Table

```
<Table CellSpacing="6">
    <TableHeader>
        <TableRow FontSize="24" FontWeight="Bold">
            <TableCell ColumnSpan="3" TextAlignment="Center" >
                Ice Cream
            </TableCell>
        </TableRow>
        <TableRow FontWeight="Bold" FontSize="18" Background="LightGray">
            <TableCell>Type</TableCell>
            <TableCell>Description</TableCell>
            <TableCell>Availability</TableCell>
        </TableRow>
    </TableHeader>
    <TableBody>
        <TableRow>
            <TableCell>Chocolate</TableCell>
            <TableCell>Yummy</TableCell>
            <TableCell>Widespread</TableCell>
        </TableRow>
        <TableRow>
            <TableCell>Cookie Dough</TableCell>
            <TableCell>Extra yummy</TableCell>
            <TableCell>Scarce - Ian ate it all</TableCell>
        </TableRow>
        <TableRow>
            <TableCell>Artichoke</TableCell>
            <TableCell>Gruesome</TableCell>
            <TableCell>Rarely available</TableCell>
        </TableRow>
    </TableBody>
</Table>
```

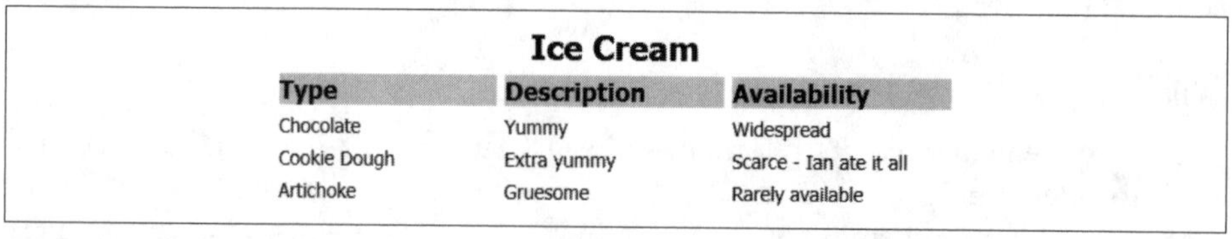

Ice Cream		
Type	**Description**	**Availability**
Chocolate	Yummy	Widespread
Cookie Dough	Extra yummy	Scarce - Ian ate it all
Artichoke	Gruesome	Rarely available

Figure 2-34. Table

Floater

A Floater is a block that is not laid out as part of the overall flow of the text. It is usually arranged to one side, and the rest of the content of the TextFlow flows around it.

Example 2-28 shows a typical use of a Floater. This TextFlow contains some Paragraphs of text. It has one Floater acting as a sidebar. Figure 2-35 shows the results.

Example 2-28. TextFlow with Floater

```
<TextFlow>
    <Paragraph FontWeight="Bold">Metasyntactic Variables</Paragraph>

    <Paragraph>
        <Floater Background="LightBlue" Margin="10" Width="230">
            <Paragraph FontWeight="Bold">Foo and Bar</Paragraph>
            <Paragraph>
                Many developers are unaware of the origin of
                the most popular placeholders,'Foo' and 'Bar'.
            </Paragraph>
            <Paragraph>
                They originate from the Air Force. They are a
                corruption of FUBAR, the polite expansion of
                which is 'Fouled Up Beyond All Recognition.'
            </Paragraph>
        </Floater>
    </Paragraph>
    <Paragraph>
        In describing software, we must often describe
        constructs or processes in the most general of
        terms. Using concrete examples is not always wise,
        because specific details of the example can get
        in the way.
    </Paragraph>

    <Paragraph>
        English offers only a limited number of nouns
        suitable for discussing abstract constructs.
        You can only use the word 'thing' so many times
        without sounding stupid, so most software
        practitioners use words such as 'Foo' and 'Bar'
        to augment the number of abstract nouns available.
        These words are sometimes referred to as
        'metasyntactic variables'
    </Paragraph>
</TextFlow>
```

By default, a Floater will appear to the right of the main text. However, you can change this with the HorizontalAlignment property, which supports three options: Left, Center, and Right. Example 2-29 shows all three in use, and Figure 2-36 shows the results.

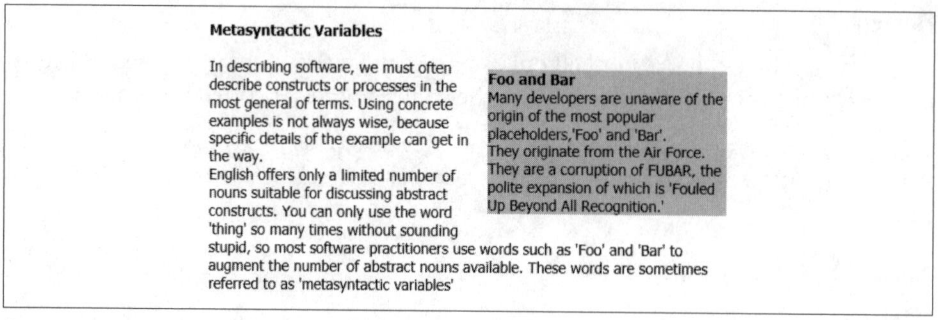

Metasyntactic Variables

In describing software, we must often describe constructs or processes in the most general of terms. Using concrete examples is not always wise, because specific details of the example can get in the way.

English offers only a limited number of nouns suitable for discussing abstract constructs. You can only use the word 'thing' so many times without sounding stupid, so most software practitioners use words such as 'Foo' and 'Bar' to augment the number of abstract nouns available. These words are sometimes referred to as 'metasyntactic variables'

Foo and Bar
Many developers are unaware of the origin of the most popular placeholders,'Foo' and 'Bar'. They originate from the Air Force. They are a corruption of FUBAR, the polite expansion of which is 'Fouled Up Beyond All Recognition.'

Figure 2-35. TextFlow with Floater

Example 2-29. Floater alignment

```
<TextFlow>

    <Paragraph>
        <Floater Background="Yellow" Margin="10,0" HorizontalAlignment="Left">
            <Paragraph FontWeight="Bold">Left Floater</Paragraph>
        </Floater>
    </Paragraph>
    <Paragraph>
        This is some normal text.
    </Paragraph>
    <Paragraph>
        <Floater Background="Yellow" Margin="10,5" HorizontalAlignment="Center">
            <Paragraph FontWeight="Bold">Center Floater</Paragraph>
        </Floater>
    </Paragraph>
    <Paragraph>
        This is some more normal text. Notice how it flows both
        sides of the centered floater.
    </Paragraph>
    <Paragraph>
        <Floater Background="Yellow" Margin="10,0" HorizontalAlignment="Right">
            <Paragraph FontWeight="Bold">Right Floater</Paragraph>
        </Floater>
    </Paragraph>
    <Paragraph>
        This is yet more normal text.
    </Paragraph>

</TextFlow>
```

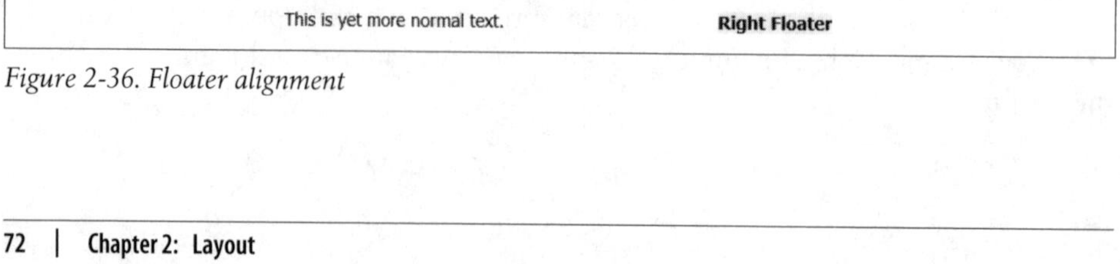

Left Floater This is some normal text.

This is some more normal   **Center Floater**   text. Notice how it flows
both sides of the   centered floater.

This is yet more normal text.   **Right Floater**

Figure 2-36. Floater alignment

Figure

Figure provides a similar service to Floater; it allows a block to be put outside of the main text, which the main text will flow around. However, you can give the TextFlow more freedom to decide where to position a Figure than a Floater.

Figure has a HorizontalAnchor property that indicates where the figure should appear. This does a very similar job to the floater's HorizontalAlignment, and offers the same three options: left, middle and center. However, unlike the floater, you can specify how far the figure can be moved vertically in order to fit it into the text. By allowing WPF some flexibility for vertical placement, it may be able to do a better job of arranging the document onto the available screen space than would otherwise be possible.

For example, you can specify PageLeft, PageCenter, or PageRight. These indicate that the figure should be placed to the left of, in the center of, or to the right of the page, respectively. This tells the TextFlow that any vertical position is allowed so long as it the figure is displayed on the same page as the paragraph after the figure. ContentLeft, ContentCenter, and ContentRight allow the figure to appear at any vertical location. (Pagination is only relevant when printing, or using a paginating control such as the DocumentViewer. When viewing text without pagination, Page and Content positioning are equivalent.)

You can choose to be more restrictive by specifying ParagraphLeft, ParagraphCenter, or ParagraphRight anchor values. These require the figure to be displayed next to the paragraph that follows the figure. These horizontal anchor values are equivalent to the three HorizontalAlignment options we saw with Floater.

There is also a VerticalAnchor property. This lets you specify the vertical positioning you require, allowing WPF some latitude with the vertical location. The available options are essentially the same as for the horizontal anchor, but with Left, Center, and Right replaced with Top, Center, and Bottom.

Armed with the TextFlow, we are now in a position to complete the layout of our document viewer. The TextFlow offers all of the layout features we require to provide richly formatted text. All we need to do is wrap it in a ScrollViewer to enable scrolling through long documents.

Common Layout Properties

All user-interface elements have a standard set of layout properties, inherited from the FrameworkElement base class. We have seen a few of these in passing in the preceding section, but we will now look at them all in a little more detail.

Width and Height

You can set these properties to specify an exact width and height for your element. You should try to avoid using these—in general it is preferable to let elements determine their own size where possible. Allowing elements to size to content makes changing your user interface less effort. It can also simplify localization. However, you will occasionally need to provide a specific size.

If you specify a Width or Height, the layout system will always attempt to honor your choices. Of course if you make an element wider than the screen, WPF can't make the screen any wider, but as long as what you request is possible, it will be done.

MinWidth, MaxWidth, MinHeight, and MaxHeight

These properties allow you to specify upper and lower limits on the size of an element. If you need to constrain your user interface's layout, it is usually better to use these than Width and Height where possible. By specifying upper and lower limits, you can still allow WPF some latitude to automate the layout.

It is possible to mandate limits that simply cannot be fulfilled. For example, if you request a MinWidth of 10000, WPF won't be able to honor that request unless you have some very exotic display hardware. In these cases, your element will be truncated to fit the space available.

HorizontalAlignment and VerticalAlignment

These properties control how an element is placed inside a parent when there is more room available than necessary. For example, a vertical StackPanel will be as wide as the widest element, meaning that any narrower elements are given excess space. A DockPanel will provide enough space for an element to fill an edge or all the remaining space. Alignment is for these sorts of scenarios, enabling you to determine what the child element does with the extra space.

The default setting for both of these properties is Stretch: when excess space is available, the element will be enlarged to fill that space. The alternatives are Left, Center, and Right for HorizontalAlignment, and Top, Center, and Bottom for VerticalAlignment. If you choose any of these, the element will not be stretched—it will use its natural height or width and will then be positioned to one side or in the center.

Margin

This property determines the amount of space that should be left around the element during layout.

`Margin` can be specified as a single number, a pair of numbers, or a list of four numbers. When one number is used, this indicates that the same amount of space should be left on all sides. With two numbers, the first indicates the space to the left and right while the second indicates the space above and below. When four numbers are specified, they indicate the amount of space on the left, top, right, and bottom sides, respectively.

Padding

`Padding` is similar to `Margin`, except it is internal rather than external. While `Margin` indicates how much space should be left around the outside of an element, `Padding` specifies how much space should be left between a control's outside, and its internal content.

`Padding` is not present on all WPF elements, since not all elements have internal content. It is defined by the `Control` base class.

Example 2-30 shows three buttons, one with just margin, one with both margin and padding, and one with just padding. It also fills the area behind the buttons with color so the effects of the margin can be seen.

Example 2-30. Margin versus padding

```
<Grid ShowGridLines="True">
    <Grid.ColumnDefinitions>
        <ColumnDefinition Width="Auto" />
        <ColumnDefinition Width="Auto" />
        <ColumnDefinition Width="Auto" />
    </Grid.ColumnDefinitions>
    <Grid.RowDefinitions>
        <RowDefinition Height="Auto" />
    </Grid.RowDefinitions>

    <Rectangle Grid.ColumnSpan="2" Fill="Cyan" />

    <Button Grid.Column="0" Margin="20">Click me!</Button>
    <Button Grid.Column="1" Margin="10" Padding="10">Click me!</Button>
    <Button Grid.Column="2" Padding="20">Click me!</Button>

</Grid>
```

Figure 2-37 shows the results. The button with margin but no padding has appeared at its normal size, but has space around it. The middle button is larger, because the padding causes space to be added around its content. The third button is larger still because it has more padding, but it has no space around it since it has no margin.

Figure 2-37. Buttons with margin and padding

FlowDirection

The FlowDirection property controls how text flows. The default is left to right, then top to bottom. Many cultures use the alternative right-to-left then top-to-bottom flow style.

RenderTransform and LayoutTransform

The RenderTransform and LayoutTransform properties can both be used to apply a transform, such as scaling or rotation, to an element and all of its children. The use of transforms is described in Chapter 7, but it is useful to understand their impact on layout.

If you apply a transform that doubles the size of an element, the element will appear to be twice as large onscreen. You would normally want the layout system to take this into account—if a Rectangle with a Width of 100 is scaled up to twice its size, it will normally make sense for the layout system to treat it as having an effective width of 200. However, you might sometimes want the transformation to be ignored for layout purposes. For example, if you are using a transform in a short animation designed to draw attention to a particular part of the UI, you probably don't want the entire UI's layout to be changed as a result of that animation.

You can apply a transform to an object using either LayoutTransform or RenderTransform. The former causes the transform to be taken into account by the layout system, while the latter causes it to be ignored. Example 2-31 shows three buttons, one containing untransformed content and the other two containing content transformed with these two properties.

Example 2-31. RenderTransform and LayoutTransform

```
<Button><TextBlock>Foo bar</TextBlock></Button>
<Button><TextBlock RenderTransform="scale 3">Foo bar</TextBlock></Button>
<Button><TextBlock LayoutTransform="scale 3">Foo bar</TextBlock></Button>
```

The results are shown in Figure 2-38. As you can see, the button with content scaled by RenderTransform is the same size as the unscaled one. The presence of the transform has had no effect on layout, and the content no longer fits inside the space allocated for it. However, the LayoutTransform has been taken into account by the layout system—the third button has been enlarged in order for the scaled content to fit.

Figure 2-38. RenderTransform and LayoutTransform

The way in which LayoutTransform is dealt with by the layout system is straightforward for simple scaling transforms. The size allocated for the content is scaled up accordingly. But what about rotations? Figure 2-39 shows a button whose content has a LayoutTransform of "rotate 30". This is not a scaling transform, but notice that the button has grown to accommodate the content: it is taller than a normal button.

Figure 2-39. LayoutTransform and rotation

When it encounters a LayoutTransform, the layout system simply applies that transform to the bounding box, and makes sure that it provides enough space to hold the transformed bounding box. This can occasionally lead to surprising results. Consider the two buttons in Example 2-32.

Example 2-32. Rotation of content

```
<Button>
    <Line Stroke="Blue" Y1="30" X2="100" />
</Button>
<Button>
    <Line LayoutTransform="rotate 50" Stroke="Blue" Y1="30" X2="100" />
</Button>
```

These are shown in Figure 2-40. The top button looks as you would expect: the button is large enough to contain the graphical content. But the bottom one is rather surprising—the button appears to be much larger than necessary.

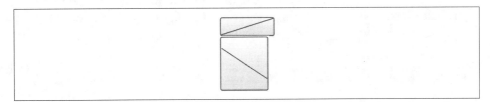

Figure 2-40. Rotated content

This result only makes sense when you consider the bounding box—remember that the layout system decides how much space to allocate by applying the LayoutTransform to the bounding box. So let's look at it again, this time with the bounding boxes shown. Example 2-33 is a modified version of Example 2-32, with Border elements added to show the bounding box of the lines.

Example 2-33. Rotation showing bounding box

```
<Button>
    <Border BorderBrush="Black" BorderThickness="1">
        <Line Stroke="Blue" Y1="30" X2="100" />
```

Example 2-33. Rotation showing bounding box (continued)

```
        </Border>
</Button>
<Button>
    <Border BorderBrush="Black" BorderThickness="1"
            LayoutTransform="rotate 50" >
        <Line Stroke="Blue" Y1="30" X2="100" />
    </Border>
</Button>
```

In Figure 2-41, we can now see the bounding box of the content. The button on the bottom shows this bounding box with the same 30 degree rotation as has been applied to the line. This makes it clear that the button is exactly large enough to hold this rotated bounding box.

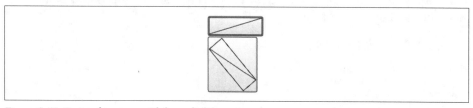

Figure 2-41. Rotated content with bounding boxes

You might be wondering why WPF doesn't simply calculate a new bounding box for the transformed content instead of transforming the existing one. The reason is that calculating a new bounding box may not be possible. Some elements, such as Canvas, can declare a width and height that does not directly reflect their apparent size. The only sensible way in which the layout system can deal with such elements is to treat their logical shape as being rectangular. Using this approach of transforming the bounding box everywhere ensures consistent behavior.

When Content Doesn't Fit

Sometimes, WPF will not be able to honor your requests because you have asked the impossible. Example 2-34 creates a StackPanel with a Height of 100, which contains a Button with a Height of 195.

Example 2-34. Asking the impossible

```
<StackPanel Height="100" Background="Yellow" Orientation="Horizontal">
    <Button>Foo</Button>
    <Button Height="30">Bar</Button>
    <Button Height="195">Spong</Button>
</StackPanel>
```

Clearly that last button is too big to fit—it is taller than its containing panel. Figure 2-42 shows how WPF deals with this.

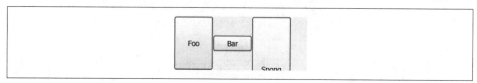

Figure 2-42. Truncation when content is too large

The StackPanel has dealt with the anomaly by truncating the element that was too large. When confronted with contradictory hardcoded sizes like these, most panels take a similar approach and will crop content where it simply cannot fit.

There is some variation in the way that panels handle overflow in situations where sizes are not hardcoded but there is still too much content to fit. Example 2-35 puts the three copies of a TextBlock and its content into a StackPanel, a DockPanel, and a Grid cell.

Example 2-35. Handling overflow

```
<Grid>
    <Grid.RowDefinitions>
        <RowDefinition />
        <RowDefinition />
        <RowDefinition />
    </Grid.RowDefinitions>

    <StackPanel Height="100" Background="Yellow" Orientation="Horizontal">
        <TextBlock TextWrap="Wrap" FontSize="20">
            This is some text that is too long to fit.
        </TextBlock>
    </StackPanel>

    <DockPanel Grid.Row="1" Height="100" Background="Yellow" LastChildFill="False">
        <TextBlock TextWrap="Wrap" FontSize="20">
            This is some text that is too long to fit.
        </TextBlock>
    </DockPanel>

    <TextBlock Grid.Row="2" TextWrap="Wrap" FontSize="20">
        This is some text that is too long to fit.
    </TextBlock>
</Grid>
```

Figure 2-43 shows what happens when the available space is too narrow to hold the TextBlock at its natural length.

The StackPanel has simply truncated the TextBlock. The DockPanel and Grid have been slightly more intelligent. They have exploited the fact that the TextBlock had wrapping enabled and were able to flow the text into the narrow space available.

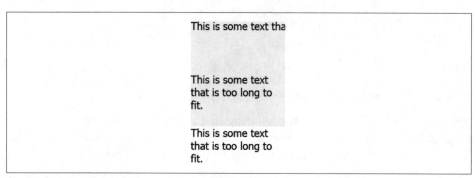

Figure 2-43. Overflow handling

Custom Layout

Although WPF supplies a flexible set of layout elements, you might decide that none of them suits your requirements. Fortunately, the layout system is extensible, and it is fairly straightforward to implement your own custom panel. To write a panel, you need to understand how the layout system works.

Layout occurs in two phases: *measure* and *arrange*. Your custom panel will first be asked how much space it would like to have—that's the measure phase. The panel should measure each of its children to find out how much space they require and then decide how much space the panel needs in total.

Of course, you can't always get what you want. If your panel's measure phase decides it needs an area twice the size of the screen, it won't get that in practice. (Unless its parent happens to be a ScrollViewer.) Moreover, even when there is enough space onscreen, your panel's parent could still choose not to give it to you. For example, if your custom panel is nested inside a Grid, the Grid may well have been set up with a hardcoded width for the column your panel occupies, in which case that's the width you'll get regardless of what you asked for during the measure phase.

It is only in the "arrange" phase that we find out how much space we have. During this phase, we must decide where to put all of our children as best we can in the space available.

You might be wondering why layout bothers with the measure phase when the amount of space we get during the arrange phase may be different. The reason for having both is that most panels try to take the measured size of their children into account during the arrange phase. You can think of the measure phase as asking every element in the tree what it would like, and the arrange phase as honoring those measurements where possible, compromising only where physical or configured constraints come into play.

Let's create a new panel type to see how the measure and arrange phases work in practice. We'll call this new panel DiagonalPanel, and it will arrange elements diagonally from the top left of the panel down to the bottom right, as Figure 2-44 shows. Each element's top-left corner will be placed where the previous element's bottom-right corner went.

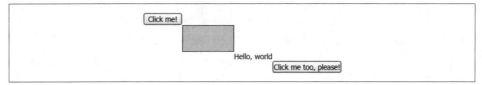

Figure 2-44. Custom DiagonalPanel in action

You don't really need to write a new panel type to achieve this layout—you could get the same effect with a Grid, setting every row and column's size to Auto. However, the same argument could be made for StackPanel and DockPanel: neither of those do anything that couldn't be done with the Grid. It's just convenient to have a simple single-purpose panel, as the Grid equivalent is a little more verbose.

To implement this custom layout, we must write a class that derives from Panel and implements the measure and arrange phases. As Example 2-36 shows, we do this by overriding the MeasureOverride and ArrangeOverride methods.

Example 2-36. Custom DiagonalPanel

```
using System;
using System.Windows.Controls;
using System.Windows;

namespace CustomPanel {
    public class DiagonalPanel : Panel {

        protected override Size MeasureOverride( Size availableSize ) {
            double totalWidth = 0;
            double totalHeight = 0;

            foreach( UIElement child in Children ) {
                child.Measure( new Size( double.PositiveInfinity,
                                         double.PositiveInfinity ) );
                Size childSize = child.DesiredSize;
                totalWidth += childSize.Width;
                totalHeight += childSize.Height;
            }

            return new Size( totalWidth, totalHeight );
        }

        protected override Size ArrangeOverride( Size finalSize ) {
```

Example 2-36. Custom DiagonalPanel (continued)

```
        Point currentPosition = new Point( );

        foreach( UIElement child in Children ) {
            Rect childRect = new Rect( currentPosition, child.DesiredSize );
            child.Arrange( childRect );
            currentPosition.Offset( childRect.Width, childRect.Height );
        }

        return new Size( currentPosition.X, currentPosition.Y );
    }
  }
}
```

Notice that the MeasureOverride method is passed a Size parameter. If the parent is aware of size constraints that will be need to be applied during the arrange phase, it passes them here during the measure phase. For example, if this panel's parent was a Window with a specified size, the Window would pass in the size of its client area during the measure phase. However, not all panels will do this. You may find the available size is specified as being Double.PositiveInfinity in both dimensions, indicating that the parent is not informing us of any fixed constraints at this stage. An infinite available size indicates that we should simply pick whatever size is appropriate for our content.

Some elements ignore the available size, because their size is always determined by their contents. For example, our panel's simple layout is driven entirely by the natural size of its children, so it ignores the available size. Our MeasureOverride simply loops through all of the children, adding up their widths and heights. We pass in an infinite size when calling Measure on each of the children in order to use their preferred size.

 You must call Measure on all of your panel's children. If your MeasureOverride fails to Measure all of its children, the layout process may not function correctly. All elements expect to be measured before they are arranged. Their arrange logic might rely on the results of calculations performed during the measure phase. When you write a custom panel, it is your responsibility to ensure that child elements are measured and arranged at the appropriate times.

In our ArrangeOverride, we loop through all of the child elements, setting them to their preferred size, basing the position on the bottom right-hand corner of the previous element. Since this very simple layout scheme cannot adapt, it ignores the amount of space it has been given. Any child elements that do not fit will be cropped, as happens with StackPanel.

This measure-and-arrange sequence traverses the entire user interface tree—all elements use this mechanism, not just panels. A custom panel is the most appropriate place to write custom layout logic for managing the arrangement of controls. However, there is one other situation in which you might want to override the MeasureOverride and ArrangeOverride methods. If you are writing a graphical element that uses the low-level visual APIs described in Chapter 7, you will need to override these methods in order for the layout system to work with your element. The code will typically be simpler than for a panel, because you will not have child elements to arrange. Your MeasureOverride will simply need to report how much space it needs, and ArrangeOverride will tell you how much space you have been given.

Where Are We?

WPF provides a wide range of options for layout. Many panel types are available, each offering its own layout style. These can then be composed into a single application in any number of ways, supporting many different user interface styles. The top-level layout will usually be set with either a DockPanel or a Grid. The other panels are typically used to manage the details. You can use the common layout properties on child elements to control how they are arranged; these properties work consistently across all panel types. The TextBlock and TextFlow provide great support for embedding text into your application. And if none of the built-in layout features meet your requirements, you can write your own custom panel.

CHAPTER 3

Controls

Windows applications present a graphical interface that users interact with. Most users are familiar with certain common GUI features. For example, they recognize buttons as things that can be clicked, and they know that they can type into text boxes. These features are often made up of many individual visual pieces. For example, a text box consists of an outlined rectangle, a sequence of characters representing the text, and a blinking vertical line showing where the next character will appear. Users recognize that these parts form a single entity that offers certain functionality. In WPF, such composite entities are called controls.

There are many ways to alter the appearance of a control. We can adjust properties to make simple alterations, such as setting foreground and background colors. With controls that support the content model, we can put any mixture of graphics and text inside the control. We can even using templates to replace the whole look of the control. However, even if we replace the visuals of, say, a scrollbar, we have not changed its fundamental role as an element for performing scrolling. In WPF, it is this behavior that forms the essence of a control.

In this chapter we will examine how to use controls to handle input, and we will explore the set of behaviors offered by the built-in controls.

What Are Controls?

Controls are the building blocks of an application's user interface. They are interactive features such as text boxes, buttons, or listboxes. You may be familiar with similar constructs from other user-interface technologies—most UI frameworks offer an abstraction similar to a control. However, WPF is somewhat unusual, in that controls are typically not directly responsible for their own appearance. Many GUI frameworks require you to write a custom control when customizing a control's appearance. In WPF, this is not necessary: nested content, and templates offer powerful yet simpler solutions. You only need to write a custom control if you need behavior that is different from any of the built-in controls.

Many WPF user-interface elements are not controls. For example, shapes like `Rectangle` and `Ellipse` have no intrinsic behavior—they are just about appearance.

Figure 3-1 shows how a control fits into a program. As you can see, the visible parts of the control are provided by its template, rather than the control itself. The control is not completely disconnected from these visuals, of course. It uses them to present information to the user. Moreover, since the visuals are all that the user can see, they will be the immediate target of any user input. This means that although visuals can be replaced, the replacement has certain responsibilities—there is a form of contract between the control and its visuals. The use of templates to replace visuals is discussed in Chapter 5.

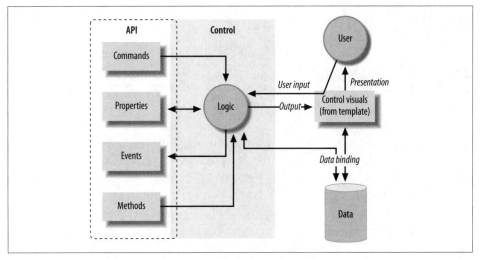

Figure 3-1. A control's relationship with its visuals and data

You may be familiar with the Model View Controller (MVC) concept. This is a way of structuring the design of interactive systems. MVC has been interpreted in many different ways over the years, but broadly speaking, it always breaks the design down into objects representing the underlying data (the Model), objects that display that data (the View), and objects that manage input from the user and interactions between the model and view (the Controller).

MVC is a concept that can be used at many different scales, and it is somewhat unusual to apply it at the level of an individual control. However, if you are accustomed to the MVC way of looking at things, you may find it helpful to think of data binding as a way of attaching a Model, the visuals as the View, and the control as the Controller.

While the control makes itself visible to the user through its visuals, it makes its services available to developers mainly through an API, shown on the left of Figure 3-1. Controls offer *commands* to represent supported operations. For example, a text box might offer Cut, Copy, and Paste commands. Controls offer *properties* to provide a means of modifying either behavior or appearance. Controls raise *events* when something important happens, such as receiving some form of input. Finally, some functionality may be exposed through *methods*. Commands, properties, and events are preferred because they are easier to use from markup, and will be supported by design tools. However, for features that would only ever be used from code, methods may be a more appropriate form of API.

Of course developers and designers are not the only people who will use controls. Controls also need to respond to users, so let's look at how input is handled in WPF.

Handling Input

There are three main kinds of user input for a Windows application: mouse, keyboard, and ink.* There is also a higher-level concept of a *command*: a particular action that might be accessible through several different inputs such as keyboard shortcuts, toolbar buttons, and menu items.

Although controls typically act as the principal target for input, all elements in a user interface can receive input. This is unsurprising because controls rely entirely on the services of lower-level elements like Rectangle and TextBlock in order to provide visuals. All of the input mechanisms described in the following sections are therefore available on all user-interface element types.

Routed Events

The .NET Framework defines a standard mechanism for exposing events. A class may expose several events, and each event may have any number of subscribers. Although WPF uses this standard mechanism, it augments it to overcome a limitation: if a normal .NET event has no registered handlers, it is effectively ignored.

Consider what this would mean for a typical WPF control. Most controls are made up of multiple visual components. For example, even if you give a button a very plain visual tree consisting of a single Rectangle and provide a simple piece of text as the content, there are still two elements present: the text and the rectangle. The button should respond to a mouse click whether the mouse is over the text or the rectangle. In the standard .NET event-handling model, this would mean registering a MouseLeftButtonUp event handler for both elements.

---

* *Ink* is input written with a stylus. You will usually only see this on Tablet PCs and handheld devices.

This problem would get much worse when taking advantage of WPF's content model. A Button is not restricted to having just simple text as a caption—it can contain any markup. The example in Figure 3-2 is fairly unambitious, but even this has six elements: the yellow outlined circle, the two dots for the eyes, the curve for the mouth, the text, and the button background itself. Attaching event handlers for every single element would be tedious and inefficient. Fortunately, it's not necessary.

Figure 3-2. A button with nested content

WPF uses *routed events*, which are more thorough than normal events. Instead of just calling handlers attached to the element that raised the event, a routed event will call all of the handlers attached to any given node, from the originating element right up to the root of the user-interface tree.

Example 3-1 shows markup for the button shown in Figure 3-2. If one of the Ellipse elements inside the Canvas were to receive input, event routing would enable the Button, Grid, Canvas and Ellipse to receive the event, as Figure 3-3 shows.

Example 3-1. Handling events in a user interface tree

```
<Button MouseLeftButtonDown="MouseButtonDownButton"
        PreviewMouseLeftButtonDown="PreviewMouseButtonDownButton">
    <Grid MouseLeftButtonDown="MouseButtonDownGrid"
            PreviewMouseLeftButtonDown="PreviewMouseButtonDownGrid">
        <Grid.ColumnDefinitions>
            <ColumnDefinition />
            <ColumnDefinition />
        </Grid.ColumnDefinitions>

        <Canvas MouseLeftButtonDown="MouseButtonDownCanvas"
                PreviewMouseLeftButtonDown="PreviewMouseButtonDownCanvas"
                Width="20" Height="18" VerticalAlignment="Center">

            <Ellipse MouseLeftButtonDown="MouseButtonDownEllipse"
                    PreviewMouseLeftButtonDown="PreviewMouseButtonDownEllipse"
                    Canvas.Left="1" Canvas.Top="1" Width="16" Height="16"
                    Fill="Yellow" Stroke="Black" />
            <Ellipse Canvas.Left="4.5" Canvas.Top="5" Width="2.5" Height="3"
                    Fill="Black" />
            <Ellipse Canvas.Left="11" Canvas.Top="5" Width="2.5" Height="3"
                    Fill="Black" />
            <Path Data="M 5,10 A 3,3 0 0 0 13,10" Stroke="Black" />
        </Canvas>

        <TextBlock Grid.Column="1">Foo</TextBlock>
    </Grid>
</Button>
```

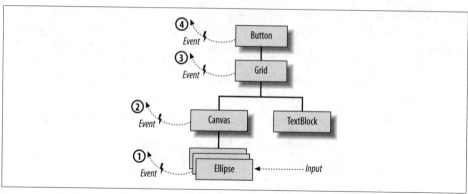

Figure 3-3. Routed events

A routed event can be bubbling, tunneling, or direct. A *bubbling event* starts by looking for event handlers attached to the element that raised the event, and then looks at its parent, and then its parent's parent, and so on, until it reaches the root of the tree—this order is indicated by the numbers on Figure 3-3. A *tunneling event* works in reverse—it looks for handlers at the root of the tree first and works its way down, finishing with the originating element.

Direct events are routed in the same way as normal .NET event handling—only handlers attached directly to the originating element are notified. This is typically used for events that make sense only in the context of their originating element. For example, it would be unhelpful if mouse enter and leave events were bubbled or tunneled—the parent element is unlikely to care when the mouse moves from one child element to another. At the parent element, you would expect "mouse leave" to mean "the mouse has left the parent element," and because direct event routing is used, that's exactly what it does mean. If bubbling were used, the event would effectively mean "the mouse has left an element that is inside the parent, and is now inside another element that may or may not be inside the parent."

With the exception of direct events, WPF defines most routed events in pairs—one bubbling and one tunneling. The tunneling event name always begins with Preview and is raised first. This gives parents of the originating element the chance to see the event before it reaches the child. (Hence the "Preview" prefix.) The tunneling preview event is followed directly by a bubbling event. In most cases, you will only handle the bubbling event—the preview would usually only be used if you wanted to be able to block the event, or if you needed a parent to do something in advance of normal handling of the event.

In Example 3-1, most of the elements have event handlers that are specified for the MouseLeftButtonDown and PreviewMouseLeftButtonDown events—the bubbling and tunneling events respectively. Example 3-2 shows the corresponding code-behind file.

Example 3-2. Handling events

```
using System;
using System.Windows;
using System.Diagnostics;


namespace EventRouting {
    public partial class Window1 : Window {
        public Window1( ) {
            InitializeComponent( );
        }

        private void MouseButtonDownButton(object sender, RoutedEventArgs e)
        { Debug.WriteLine("MouseButtonDownButton"); }

        private void PreviewMouseButtonDownButton(object sender, RoutedEventArgs e)
        { Debug.WriteLine("PreviewMouseButtonDownButton"); }


        private void MouseButtonDownGrid(object sender, RoutedEventArgs e)
        { Debug.WriteLine("MouseButtonDownGrid"); }

        private void PreviewMouseButtonDownGrid(object sender, RoutedEventArgs e)
        { Debug.WriteLine("PreviewMouseButtonDownGrid"); }


        private void MouseButtonDownCanvas(object sender, RoutedEventArgs e)
        { Debug.WriteLine("MouseButtonDownCanvas"); }

        private void PreviewMouseButtonDownCanvas(object sender, RoutedEventArgs e)
        { Debug.WriteLine("PreviewMouseButtonDownCanvas"); }


        private void MouseButtonDownEllipse(object sender, RoutedEventArgs e)
        { Debug.WriteLine("MouseButtonDownEllipse"); }

        private void PreviewMouseButtonDownTextBlock(object sender,
                                                RoutedEventArgs e)
        { Debug.WriteLine("PreviewMouseButtonDownEllipse"); }

    }
}
```

Each of the handlers prints out a debug message. Here is the debug output we get when clicking on the TextBlock inside the Canvas:

```
PreviewButtonDownButton
PreviewButtonDownGrid
PreviewButtonDownCanvas
PreviewButtonDownEllipse
ButtonDownEllipse
ButtonDownCanvas
ButtonDownGrid
ButtonDownButton
```

This confirms that the Preview event is raised first. It also shows that it starts from the Button element and works down, as we would expect with a tunneling event. The bubbling event that follows starts from the Ellipse element and works up.

This bubbling routing offered for most events means that you can register a single event handler on a control, and it will receive events for any of the elements nested inside of the control. You do not need any special handling to deal with nested content or custom visual tree contents—events simply bubble up to the control and can all be handled there.

Halting event handling

There are some situations in which you might not want events to bubble up. For example, you may wish to convert the event into something else—the Button element effectively converts MouseLeftButtonDown and MouseLeftButtonUp events into Click events. It suppresses the lower-level events so that only the Click event bubbles up out of the control.

Any handler can prevent further processing of a routed event by setting the Handled property of the RoutedEventArgs, as shown in Example 3-3.

Example 3-3. Halting event routing with Handled

```
private void ButtonDownCanvas(object sender, RoutedEventArgs e) {
    Debug.WriteLine("ButtonDownCanvas");
    e.Handled = true;
}
```

Another reason for setting the Handled flag would be if you wanted to prevent normal event handling. If you do this in a Preview handler, not only will the tunneling of the Preview event stop, the corresponding bubbling event that would normally follow will not be raised at all, so it appears as though the event never occurred.

Determining the target

Although it is convenient to be able to handle events from a group of elements in a single place, your handler might need to know which element caused the event to be raised. You might think that this is the purpose of the sender parameter of your handler. In fact, the sender always refers to the object to which you attached the event handler. In the case of bubbled and tunneled events, this often isn't the element that caused the event to be raised. In Example 3-1, the ButtonDownWindow handler's sender will always be the Window itself.

Fortunately, it's easy to find out which element was the underlying cause of the event. The RoutedEventArgs object passed as the second parameter offers an OriginalSource property.

Routed events and normal events

Normal .NET events (or, as they are sometime called, *CLR events*) offer one advantage over routed-event syntax: many .NET languages have built-in support for handling CLR events. Because of this, most routed events are also exposed as CLR events. This provides the best of both worlds: you can use your favorite language's event-handling syntax while taking advantage of the extra functionality offered by routed events.

 This is possible thanks to the flexible design of the CLR event mechanism. Although there is a standard simple behavior associated with CLR events, the CLR designers had the foresight to realize that some applications would require more sophisticated behavior. Classes are therefore free to implement events however they like. WPF reaps the benefits of this design by defining CLR events that are implemented internally as routed events.

Example 3-1 and Example 3-2 arranged for the event handlers to be connected by using attributes in the markup. But we could have used the normal C# event-handling syntax to attach handlers in the constructor instead. For example, we could remove the `MouseLeftButtonDown` and `PreviewMouseLeftButtonDown` attributes from Example 3-1 and then modify the constructor from Example 3-2 as follows in Example 3-4.

Example 3-4. Attaching event handlers in code

```
...
public Window1( ) {
    InitializeComponent( );

    this.MouseLeftButtonDown += MouseButtonDownWindow;
    this.PreviewMouseLeftButtonDown += PreviewMouseButtonDownWindow;
}
...
```

We could also do the same for the events from the nested elements. We would just have to apply x:Name attributes in order to be able to access those elements from C#.

The code-behind is usually the best place to attach event handlers. If your user interface has unusual and creative visuals, there's a good chance that the XAML file will effectively be owned by a graphic designer. A designer shouldn't have to know what events a developer needs to handle, or what the handler functions are called. So you will normally get the designer to give elements names in the XAML, and the developer will attach handlers in the code-behind.

Mouse Input

Mouse input is directed to whichever element is directly under the mouse cursor. All user-interface elements derive from the UIElement base class, which defines a number of mouse input events. These are listed in Table 3-1.

Table 3-1. Mouse input events

Event	Routing	Meaning
GotMouseCapture	Bubble	Element captured the mouse.
LostMouseCapture	Bubble	Element lost mouse capture.
MouseEnter	Direct	Mouse pointer moved into element.
MouseLeave	Direct	Mouse pointer moved out of element.
PreviewMouseLeftButtonDown, MouseLeftButtonDown	Tunnel, Bubble	Left mouse button pressed while cursor inside element.
PreviewMouseLeftButtonUp, MouseLeftButtonUp	Tunnel, Bubble	Left mouse button released while cursor inside element.
PreviewMouseRightButtonDown, MouseRightButtonDown	Tunnel, Bubble	Right mouse button pressed while cursor inside element.
PreviewMouseRightButtonUp, MouseRightButtonUp	Tunnel, Bubble	Right mouse button released while cursor inside element.
PreviewMouseMove, MouseMove	Tunnel, Bubble	Mouse cursor moved while cursor inside element.
PreviewMouseWheel, MouseWheel	Tunnel, Bubble	Mouse wheel moved while cursor inside element.
QueryCursor	Bubble	Mouse cursor shape to be determined while cursor inside element.

UIElement also defines a pair of properties that indicate whether the mouse cursor is currently over the element: IsMouseOver and IsMouseDirectlyOver. The distinction between these two properties is that the former will be true if the cursor is over the element in question or over any of its child elements, but the latter will be true only if the cursor is over the element in question but not one of its children.

Note that the basic set of mouse events shown above does not include a click event. This is because clicks are a higher-level concept than basic mouse input—a button can be "clicked" with either the mouse or the keyboard. Moreover, clicking doesn't necessarily correspond directly to a single mouse event—usually, the user has to press and release the mouse button while the mouse is over the control to register as a click. Accordingly, these higher-level events are provided by more specialized element types. The Control class adds a MouseDoubleClick and PreviewMouseDoubleClick event pair. ButtonBase, the base class of Button, CheckBox, and RadioButton, goes on to add a Click event.

If you use a Shape (such as a Rectangle or Path) with a Fill that uses transparency, the shape will act as the target of the input if the mouse is over the shape. This can be slightly surprising if you use a completely transparent brush—the shape will not be visible, but it will still be the input target, regardless of what the mouse may appear to be over. If you want a shape with a transparent fill that does not capture mouse input, simply supply no Fill at all—if the Fill is null, (as opposed to being a completely transparent brush), the shape will not act as an input target.

Remember that if the reason you are considering handling a mouse event is simply to provide some visible feedback to the user, writing an event handler may be overkill. It is often possible to achieve the visible effects you require entirely within the markup for a style by using declarative property triggers and event triggers. (Triggers are discussed in Chapter 5.)

Keyboard Input

Keyboard input introduces the idea of *focus*. Unlike the mouse, there is no way for the user to move the keyboard over an element in order to indicate the target for input. In Windows, a particular element is designated as having the *focus*, meaning that it acts as the target for keyboard input. The user sets the focus by clicking the mouse or tapping the stylus on the control in question, or by using navigation keys such as the Tab and cursor keys.

 In principle, any user interface element can receive the focus—the IsFocused property is defined on UIElement, the base class of FrameworkElement. However, the Focusable property determines whether this feature is enabled on any particular element. By default, this is true for controls and false for other elements.

Table 3-2 shows the keyboard input events offered on user-interface elements. All of these items use tunnel and bubble routing for the Preview and main events, respectively.

Table 3-2. Keyboard input events

Event	Routing	Meaning
PreviewGotFocus, GotFocus	Tunnel, Bubble	Element received the focus.
PreviewLostFocus, LostFocus	Tunnel, Bubble	Element lost the focus.
PreviewKeyDown, KeyDown	Tunnel, Bubble	Key pressed.
PreviewKeyUp, KeyUp	Tunnel, Bubble	Key released.
PreviewTextInput, TextInput	Tunnel, Bubble	Element received text input.

Note that TextInput is not necessarily keyboard input. It represents textual input in a device-independent way, so this event can also be raised as a result of ink input.

Ink Input

The stylus used on tablet PCs and other ink-enabled systems has its own set of events. Table 3-3 shows the ink input events offered on user-interface elements.

Table 3-3. Stylus and ink events

Event	Routing	Meaning
GotStylusCapture	Bubble	Element captured stylus.
LostStylusCapture	Bubble	Element lost stylus capture.
PreviewStylusDown, StylusDown	Tunnel, Bubble	Stylus touched screen over element.
PreviewStylusUp, StylusUp	Tunnel, Bubble	Stylus left screen while over element.
PreviewStylusEnter, StylusEnter	Tunnel, Bubble	Stylus moved into element.
PreviewStylusLeave, StylusLeave	Tunnel, Bubble	Stylus left element.
PreviewStylusInRange, StylusInRange	Tunnel, Bubble	Stylus moved close enough to screen to be detected.
PreviewStylusOutOfRange, StylusOutOfRange	Tunnel, Bubble	Stylus moved out of detection range.
PreviewStylusMove, StylusMove	Tunnel, Bubble	Stylus moved while over element.
PreviewStylusInAirMove, StylusInAirMove	Tunnel, Bubble	Stylus moved while over element but not in contact with screen.
PreviewStylusSystemGesture, StylusSystemGesture	Tunnel, Bubble	Stylus performed a gesture.
PreviewTextInput, TextInput	Tunnel, Bubble	Element received text input.

Commands

Many applications provide more than one way of performing certain actions. For example, consider the act of creating a new file. You might choose the File → New menu item, or you could click the corresponding toolbar button. Alternatively, you might use a keyboard shortcut such as Ctrl+N. If the application provides a scripting system, a script could provide yet another way to perform the action. The outcome is the same whichever mechanism you use, because these are all just different ways of invoking the same underlying *command*.

WPF has built-in support for this idea. The RoutedCommand class represents a logical action that could be invoked in several ways. In a typical WPF application, each menu item and toolbar button is associated with an underlying RoutedCommand object.

RoutedCommand works in a very similar way to lower-level forms of input. When a command is invoked, it raises two events: PreviewExecuteEvent and ExecuteEvent.

These tunnel and bubble through the element tree in the same way as input events. The target of the command is determined by the way in which the command was invoked. Typically, the target will be whichever element currently has the focus, but RoutedCommand also provides an overloaded Execute method, which may be passed a specific target element.

There are several places from which you can get hold of a RoutedCommand. A few controls offer commands. For example, the ScrollBar control defines commands for each of its actions and makes these available in static fields, such as LineUpCommand and PageDownCommand. However, most commands are not unique to a particular control. Some correspond to application-level actions such as "new file" or "open." Others represent actions that would be invoked on a control, but could be implemented by several different controls. For example, both TextBox and RichTextBox can handle clipboard operations.

There is a set of classes that provide standard commands. These classes are shown in Table 3-4. This means you don't need to create your own RoutedCommand objects to represent the most common operations. Moreover, many of these commands are understood by built-in controls. For example, TextBox and RichTextBox support many of these standard operations, including clipboard, undo, and redo commands.

Table 3-4. Standard command classes

Class	Command types
ApplicationCommands	Commands common to almost all applications. Includes clipboard commands, undo and redo, and document-level operations (open, close, print, etc.).
ComponentCommands	Operations for moving through information such as scroll up and down, move to end, and text selection.
EditCommands	Text-editing commands such as bold, italic, and alignment.
MediaCommands	Media-playing operations such as transport (play, pause, etc.), volume control, and track selection.

Handling commands

For a command to be of any use, something must respond to it. This works slightly differently from handling normal input events, because most commands are not defined by the controls that will handle them. The classes in Table 3-4 define 95 commands, so if Control defined CLR events for each distinct command, that would require 190 events once you include previews. Not only would this be extremely unwieldy, it wouldn't even be a complete solution—most applications define their own custom commands as well as using standard ones. The obvious alternative would be for the RoutedCommand itself to raise events. However, each command is a singleton—there is only one ApplicationCommands.New object, for example. If you were able to add a handler to a command object directly, that handler would run any time the command was invoked anywhere in your application. What if you just want to handle the command when it is executed in a particular window?

The CommandBinding class solves these problems. A CommandBinding object maps a specific RoutedCommand onto a handler function in the scope of a particular user-interface element. It is this CommandBinding that raises the PreviewExecute and Execute events, rather than the UI element. These bindings are held in the CommandBindings property defined by UIElement. Example 3-5 shows how to handle the ApplicationCommands.New command in the code-behind file for a window.

Example 3-5. Handling a command

```
public partial class Window1 : Window {
    public Window1( ) {
        InitializeComponent( );

        CommandBinding cmdBindingNew = new CommandBinding(ApplicationCommands.New);
        cmdBindingNew.Execute +=  NewCommandHandler;
        CommandBindings.Add(cmdBindingNew);
    }

    private void NewCommandHandler(object sender, ExecuteEventArgs e) {
        if (unsavedChanges) {
            MessageBoxResult result = MessageBox.Show(this,
                "Save changes to existing document?", "New",
                MessageBoxButton.YesNoCancel);

            if (result == MessageBoxResult.Cancel) {
                return;
            }
            if (result == MessageBoxResult.Yes) {
                SaveChanges( );
            }
        }

        // Reset text box contents
        inputBox.Clear( );
    }
}
```

This code relies on the bubbling nature of command routing—the top-level Window element is unlikely to be the target of the command, as the focus will usually belong to some child element inside the window. However, the command will bubble up to the top. This routing makes it easy to put the handling for commands in just one place.

The command that Example 3-5 handles is ApplicationCommands.New. If the set of standard commands does not meet all of your application's needs, you can define custom commands for specialized operations.

Defining commands

Example 3-6 shows how to define a command. WPF uses object instances to establish the identity of commands. If you were to create a second command of the same name, it would not be treated as the same command. For this reason, commands are usually put in static fields or properties.

Example 3-6. Creating a custom command

```
public partial class Window1 : Window {
    public static RoutedCommand FooCommand;

    static Window1() {
        InputGestureCollection fooInputs = new InputGestureCollection();
        fooInputs.Add(new KeyGesture(Key.F,
                                ModifierKeys.Control|ModifierKeys.Shift));
        FooCommand = new RoutedCommand("Foo", typeof(Window1), fooInputs);
    }
    ...
}
```

The Foo command created in Example 3-6 would be handled using a CommandBinding just like any other command. Of course, the user needs some way of invoking the command.

Invoking commands

As well as defining a custom command, Example 3-6 also shows one way in which a command can be associated with user input. This particular command has been configured to be invoked by a specific *input gesture*. Two input-gesture types are currently supported: a MouseGesture is a particular shape made with the mouse or stylus; a KeyGesture, as used in Example 3-6, is a particular keyboard shortcut. Many of the built-in commands are associated with standard gestures. For example, ApplicationCommands.Copy is associated with the standard keyboard shortcut for copying. (Ctrl+C in most locales.)

Although a command can be associated with a set of gestures when it is created, you may wish to assign additional shortcuts for the command in the context of a particular window. To allow this, user-interface elements have an InputBindings property. This collection contains InputBinding objects, which associate input gestures with commands. These augment the default gestures associated with the command.

Input gestures such as keyboard shortcuts are not the only way in which commands can be invoked. You can call the Execute method on the command in order to invoke it from code. As Example 3-7 shows, Execute is overloaded. If you pass no parameters, the command target will be whichever element has the focus, just as it would be if the command had been invoked using an input gesture. But you can pass in a target element if you want.

Example 3-7. Invoking a command from code

```
ApplicationCommands.New.Execute( );
...or...
ApplicationCommands.New.Execute(targetElement);
```

You might think that you would write code like this in click handlers for menu items or toolbar buttons. However, since commands are so often associated with menu items or buttons on a toolbar, Button and MenuItem both offer a Command property. This identifies the command to invoke when the element is clicked. This provides a declarative way of connecting user-interface elements to commands. You only need to write an event handler for the command itself, rather than a handler for each UI element bound to the command. Example 3-8 shows a Button associated with the standard Copy command.

Example 3-8. Invoking a command with a Button

```
<Button Command="Copy">Copy</Button>
```

Because this example uses a standard command from the ApplicationCommands class, we can use this short-form syntax, specifying nothing but the command name. For commands not defined by the classes in Table 3-4, a little more information is required. The full syntax for a command attribute in XAML is:

```
[[xmlNamespacePrefix:]ClassName.]EventName
```

If only the event name is present, the event is presumed to be one of the standard ones. For example, Undo is shorthand for ApplicationCommands.Undo. Otherwise, you must also supply a class name, and possibly a namespace prefix. The namespace prefix is required if you are using either custom commands or commands defined by some third-party component. This is used in conjunction with the Mapping XML processing instruction used to make external types available in a XAML file. (See Appendix A for more information on the Mapping processing instruction.)

Example 3-9 shows the use of the command-name syntax with all the parts present. The value of m:MyCommands.Foo means that the command in question is defined in the MyLib.Commands.MyCommands class in the mylib component and is stored in either a field or a property called Foo.

Example 3-9. Using a custom command in XAML

```
<?Mapping ClrNamespace="MyLib.Commands" Assembly="mylib"
          XmlNamespace="urn:mylib" ?>

<Window xmlns:m="urn:mylib" ...>
    ...
```

Example 3-9. Using a custom command in XAML (continued)

```
<Button Command="m:MyCommands.Foo">Custom Command</Button>
...
```

Enabling commands

As well as being executable, commands also offer a `QueryEnabled` method. This returns a Boolean indicating whether the command can be invoked right now; certain commands are only valid in particular contexts. This feature can be used to determine whether items in a menu or toolbar should be grayed out. Calls to the `QueryEnabled` method are handled in much the same way as calls to `Execute`; `CommandBinding` objects are used to handle the query. The binding raises a `PreviewQueryEnabled` and `QueryEnabled` pair of events, which tunnel and bubble in the same way as the `PreviewExecute` and `Execute` events. Example 3-10 shows how to handle this event for the system-defined `Redo` command.

Example 3-10. Handling QueryEnabled

```
public Window1( ) {
    InitializeComponent( );

    CommandBinding redoCommandBinding =
            new CommandBinding(ApplicationCommands.Redo);
    redoCommandBinding.QueryEnabled += RedoCommandQueryEnabled;
    CommandBindings.Add(redoCommandBinding);
}

void RedoCommandQueryEnabled(object sender, QueryEnabledEventArgs e) {
    if (!CanRedo( )) {
        e.IsEnabled = false;
    }
}
```

 Unfortunately, the current build of WPF at the time of writing does not gray out menu or toolbar items. It raises the `QueryEnabled` event when a menu item is invoked and prevents the command from executing if it is disabled, but does not currently provide any visual indication that a menu item is disabled. We hope this will be addressed in a future release.

We've seen all of the various ways in which controls handle input in WPF. Now let's look at the set of controls built into WPF.

Built-In Controls

WPF provides a range of built-in controls. Most of these correspond to standard Windows control types that you will already be familiar with. Note that none of these controls are wrappers around old Win32 controls. Although they look like their Win32 counterparts, they are all native WPF controls. This means that they offer full support for all of the WPF functionality described in this book, including styling, resolution independence, data binding, composition, and fully integrated support for WPF's graphical capabilities.

Buttons

Buttons are controls that a user can click. The result of the click is up to the application developer, but there are common expectations, depending on the type of button. For example, clicking on a CheckBox or RadioButton is used to express a choice and does not normally have any immediate effect beyond visually reflecting that choice. By contrast, clicking on a normal Button usually has some immediate effect.

Using buttons is straightforward. Example 3-11 shows markup for a Button element:

Example 3-11. Markup for a Button

```
<Button Click="ButtonClicked">Button</Button>
```

The contents of the element (the text "Button" in this case) are used as the button caption. A handler for the Click event has been specified with an attribute. This indicates that the code-behind for the XAML must contain a method with the name specified in the markup, such as that shown in Example 3-12. (Of course we could also attach the event handler by giving the button an x:Name and using normal C# event-handling syntax.)

Example 3-12. Handling a Click event

```
private void ButtonClicked(object sender, RoutedEventArgs e) {
    MessageBox.Show("Button was clicked");
}
```

Alternatively, a button's Command property may be set, in which case the specified command will be invoked when the button is clicked. Example 3-13 shows a button that invokes the standard ApplicationCommands.Copy command.

Example 3-13. Invoking a command with a Button

```
<Button Command="Copy">Copy</Button>
```

Figure 3-4 shows the three button types provided by WPF. These all derive from a common base class, ButtonBase. This in turn derives from ContentControl, meaning that they all support the content model: you are not restricted to using simple text as the label for a button.

Figure 3-4. Button types

As Figure 3-5 shows, you can use whatever content you like, although you will still get the default look for the button around or alongside your chosen content. (If you wish to replace the whole appearance of the button rather than just customize its caption, you can use a control template. See Chapter 5 for more information on templates.)

Figure 3-5. Buttons with nested content (Color Plate 4)

Although the buttons derive from the common `ButtonBase` base class, `RadioButton` and `CheckBox` derive from it indirectly via the `ToggleButton` class. This defines an `IsChecked` property, indicating whether the user has checked the button.

Radio buttons are normally used in groups in which only one button may be selected at any time. Use the `RadioButtonList` element to indicate that a set of radio buttons act as a group, as shown in Example 3-14.

Example 3-14. Grouping radio buttons

```
<RadioButtonList>
    <RadioButton>To be</RadioButton>
    <RadioButton>Not to be</RadioButton>
</RadioButtonList>
```

Slider and Scroll Controls

WPF provides controls that allow a value to be selected from a range. They all offer a similar appearance and usage: they show a track, indicating the range, and a draggable "thumb" with which the value can be adjusted. There are two slider controls, `HorizontalSlider` and `VerticalSlider`, shown in Figure 3-6. There are also two scrollbar controls, `HorizontalScrollBar` and `VerticalScrollBar`, shown in Figure 3-7. The main difference is one of convention rather than functionality—the scrollbar controls are commonly used in conjunction with some scrolling viewable area, while the sliders are used to adjust values.

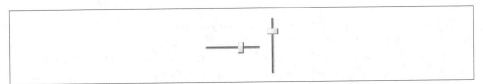

Figure 3-6. Horizontal and vertical sliders

Both the sliders and the scrollbars are very similar in use. They all derive from a common base class, `RangeBase`. This class provides `Minimum` and `Maximum` properties, which define the range of values the control represents, and a `Value` property holding the

Figure 3-7. Horizontal and vertical ScrollBars

currently selected value. It also defines SmallChange and LargeChange properties, which determine by how much the Value changes when adjusted with the arrow keys, or the PageUp and PageDown keys, respectively. The LargeChange value is also used when the part of the slider track on either side of the thumb is clicked.

While slider controls have a fixed-size thumb, the thumb on a scrollbar can change in size. If the slide is used in conjunction with a scrollable view, the size of the thumb relative to the track is proportional to the size of the visible area relative to the total scrollable area. For example, if the thumb is about one third of the length or height of the scrollbar, this indicates that one third of the scrollable area is currently in view.

You can control the size of a scrollbar's thumb with the ViewPortSize property. This can be anywhere from 0 to the Maximum property value. If the ViewPortSize is equal to Maximum, the thumb will fill the track, and will not be moveable. The smaller ViewPortSize is, the smaller the thumb will be.

If you want to provide a scrollable view of a larger user-interface area, you would not normally use the scrollbar controls directly. It is usually easier to use the ScrollViewer control.

A ScrollViewer element has a single child. Example 3-15 uses an Ellipse element, but it could be anything. If you want to put multiple elements into a scrollable view, you would nest them inside one of the panels discussed in Chapter 2.

Example 3-15. ScrollViewer

```
<ScrollViewer HorizontalScrollBarVisibility="Auto">
    <Ellipse Fill="VerticalGradient Green DarkGreen" Height="1000" Width="2000" />
</ScrollViewer>
```

If the content of a ScrollViewer is larger than the space available, the ScrollViewer can provide scrollbars to allow the user to scroll around the content, as Figure 3-8 shows. By default, a ScrollViewer provides a vertical scrollbar, but not a horizontal one. In Example 3-15, the HorizontalScrollBarVisibility property has been set to Auto, indicating that a horizontal scrollbar should be added if required.

This Auto visibility we've chosen for the horizontal scrollbar is different from the default vertical behavior. The VerticalScrollBarVisibility defaults to Visible, meaning that the scrollbar is present whether it is required or not.

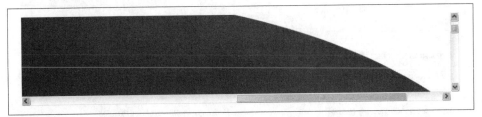

Figure 3-8. ScrollViewer

There are two ways to make sure a scrollbar does not appear. You can set its visibility either to Disabled (the default for horizontal scrollbars) or to Hidden. The distinction is that Disabled constrains the logical size of the ScrollViewer's contents to be the same as the available space. Hidden allows the logical size to be unconstrained, even though the user has no way of scrolling into the excess space. This can change the behavior of certain layout styles.

To examine how these settings affect the behavior of a ScrollViewer, we'll look at what happens to Example 3-16 as we change the ScrollViewer properties.

Example 3-16. A resizable layout

```
<ScrollViewer ...>
    <Grid>
        <Grid.ColumnDefinitions>
            <ColumnDefinition />
            <ColumnDefinition />
            <ColumnDefinition />
        </Grid.ColumnDefinitions>

        <RowDefinition Height="Auto" />

        <Button Grid.Column="0">Stretched</Button>
        <Button Grid.Column="1">Stretched</Button>
        <Button Grid.Column="2">Stretched</Button>
    </Grid>
</ScrollViewer>
```

This example shows a Grid containing three Button elements in a row. If the Grid is given more space than it requires, it will stretch the buttons to be wider than necessary. If it is given insufficient space, it will crop the buttons. If it is placed inside a ScrollViewer, it will be possible for the ScrollViewer to provide enough virtual, scrollable space for it, even if the space onscreen is insufficient.

Figure 3-9 shows how the Grid in Example 3-16 appears in a ScrollViewer when there is more than enough space. All four options for HorizontalScrollBarVisibility are shown, and in all four cases, the buttons have been stretched to fill the space.

Figure 3-10 shows the same four arrangements, but with insufficient horizontal space. The top two ScrollViewer elements have horizontal scrolling enabled, with

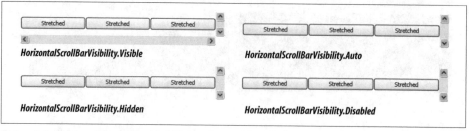

Figure 3-9. HorizontalScrollBarVisibility settings with enough space

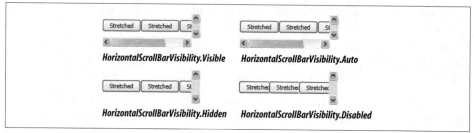

Figure 3-10. HorizontalScrollBarVisibility settings with insufficient space

Visible and Auto respectively. As you would expect, the ScrollViewer has provided enough space to hold all of the content and allows the user to scroll the cropped part into view. At the bottom left, where the horizontal scrollbar is set to Hidden, the layout behavior is the same—it has arranged the elements as though there were enough space to hold all of them. The only difference is that it has not shown a scrollbar. At the bottom right, we can see that the behavior resulting from Disabled is different. Here, not only is a scrollbar not shown, but horizontal scrolling is disabled completely. The Grid has therefore been forced to crop the buttons to fit into the available space.

Text Controls

WPF provides controls for editing and displaying text. The simplest text editing control is TextBox. By default, it allows a single line of text to be edited, but by setting AcceptReturn to true, it can edit multiple lines. It provides standard basic text editing facilities: selection support, system clipboard integration (cut, paste, etc.) and multi-level undo support.

Example 3-17 shows two TextBox elements, one with default settings and one in multi-line mode. It also shows PasswordBox, which is similar but is designed for entering passwords. Figure 3-11 shows the results. As you can see, the text in the PasswordBox has been displayed as a line of asterisks. This is common practice, to prevent passwords from being visible to anyone who can see the screen. The PasswordBox also opts out of the ability to copy its contents to the clipboard.

Example 3-17. TextBox and PasswordBox

```
<StackPanel Orientation="Horizontal">

    <TextBox Margin="5" VerticalAlignment="Center">Single line textbox</TextBox>

    <TextBox AcceptsReturn="True" Margin="5"
            VerticalAlignment="Center">Multiline textbox</TextBox>

    <PasswordBox Margin="5" VerticalAlignment="Center" />
</StackPanel>
```

Figure 3-11. TextBox and PasswordBox

TextBox and PasswordBox only support plain text. They do not support any kind of nested content—attempting to nest anything other than plain text will cause an error at runtime. This makes them easy to use for entering and editing simple data. TextBox provides a Text property that represents the control's contents as a String.

> PasswordBox does not have a Text property. Instead, it has a Password property. Rather than returning a String, this returns a SecureString. This still supports only plain-text values. However, it provides two mechanisms to prevent accidental leakage of password data.
>
> First, it stores the string in encrypted form. This means that should the memory containing the string be paged out to the system paging file, its contents will not be readable. (.NET generates a random encryption key at runtime and stores it in a memory location that is locked to prevent it from being written to the paging file.) If a normal string were used, an attacker might be able to retrieve its contents by making a copy of your system swapfile. Various .NET security APIs can be passed a SecureString, meaning that your code never has to deal with the decrypted version.
>
> Secondly, you can call Dispose on a SecureString, which overwrites the password data. This means that even in its encrypted form, the sensitive data can be wiped on demand. With a normal String, data can remain in memory long after you have finished with it, being destroyed only when the garbage collector happens to run.
>
> Be aware that a new SecureString is returned each time you read the Password property, so if you plan to take advantage of this wipe-on-demand behavior, you must Dispose after each time you read this property. The PasswordBox maintains its own internal copy of the string, which it disposes of for you when the control is destroyed.

The simplicity of plain text is good if you require nothing more than plain text as input. However, it is sometimes useful to allow more varied input. WPF therefore offers the RichTextBox.

RichTextBox is very flexible—it can contain almost any content. Example 3-18 shows markup for a RichTextBox containing a mixture of text, graphics, and controls. The results are shown in Figure 3-12.

Example 3-18. RichTextBox with mixed content

```
<RichTextBox>
    RichTextBox
    <Ellipse Fill="Red" Width="100" Height="25" />
    containing
    <Polyline Stroke="Blue" Points="0,0 10,30 20,33 30,28 40,35 50,10" />
    <Bold>rich</Bold>
    <Button>
        <TextBlock>and <Italic>varied</Italic></TextBlock>
    </Button>
    content!
</RichTextBox>
```

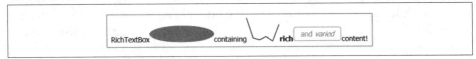

Figure 3-12. RichTextBox with mixed content (Color Plate 5)

The non-text elements are treated in the same way as characters of text—you can insert text before or after them, or move them around using cut and paste. Windows doesn't define a standard way for a user to "type" an ellipse with the keyboard, so although we can preload the RichTextBox with these elements in markup, it doesn't provide any way for the user to add such elements. However, it is easy enough to write a program that provides such a facility.

Example 3-19 shows the markup for an application that uses a RichTextBox. At the top of the screen, it provides a panel containing controls allowing the user to add rectangles and ellipses. The application is shown in Figure 3-13.

Example 3-19. Adding non-text elements

```
<Window x:Class="RichEditApp.Window1"
    xmlns="http://schemas.microsoft.com/winfx/avalon/2005"
    xmlns:x="http://schemas.microsoft.com/winfx/xaml/2005"
    Text="RichEditApp"
    >
    <Grid>
        <Grid.RowDefinitions>
            <RowDefinition Height="Auto" />
            <RowDefinition Height="*" />
        </Grid.RowDefinitions>

        <StackPanel Orientation="Horizontal">
            <Label x:Name="widthLabel" Target="{Binding ElementName=widthBox}">
                <TextBlock><AccessKey>W</AccessKey>idth:</TextBlock>
```

Example 3-19. Adding non-text elements (continued)

```
        </Label>
        <TextBox x:Name="widthBox">100</TextBox>
        <Label x:Name="heightLabel" Target="{Binding ElementName=heightBox}">
            <TextBlock><AccessKey>H</AccessKey>eight:</TextBlock>
        </Label>
        <TextBox x:Name="heightBox">10</TextBox>
        <Label x:Name="fillLabel" Target="{Binding ElementName=fillBox}">
            <TextBlock><AccessKey>F</AccessKey>ill:</TextBlock>
        </Label>
        <TextBox x:Name="fillBox">Red</TextBox>
        <Label x:Name="strokeLabel" Target="{Binding ElementName=strokeBox}">
            <TextBlock><AccessKey>S</AccessKey>troke:</TextBlock>
        </Label>
        <TextBox x:Name="strokeBox">Black</TextBox>
        <Button Click="AddRectangleClick">
            <TextBlock><AccessKey>R</AccessKey>ectangle</TextBlock>
        </Button>
        <Button Click="AddEllipseClick">
            <TextBlock><AccessKey>E</AccessKey>llipse</TextBlock>
        </Button>
    </StackPanel>
    <RichTextBox VerticalScrollBarVisibility="Visible" Grid.Row="1"
                x:Name="inputBox" Wrap="True" />

  </Grid>
</Window>
```

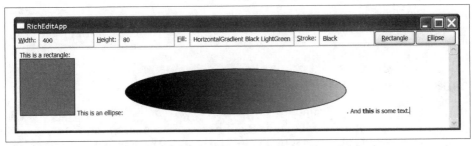

Figure 3-13. Adding non-text elements to a RichTextBox (Color Plate 6)

The code to add these elements is fairly straightforward. It is in the code-behind file shown in Example 3-20. The code creates a shape; sets the Width, Height, Fill, and Stroke properties; and then adds it to the RichTextBox content. The RichTextBox provides a TextSelection property indicating the current selection or insertion point. The code simply inserts the shape at the start of that region.

Example 3-20. Adding content to a RichTextBox

```
using System;
using System.Windows;
using System.Windows.Media;
using System.Windows.Shapes;
```

Example 3-20. Adding content to a RichTextBox (continued)

```
namespace RichEditApp {
    public partial class Window1 : Window {
        public Window1() {
            InitializeComponent();
        }

        private void AddRectangleClick(object sender, RoutedEventArgs e) {
            Rectangle rect = new Rectangle();
            SetShapeParams(rect);
            inputBox.TextSelection.Start.InsertEmbeddedElement(rect);
        }

        private void AddEllipseClick(object sender, RoutedEventArgs e) {
            Ellipse ellipse = new Ellipse();
            SetShapeParams(ellipse);
            inputBox.TextSelection.Start.InsertEmbeddedElement(ellipse);
        }

        private void SetShapeParams(Shape s) {
            s.Width = double.Parse(widthBox.Text);
            s.Height = double.Parse(heightBox.Text);
            BrushConverter b = new BrushConverter();
            if (fillBox.Text.Length > 0) {
                s.Fill = (Brush) b.ConvertFromString(fillBox.Text);
            }
            if (strokeBox.Text.Length > 0) {
                s.Stroke = (Brush) b.ConvertFromString(strokeBox.Text);
            }
        }
    }
}
```

Label

In the previous section, Example 3-19 used the Label control. It is typically used to provide a caption for a control that does not have its own built-in caption—the most common example being the TextBox control. Label might appear to be redundant, since the same visual effect can be achieved without a full control; you could just use the low-level TextBlock element. However, Label has an important focus-handling responsibility.

Well-designed user interfaces should be easy to use from the keyboard. A common way of achieving this is to provide *access keys*. An access key is a letter associated with a control, so that if you hold down the Alt key and then press the access key, the behavior is the same as if you had clicked the control in question. Applications advertise their access keys to the user by underlining the relevant letter in the control's caption when the Alt key is held down. (You can also configure Windows to show access key underlines at all times, whether Alt is pressed or not.) The AccessKey inline element used in Example 3-19 manages this underlining for us.

Figure 3-14 shows a close-up of part of the user interface defined by Example 3-19, showing the access keys underlined, as the user would see if she were holding down the Alt key. With a Button, no special code is required to make the access key work. All you need to do is use the AccessKey inline modifier within the markup of the control. In this case, hitting Alt+R or Alt+E will automatically have the same effect as clicking on the Rectangle or Ellipse buttons.

Figure 3-14. Access key underlines

The TextBox poses slightly more of a challenge. It does not have a caption—the only text it displays is the text being edited. The caption is supplied by a separate element to the left of the TextBox. This is where the Label control comes in. The purpose of the Label control is to provide a place to put the caption with its AccessKey element. When the access key is pressed, the Label will redirect the input to the relevant control, which in this case is a TextBox.

How does the Label know which control it should redirect its access key to? Label has a Target property, indicating the intended target of the access key. We use a binding expression to connect the label to its target. Binding expressions are discussed in detail in Chapter 4. The expression here simply sets the Target property to refer to the named element.

Selectors

Several kinds of controls allow the user to select from a set of items. In some cases, such as the RadioButtonList and TabControl, there is usually exactly one selected item. ComboBox extends this functionality with the option to have no current selection. ListBox goes one step further, with the ability to select multiple items simultaneously. All of these controls inherit their common list and selection functionality from the Selector base class.

The simplest way to use any of these controls is to add content to their Items property. Example 3-21 shows the markup for a ComboBox with various elements added to its Items.

Example 3-21. Content in Items

```
<ComboBox>
    <ComboBox.Items>
        <Button>Click!</Button>
        <TextBlock>Hello, world</TextBlock>
        <StackPanel Orientation="Horizontal">
            <TextBlock>Ellipse:</TextBlock><Ellipse Fill="Blue" Width="100" />
```

Example 3-21. Content in Items (continued)

```
        </StackPanel>
    </ComboBox.Items>
</ComboBox>
```

This same technique can also be used with ListBox, TabControl, and RadioButtonList. As you can see in Figure 3-15, each of the controls presents the items in its own way. The RadioButtonList generates a RadioButton for each item, using the item as the caption. The TabControl puts each element in its own TabItem, in order to present it on its own tab page. (Figure 3-15 just shows the first item, but the other three are accessible through the three tab headers.)

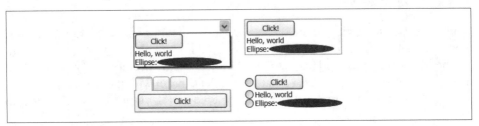

Figure 3-15. Content in selectors (left to right, top to bottom: ComboBox, ListBox, TabControl, and RadioButtonList)

All selector controls wrap our items in order to present them in a suitable way. Although this can be convenient, in some cases you will want a little more control. For example, the TabControl shown above isn't particularly useful—it has wrapped our items with tabs that have no title. To fix this, we simply provide our own TabItem elements instead of letting the TabControl generate them for us. We can then set the Header property in order to control the tab-page caption. These techniques are illustrated in Example 3-22.

Example 3-22. Setting tab page headers

```
<TabControl Grid.Row="3" Grid.Column="1">
    <TabControl.Items>

        <TabItem Header="Button">
            <Button>Click!</Button>
        </TabItem>

        <TabItem>
            <TabItem.Header>
                <TextBlock FontSize="18"
                    FontFamily="Palatino Linotype">Text</TextBlock>
            </TabItem.Header>
            <TextBlock>Hello, world</TextBlock>
        </TabItem>

        <TabItem>
```

Example 3-22. Setting tab page headers (continued)

```
        <TabItem.Header>
            <Ellipse Fill="Blue" Width="30" Height="20" />
        </TabItem.Header>

        <StackPanel Orientation="Horizontal">
            <TextBlock>Ellipse:</TextBlock>
            <Ellipse Fill="Blue" Width="100" />
        </StackPanel>
    </TabItem>

  </TabControl.Items>
</TabControl>
```

Example 3-22 shows the markup for a TabControl with the same three items as before, but this time with the TabItem elements specified explicitly. In the first of these, the Header property has been set to the text "Button." The other two items illustrate that these headers support nested content—the first uses a TextBlock to control the text appearance, and the second puts an Ellipse into the header instead of text. Figure 3-16 shows the results.

Figure 3-16. TabItem headers

Providing a fixed set of elements through the Items property makes sense for tab pages and radio buttons, where you are likely to know what elements are required when you design the user interface. But this may not be the case for combo boxes and lists. To enable you to decide at runtime what items will appear, all selector controls offer an alternative means of populating the list: data binding. Instead of using Items, you can provide a data-source object with the ItemsSource property and use data styling to determine how the elements appear. These techniques are described in Chapters 4 and 5.

Regardless of whether you use a fixed set of items or a bound data source, you can always find out when the selected item changes by handling the SelectionChanged event. You can then use either the SelectedIndex or SelectedItem property to find out which item is currently selected.

Menus

Many Windows applications provide access to their functionality through a hierarchy of menus. These are typically presented as either a main menu at the top of the window or as a pop-up "context" menu. WPF provides two menu controls. Menu is for permanently visible menus (such as a main menu), and ContextMenu is for context menus.

Menus in Windows today are typically treated differently from other user-interface elements. There is a special handle type for them. Event handling makes special provisions for menus. In Windows Forms, most visible elements derive from a Control base class, but menus do not. This means that menus tend to be somewhat inflexible—some user interface toolkits choose not to use the built-in menu handling in Windows simply to avoid the shortcomings. In WPF, menus are just normal controls, so they do not have any special features or restrictions.

Both kinds of menus are built in the same way—their contents consist of a hierarchy of MenuItem elements. Example 3-23 creates a typical menu. The results are shown in Figure 3-17.

Example 3-23. A main menu

```
<Menu>
    <MenuItem Header="File">
        <MenuItem Header="New" />
        <MenuItem Header="Open..." />
        <MenuItem Header="Save" />
        <MenuItem Header="Save As..." />
        <MenuItem Mode="Separator" />
        <MenuItem Header="Page Setup..." />
        <MenuItem Header="Print..." />
        <MenuItem Mode="Separator" />
        <MenuItem Header="Exit" />
    </MenuItem>
    <MenuItem Header="Edit">
        <MenuItem Header="Undo" />
        <MenuItem Header="Redo" />
        <MenuItem Mode="Separator" />
        <MenuItem Header="Cut" />
        <MenuItem Header="Copy" />
        <MenuItem Header="Paste" />
        <MenuItem Header="Delete" />
        <MenuItem Mode="Separator" />
        <MenuItem Header="Select All" />
    </MenuItem>
    <MenuItem Header="Help">
        <MenuItem Header="Help Topics" />
        <MenuItem Header="About..." />
    </MenuItem>
</Menu>
```

ContextMenu is used in a very similar way. The main differences are the appearance—Menu has a horizontal bar at the top—and the fact that a Menu can be used anywhere in the UI, while a ContextMenu can be used only as the value of an element's ContextMenu property. Example 3-24 shows a Grid element with a ContextMenu.

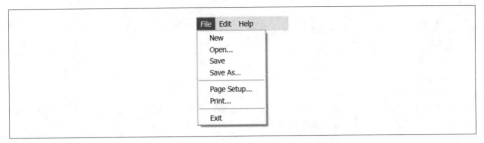

Figure 3-17. Menu

Example 3-24. Grid with ContextMenu

```
<Grid>
    <Grid.ContextMenu>
        <ContextMenu>
            <MenuItem Header="Foo" />
            <MenuItem Header="Bar" />
        </ContextMenu>
    </Grid.ContextMenu>
...
</Grid>
```

With this context menu in place, a right-click anywhere on the grid will bring up the context menu. Figure 3-18 shows the context menu in action.

Figure 3-18. Context menu

Each `MenuItem` has a `Header` property. For children of a `Menu`, the header determines the label shown on the menu bar. For a `MenuItem` nested in either a `ContextMenu` or inside another `MenuItem`, the `Header` contains the content for that menu line. The `Header` property allows either plain text, as shown in Example 3-23, or nested content. Example 3-25 shows a modified version of one of the menu items, exploiting the ability to add structure in order to mark a letter as an access key. Figure 3-19 shows the results.

Example 3-25. Nesting content inside MenuItem.Header

```
<MenuItem>
    <MenuItem.Header>
        <TextBlock>
            <AccessKey>N</AccessKey>ew...
        </TextBlock>
    </MenuItem.Header>
</MenuItem>
```

Figure 3-19. Menu item with access key

The menu in Example 3-23 doesn't do anything useful, because there are no event handlers or commands specified. There are two ways you can hook up a MenuItem to some code. You can handle its Click event in much the same way that you would handle a button click. Alternatively, you can set the Command property on the MenuItem, using the same syntax we saw earlier in Example 3-8.

Example 3-26 shows a modified version of the Edit submenu, with menu items associated with the relevant standard commands. As long as the focus is in a control such as TextBox or RichTextBox that understands these standard commands, these commands will be handled without needing any explicit coding. (If the focus is not in such a control, the commands will simply bubble up. If nothing handles the command, it will be ignored.)

Example 3-26. MenuItems with Commands

```
<MenuItem Header="Edit">
    <MenuItem Header="Undo" Command="Undo" />
    <MenuItem Header="Redo" Command="Redo"/>
    <MenuItem Mode="Separator" />
    <MenuItem Header="Cut" Command="Cut" />
    <MenuItem Header="Copy" Command="Copy" />
    <MenuItem Header="Paste" Command="Paste" />
    <MenuItem Header="Delete" Command="Delete" />
    <MenuItem Mode="Separator" />
    <MenuItem Header="Select All" Command="SelectAll" />
</MenuItem>
```

Menus often have a shortcut key as well as an accelerator. The accelerator works only when the menu is open. A shortcut, such as Ctrl+S for save, works whether the menu is open or not. The menu isn't responsible for binding the control shortcut to the key gestured—as we saw earlier, we do this with CommandBindings, which associate inputs with commands. However, menus conventionally display the shortcut in order to help users discover them.

If a menu item's Command has an associated key-gestured binding, WPF will automatically display this shortcut in the menu. Since Example 3-26 uses standard clipboard and undo/redo commands, the menu it produces has shortcuts associated, as you can see in Figure 3-20.

If for some reason you choose not to use WPF's command system, you can still display a shortcut. MenuItem provides an InputGestureText property that lets you choose the text that appears in the normal place for such shortcuts. Example 3-27 shows a menu item with both a shortcut and an access key.

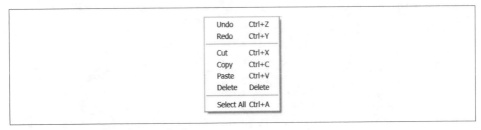

Figure 3-20. Automatic shortcut display

Example 3-27. Menu item with shortcut and access key

```
<MenuItem InputGestureText="Ctrl+N">
    <MenuItem.Header>
        <TextBlock><AccessKey>N</AccessKey>ew</TextBlock>
    </MenuItem.Header>
</MenuItem>
```

Note that `Menu` and `ContextMenu` both derive indirectly from `ItemsControl`, the same base class as all of the selector controls. This means that you can use the `ItemsDataSource` property to populate a menu using data binding, rather than using fixed content. This could be useful if you want to make your menu structure reconfigurable. See Chapter 4 for more details on how to use data binding.

Toolbars

Most Windows applications offer toolbars as well as menus. Toolbars provide faster access for frequently used operations, because the user does not need to navigate through the menu system—the toolbar is always visible onscreen, as shown in Figure 3-21.

Figure 3-21. Application with menu and toolbar (Color Plate 7)

WPF supports toolbars through the `ToolBarTray` and `ToolBar` controls. `ToolBarTray` provides a container into which you can add multiple `ToolBar` elements. Example 3-28 shows a simple example, which provides the markup for Figure 3-21.

Example 3-28. ToolBarTray and ToolBar

```
<ToolBarTray Grid.Row="1" Margin="2">
    <ToolBar>
        <Button>
            <Canvas Width="16" Height="16">
```

Example 3-28. ToolBarTray and ToolBar (continued)

```
                <Polygon Stroke="Black" StrokeThickness="0.5"
                        Fill="LinearGradient 1,1 0.2,0.7 #AAA White"
                        Points="3,1 10,1 13,5 13,15 3,15" />
                <Polygon Stroke="Black" Fill="DarkGray" StrokeThickness="0.5"
                        StrokeLineJoin="Bevel" Points="10,1 10,5 13,5" />
            </Canvas>
        </Button>

        <Button>
            <Canvas Width="16" Height="16">
                <Polygon Stroke="Black" StrokeThickness="0.5"
                        Fill="VerticalGradient Khaki Beige"
                        Points="1,15 1,4 5.5,4 7.5,6 12,6 12,15" />
                <Polygon Stroke="Black" Fill="VerticalGradient Khaki #DB7"
                        StrokeThickness="0.5"
                        Points="1.5,15 4,8 15,8 12,15" />
                <Path    Stroke="Blue" StrokeThickness="1"
                        Data="M 8,2 C 9,1 12,1 14,3"  />
                <Polygon Fill="Blue" Points="15,1 15.5,4.5 12,4" />
            </Canvas>
        </Button>
    </ToolBar>
  </ToolBarTray>
```

This creates just one toolbar, with a couple of buttons. When you add a button to a toolbar, its size defaults to 17 × 17 logical pixels. If the content is too large, it will be cropped. This is because toolbar buttons are usually expected to be images rather than text. The toolbar sets all the buttons to the same size to ensure consistent spacing. If you provide content that is smaller than 17 × 17, it will be centered. (If you want a larger button, you can set the size explicitly; 17 × 17 is simply the default.)

In this example, we have used some simple vector graphics to draw the usual New and Open... icons. The graphical elements used are explained in more detail in Chapter 7. In practice, you would rarely put graphics inline like this—you would usually expect drawings to be resources that are simply referred to by the buttons in the toolbar. See Chapter 6 for more details.

Since toolbar buttons are just normal Button elements with specialized visuals, there is nothing particularly special about their behavior. Toolbars really just provide a particular way of arranging and presenting controls. You can also add other elements to toolbars, such as a TextBox or ComboBox. These will just be arranged on the toolbar along with the buttons.

Where Are We?

Controls are the building blocks of applications. They represent the features of the interface that the user interacts with. Controls provide behavior and rely on styling and templates to present an appearance. Input is handled through events and commands, which use a routing system to allow simple, uniform event handling regardless of how complex the detailed structure of the user-interface visuals might be. WPF provides a set of built-in controls based on the controls commonly used in Windows applications.

CHAPTER 4

Data Binding

Any application has data that it's allowing the user to manipulate, whether it's from object, hierarchical or relational sources. Regardless of where it comes from or the format it's in, there are several things that you'll most likely need to do with the data, including showing it, converting it, sorting it, filtering it, relating one part of it to another part and, more often then not, editing it. Without some kind of data-binding engine, you're going to be writing a great deal of code to manually shuttle the data back and forth between the data and the UI. With data binding in place, you get more features with less code, which is always a nice place to be.

Without Data Binding

Consider a very simple application for editing a single person's name and age, as shown in Figure 4-1.

Figure 4-1. An exceedingly simple application

Figure 4-1 can be implemented with the simple XAML shown in Example 4-1.

Example 4-1. A simple Person editor layout

```
<!-- Window1.xaml -->
<Window ...>
  <Grid>
    ...
    <TextBlock ...>Name:</TextBlock>
```

Example 4-1. A simple Person editor layout (continued)

```
    <TextBox x:Name="nameTextBox" ... />
    <TextBlock ...>Age:</TextBlock>
    <TextBox x:Name="ageTextBox" ... />
    <Button x:Name="birthdayButton" ...>Birthday</Button>
  </Grid>
</Window>
```

The data to be shown in our simple application can be represented in a simple class, as shown in Example 4-2.

Example 4-2. A simple Person class

```
public class Person {
  string name;
  public string Name {
    get { return this.name; }
    set { this.name = value; }
  }

  int age;
  public int Age {
    get { return this.age; }
    set { this.age = value; }
  }

  public Person( ) {}
  public Person(string name, int age) {
    this.name = name;
    this.age = age;
  }
}
```

With this class, a naive implementation of the behavior of our application could look like Example 4-3.

Example 4-3. Naive Person editor code

```
// Window1.xaml.cs
...
public class Person {...}

public partial class Window1 : Window {
  Person person = new Person("Tom", 9);

  public Window1( ) {
    InitializeComponent( );

    // Fill initial person fields
    this.nameTextBox.Text = person.Name;
    this.ageTextBox.Text = person.Age.ToString( );

    this.birthdayButton.Click += birthdayButton_Click;
  }
```

Example 4-3. Naive Person editor code (continued)

```
void birthdayButton_Click(object sender, RoutedEventArgs e) {
  ++person.Age;
  MessageBox.Show(
    string.Format(
      "Happy Birthday, {0}, age {1}!",
      person.Name,
      person.Age),
    "Birthday");
  }
}
```

The code in Example 4-3 creates a Person object and initializes the text boxes with
the Person object properties. When the Birthday button is pressed, the Person
object's Age property is incremented, and the updated Person data is shown in a message box, as shown in Figure 4-2.

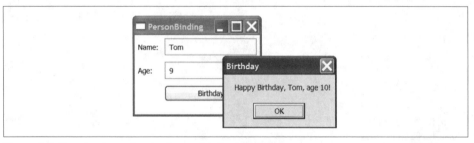

Figure 4-2. Our simple application is too simple

Our simple application implementation is, in fact, too simple. The change in the
Person Age property does show up in the message box, but it does not show up in the
main window. One way to keep the application's UI up to date is to write the code
so that whenever a Person object is updated, it manually updates the UI at the same
time, as shown in Example 4-4.

Example 4-4. Manually updating the UI when a Person is updated

```
void birthdayButton_Click(object sender, RoutedEventArgs e) {
  ++person.Age;

  // Manually update the UI
  this.ageTextBox.Text = person.Age.ToString();

  MessageBox.Show(
    string.Format(
      "Happy Birthday, {0}, age {1}!",
      person.Name,
      person.Age),
    "Birthday");
}
```

With a single line of code, we've "fixed" our application. This is a seductive and popular road, but it does not scale as the application gets more complicated and requires more of these "single" lines of code. To get beyond the simplest of applications, we'll need a better way.

Object Changes

A more robust way for the UI to track object changes is for the object to raise an event when a property changes. As of .NET 2.0, the right way for an object to do this is with an implementation of the INotifyPropertyChanged interface, as shown in Example 4-5.

Example 4-5. A class that supports property-change notification

```
using System.ComponentModel; // INotifyPropertyChanged
...
public class Person : INotifyPropertyChanged {
  // INotifyPropertyChanged Members
  public event PropertyChangedEventHandler PropertyChanged;
  protected void OnPropertyChanged(string propName) {
    if( this.PropertyChanged != null ) {
      PropertyChanged(this, new PropertyChangedEventArgs(propName));
    }
  }

  string name;
  public string Name {
    get { return this.name; }
    set {
      this.name = value;
      OnPropertyChanged("Name");
    }
  }

  int age;
  public int Age {
    get { return this.age; }
    set {
      this.age = value;
      OnPropertyChanged("Age");
    }
  }

  public Person( ) {}
  public Person(string name, int age) {
    this.name = name;
    this.age = age;
  }
}
```

In Example 4-5, when either of the Person properties changes (as is caused by the implementation of the Birthday button), a Person object raises the PropertyChanged event. We can use this event to keep the UI synchronized with the Person properties, as in Example 4-6.

Example 4-6. Simple Person editor code

```
// Window1.xaml.cs
...
public class Person : INotifyPropertyChanged {...}
public partial class Window1 : Window {
  Person person = new Person("Tom", 9);

  public Window1() {
    InitializeComponent();

    // Fill initial person fields
    this.nameTextBox.Text = person.Name;
    this.ageTextBox.Text = person.Age.ToString();

    // Watch for changes in Tom's properties
    person.PropertyChanged += person_PropertyChanged;

    this.birthdayButton.Click += birthdayButton_Click;
  }

  void person_PropertyChanged(
    object sender,
    PropertyChangedEventArgs e) {

    switch( e.PropertyName ) {
      case "Name":
      this.nameTextBox.Text = person.Name;
      break;

      case "Age":
      this.ageTextBox.Text = person.Age.ToString();
      break;
    }
  }

  void birthdayButton_Click(object sender, RoutedEventArgs e) {
    ++person.Age; // person_PropertyChanged will update ageTextBox
    MessageBox.Show(
      string.Format(
        "Happy Birthday, {0}, age {1}!",
        person.Name,
        person.Age),
      "Birthday");
  }
}
```

Example 4-6 shows a single instance of the Person class that's created when the main window first comes into existence, initializing the name and age text boxes with the initial person values and then subscribing to the property-change event to keep the text boxes up to date as the Person object changes. With this code in place, the birthday-button click event handler doesn't have to manually update the text boxes when it updates Tom's age; instead, updating the Age property causes a cascade of events that keeps the age text box up to date with the Person object's changes, as shown in Figure 4-3.

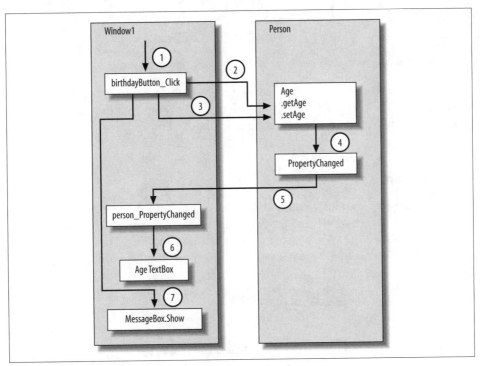

Figure 4-3. Keeping the UI up to date with changes in the object

The steps are as follows:

1. User clicks on button, which causes Click event to be raised.
2. Click handler gets the age (9) from the Person object.
3. Click handler sets the age (10) on the Person object.
4. Person Age property setter raises the PropertyChanged event.
5. PropertyChanged event is routed to event handler in the UI code.
6. UI code updates the age TextBox from "9" to "10".
7. Button click event handler displays a message box showing the new age ("10").

By the time the message box is shown with Tom's new age, the age text box on the form has already been updated, as shown in Figure 4-4.

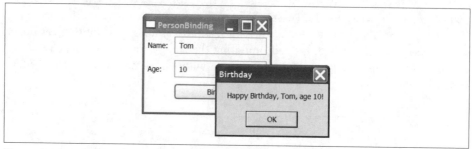

Figure 4-4. Manually populating two WPF controls with two object properties

With the handling of the `INotifyPropertyChanged` event, when the data in the object changes, the UI is updated to reflect that change. However, that only solves half the problem; we still need to handle changes in the UI and reflect them back to the object.

Control Changes

Without some way to track changes from the UI back into the object, we could easily end up with a case where the user has made some change (like changing the person's name), shows the object (as happens when pressing the `Birthday` button) and expects the change to have been made, only to be disappointed with Figure 4-5.

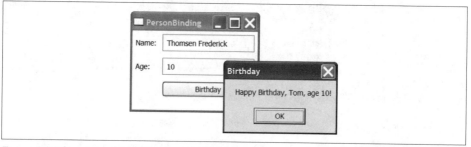

Figure 4-5. The need to keep controls and objects in sync

Notice in Figure 4-5 that the `Name` is "Thomsen Frederick" in the form, but "Tom" in the message box, which shows that while one part of the UI has been updated, the underlying object has not. To fix this problem, we have but to watch for the `Text` property in our `TextBox` object to change, updating the `Person` object as appropriate, as in Example 4-7.

Example 4-7. Tracking changes in the UI

```
public partial class Window1 : Window {
  Person person = new Person("Tom", 9);

  public Window1() {
    InitializeComponent();

    // Fill initial person fields
    this.nameTextBox.Text = person.Name;
    this.ageTextBox.Text = person.Age.ToString();

    // Watch for changes in Tom's properties
    person.PropertyChanged += person_PropertyChanged;

    // Watch for changes in the controls
    this.nameTextBox.TextChanged += nameTextBox_TextChanged;
    this.ageTextBox.TextChanged += ageTextBox_TextChanged;

    this.birthdayButton.Click += birthdayButton_Click;
  }

  ...

  void nameTextBox_TextChanged(object sender, TextChangedEventArgs e) {
    person.Name = nameTextBox.Text;
  }

  void ageTextBox_TextChanged(object sender, TextChangedEventArgs e) {
    int age = 0;
    if( int.TryParse(ageTextBox.Text, out age) ) {
      person.Age = age;
    }
  }

  void birthdayButton_Click(object sender, RoutedEventArgs e) {
    ++person.Age;

    // nameTextBox_TextChanged and ageTextBox_TextChanged
    // will make sure the Person object is up to date
    MessageBox.Show(
      string.Format(
        "Happy Birthday, {0}, age {1}!",
        person.Name,
        person.Age),
      "Birthday");
  }
}
```

Now, no matter where the data changes, both the Person object and the UI showing the Person object are kept synchronized. Figure 4-6 shows the name changes in the UI correctly propagating to the Person object.

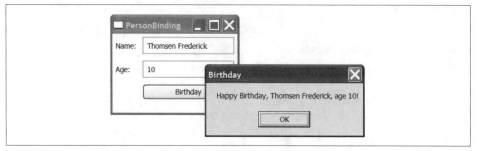

Figure 4-6. Manually keeping properties and controls in sync

While we've gotten the functionality we wanted, we had to write quite a bit of code to make it happen:

- Window1 constructor code to set controls to initial values
- Window1 constructor code to hook up the PropertyChanged event to track the Person object's property changes
- PropertyChanged event handler to grab the updated data from the Person object, converting data to strings as appropriate
- Window1 constructor code to hook up the TextBox object's TextChanged event to track the UI changes
- TextChanged event handlers to push the updated TextBox data into the Person object, converting the data as appropriate

This code allows us to write our birthday button event handler safe in the knowledge that all changes are synchronized when we display the message box. However, it's easy to imagine how this code could quickly get out of hand as the number of object properties gets beyond two or as the number of objects we're managing grows. Plus, this seems like such a common thing to want to do that someone must have already provided a simpler way to do this. And, in fact, they have; it's called data binding.

Data Binding

Our manual code to keep the UI and the data synchronized has the effect of implicitly binding together two sets of properties, one from the Person object and one from the controls showing the Person object. *Data binding* is the act of explicitly binding properties from one object to another, keeping them synchronized and converting types as appropriate, as shown in Figure 4-7.

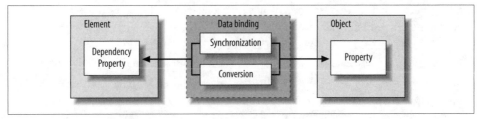

Figure 4-7. The synchronization and conversion duties of data binding

Bindings

Instead of setting the Text property of the TextBox objects manually in code and then keeping them up to date, data binding allows us to set the Text property using an instance of a Binding object, as in Example 4-8.

Example 4-8. Binding a dependency property to a CLR property

```
<TextBox ...>
  <TextBox.Text>
    <Binding Path="Age" />
  </TextBox.Text>
</TextBox>
```

In Example 4-8, we've used the property-element syntax introduced in Chapter 1 to create an instance of the Binding class, initialize its Path property to the string "Age" and set the Binding object as the value of the TextBox object's Text property. Using the binding markup extension (also introduced in Chapter 1), we can shorten Example 4-8 to Example 4-9.

Example 4-9. The shortcut binding syntax

```
<TextBox TextContent="{Binding Path=Age}" />
```

As an even shorter cut, you can drop the Path designation altogether, and the Binding will still know what you mean, as in Example 4-10.

Example 4-10. The shortest cut binding syntax

```
<TextBox TextContent="{Binding Age}" />
```

I prefer to be more explicit, so I won't use the syntax in Example 4-10, but I won't judge if you like it.

The Binding class has all kinds of interesting facilities for managing the binding between properties, but the one that we're most interested in is the Path property. For most cases, you can think of the Path as the name of the property on the object serving as the data source. So, the binding statement in Example 4-10 is creating a binding between the Text property of the TextBox and the Name property of some object to be named later, as shown in Figure 4-8.

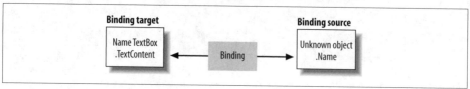

Figure 4-8. Binding targets and sources

In this binding, the TextBox control is the *binding target*, as it acts as a consumer of changes to the *binding source*, which is the object that provides the data. The binding target can be a WPF element, but you're only allowed to bind to the element's dependency properties (described in Chapter 9).

On the other hand, you can bind to any public CLR property on the binding source object; the binding source is not named in this example specifically so that we can have some freedom as to where it comes from at runtime and so that it's easier to bind multiple controls to the same object (like our name and age text-box controls bound to the same Person object).

Commonly, the binding source data comes from a data context.

Implicit Data Source

A *data context* is a place for bindings to look for the data source if they don't have any other special instructions (which we'll discuss later). In WPF, every FrameworkElement and every FrameworkContentElement has a DataContext property. The DataContext property is of type object so you can plug anything you like into it—e.g., string, Person, List<Person>, etc. When looking for an object to use as the binding source, the binding object traverses up the tree from where it's defined, looking for a non-null DataContext property.

This traversal is handy because it means that any two controls with a common logical parent can bind to the same data source. For example, both of our text box controls are children of the grid, and they each search for a data context, as shown in Figure 4-9.

The steps work like this:

1. The binding looks for a non-null DataContext on the TextBox itself
2. The binding looks for a non-null DataContext on the Grid
3. The binding looks for a non-null DataContext on the Window

Providing a non-null DataContext for both of the text box controls is a matter of setting the shared Person object as the value of the grid's DataContext property in the Window1 constructor, as in Example 4-11.

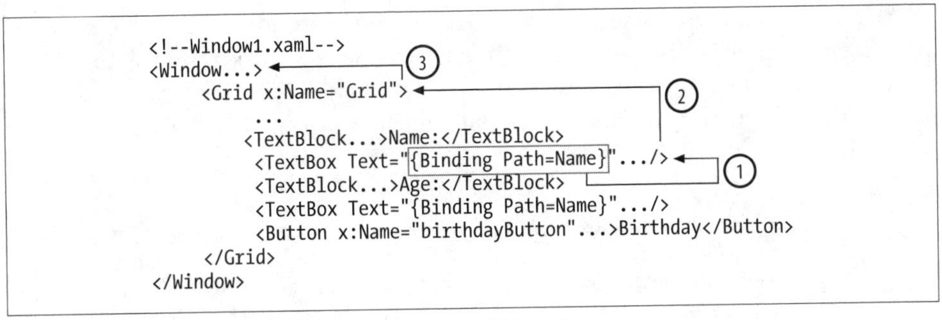

```
<!--Window1.xaml-->
<Window...>  ◄─────────────────┐ ③
    <Grid x:Name="Grid">  ◄───────────────┐ ②
        ...
        <TextBlock...>Name:</TextBlock>
        <TextBox Text="{Binding Path=Name}"...>  ◄───────┐ ①
        <TextBlock...>Age:</TextBlock>
        <TextBox Text="{Binding Path=Name}"...>
        <Button x:Name="birthdayButton"...>Birthday</Button>
    </Grid>
</Window>
```

Figure 4-9. *Searching the element tree for a non-null DataContext*

Example 4-11. Editor code simplified with data binding

```
// Window1.xaml.cs
using System;
using System.Windows;
using System.Windows.Controls;

namespace PersonBinding {
  public partial class Window1 : Window {
    Person person = new Person("Tom", 9);

    public Window1() {
      InitializeComponent();

      // Let the grid know its data context
      grid.DataContext = person;

      this.birthdayButton.Click += birthdayButton_Click;
    }

    void birthdayButton_Click(object sender, RoutedEventArgs e) {
      // Data binding keeps person and the text boxes synchronized
      ++person.Age;
      MessageBox.Show(
        string.Format(
          "Happy Birthday, {0}, age {1}!",
          person.Name,
          person.Age),
        "Birthday");
    }
  }
}
```

So, while the functionality of our app is the same as shown in Figure 4-9, the data-synchronization code has been reduced to a binding object for each property in the XAML where data is to be shown, and a data context for the bindings to find the data. There is no need for the UI initialization code or the event handlers that copy and convert the data (notice the lack of ellipses in Example 4-11).

To be clear, *the use of the* `INotifyPropertyChanged` *implementation is not an accident.* This is the interface that WPF's data-binding engine uses to keep the UI synchronized when an object's properties change. Without it, a UI change can still propagate to the object, but the binding engine will have no way of knowing when to update the UI.

It's not quite true that the binding engine will have *no* way of knowing when a change happens on an object that does not implement the `INotifyPropertyChanged` interface. One way it can know is if the object implements the `PropertyNameChanged` events as prescribed in .NET 1.x data binding—e.g. `SizeChanged`, `TextChanged`, etc.—with which WPF maintains backward compatibility. Another way is a manual call to the `UpdateTarget` method on the `BindingExpression` object associated with the Binding in question.

However, it's safe to say that implementing `INotifyPropertyChanged` is the recommended way to enable property change notifications in WPF data binding.

Declarative Data

While our application is attempting to simulate a more complicated application that, perhaps, loads its "person data" from some persisted form and saves it between application sessions, it's not hard to imagine cases where some data is known at compile time. Maybe it's sample data (like our Tom) or well-known data that doesn't change between sessions, such as application settings defaults or error messages. Lots of applications have string resources that are kept separate from the workings of the UI, but are still bundled with the application. Keeping the data bundled with the app makes it easier to maintain and localize, while keeping it out of the UI logic itself reduces coupling between the data and the UI. In our sample thus far, we've been keeping this well-known data in the code, but XAML is a better choice, both because of the ease of maintaining data in XAML and XAML's support for localization (as described in Chapter 6).

As discussed in Chapter 1, XAML is a language for describing object graphs, so practically any type with a default constructor can be initialized in XAML. Luckily, as you'll recall from Example 4-2, our `Person` class has a default constructor, so we can create an instance of it in our application's XAML, as shown in Example 4-12.

Example 4-12. Creating an instance of a custom type in XAML

```
<?Mapping XmlNamespace="local" ClrNamespace="PersonBinding" ?>
<Window ... xmlns:local="local">
  <Window.Resources>
    <local:Person x:Key="Tom" Name="Tom" Age="9" />
  </Window.Resources>
  <Grid>...</Grid>
</Window>
```

Here we've created a little "data island" inside the window's resources element, bringing the Person type in using the XAML mapping syntax described in Chapter 1.

With a named Person in our XAML code, we can declaratively set the grid's DataContext, instead of setting it in the code-behind file programmatically, as in Example 4-13.

Example 4-13. Binding to an object declared in XAML

```
<!-- Window1.xaml -->
<?Mapping XmlNamespace="local" ClrNamespace="PersonBinding" ?>
<Window ... xmlns:local="local">
  <Window.Resources>
    <local:Person x:Key="Tom" Name="Tom" Age="9" />
  </Window.Resources>
  <Grid DataContext="{StaticResource Tom}">
    ...
    <TextBlock ...>Name:</TextBlock>
    <TextBox ... Text="{Binding Path=Name}" />
    <TextBlock ...>Age:</TextBlock>
    <TextBox ... Text="{Binding Path=Age}" />
    <Button ... x:Name="birthdayButton">Birthday</Button>
  </Grid>
</Window>
```

Now that's we've moved the creation of the Person object to the XAML, we have to update our Birthday button click handler from using a member variable to using the data defined in the resource, as in Example 4-14.

Example 4-14. Binding to an object declared in XAML

```
public partial class Window1 : Window {
  ...
  void birthdayButton_Click(object sender, RoutedEventArgs e) {
    Person person = (Person)this.FindResource("Tom"));
    ++person.Age;
    MessageBox.Show(...);
  }
}
```

In Example 4-14, we're using the FindResource method (introduced in Chapter 1 and further detailed in Chapter 6) to pull the Person object from the main window's resources. With this minor change, the result is brought again into parity with Figure 4-6. The only thing that's different is that you don't have to touch the code-behind file to maintain or localize the data known at compile time. (Chapter 6 discusses the localization of XAML resources.)

Explicit Data Source

Once you've got yourself a named source of data, you can be explicit in the XAML about the source in the binding object instead of relying on implicitly binding to a non-null `DataContext` property somewhere in the tree. Being explicit is useful if you've got more than one source of data—e.g., two `Person` objects. Setting the source explicitly is accomplished with the `Source` property in the binding, as in Example 4-15.

Example 4-15. Data binding using the Source property

```
<!-- Window1.xaml -->
<Window ...>
  <Window.Resources>
    <local:Person x:Key="Tom" ... />
    <local:Person x:Key="John" ... />
  </Window.Resources>
  <Grid>
    ...
    <TextBox x:Name="tomTextBox"
      Text="
        {Binding
          Path=Name,
          Source={StaticResource Tom}}" />

    <TextBox x:Name="johnTextBox"
      Text="
        {Binding
          Path=Name,
          Source={StaticResource John}}" />
    ...
  </Grid>
</Window>
```

In Example 4-15, we're binding two text boxes to two different person objects, using the `Source` property of the `Binding` object to bind each person explicitly.

Implicit Versus Explicit Binding

In general, I find implicit binding to be most useful when I'm sharing the same data between multiple controls, because all that's needed is a bit of code to set the the `DataContext` property on a single parent element. On the other hand, if I've got multiple data sources, I really like using the `Source` property on my `Binding` objects to make it clear where the data is coming from.

Value Conversion

So far, our sample application has shown the bound data as text in text boxes. However, there's absolutely nothing stopping you from binding to other properties of a control—e.g., `Foreground`, `FontWeight`, `Height`, etc. For example, we might decide that anyone over age 25 is cool, so should be marked in the UI as red (or, they're in danger of dying sooner—whichever makes you more likely to recommend this book to your friends...). As someone ages at the press of the `Birthday` button, we want to keep the UI up to date, which means we've got ourselves a perfect candidate for data binding. Imagine the ability to do the following in Example 4-16.

Example 4-16. Binding to a non-Text property

```
<!-- Window1.xaml -->
<Window ...>
  <Window.Resources>
    <local:Person x:Key="Tom" ... />
  </Window.Resources>
  <Grid>
    ...
    <TextBox
      Text="{Binding Path=Age}"
      Foreground="{Binding Path=Age, ...}"
      ...
    />
    ...
  </Grid>
</Window>
```

In Example 4-16, we've bound the age text box's Text property to the Person object's Age property, as we've already seen, but we're also binding the Foreground property of the text box to the exact same property on the Person object. As Tom's age changes, we want to update the foreground color of the age text box. However, since the Age is of type Int32 and Foreground is of type Brush, there needs to be a mapping from Int32 to Brush applied to the data binding from Age to Foreground. That's the job of a value converter.

A *value converter* (or just "converter" for short) is an implementation of the IValueConverter interface, which contains two methods: Convert and ConvertBack. The Convert method is called when converting from the source data to the target UI data—e.g., from Int32 to Brush. The ConvertBack method is called to convert back from the UI data to the source data. In both cases, the current value and the type wanted for the target data is passed to the method.

To convert an Age Int32 into a Foreground Brush, we can implement whatever mapping in the Convert function we feel comfortable with, as in Example 4-17.

Example 4-17. A simple value converter

```
public class AgeToForegroundConverter : IValueConverter {
  // Called when converting the Age to a Foreground brush
  public object Convert(object value, Type targetType, ...) {
    Debug.Assert(targetType == typeof(Brush));

    // DANGER! After 25, it's all down hill...
    int age = int.Parse(value.ToString());
    return (age > 25 ? Brushes.Red : Brushes.Black);
  }
```

Example 4-17. A simple value converter (continued)

```
// Called when converting a Foreground brush back to an Age
public object ConvertBack(object value, ...) {
  // should never be called
  throw new NotImplementedException( );
}
}
```

In Example 4-17, we've implemented the Convert method to double-check that we're after a Foreground brush and then we hand out the brush that's appropriate for the age being displayed. Since we haven't provided any facility to change the Foreground brush being used to display the age, there's no reason to implement the ConvertBack method.

 I chose the name AgeToForegroundConverter because I have specific semantics I'm building into my converter class that go above simply converting an Int32 to a Brush. Even though this converter could be plugged in anywhere that converted an Int32 to a Brush, I might have very different requirements for a HeightToBackgroundConverter, as just one example.

Once you've got a converter class, it's easy to create an instance of one in the XAML, just like we've been doing with our Person object, as shown in Example 4-18.

Example 4-18. Binding with a value converter

```
<!-- Window1.xaml -->
<?Mapping XmlNamespace="local" ClrNamespace="PersonBinding" ?>
<Window ... xmlns:local="local">
  <Window.Resources>
    <local:Person x:Key="Tom" ... />
    <local:AgeToForegroundConverter
      x:Key="AgeToForegroundConverter" />
  </Window.Resources>
  <Grid DataContext="{StaticResource Tom}">
    ...
    <TextBox
      Text="{Binding Path=Age}"
      Foreground="
        {Binding
          Path=Age,
          Converter={StaticResource AgeToForegroundConverter}}"
      ... />
    ...
  </Grid>
</Window>
```

In Example 4-18, once we have a named converter object in our XAML, we establish it as the converter between the Age property and the Foreground brush by setting the Converter property of the binding object. Figure 4-10 shows the result of our conversion.

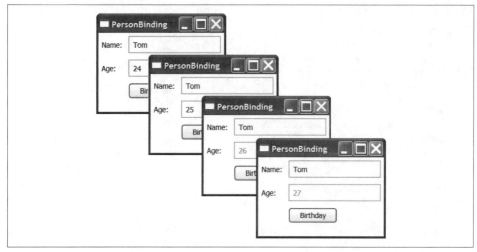

Figure 4-10. A value converter in action (Color Plate 8)

In Figure 4-10, notice that as Tom's age increases past the threshold, the converter switches the foreground brush from black to red. This change happens immediately as the data changes without any explicit code to force it, just as with any other kind of data binding.

Binding to List Data

So far, you've seen several examples of binding a control to a single object. However, a more traditional use of binding is to a list of objects. For example, imagine a new type that our object data source can create that presents a list of Person objects, as in Example 4-19.

Example 4-19. Declaring a custom list type

```
using System.Collections.Generic; // List<T>
...
namespace PersonBinding {
  // XAML doesn't (yet) have a syntax
  // for generic class instantiation
  class People : List<Person> {}
}
```

We can hook this new list data source and bind to it in exactly the same way as if we were binding to a single object data source, as in Example 4-20.

Example 4-20. Declaring a collection in XAML

```
<!-- Window1.xaml -->
<?Mapping XmlNamespace="local" ClrNamespace="PersonBinding" ?>
<Window ... xmlns:local="local">
```

Example 4-20. Declaring a collection in XAML (continued)

```
<Window.Resources>
  <local:People x:Key="Family">
    <local:Person Name="Tom" Age="9" />
    <local:Person Name="John" Age="11" />
    <local:Person Name="Melissa" Age="36" />
  </local:People>
  <local:AgeToForegroundConverter
    x:Key="AgeToForegroundConverter" />
</Window.Resources>
<Grid DataContext="{StaticResource Family}">
  ...
  <TextBlock ...>Name:</TextBlock>
  <TextBox Text="{Binding Path=Name}" ... />
  <TextBox
    Text="{Binding Path=Age}"
    Foreground="{Binding Path=Age, Converter=...}" ... />
  <Button ...>Birthday</Button>
</Grid>
</Window>
```

In Example 4-20, we've created an instance of the People collection and populated it with three Person objects. However, running it will still look just like Figure 4-6.

Current Item

While the text box properties can only be bound to a single object at a time, the binding engine is giving them the *current item* in the list of possible objects they could bind against, as illustrated in Figure 4-6.

By default, the first item in the list starts as the current item. Since the first item in our list example is the same as the only item to which we were binding before, things look and act in exactly the same way as shown in Figure 4-11, except for the Birthday button.

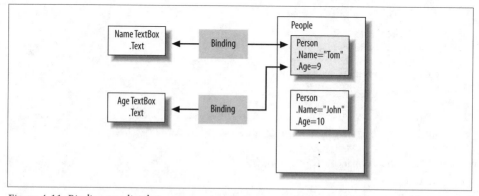

Figure 4-11. Binding to a list data source

Getting the current item

Recall the current `Birthday` button click event handler (Example 4-21).

Example 4-21. Finding a custom object declared in XAML

```
public partial class Window1 : Window {
  ...
  void birthdayButton_Click(object sender, RoutedEventArgs e) {
    Person person = (Person)this.FindResource("Tom"));
    ++person.Age;
    MessageBox.Show(...);
  }
}
```

Our `Birthday` button has always been about celebrating the birthday of the current person, but so far the current person has always been the same, so we could just shortcut things and go directly to the single `Person` object. Now that we've got a list of objects, this no longer works (unless you consider a message box containing the word "InvalidCastException" acceptable behavior). Further, casting to `People`, our collection class, won't tell us which `Person` is currently being shown in the UI, because it has no idea about such things (nor should it). For this information, we're going to have to go to the broker between the data-bound control and the collection of items, the *view*.

The job of the view is to provide services on top of the data, including sorting, filtering and, most importantly for our purposes at the moment, control of the current item. A view is an implementation of a data-specific interface, which, in our case, is going to be the `ICollectionView` interface. We can access a view over our data with the static `GetDefaultView` method of the `BindingOperations` class, as in Example 4-22.

Example 4-22. Getting a collection's view

```
public partial class Window1 : Window {
  ...
  void birthdayButton_Click(object sender, RoutedEventArgs e) {
    People people = (People)this.FindResource("Family");
    ICollectionView view =
      BindingOperations.GetDefaultView(people);
    Person person = (Person)view.CurrentItem;

    ++person.Age;
    MessageBox.Show(...);
  }
}
```

To retrieve the view associated with the Family collection, Example 4-22 makes a call to the `GetDefaultView` method of `BindingOperations`, which provides us with an implementation of the `ICollectionView` interface. With it, we can grab the current item, cast it into an item from our collection (the `CurrentItem` property returns an object), and use it for display.

Navigating between items

In addition to getting the current item, we can also change which item is current using the MoveCurrentTo methods of the ICollectionView interface, as in Example 4-23.

Example 4-23. Navigating between items via the view

```
public partial class Window1 : Window {
  ...
  ICollectionView GetFamilyView( ) {
    People people = (People)this.FindResource("Family");
    return BindingOperations.GetDefaultView(people);
  }

  void birthdayButton_Click(object sender, RoutedEventArgs e) {
    ICollectionView view = GetFamilyView( );
    Person person = (Person)view.CurrentItem;

    ++person.Age;
    MessageBox.Show(...);
  }

  void backButton_Click(object sender, RoutedEventArgs e) {
    ICollectionView view = GetFamilyView( );
    view.MoveCurrentToPrevious( );
    if( view.IsCurrentBeforeFirst ) {
      view.MoveCurrentToFirst( );
    }
  }

  void forwardButton_Click(object sender, RoutedEventArgs e) {
    ICollectionView view = GetFamilyView( );
    view.MoveCurrentToNext( );
    if( view.IsCurrentAfterLast ) {
      view.MoveCurrentToLast( );
    }
  }
}
```

The ICollectionView methods MoveCurrentToPrevious and MoveCurrentToNext change which item is currently selected by going backward and forward through the collection. If we walk off the end of the list in one direction or the other, the IsCurrentBeforeFirst or IsCurrentAfterLast properties will tell us that. The MoveCurrentToFirst and MoveCurrentToLast help us recover after walking off the end of the list and would be useful for implementing the Back and Forward buttons shown in Figure 4-12, as well as First and Last buttons (which would be an opportunity for you to apply what you've learned...).

Figure 4-12 shows the effect of moving forward from the first Person in the collection, including the color changes based on the Person object's Age property (which still works in exactly the same way).

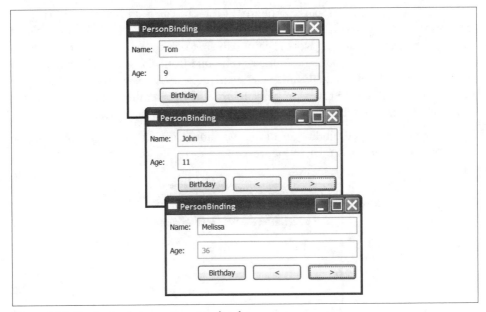

Figure 4-12. Navigating between items in a list data source

List Data Targets

Of course, there's only so far we can push the user of list data without providing them a control that can actually show more than one item at a time, such as the ListBox control in Example 4-24.

Example 4-24. Binding a list element to a list data source

```
<!-- Window1.xaml -->
<?Mapping XmlNamespace="local" ClrNamespace="PersonBinding" ?>
<Window ... xmlns:local="local">
  <Window.Resources>
    <local:People x:Key="Family">...</local:People>
    <local:AgeToForegroundConverter
      x:Key="AgeToForegroundConverter" />
  </Window.Resources>
  <Grid DataContext="{StaticResource Family}">
    ...
    <ListBox
      ItemsSource="{Binding}"
      IsSynchronizedWithCurrentItem="True" ... />
    <TextBlock ...>Name:</TextBlock>
    <TextBox Text="{Binding Path=Name}" ... />
    ...
</Window>
```

In Example 4-24, the ItemsSource property of the ListBox is a Binding with no path, which is the same as saying "bind to the entire current object." Notice that there's no source, either, so the binding works against the first non-null data context it finds. In this case, the first non-null data context is the one from the Grid, the same one as shared between both name and age text boxes. Also, we are setting the IsSynchronizedWithCurrentItem property to true so that as the selected item of the listbox changes, it updates the current item in the view and vice versa.

With our item's source binding in place, we should expect to see all three Person objects in the listbox, as shown in Figure 4-13.

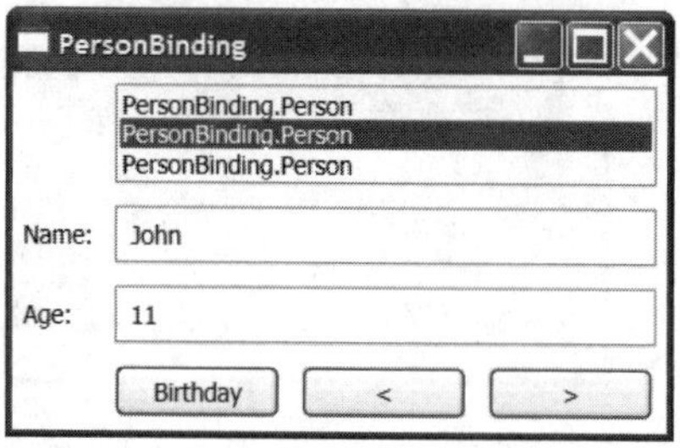

Figure 4-13. Person objects being displayed in a ListBox without help

As you might have noticed, everything is not quite perfect in Figure 4-13. What's happening is that when you bind against a whole object, data binding is doing its best to display each Person object. Without special instructions, it'll use a type converter to get a string representation. For name and age, which are of built-in types with built-in conversions, this works just fine, but it doesn't work very well at all for a custom type without a visual rendering, as is the case with our Person type.

Data Templates

The right way to solve this problem is with a *data template*. A data template is a tree of elements to expand in a particular context. For example, for each Person object, we'd really like to be able to concatenate the name and age together in a string like the following:

Tom (age:**9**)

We can think of this as a logical template that looks like this:

Name (age:*Age*)

To define this template for items in the listbox, we create a DataTemplate element, as in Example 4-25.

Example 4-25. Using a data template

```
<ListBox ... ItemsSource="{Binding}">
  <ListBox.ItemTemplate>
    <DataTemplate>
      <StackPanel Orientation="Horizontal">
        <TextBlock TextContent="{Binding Path=Name}" />
        <TextBlock TextContent=" (age: " />
        <TextBlock
          TextContent="{Binding Path=Age}"
          Foreground="
            {Binding
              Path=Age,
              Converter={StaticResource AgeToForegroundConverter}}" />
        <TextBlock TextContent=")" />
      </StackPanel>
    </DataTemplate>
  </ListBox.ItemTemplate>
</ListBox>
```

In this case, the ListBox control has an ItemTemplate property, which accepts an instance of a DataTemplate object. The DataTemplate allows us to specify a single child element to repeat for every item that the ListBox control binds against. In our case, we're using a StackPanel to gather together four TextBlock controls in a row, two for text bound to properties on each Person object and two for the constant text. Notice that we're also binding the Foreground to the Age property using the AgeToForegroundConverter so that Age properties show up in black or red, so that the listbox is consistent with the age text box.

With the use of the data template, our experience goes from Figure 4-13 to Figure 4-14.

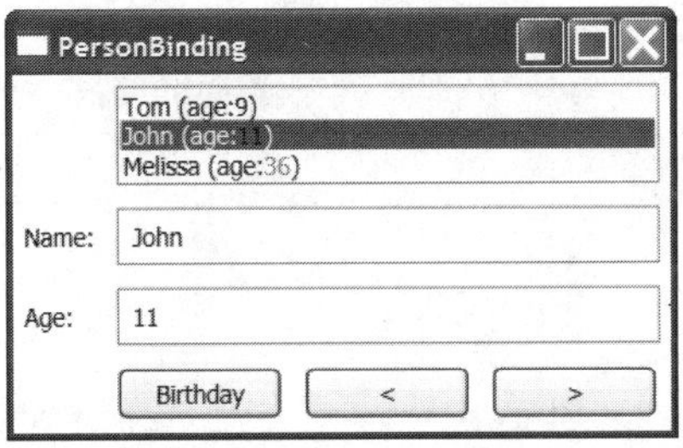

Figure 4-14. Person objects being displayed in a ListBox with a data template

Notice that the listbox shows all of the items in the collection and keeps the view's idea of current item synchronized with it as the selection moves or the back and forward buttons are pressed (actually, you can't really "notice" this based on the screenshot in Figure 4-14, but trust me, that's what happens). In addition, as data changes in Person objects, the listbox, and the text boxes are all kept in sync, including the Age color.

Typed data templates

In Example 4-25, we explicitly set the data template for items in our listbox. However, if a Person object showed up in a button or in some other element, we'd have to specify the data template for those Person objects separately. On the other hand, if you'd like a Person object to have a specific template no matter where it shows up, you can do so with a typed data template, as in Example 4-26.

Example 4-26. A typed data template

```
<Window.Resources>
  <local:AgeToForegroundConverter
    x:Key="AgeToForegroundConverter" />
  <local:People x:Key="Family">...</local:People>
  <DataTemplate DataType="{x:Type local:Person}">
    <StackPanel Orientation="Horizontal">
      <TextBlock TextContent="{Binding Path=Name}" />
      <TextBlock TextContent=" (age: " />
      <TextBlock TextContent="{Binding Path=Age}" ... />
      <TextBlock TextContent=")" />
    </StackPanel>
  </DataTemplate>
</Window.Resources>
...
<!-- no need for an ItemTemplate setting -->
<ListBox ItemsSource="{Binding}" ...>
```

In Example 4-26, we've hoisted the data template definition into a resources block and tagged it with a type using the DataType property. Now, unless told otherwise, whenever WPF sees an instance of the Person object, it will apply the appropriate data template. This is a handy way to make sure that data is displayed in a consistent way throughout your application without worrying about just where it shows.

List Changes

Thus far, we've got a list of objects that we can edit in place and navigate among, even highlighting certain data values with ease and providing an automatic look for data that wasn't shipped with a rendering from the manufacturer. In the spirit of how far we've come, you might suspect that providing an Add button would be a breeze, as in Example 4-27.

Example 4-27. Adding an item to a data bound collection

```
public partial class Window1 : Window {
  ...
  void addButton_Click(object sender, RoutedEventArgs e) {
    People people = (People)this.FindResource("Family");
    people.Add(new Person("Chris", 35));
  }
}
```

The problem with this implementation is that while the view can figure out the existence of new items on the fly as you move to it, the listbox itself has no idea that something new has been added to the collection, as shown in Figure 4-15.

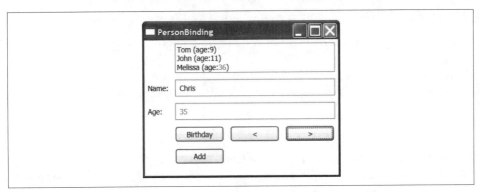

Figure 4-15. The ListBox doesn't know the collection has gotten bigger

In interacting with the state of the application shown in Figure 4-15, I ran the application, pressed the Add button and used the Forward button to navigate to it. However, even though the new person is shown in the text boxes, the listbox still has no idea something was added. Likewise, it wouldn't have any idea if something was removed. Just like data-bound *objects* need to implement the INotifyPropertyChanged interface, data-bound *lists* need to implement the INotifyCollectionChanged interface, as in Example 4-28.

Example 4-28. The INotifyCollectionChanged interface

```
namespace System.Collections.Specialized {
  public interface INotifyCollectionChanged {
    event NotifyCollectionChangedEventHandler CollectionChanged;
  }
}
```

The INotifyCollectionChanged interface is used to notify the data-bound control that items have been added or removed from the bound list. While it's common to implement INotifyPropertyChanged in your custom types to enable two-way data binding on your type's properties, it's less common to implement your own collection classes, which leaves you less opportunity to implement the INotifyCollectionChanged interface. Instead, you'll most likely be relying on one of the collection classes in the .NET Framework Class Library to implement INotifyCollectionChanged for you. The number of such classes is small, and unfortunately, List<T>, the collection class we're using to hold Person objects, is not among them. While you're more than welcome to spend your evenings and weekends implementing INotifyCollectionChanged, WPF provides the ObservableCollection<T> class for those of us with more pressing duties, as in Example 4-29.

Example 4-29. WPF's implementation of INotifyCollectionChanged

```
namespace System.Windows.Data {
  public class ObservableCollection<T> :
    Collection<T>, INotifyCollectionChanged, INotifyPropertyChanged {
    ...
  }
}
```

Since ObservableCollection<T> derives from Collection<T> and implements the INotifyCollectionChanged interface, we can use it instead of List<T> for our Person collection, as in Example 4-30.

Example 4-30. ObservableCollection<T> in action

```
namespace PersonBinding {
  class Person : INotifyPropertyChanged {...}
  class People : ObservableCollection<Person> {}
}
```

Now, when an item is added to or removed from the Person collection, those changes will be reflected in the list data-bound controls, as shown in Figure 4-16.

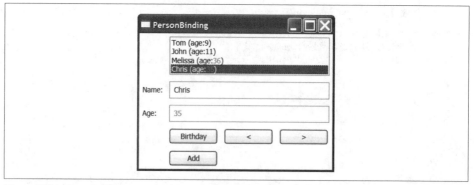

Figure 4-16. Keeping the ListBox in sync with INotifyCollectionChanged

Sorting

Once we have data targets showing more than one thing at a time properly, a young person's fancy turns to more, well, fancy things, such as sorting the view of the data or filtering it. Recall that the view always sits between the data-bound target and the data source. This means that it's possible to skip data that we don't want to show (this is called *filtering*, and it will be covered directly), and it's possible to change the order in which the data is shown, a.k.a. *sorting*. The simplest way to sort is by manipulating the Sort property of the view, as in Example 4-31.

Example 4-31. Sorting

```
public partial class Window1 : Window {
  ...
  ICollectionView GetFamilyView( ) {
    People people = (People)this.FindResource("Family");
    return BindingOperations.GetDefaultView(people);
  }

  void sortButton_Click(object sender, RoutedEventArgs e) {
    ICollectionView view = GetFamilyView( );
    if( view.Sort.Count == 0 ) {
      view.Sort.Add(
        new SortDescription("Name", ListSortDirection.Ascending));
      view.Sort.Add(
        new SortDescription("Age", ListSortDirection.Descending));
    }
    else {
      view.Sort.Clear( );
    }
  }
}
```

Here we are toggling between sorted and unsorted views by checking the SortDescriptionCollection exposed by the ICollectionView Sort property. If there are no sort descriptions, we sort first by the Name property in ascending order, then by the Age property in Descending order. If there are sort descriptions, we clear them, restoring the order to whatever it was before we applied our sort. While the sort descriptions are in place, any new objects added to the collection will be inserted into their proper sort position, as Figure 4-17 shows.

A collection of SortDescription objects should cover most cases, but if you'd like a bit more control, you can provide the view with a custom sorting object by implementing the IComparer interface, as in Example 4-32.

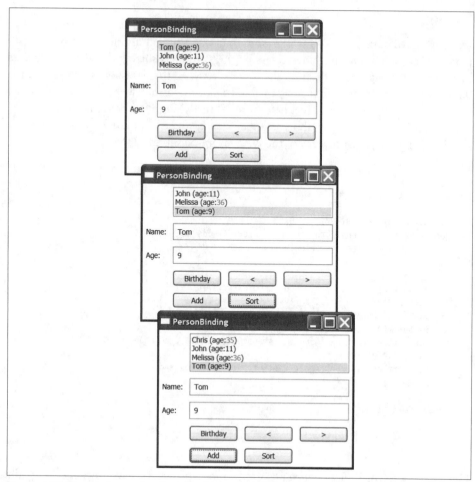

Figure 4-17. Unsorted, sorted with original data, and adding to a sorted view

Example 4-32. Custom sorting

```
class PersonSorter : IComparer {
  public int Compare(object x, object y) {
    Person lhs = (Person)x;
    Person rhs = (Person)y;

    // Sort Name ascending and Age descending
    int nameCompare = lhs.Name.CompareTo(rhs.Name);
    if( nameCompare != 0 ) return nameCompare;
    return rhs.Age - lhs.Age;
  }
}

public partial class Window1 : Window {
  ...
  ICollectionView GetFamilyView( ) {
```

Example 4-32. Custom sorting (continued)

```
    People people = (People)this.FindResource("Family");
    return BindingOperations.GetDefaultView(people);
  }

  void sortButton_Click(object sender, RoutedEventArgs e) {
    ListCollectionView view = (ListCollectionView)GetFamilyView( );
    if( view.CustomSort == null ) {
      view.CustomSort = new PersonSorter( );
    }
    else {
      view.CustomSort = null;
    }
  }
}
```

In the case of setting a custom sorter, we have to make an assumption about the implementation of ICollectionView—specifically, that it is a ListCollectionView, which is what WPF wraps around an implementation of IList (which our ObserverableCollection provides) to provide view functionality. There are other implementations of ICollectionView that don't provide custom sorting, so you'll want to test this code before shipping it.[*]

 While I'm sure this will get better as we approach v1.0 of WPF, as of right now, the view implementations associated with specific data characteristics—such as the matching of ListCollectionView to IList— are undocumented (at least as far as I could tell). Also, it seems somewhat funny that CustomSort was part of the view implementation class and not part of the ICollectionView interface, so let's keep our fingers crossed that this will also change as Microsoft moves toward the release of WPF.

Filtering

Just because all of the objects are shown in an order that makes you happy doesn't mean that you want all of the objects to be shown. For those rogue objects that happen to be in the data but that don't belong in the view, we need to feed the view an implementation of the CollectionFilterCallback delegate[†] that takes a single object parameter and returns a Boolean indicating whether the object should be shown or not, as in Example 4-33.

---

[*] Hopefully you'll test the rest of your code before shipping it, too, but it never hurts to point these things out…

[†] Sorting uses a single-method interface implementation because of history, and filtering uses a delegate because with the addition of anonymous delegates in C# 2.0, delegates are all the rage.

Example 4-33. Filtering

```
public partial class Window1 : Window {
  ...
  ICollectionView GetFamilyView( ) {
    People people = (People)this.FindResource("Family");
    return BindingOperations.GetDefaultView(people);
  }

  void filterButton_Click(object sender, RoutedEventArgs e) {
    ICollectionView view = GetFamilyView( );
    if( view.Filter == null ) {
      view.Filter = delegate(object item) {
        return ((Person)item).Age >= 18;
      };
    }
    else {
      view.Filter = null;
    }
  }
}
```

Like sorting, with a filter in place, new things are filtered appropriately, as Figure 4-18 shows.

The top window in Figure 4-18 shows no filtering, the middle window shows filtering of the initial list, and the bottom window shows adding a new adult with filtering still in place.

Data Sources

So far, we've been dealing simply with objects. However, that's not the only place that data can come from; XML and relational databases spring to mind as popular alternatives. Further, since neither XML nor relational databases store their data as .NET objects, some translation is going to be needed to support data binding which, as you recall, requires .NET properties on data-source objects. And even if we can declare objects directly in XAML, we'd still like a layer of indirection for pulling objects from other sources and even pushing that work off to a worker thread if said retrieval is a ponderous operation.

In short, we'd like some indirection away from the direct declaration of objects for translation and loading. For this indirection, we have but to turn to IDataSource implementations, one of which is the object data source.

Object Data Source

An implementation of the IDataSource interface provides a layer of indirection for all kinds of operations that produce objects against which to data-bind. For example, if we wanted to load a set of Person objects over the Web, we could encapsulate that logic into a bit of code, such as Example 4-34.

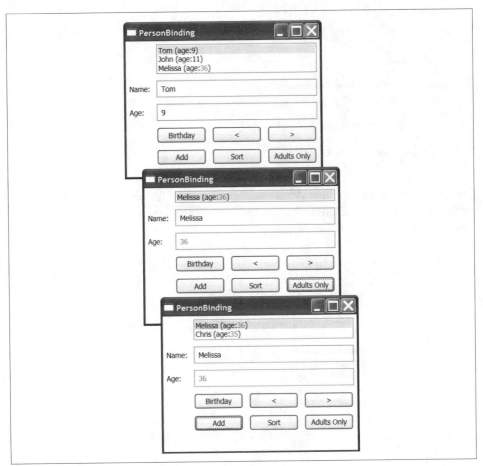

Figure 4-18. Unfiltered, filtered for adults, and adding to a filtered view

Example 4-34. A type to be used by ObjectDataSource

```
namespace PersonBinding {
  public class Person : INotifyPropertyChanged {...}
  public class People : ObservableCollection<Person> {}

  public class RemotePeopleLoader : People {
    public RemotePeopleLoader() {
      // Load people from afar
      ...
    }
  }
}
```

In Example 4-34, the RemotePeopleLoader class derives from the People collection class, retrieving the data in the constructor, because the object data source expects the object it creates to be the collection, as in Example 4-35.

Example 4-35. Using the ObjectDataSource

```
<Window.Resources>
  ...
  <ObjectDataSource
    x:Key="Family"
    TypeName="PersonBinding.RemotePeopleLoader"
    Asynchronous="True" />
</Window.Resources>
<Grid DataContext="{StaticResource Family}">
  ...
  <ListBox ItemsSource="{Binding}" ...>
</Grid>
```

The ObjectDataSource element is most often placed in a resource block to be used by
name elsewhere in the XAML. The TypeName property refers to the fully qualified type
name of the class that will be the collection.

Most of the classes in WPF that take type parameters, such as the
DataType property of the DataTemplate element, can be set with the
type markup extension, which includes class, namespace, and assembly information using the mapping syntax:

```
<!-- set up DataTemplate for Bar.Quux in assembly foo -->
<?Mapping
  XmlNamespace="local"
  ClrNamespace="Bar"
  Assembly="foo" />
<Window ... xmlns="local">
  <Window.Resources>
    <DataTemplate
      DataType="{x:Type local:Quux}">...</DataTemplate>
  </Window.Resources>
  ...
</Window>
```

However, the ObjectDataSource takes its type information in its own
form:

```
<!-- set up ObjectDataSource for Bar.Quux in assembly foo -->
<ObjectDataSource x:Key="foo" TypeName="Bar.Quux, foo" />
```

One can only hope that the two techniques will be rationalized by
RTM.

With an object data source acting as an intermediary between the data and the bindings, we need to update our code when we're retrieving the People collection (now a
base class of the RemotePeopleLoader, but still the container of our Person objects), as
in Example 4-36.

Example 4-36. Accessing the data held by an object data source

```
public partial class Window1 : Window {
  ...
  ICollectionView GetFamilyView() {
```

Example 4-36. Accessing the data held by an object data source (continued)

```
    IDataSource ds = (IDataSource)this.FindResource("Family");
    People people = (People)ds.Data;
    return BindingOperations.GetDefaultView(people);
}

void birthdayButton_Click(object sender, RoutedEventArgs e) {
  ICollectionView view = GetFamilyView( );
  Person person = (Person)view.CurrentItem;

  ++person.Age;
  MessageBox.Show(...);
}

void addButton_Click(object sender, RoutedEventArgs e) {
  IDataSource ds = (IDataSource)this.FindResource("Family");
  People people = (People)ds.Data;
  people.Add(new Person("Chris", 35));
}
}
```

Since the Family resource is now an `ObjectDataSource`, itself an implementation of the `IDataSource`, in Example 4-36, when we need the `People` collection, we're casting to `IDataSource` on the `Family` resource and pulling the collection out of the `Data` property.

> Even though the object data source exposes its data from the `Data` property, that doesn't mean that you should bind to it. If you notice from Example 4-35, we're still binding the listbox as before:
>
> ```
> <!-- do not bind to Path=Data -->
> <ListBox ItemsSource="{Binding}" ...>
> ```
>
> The reason this works is because WPF has built-in knowledge of `IDataSource`, so there's no need for you to do the indirection yourself.

Asynchronous data retrieval

In Example 4-35, we applied the `Asynchronous` property, which is easily the most interesting piece of functionality that the object data source gives us that we lack when we declare object graphs directly in XAML. When the `Asynchronous` property is set to true (the default is false), the task of creating the object specified by the `TypeName` property is handled on a worker thread, only performing the binding on the UI thread when the data has been retrieved. This is not the same as binding to the data as its retrieved—e.g., from a stream over the network—but it's better than blocking the UI thread while a long retrieval happens.

Passing parameters

In addition to the `Asynchronous` property, the object data source also provides the `Parameters` property, which is a comma-delimited list of strings to be passed as string arguments to the type created by the object data source. For example, if we wanted to pass in a set of URLs from which to try and retrieve the data, we could use the Parameters property as in Example 4-37.

Example 4-37. Passing parameters via ObjectDataSource

```
<ObjectDataSource
  x:Key="Family"
  TypeName="PersonBinding.RemotePeopleLoader"
  Asynchronous="True"
  Parameters="http://sellsbrothers.com/sons.dat,
              http://sellssisters.com/daughters.dat" />
```

In Example 4-37, we've added a list of two URLs, which will be translated into a call to the RemotePeopleLoader constructor that takes two strings, as in Example 4-38.

Example 4-38. Accepting arguments passed by ObjectDataSource

```
namespace PersonBinding {
  public class RemotePeopleLoader : People {
    public RemotePeopleLoader(string url1, string url2) {
      // Load People from afar using two URLs
      ...
    }
  }
}
```

Unfortunately, if we put other data types into the list of parameters supported by the object data source's Parameters property, like integers, they will not be translated, even if constructors of the appropriate types are available; the object data source only supports the creation of objects with constructors taking zero or more strings. If any data conversion is necessary, you will have to do it.

XmlDataSource

As I mentioned, while objects are the only thing that data binding supports, data isn't only stored as objects in the world. In fact, most data isn't stored in objects. One increasingly popular way to store data is XML. For example, Example 4-39 shows our family data represented in XML.

Example 4-39. My family rendered in XML

```
<!-- family.xml -->
<Family xmlns="">
  <Person Name="Tom" Age="9" />
  <Person Name="John" Age="11" />
  <Person Name="Melissa" Age="36" />
</Family>
```

With this file available in the same folder as the executing application, we can bind to it using the XmlDataSource, as shown in Example 4-40.

Example 4-40. An XmlDataSource in action

```
<!-- Window1.xaml -->
<Window ...>
  <Window.Resources>

    ...

    <XmlDataSource
      x:Key="Family"
      Source="family.xml"
      XPath="/Family/Person" />
  </Window.Resources>
  <Grid DataContext="{StaticResource Family}">

    ...

    <ListBox ... ItemsSource="{Binding}">
      <ListBox.ItemTemplate>
        <DataTemplate>
          <StackPanel Orientation="Horizontal">
            <TextBlock TextContent="{Binding XPath=@Name}" />
            <TextBlock TextContent=" (age: " />
            <TextBlock TextContent="{Binding XPath=@Age}" ... />
            <TextBlock TextContent=")" />
          </StackPanel>
        </DataTemplate>
      </ListBox.ItemTemplate>
    </ListBox>

    <TextBlock ...>Name:</TextBlock>
    <TextBox Text="{Binding XPath=@Name}" .../>
    <TextBlock ...>Age:</TextBlock>
    <TextBox Text="{Binding XPath=@Age}" ... />

    ...
  </Grid>
</Window>
```

Notice the use of the XmlDataSource with a relative URL that points to the *family.xml* file and the XPath expression* that pulls out the Person elements under the Family element root. The only other thing that changes in the XAML file from the use of the ObjectDataSource is that when binding Name and Age to TextBlock and TextBox controls, we use XPath statements instead of Path statements.

XML island data

If you happen to know your data at compile time, the XML data source also supports "data islands" in the same way that XAML creating objects directly does, as in Example 4-41.

---

* An explanation of the XPath syntax is beyond the scope of this book, but for a good reference, I'd start with *Essential XML Quick Reference* by Aaron Skonnard and Martin Gudgin (Addison Wesley).

Example 4-41. An XML data island in XAML

```
<XmlDataSource x:Key="Family" XPath="/Family/Person">
  <Family xmlns="">
    <Person Name="Tom" Age="9" />
    <Person Name="John" Age="11" />
    <Person Name="Melissa" Age="36" />
  </Family>
</XmlDataSource>
```

In Example 4-41, we've just copied the contents of *family.xml* under the XmlDataSource element, dropping the Source attribute but leaving the XPath statement.

However, now that we're using XML instead of object data, some of the operations in our sample application need changing, such as accessing and/or changing the current item (as we do in the Birthday button implementation), adding a new item, and sorting items or filtering items. In short, anything where we assumed a collection of Person objects needs to change. On the other hand, moving between items using the ICollectionView.MovingCurrentToXxx( ) family of methods continues to work just fine, as does our AgeToForegroundValueConverter.

 Our implementation of IValueConverter.Convert continues to work because we parsed the string value of the object instead of casting directly to an Int32. A cast would have been preferred in the Person object case, because Age was of type Int32 and parsing it was unnecessary. However, in the XML case and in the absence of any application of an XSD, Age is of type String, so the parsing is necessary.

XML data sources and item access

To access and manipulate items in an XML data source, instead of instances of your custom type, you'll be using instances of the XmlElement class from the System.Xml namespace, as in Example 4-42.

Example 4-42. Accessing XML from an XML data source

```
// Window1.xaml.cs
...
namespace PersonBinding {
  public partial class Window1 : Window {
    ...

    ICollectionView GetFamilyView( ) {
      IDataSource ds = (IDataSource)this.FindResource("Family");
      IEnumerable people = (IEnumerable)ds.Data;
      return BindingOperations.GetDefaultView(people);
    }

    void birthdayButton_Click(object sender, RoutedEventArgs e) {
      ICollectionView view = GetFamilyView( );
```

Example 4-42. Accessing XML from an XML data source (continued)

```
    XmlElement person = (XmlElement)view.CurrentItem;
    person.SetAttribute("Age",
      (int.Parse(person.Attributes["Age"].Value) + 1).ToString( ));
    MessageBox.Show(
      string.Format(
        "Happy Birthday, {0}, age {1}!",
        person.Attributes["Name"].Value,
        person.Attributes["Age"].Value),
      "Birthday");
  }
  ...
 }
}
```

The first thing to notice in Example 4-42 is that in our implementation of GetFamilyView, we're no longer looking for the People collection directly but rather some implementation of IEnumerable provided by the XML data source. IEnumerable is the simplest thing you can have in .NET and still have a collection, so that's what the GetDefaultView method requires.

Also notice in Example 4-42 that the CurrentItem property of the collection view is an instance of the XmlElement. To increment the age, we access the element's Age attribute, pull out its value, parse it as an integer, increment it, convert the whole thing back to a string, and set it as the new Age attribute value of the current element. Showing each attribute is merely another couple of attribute accesses.

XML data sources and adding items

When adding (or removing) items, it's best to get access to the XmlDataSource itself so that you can access the Document property for creating and adding new elements, as in Example 4-43.

Example 4-43. Adding an item to an XML data source

```
void addButton_Click(object sender, RoutedEventArgs e) {
  XmlDataSource xds = (XmlDataSource)this.FindResource("Family");
  XmlElement person = xds.Document.CreateElement("Person");
  person.SetAttribute("Name", "Chris");
  person.SetAttribute("Age", "35");
  xds.Document.ChildNodes[0].AppendChild(person);
}
```

Here, we're using the XmlDataSource to get to the XmlDocument and then using the XmlDocument to create a new element called Person (to fit in with the rest of our Person elements), setting the Name and Age attributes, and adding the element under the Family root element (available at ChildNodes[0] on the top-level Document object).

XML data sources and sorting

Sorting XML data-source items is a matter of remembering that we're dealing with XmlElements, as in Example 4-44.

Example 4-44. Sorting XML

```
class PersonSorter : IComparer {
  public int Compare(object x, object y) {
    XmlElement lhs = (XmlElement)x;
    XmlElement rhs = (XmlElement)y;

    // Sort Name ascending and Age descending
    int nameCompare =
      lhs.Attributes["Name"].Value.CompareTo(
        rhs.Attributes["Name"].Value);

    if( nameCompare != 0 ) {
      return nameCompare;
    }

    return int.Parse(rhs.Attributes["Age"].Value) -
           int.Parse(lhs.Attributes["Age"].Value);
  }
}

void sortButton_Click(object sender, RoutedEventArgs e) {
  ListCollectionView view = (ListCollectionView)GetFamilyView();

  // Managing the view.Sort collection would work, too
  if( view.CustomSort == null ) {
    view.CustomSort = new PersonSorter();
  }
  else {
    view.CustomSort = null;
  }
}
```

In Example 4-44, we're sorting just like before, but we're pulling out the Name and Age attributes and converting as appropriate to do so.

XML data sources and filtering

XML filtering is very much like object filtering, except that we're dealing with XmlElements, as in Example 4-45.

Example 4-45. Filtering XML

```
void filterButton_Click(object sender, RoutedEventArgs e) {
  ICollectionView view = GetFamilyView();

  if( view.Filter == null ) {
    view.Filter = delegate(object item) {
```

Example 4-45. Filtering XML

```
      return
        int.Parse(((XmlElement)item).Attributes["Age"].Value) >= 18;
    };
  }
  else {
    view.Filter = null;
  }
}
```

Here our filter delegate casts each item to an XmlElement to do the filtering.

Relational Data Source

As of the current build, WPF has no direct support for binding to relational databases, and the indirect support is not in such great shape, either. For an example of the current state of binding to relational data in WPF, I recommend the WinFX SDK sample entitled "Binding with Data in an ADO DataSet Sample."

Custom Data Sources

If you'd like to take advantage of the indirection that data sources provide for retrieving objects, but none of the built-in data sources tickles you, a custom implementation of IDataSource should do the trick. For example, instead of creating the RemotePersonLoader collection to load the remove family data (it was kind of hokey to add collection items in the collection's constructor, anyway), we could have created a custom implementation of IDataSource to do the magic, as in Example 4-46.

Example 4-46. A simple custom data source

```
namespace PersonBinding {
  public class Person : INotifyPropertyChanged {...}
  public class People : ObservableCollection<Person> {}

  public class RemotePeopleSource : IDataSource {
    People people = null;

    public RemotePeopleSource() {
      // Load People from afar
      ...

      // Let data binding know we've got data
      if( DataChanged != null ) {
        DataChanged(this, EventArgs.Empty);
      }
    }

    // IDataSource Members

    // Gets the underlying data object
```

Example 4-46. A simple custom data source (continued)

```
    public object Data {
      get { return people; }
    }

    // Occurs when a new data object becomes available
    // Especially handy for async object retrieval
    public event EventHandler DataChanged;

    // Refreshes the data source object using the most current
    // values for the object's configuration properties
    public void Refresh() {
      // Not needed in our case...
    }
  }
}
```

In Example 4-46, we've implemented IDataSource by creating an instance of the People collection, and, after some mysterious data retrieval process in the constructor, we fire off an event to let data binding know that we've got data[*] and that it should now recheck the Data property. This protocol is especially useful if you're doing asynchronous data retrieval like the object data source does.

If your data source provides custom properties—e.g., Asynchronous—it's possible that one or more of the properties could be changed at runtime. If you've got more than one property that affects data retrieval, you may not want to kick off the search for the new data until the Refresh method is called; otherwise, you may start things off after one property is changed but before the client has a chance to change the rest of them.

Master-Detail Binding

We've seen binding to a single object. We've seen binding to a single list of objects. One other very popular thing to do is to bind to more than one list, especially related lists. For example, if you're showing your users a list of customers and then, when they select one, you'd like to show that customer's related orders, you'll want master-detail binding.

Master-detail binding is a form of filtering, where the selection in the master list—e.g., customer 452—sets the filtering parameters for the associated detail data—e.g., orders for customer 452.

In our discussion thus far, we don't have customers and orders, but we do have families and people, which we could further formalize as shown in Example 4-47.

---

[*] Wouldn't "Got Data?" look nice on a T-shirt?

Example 4-47. Master-detail data for binding

```
public class Families : ObservableCollection<Family> {}

public class Family {
  string familyName;
  public string FamilyName {
    get { return familyName; }
    set { familyName = value; }
  }

  People members;
  public People Members {
    get { return members; }
    set { members = value; }
  }
}

public class People : ObservableCollection<Person> {}

public class Person {
  string name;
  public string Name {
    get { return name; }
    set { name = value; }
  }

  int age;
  public int Age {
    get { return age; }
    set { age = value; }
  }
}
```

In Example 4-47, we've got our familiar Person class with Name and Age properties, collected into a familiar People collection. Further, we have a Family class with a FamilyName property and a Members property of type People. Finally, we have a Families collection, which collects Family objects. In other words, families have members, which consist of people with names and ages.

You could imagine instances of Families, Family, People, and Person that looked like Figure 4-19.

In Figure 4-19, the Families collection forms the master data, holding instances of the Family class, each of which holds a Members property of type People, which holds the detail Person data. You could populate instances of these data structures, as shown in Example 4-48.

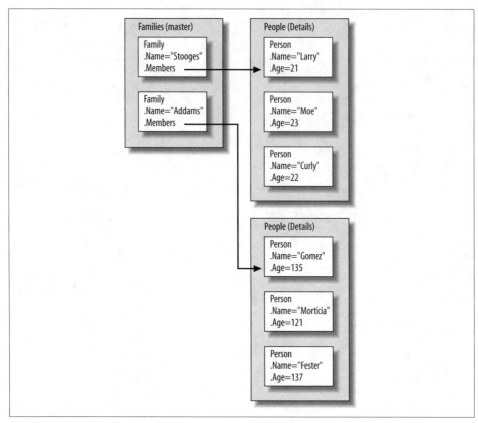

Figure 4-19. Sample master-detail data

Example 4-48. Declaring sample master-detail data

```
<!-- Window1.xaml -->
<?Mapping
  XmlNamespace="local" ClrNamespace="MasterDetailBinding" ?>
<Window ... xmlns:local="local">
  <Window.Resources>
    <local:Families x:Key="Families">
      <local:Family FamilyName="Stooge">
        <local:Family.Members>
          <local:People>
            <local:Person Name="Larry" Age="21" />
            <local:Person Name="Moe" Age="22" />
            <local:Person Name="Curly" Age="23" />
          </local:People>
        </local:Family.Members>
      </local:Family>
      <local:Family FamilyName="Addams">
        <local:Family.Members>
          <local:People>
            <local:Person Name="Gomez" Age="135" />
```

Example 4-48. Declaring sample master-detail data (continued)

```
                <local:Person Name="Morticia" Age="121" />
                <local:Person Name="Fester" Age="137" />
            </local:People>
        </local:Family.Members>
    </local:Family>
  </local:Families>
 </Window.Resources>
 ...
</Window>
```

Binding to this data at the top level—i.e., to show the family names—could look like Example 4-49.

Example 4-49. Binding to master Family data

```
<!-- Window1.xaml -->
<?Mapping ... ?>
<Window ...>
  <Window.Resources>
    <local:Families x:Key="Families">...</local:Families>
  </Window.Resources>
  <Grid DataContext="{StaticResource Families}">

    ...
    <!-- Families Column -->
    <TextBlock Grid.Row="0" Grid.Column="0">Families:</TextBlock>
    <ListBox Grid.Row="1" Grid.Column="0"
      IsSynchronizedWithCurrentItem="True"
      ItemsSource="{Binding}">
      <ListBox.ItemTemplate>
        <DataTemplate>
          <TextBlock TextContent="{Binding Path=FamilyName}" />
        </DataTemplate>
      </ListBox.ItemTemplate>
    </ListBox>
</Window>
```

In Example 4-49, we're setting two things in the Families column (column 0). The first is the header, which is set to the constant string "Families". The second forms the body, which is a list of Family objects in the Families collection, showing each family's FamilyName property, as shown in Figure 4-20.

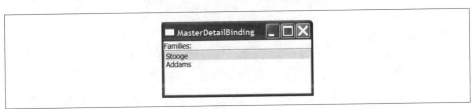

Figure 4-20. Showing family data

Figure 4-20 isn't master-detail, of course, since selecting a master family doesn't show its associated details. To do that, we need to bind to the next level, as in Example 4-50.

Example 4-50. Binding to detail Person data

```
<Grid DataContext="{StaticResource Families}">
  ...
  <!-- Families Column -->
  ...
  <!-- Members Column -->
  <StackPanel Grid.Row="0" Grid.Column="1" Orientation="Horizontal">
    <TextBlock TextContent="{Binding Path=FamilyName}" />
    <TextBlock TextContent=" Family Members:" />
  </StackPanel>
  <ListBox Grid.Row="1" Grid.Column="1"
    IsSynchronizedWithCurrentItem="True"
    ItemsSource="{Binding Path=Members}" >
    <ListBox.ItemTemplate>
      <DataTemplate>
        <StackPanel Orientation="Horizontal">
          <TextBlock TextContent="{Binding Path=Name}" />
          <TextBlock TextContent=" (age: " />
          <TextBlock TextContent="{Binding Path=Age}" />
          <TextBlock TextContent=" )" />
        </StackPanel>
      </DataTemplate>
    </ListBox.ItemTemplate>
  </ListBox>
```

In the Members column (column 1), we're also setting a header and body, but this time the header is bound to the FamilyName of the currently selected Family object.

Also, recall that in the Families column, our listbox's items source was bound to the entire collection via a Binding statement without a Path. In the details case, however, we want to tell the data-binding engine that we'd like to bind to the Members property of the currently selected Family object, which is itself a collection of Person objects. Figure 4-21 shows master-detail binding in action.

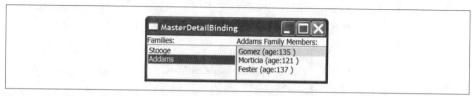

Figure 4-21. Showing master Family and detail Person data

But, wait: there's more! Master-detail binding doesn't stop at just two levels, oh no. You can go as deep as you like, with each detail binding becoming the master binding for the next level. To see this in action, let's add one more level of detail to our data classes, as in Example 4-51.

Example 4-51. Adding a 3rd level of detail

```
public class Person {
  string name;
  public string Name {
    get { return name; }
    set { name = value; }
  }

  int age;
  public int Age {
    get { return age; }
    set { age = value; }
  }

  Traits traits;
  public Traits Traits {
    get { return traits; }
    set { traits = value; }
  }
}

public class Traits : ObservableCollection<Trait> {}

public class Trait {
  string description;
  public string Description {
    get { return description; }
    set { description = value; }
  }
}
```

Now, not only do families have family names and members which consist of people with names and ages, but each person also has a set of traits, each with their own description. Expanding our XAML a bit to include traits would look like Example 4-52.

Example 4-52. Declaring a third level of detail

```
<local:Families x:Key="Families">
  <local:Family FamilyName="Stooge">
    <local:Family.Members>
      <local:People>
        <local:Person Name="Larry" Age="21">
          <local:Person.Traits>
            <local:Traits>
              <local:Trait Description="In Charge" />
              <local:Trait Description="Mean" />
              <local:Trait Description="Ugly" />
            </local:Traits>
          </local:Person.Traits>
        </local:Person>
        <local:Person Name="Moe" Age="22" >...</local:Person>

        ...
```

Example 4-52. Declaring a third level of detail (continued)

```
        </local:People>
      </local:Famil.Members>
      ...
    </local:Family>
  ...
</local:Families>
```

With a third level of detail, we bind as shown in Example 4-53.

Example 4-53. Binding to a third level of detail data

```
<Grid DataContext="{StaticResource Families}">
  ...

  <!-- Families Column -->
  ...

  <!-- Members Column -->
  ...

  <!-- Traits Column -->
  <StackPanel Grid.Row="0" Grid.Column="2" Orientation="Horizontal">
    <TextBlock TextContent="{Binding Path=Members/Name}" />
    <TextBlock TextContent=" Traits:" />
  </StackPanel>
  <ListBox Grid.Row="1" Grid.Column="2"
    IsSynchronizedWithCurrentItem="True"
    ItemsSource="{Binding Path=Members/Traits}" >
    <ListBox.ItemTemplate>
      <DataTemplate>
        <TextBlock TextContent="{Binding Path=Description}" />
      </DataTemplate>
    </ListBox.ItemTemplate>
  </ListBox>
</Grid>
```

In the case of the Families column header, recall that we had no binding at all; the
text was hardcoded:

```
<TextBlock ...>Families:</TextBlock>
```

In the case of the Members column header, we bound to the FamilyName of the currently selected Family object like so:

```
<TextBlock ... TextContent="{Binding Path=FamilyName}" />
```

Logically, you could think of this as expanding to the following:

```
<TextBlock ... TextContent="{Binding Path=family.FamilyName}" />
```

where family is the currently selected Family object.

Taking this one level deeper, in the case of the traits column header, we're binding to the `Name` property of the currently selected `Person` from the `Members` property of the currently selected `Family`, which binds like this:

```
<TextBlock ...
   TextContent="{Binding Path=Members/Name}" />
```

Again, logically you could think of it expanding like this:

```
<TextBlock ...
   TextContent="{Binding Path=family.Members.person.Name}" />
```

where `family` is the currently selected `Family` object and `person` is the currently selected `Person` object. The / in the binding statement acts as the separator between objects, with the object at each level assumed to be "currently selected."

The binding for the listbox's items source works the same way, except we want the `Traits` collection from the currently selected `Person`, not the `Name`. Our tri-level master-detail example looks like Figure 4-22.

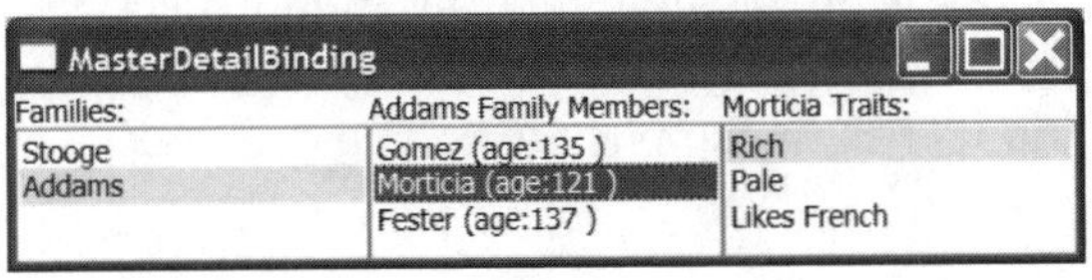

Figure 4-22. Showing master-detail-more detail data

Where Are We?

Fundamentally, data binding is about keeping data in one place—e.g., a property on an object—in sync with data in another place—e.g., a property on a control. In this chapter, we've traveled the length and breadth of the data-binding engine that supports this fundamental notion, and a great many of the implications as well, including item and list data sources in object and XML data formats, item and list data targets, managing the current item, value conversion, sorting, filtering, data templates, and even master-detail relationships.

The thorough support for data binding at every level of WPF makes it a first-class feature in a way that data binding has never been before. You'll find that it permeates pretty much every aspect of your WPF programming, including styles, which is the topic of the next chapter.

CHAPTER 5

Styles and Control Templates

In a word processing document, a "style" is a set of properties to be applied to ranges of content—e.g., text, images, etc. For example, the name of the style I'm using now is called "Normal,Body,b" and for this document in pre-publication, that means a font family of Times, a size of 10, and full justification. Later on in the document, I'll be using a style called "Code,x,s" that will use a font family of Courier New, a size of 9, and left justification. Styles are applied to content to produce a certain look when the content is rendered.

In WPF, a *style* is also a set of properties applied to content used for visual rendering. A style can be used to set properties on an existing visual element, such as setting the font weight of a Button control, or it can be used to define the way an object looks, such as showing the name and age from a Person object. In addition to the features in word processing styles, WPF styles have specific features for building applications, including the ability to associate different visual effects based on user events, provide entirely new looks for existing controls, and even designate rendering behavior for non-visual objects. All of these features come without the need to build a custom control (although that's still a useful thing to be able to do, as discussed in Chapter 9).

Without Styles

As an example of how styles can make themselves useful in WPF, let's take a look at a simple implementation of tic-tac-toe in Example 5-1.

Example 5-1. A simple tic-tac-toe layout

```
<!-- Window1.xaml -->
<Window
    x:Class="TicTacToe.Window1"
    xmlns="http://schemas.microsoft.com/winfx/avalon/2005"
    xmlns:x="http://schemas.microsoft.com/winfx/xaml/2005"
    Text="TicTacToe">
```

Example 5-1. A simple tic-tac-toe layout (continued)

```
<!-- the black background lets the tic-tac-toe -->
<!-- crosshatch come through on the margins -->
<Grid Background="Black">
  <Grid.RowDefinitions>
    <RowDefinition />
    <RowDefinition />
    <RowDefinition />
  </Grid.RowDefinitions>
  <Grid.ColumnDefinitions>
    <ColumnDefinition />
    <ColumnDefinition />
    <ColumnDefinition />
  </Grid.ColumnDefinitions>
  <Button Margin="0,0,2,2" Grid.Row="0" Grid.Column="0" x:Name="cell00" />
  <Button Margin="2,0,2,2" Grid.Row="0" Grid.Column="1" x:Name="cell01" />
  <Button Margin="2,0,0,2" Grid.Row="0" Grid.Column="2" x:Name="cell02" />
  <Button Margin="0,2,2,2" Grid.Row="1" Grid.Column="0" x:Name="cell10" />
  <Button Margin="2,2,2,2" Grid.Row="1" Grid.Column="1" x:Name="cell11" />
  <Button Margin="2,2,0,2" Grid.Row="1" Grid.Column="2" x:Name="cell12" />
  <Button Margin="0,2,2,0" Grid.Row="2" Grid.Column="0" x:Name="cell20" />
  <Button Margin="2,2,2,0" Grid.Row="2" Grid.Column="1" x:Name="cell21" />
  <Button Margin="2,2,0,0" Grid.Row="2" Grid.Column="2" x:Name="cell22" />
</Grid>
</Window>
```

This grid layout arranges a set of nine buttons in a 3×3 grid of tic-tac-toe cells, using the margins on the button for the tic-tac-toe crosshatch. A simple implementation of the game logic in the XAML code-behind file looks like Example 5-2.

Example 5-2. A simple tic-tac-toe implementation

```
// Window1.xaml.cs
...
namespace TicTacToe {
  public partial class Window1 : Window {
    // Track the current player (X or O)
    string currentPlayer;

    // Track the list of cells for finding a winner etc.
    Button[] cells;

    public Window1() {
      InitializeComponent();

      // Cache the list of buttons and handle their clicks
      this.cells = new Button[] { this.cell00, this.cell01, ... };
      foreach( Button cell in this.cells ) {
        cell.Click += cell_Click;
      }

      // Initialize a new game
      NewGame();
```

Example 5-2. A simple tic-tac-toe implementation (continued)

```
    }

    // Wrapper around the current player for future expansion,
    // e.g. updating status text with the current player
    string CurrentPlayer {
      get { return this.currentPlayer; }
      set { this.currentPlayer = value; }
    }

    // Use the buttons to track game state
    void NewGame( ) {
      foreach( Button cell in this.cells ) {
        cell.Content = null;
      }
      CurrentPlayer = "X";
    }

    void cell_Click(object sender, RoutedEventArgs e) {
      Button button = (Button)sender;

      // Don't let multiple clicks change the player for a cell
      if( button.Content != null ) { return; }

      // Set button content
      button.Content = CurrentPlayer;

      // Check for winner or a tie
      if( HasWon(this.currentPlayer) ) {
        MessageBox.Show("Winner!", "Game Over");
        NewGame( );
        return;
      }
      else if( TieGame( ) ) {
        MessageBox.Show("No Winner!", "Game Over");
        NewGame( );
        return;
      }

      // Switch player
      if( CurrentPlayer == "X" ) {
        CurrentPlayer = "O";
      }
      else {
        CurrentPlayer = "X";
      }
    }

    // Use this.cells to find a winner or a tie
    bool HasWon(string player) {...}
    bool TieGame( ) {...}
  }
}
```

Our simple tic-tac-toe logic uses strings to represent the players and uses the buttons themselves to keep track of the game state. As each button is clicked, we set the content to the string indicating the current player and switch players. When the game is over, the content for each button is cleared. The middle of a game looks like Figure 5-1.

Figure 5-1. A simple tic-tac-toe game

Notice in Figure 5-1 how the grid background comes through from the margin. These spacers almost make the grid look like a drawn tic-tac-toe board (although we'll do better later). However, if we're really looking to simulate a hand-drawn game, we've got to do something about the size of the font used on the buttons; it doesn't match the thickness of the lines.

One way to fix this problem is by setting the size and weight for each of the Button objects, as in Example 5-3.

Example 5-3. Setting control properties individually

```
<Button FontSize="32" FontWeight="Bold" ... x:Name="cell00" />
<Button FontSize="32" FontWeight="Bold"... x:Name="cell01" />
<Button FontSize="32" FontWeight="Bold"... x:Name="cell02" />
<Button FontSize="32" FontWeight="Bold"... x:Name="cell10" />
<Button FontSize="32" FontWeight="Bold"... x:Name="cell11" />
<Button FontSize="32" FontWeight="Bold"... x:Name="cell12" />
<Button FontSize="32" FontWeight="Bold"... x:Name="cell20" />
<Button FontSize="32" FontWeight="Bold"... x:Name="cell21" />
<Button FontSize="32" FontWeight="Bold"... x:Name="cell22" />
```

While this will make the X's and O's look better according to my visual sensibilities today, if I want to change it later, I've now committed myself to changing both properties in nine separate places, which is a duplication of effort that offends my coding sensibilities. I'd much prefer to refactor my decisions about the look of my tic-tac-toe cells into a common place for future maintenance. That's where styles come in handy.

Inline Styles

Each "style-able" element in WPF has a `Style` property, which can be set inline using standard XAML property-element syntax (discussed in Chapter 1), as in Example 5-4.

Example 5-4. Setting an inline style

```
<Button ... x:Name="cell00" />
  <Button.Style>
    <Style>
      <Setter Property="Button.FontSize" Value="32" />
      <Setter Property="Button.FontWeight" Value="Bold" />
    </Style>
  </Button.Style>
</Button>
```

Because we want to bundle two property values into our style, we have a `Style` element with two `Setter` sub-elements, one for each property we want to set—i.e., `FontSize` and `FontWeight`—both with the `Button` prefix to indicate the class that contains the property. Properties suitable for styling are dependency properties, which are described in Chapter 9.

Due to the extra style syntax and because inline styles can't be shared across elements, inline styles actually involve more typing than just setting the properties. For this reason, inline styles aren't used nearly as often as named styles.

Named Styles

By hoisting the same inline style into a resource (as introduced in Chapter 1), we can award it a name and use it by name in our button instances, as shown in Example 5-5.

Example 5-5. Setting a named style

```
<!-- Window1.xaml -->
<Window ...>
  <Window.Resources>
    <Style x:Key="CellTextStyle">
      <Setter Property="Control.FontSize" Value="32" />
      <Setter Property="Control.FontWeight" Value="Bold" />
    </Style>
  </Window.Resources>
  ...
  <Button Style="{StaticResource CellTextStyle}" ... x:Name="cell00" />
  ...
</Window>
```

In Example 5-5, we've used the `Control` prefix on our properties instead of the `Button` prefix to allow the style to be used more broadly, as we'll soon see.

The TargetType Attribute.

As a convenience, if all of the properties can be set on a shared class, like Control in our example, we can promote the class prefix into the TargetType attribute and remove it from the name of the property, as in Example 5-6.

Example 5-6. A target-typed style

```
<Style x:Key="CellTextStyle" TargetType="{x:Type Control}">
  <Setter Property="FontSize" Value="32" />
  <Setter Property="FontWeight" Value="Bold" />
</Style>
```

When providing a TargetType attribute, you can only set properties available on that type. If you'd like to expand to a greater set of properties down the inheritance tree, you can do so by using a more derived type, as in Example 5-7.

Example 5-7. A more derived target-typed style

```
<Style x:Key="CellTextStyle" TargetType="{x:Type Button}">
  <!-- IsCancel is a Button-specific property -->
  <Setter Property="IsCancel" Value="False" />
  <Setter Property="FontSize" Value="32" />
  <Setter Property="FontWeight" Value="Bold" />
</Style>
```

In this case, the IsCancel property is only available on Button, so to set it, we need to switch the TargetType attribute for the style.

 You may be wondering why I'm setting the FontSize to "32" instead of "32pt" when the latter is more in line with how font sizes are specified and the two representations are definitely not equivalent (the former is pixels, while the latter is points). I'm using pixels because as of this writing, WPF styles using a non-prefixed property allow "32pt" to be specified for FontSize, while prefixed properties do not. For example, the following works (assuming a TargetType is set):

```
<Setter Property="FontSize" Value="32pt" />
```

whereas the following does not (regardless of whether a TargetType is set or not):

```
<Setter Property="Control.FontSize" Value="32pt" />
```

Hopefully this problem will have been fixed by the time you read this (and not replaced with others).

Reusing Styles

In addition to saving you from typing out the name of the class prefix for every property name, the TargetType attribute will also check that all classes that have the style applied are an instance of that type (or derived type). What that means is that if we leave TargetType set to Control, we can apply it to a Button element, but not to a TextBlock element, as the former derives ultimately from Control but the latter does not.

On the other hand, while Control and TextBlock both share the common ancestor FrameworkElement, the FrameworkElement class doesn't define a FontSize dependency property, so a style with a TargetType of FrameworkElement won't let us set the FontSize property because its not there, despite the fact that both Control and TextBlock have a FontSize property.

Even with the TargetType set to Control, we gain a measure of reuse of our style across classes that derive from Control—e.g., Button, Label, Window, etc. However, if we drop the TargetType attribute from the style altogether, we gain a measure of reuse of styles across controls that don't have a common base but share a dependency-property implementation. In my experimentation, I've found that dependency properties that share the same name across classes, such as Control.FontSize and TextBlock.FontSize, also share an implementation. What that means is that even though Control and TextBlock each define their own FontSize property, at runtime they share the implementation of this property, so I can write code like Example 5-8.

Example 5-8. Reusing a style between different element types

```
...
<Style x:Key="CellTextStyle">
  <Setter Property="Control.FontSize" Value="32" />
</Style>
...
<!-- derives from Control -->
<Button Style="{StaticResource CellTextStyle}" ... />

<!-- does *not* derive from Control -->
<TextBlock Style="{StaticResource CellTextStyle}" ... />
...
```

In Example 5-8, I've dropped the TargetType attribute from the style definition, using instead the class prefix on each property the style sets. This style can be applied to a Button element, as you'd expect, but can also be applied to a TextBlock control, with the FontSize set as specified by the style. The reason this works is that both the Button, which gets its FontSize dependency property *definition* from the Control class, and the TextBlock, which provides it's own FontSize dependency property *definition*, share the FontSize dependency property *implementation* with the TextElement class. Figure 5-2 shows the relationship of elements to their dependency-property implementations.

As Figure 5-2 shows, if we wanted to, we could redefine our style in terms of the TextElement class, even though it falls into the inheritance tree of neither Control nor TextBlock, as in Example 5-9.

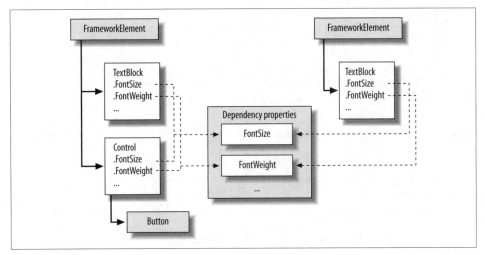

Figure 5-2. Elements and dependency properties

Example 5-9. Depending on the implementation of dependency properties

```
<Style x:Key="CellTextStyle">
  <Setter Property="TextElement.FontSize" Value="32" />
</Style>
...
<Button Style="{StaticResource CellTextStyle}" ... />
<TextBlock Style="{StaticResource CellTextStyle}" ... />
```

Taking this further, if we'd like to define a style that contains properties not shared by every element we apply them to, we can do that, too, as in Example 5-10.

Example 5-10. Styles can have properties that targets don't have

```
<Style x:Key="CellTextStyle">
  <Setter Property="TextElement.FontSize" Value="32" />
  <Setter Property="Button.IsCancel" Value="False" />
</Style>
...
<!-- has an IsCancel property -->
<Button Style="{StaticResource CellTextStyle}" ... />

<!-- does *not* have an IsCancel property -->
<TextBlock Style="{StaticResource CellTextStyle}" ... />
```

In Example 5-10, we've added the Button.IsCancel property to the CellTextStyle and applied it to the Button element, which has this property, and the TextBlock element, which doesn't. This is OK. At runtime, WPF will apply the dependency properties that exist on the elements that have them and silently swallow the ones that aren't present.

WPF's ability to apply styles to objects that don't have all of the properties defined in the style is analogous to applying the Word Normal style, which includes a font size property of its own, to both a range of text and an image. Even though Word knows that images don't have a font size, it applies the portions of the Normal style that do make sense (such as the justification property), ignoring the rest.

Getting back to our sample, we can use the CellTextStyle on a TextBlock in a new row to show whose turn it is, as in Example 5-11.

Example 5-11. Applying a style to Button and TextBlock elements

```
<Window.Resources>
  <Style x:Key="CellTextStyle">
    <Setter Property="TextElement.FontSize" Value="32" />
    <Setter Property="TextElement.FontWeight" Value="Bold" />
  </Style>
</Window.Resources>
<Grid Background="Black">
  <Grid.RowDefinitions>
    <RowDefinition />
    <RowDefinition />
    <RowDefinition />
    <RowDefinition Height="Auto" />
  </Grid.RowDefinitions>
  <Grid.ColumnDefinitions>
    <ColumnDefinition />
    <ColumnDefinition />
    <ColumnDefinition />
  </Grid.ColumnDefinitions>
  <Button Style="{StaticResource CellTextStyle}" ... />
  ...
  <TextBlock
    Style="{StaticResource CellTextStyle}"
    Foreground="White"
    Grid.Row="3"
    Grid.ColumnSpan="3"
    x:Name="statusTextBlock" />
</Grid>
</Window>
```

This reuse of the style across controls of different types gives me a consistent look in my application, as shown in Figure 5-3.

One thing you'll notice is that the status text in Figure 5-3 is white, while the text in the buttons is black. Since black is the default text color, if we want the status text to show up against a black background, we have to change the color to something else, hence the need to set the Foreground property to white on the TextBlock. Setting per-instance properties works just fine in combination with the style, and you can combine the two techniques of setting property values as you see fit.

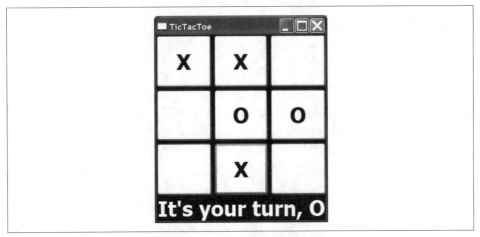

Figure 5-3. A tic-tac-toe game with style

Overriding Style Properties

Further, if we want to *override* a style property on a specific instance, we can do so by setting the property on the instance, as in Example 5-12.

Example 5-12. Overriding the FontWeight property from the style

```
<Style x:Key="CellTextStyle">
  <Setter Property="TextElement.FontSize" Value="32" />
  <Setter Property="TextElement.FontWeight" Value="Bold" />
</Style>
...
<TextBlock
  Style="{StaticResource CellTextStyle}"
  FontWeight="Thin" ... />
```

In Example 5-12, the TextBlock instance property setting of FontWeight take precedence over the style property settings of FontWeight.

Inheriting Style Properties

To complete the object-oriented triumvirate of reuse, override, and inheritance, you can *inherit* a style from a base style, adding new properties or overriding existing ones, as in Example 5-13.

Example 5-13. Style inheritance

```
<Style x:Key="CellTextStyle">
  <Setter Property="TextElement.FontSize" Value="32" />
  <Setter Property="TextElement.FontWeight" Value="Bold" />
</Style>
<Style x:Key="StatusTextStyle" BasedOn="{StaticResource CellTextStyle}">
```

Example 5-13. Style inheritance (continued)

```
  <Setter Property="TextElement.FontWeight" Value="Thin" />
  <Setter Property="TextElement.Foreground" Value="White" />
  <Setter Property="TextBlock.HorizontalAlignment" Value="Center" />
</Style>
```

The BasedOn style attribute is used to designate the base style. In Example 5-13, the StatusTextStyle style inherits all of the CellTextStyle property setters, overrides the FontWeight, and adds setters for Foreground and HorizontalAlignment. Notice that the HorizontalAlignment property uses a TextBlock prefix; this is because TextElement doesn't have a HorizontalAlignment property.

Our current use of styles causes our tic-tac-toe game to look like Figure 5-4.

Figure 5-4. A tic-tac-toe game with more style

Our application so far is pretty good, especially with the thin font weight on the status text, but we can do better.

Setting Styles Programmatically

Once a style has a name, it's easily available from our code. For example, we might decide that we'd like each player to have their own style. In this case, using named styles in XAML at compile time won't do the trick, since we want to set the style based on the content, which isn't known until runtime. However, there's nothing that requires us to set the Style property of a control statically; we can set it programmatically as well, as we do in Example 5-14.

Example 5-14. Setting styles programmatically

```
public partial class Window1 : Window {
  void cell_Click(object sender, RoutedEventArgs e) {
    Button button = (Button)sender;
```

Example 5-14. Setting styles programmatically (continued)

```
  ...
  // Set button content
  button.Content = this.CurrentPlayer;
  ...
  if( this.CurrentPlayer == "X" ) {
    button.Style = (Style)FindResource("XStyle");
    this.CurrentPlayer == "O";
  }
  else {
    button.Style = (Style)FindResource("OStyle");
    this.CurrentPlayer == "X";
  }
  ...
}
...
}
```

In Example 5-14, whenever the player clicks, in addition to setting the button's content, we pull a named style out of the window's resources and use that to set the button's style. This assumes a pair of named styles defined in the window's scope, as in Example 5-15.

Example 5-15. Styles pulled out via FindResource

```
<Window.Resources>
  <Style x:Key="CellTextStyle">
    <Setter Property="TextElement.FontSize" Value="32" />
    <Setter Property="TextElement.FontWeight" Value="Bold" />
  </Style>
  <Style x:Key="XStyle" BasedOn="{StaticResource CellTextStyle}">
    <Setter Property="TextElement.Foreground" Value="Red" />
  </Style>
  <Style x:Key="OStyle" BasedOn="{StaticResource CellTextStyle}">
    <Setter Property="TextElement.Foreground" Value="Green" />
  </Style>
</Window.Resources>
```

With these styles in place and the code to set the button style along with content, we get Figure 5-5.

Notice that the Xs and Os are colored according to the named player styles. In this particular case (and in many other cases, too), data triggers (discussed in "Data Triggers," later in this chapter) should be preferred to setting styles programmatically, but you never know when you're going to have to jam.

 As with all XAML constructs, you are free to create styles themselves programmatically. Appendix A is a good introduction on how to think about going back and forth between XAML and code.

Figure 5-5. Setting styles programmatically based on an object's content (Color Plate 9)

Element-Typed Styles

Named styles are useful when you've got a set of properties to be applied to specific elements. However, if you'd like to apply a style uniformly to all instances of a certain type of element, set the TargetType without a Key, as in Example 5-16.

Example 5-16. Element-typed styles

```
...
<!-- no Key -->
<Style TargetType="{x:Type Button}">
  <Setter Property="FontSize" Value="32" />
  <Setter Property="FontWeight" Value="Bold" />
</Style>
<!-- no Key -->
<Style TargetType="{x:Type TextBlock}">
  <Setter Property="FontSize" Value="32" />
  <Setter Property="FontWeight" Value="Thin" />
  <Setter Property="Foreground" Value="White" />
  <Setter Property="HorizontalAlignment" Value="Center" />
</Style>
...
<Button Grid.Row="0" Grid.Column="0" x:ID="cell00" />
...
<TextBlock Grid.Row="5" Grid.ColumnSpan="5" x:ID="statusTextBlock" />
...
```

In Example 5-16, we've got two styles, one with a TargetType of Button and no Key and another with a TargetType of TextBlock and no Key. Both work in the same way; when an instance of Button or TextBlock is created without an explicit Style attribute setting, it uses the style that matches the target type of the style to the type of the control. Our element-typed styles return our game to looking like Figure 5-4 again.

Element-typed styles are handy whenever you'd like all instances of a certain element to share a look, depending on the scope. For example, we've scoped the styles in our sample thus far at the top-level Window in Example 5-17.

Example 5-17. Styles scoped to the Window

```
<!-- Window1.xaml -->
<Window ...>
  <!-- every Button or TextBlock in the Window is affected -->
  <Window.Resources>
    <Style TargetType="{x:Type Button}">...</Style>
    <Style TargetType="{x:Type TextBlock}">...</Style>
  </Window.Resources>
  ...
</Window>
```

However, you may want to reduce the scope of an element-typed style. In our sample, it would work just as well to scope the styles inside the grid so that only buttons and text blocks in the grid are affected, as in Example 5-18.

Example 5-18. Styles scoped below the Window

```
<!-- Window1.xaml -->
<Window ...>
  <Grid ...>
    <!-- only Buttons or TextBlocks in the Grid are affected -->
    <Grid.Resources>
      <Style TargetType="{x:Type Button}">...</Style>
      <Style TargetType="{x:Type TextBlock}">...</Style>
    </Grid.Resources>
    ...
  </Grid>
  <!-- Buttons and TextBlocks outside the Grid are unaffected -->
  ...
</Window>
```

Or, if you want to make your styles have greater reach in your project, you can put them into the application scope, as in Example 5-19.

Example 5-19. Styles scoped to the application

```
<!-- MyApp.xaml -->
<Application ...>
  <!-- every Button or TextBlock in the Application is affected -->
  <Application.Resources>
    <Style TargetType="{x:Type Button}">...</Style>
    <Style TargetType="{x:Type TextBlock}">...</Style>
  </Application.Resources>
</Application>
```

In general it's useful to understand the scoping rules of element-typed styles so you can judge their effect on the various pieces of your WPF object model. Chapter 6 discusses resource scoping of all kinds, including styles, in more detail.

Named versus element-typed styles

When choosing between styles set by style name or by element type, one of our reviewers said that in his experience, once you get beyond 10 styles based on element type, it was too hard to keep track of where a particular control was getting its style from. This is one reason that I'm a big fan of named styles.

To me, a style is a semantic tag that will be applied to content in one place and awarded a visual representation in another. As simple as our tic-tac-toe sample is, we've already got two styles, one for the status text and one for the move cell; before we're done, we're going to have more. The major differentiating factor is going to be the kind of data we'll be showing in these elements, not the type of the element holding the data. In fact, we'll have several styles assigned to TextBox controls, which negates the use of type-based styles anyway, even for this simple application.

Data Templates and Styles

Let's imagine that we wanted to implement a version of tic-tac-toe that's more fun to play (that's an important feature in most games). For example, one variant of tic-tac-toe allows players to have only three of their pieces on at any one time, dropping the first move off when the fourth move is played, dropping the second move when the fifth is played, and so on. To implement this variant, we need to keep track of the sequence of moves, which we can do with a PlayerMove class, as in Example 5-20.

Example 5-20. A custom type suitable for tracking tic-tac-toe moves

```
namespace TicTacToe {
  public class PlayerMove {
    private string playerName;
    public string PlayerName {
      get { return playerName; }
      set { playerName = value; }
    }

    private int moveNumber;
    public int MoveNumber {
      get { return moveNumber; }
      set { moveNumber = value; }
    }

    public PlayerMove(string playerName, int moveNumber) {
      this.playerName = playerName;
      this.moveNumber = moveNumber;
    }
  }
}
```

Now, instead of using a simple string for each of the button object's content, we'll use an instance of PlayerMove in Example 5-21. Figure 5-6 shows the brilliance of such a change.

Example 5-21. Adding the PlayerMove as Button content

```
namespace TicTacToe {
  public partial class Window1 : Window {
    ...
    int moveNumber;

    void NewGame() {
      ...
      this.moveNumber = 0;
    }

    void cell_Click(object sender, RoutedEventArgs e) {
      ...
      // Set button content
      //button.Content = this.CurrentPlayer;
      button.Content =
        new PlayerMove(this.CurrentPlayer, ++this.moveNumber);
      ...
    }
    ...
  }
}
```

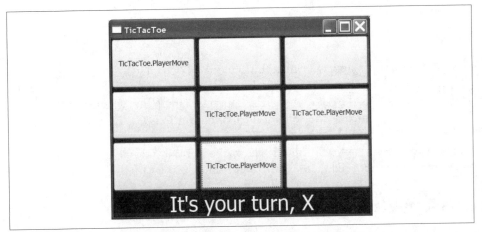

Figure 5-6. PlayerMove objects displayed without any special instructions

As you'll recall from Chapter 4, what's happening in Figure 5-6 is that the button doesn't have enough information to render a PlayerMove object, but we can fix that with a data template.

Data Templates

Recall from Chapter 4 that WPF allows you to define a data template, which is a tree of elements to expand in a particular context. Data templates are used to provide an application with the ability to render non-visual objects, as shown in Example 5-22.

Example 5-22. Setting a PlayerMove data template without styles

```
<?Mapping XmlNamespace="l" ClrNamespace="TicTacToe" ?>
<Window ... xmlns:local="local">
  <Window.Resources>
    <DataTemplate DataType="{x:Type local:PlayerMove}">
      <Grid>
        <TextBlock
          TextContent="{Binding Path=PlayerName}"
          FontSize ="32"
          FontWeight="Bold"
          VerticalAlignment="Center"
          HorizontalAlignment="Center" />
        <TextBlock
          TextContent="{Binding Path=MoveNumber}"
          FontSize="16"
          FontStyle="Italic"
          VerticalAlignment="Bottom"
          HorizontalAlignment="Right" />
      </Grid>
    </DataTemplate>
    ...
  </Window.Resources>
  ...
</Window>
```

Using the XAML mapping syntax introduced in Chapter 1, we've mapped the PlayerMover type into the XAML with the mapping directive and the xmlns attribute, which we've used as the data type of the data template. Now, whenever WPF sees a PlayerMove object, such as the content of all of our buttons, the data template will be expanded. In our case, the template consists of a grid to arrange two text blocks, one showing the player name in the middle of the button and one showing the move number in the bottom right, along with some other settings to make things pretty.

Data Templates with Style

However, these property settings are buried inside a data template several layers deep. Just as it's a good idea to take "magic numbers" out of your code, pulling them out and giving them names for easy maintenance, it's a good idea to move groups of settings into styles,[*] as in Example 5-23.

---

[*] Moving groups of settings into styles also allows for easier skinning and theming, as described in Chapter 6.

Example 5-23. Setting a PlayerMove data template with styles

```
<Window.Resources>
  <Style x:Key="CellTextStyle" TargetType="{x:Type TextBlock}">
    <Setter Property="FontSize" Value="32" />
    <Setter Property="FontWeight" Value="Bold" />
    <Setter Property="VerticalAlignment" Value="Center" />
    <Setter Property="HorizontalAlignment" Value="Center" />
  </Style>
  <Style x:Key="MoveNumberStyle" TargetType="{x:Type TextBlock}">
    <Setter Property="FontSize" Value="16" />
    <Setter Property="FontStyle" Value="Italic" />
    <Setter Property="VerticalAlignment" Value="Bottom" />
    <Setter Property="HorizontalAlignment" Value="Right" />
  </Style>
  <DataTemplate DataType="{x:Type l:PlayerMove}">
    <Grid>
      <TextBlock
        TextContent="{Binding Path=PlayerName}"
        Style="{StaticResource CellTextStyle}" />
      <TextBlock
        TextContent="{Binding Path=MoveNumber}"
        Style="{StaticResource MoveNumberStyle}" />
    </Grid>
  </DataTemplate>
</Window.Resources>
```

It's common to use styles, which set groups of properties, with data templates, which create groups of elements that have groups of properties. Figure 5-7 shows the result.

Figure 5-7. Showing objects of a custom type using data templates and styles

Still, as nice as Figure 5-7 is, the interaction is kind of boring given the capabilities of WPF. Let's see what we can do with style properties as the application is used.

Triggers

So far, we've seen styles as a collection of Setter elements. When a style is applied, the settings described in the Setter elements are applied unconditionally (unless overridden by per-instance settings). On the other hand, *triggers* are a way to wrap one or more Setter elements in a condition so that, if the condition is true, the corresponding Setter elements are executed, and when the condition becomes false, the property value reverts to its pre-trigger value.

WPF comes with three kinds of things that you can check in a trigger condition: a dependency property, a .NET property, and an event. The first two directly change values based on a condition, as I described, while the last, an event trigger, is activated when an event happens and then starts (or stops) an animation that causes properties to change.

Property Triggers

The simplest form of a trigger is a property trigger, which watches for a dependency property to have a certain value. For example, if we wanted to light up a button in yellow as the user moves the mouse over it, we can do so by watching for the IsMouseOver property to have a value of True, as in Example 5-24.

Example 5-24. A simple property trigger

```
<Style TargetType="{x:Type Button}">
  ...
  <Style.Triggers>
    <Trigger Property="IsMouseOver" Value="True" >
      <Setter Property="Background" Value="Yellow" />
    </Trigger>
  </Style.Triggers>
</Style>
```

Triggers are grouped together under the Style.Triggers element. In this case, we've added a Trigger element to the button style. When the IsMouseOver property of our button is true, the Background value of the button will be set to yellow, as shown in Figure 5-8.

You'll notice in Figure 5-8 that only the button where the mouse is currently hovering has its background set to yellow, even though other buttons have clearly been under the mouse. There's no need to worry about setting a property back when the trigger is no longer true—e.g., watching for IsMouseOver to be False. The WPF dependency-property system watches for the property trigger to become inactive and reverts to the previous value.

Figure 5-8. A property trigger in action

Property triggers can be set to watch any of the dependency properties on the control to which your style is targeted and to set any of the dependency properties on the control while the condition is true. In fact, you can use a single trigger to set multiple properties if you like, as in Example 5-25.

Example 5-25. Setting multiple properties with a single trigger

```
<Style TargetType="{x:Type Button}">
  ...
  <Style.Triggers>
    <Trigger Property="IsMouseOver" Value="True" >
      <Setter Property="Background" Value="Yellow" />
      <Setter Property="FontStyle" Value="Italic" />
    </Trigger>
  </Style.Triggers>
</Style>
```

In Example 5-25, we're setting the background to yellow and the font style to italic when the mouse is over a button.

One property that you're not allowed to set in a trigger is the Style property itself. If you try, you'll get the following error:

> A Style object is not allowed to affect the Style property of the object to which it applies.

This makes sense. Since it's the Style that's setting the property, and that participates in "unsetting" it when the trigger is no longer true, what sense would it make to change the very Style that's providing this orchestration? This would be somewhat like switching out your skis after you've launched yourself off of a jump but before you've landed.

Multiple Triggers

While you can set as many properties as you like in a property trigger, there can be more than one trigger in a style. When grouped together under the Style.Triggers element, multiple triggers act independently of each other.

For example, we can update our code so that if the mouse is hovering over one of our buttons, it'll be colored yellow and if the button has focus (the tab and arrow keys move focus around), it'll be colored green, as in Example 5-26. Figure 5-9 shows the result of one cell having focus and another with the mouse hovering.

Example 5-26. Multiple property triggers

```
<Style TargetType="{x:Type Button}">
  ...
  <Style.Triggers>
    <Trigger Property="IsMouseOver" Value="True" >
      <Setter Property="Background" Value="Yellow" />
    </Trigger>
    <Trigger Property="IsFocused" Value="True" >
      <Setter Property="Background" Value="LightGreen" />
    </Trigger>
  </Style.Triggers>
</Style>
```

Figure 5-9. Multiple property triggers in action

If multiple triggers set the same property, the last one wins. For example, in Figure 5-9, if a button has focus and the mouse is over it, the background will be light green because the trigger for the IsFocused trigger is last in the list of triggers.

Multi-Condition Property Trigger

If you'd like to check more than one property before a trigger condition is activated—e.g., the mouse is hovering over a button *and* the button content is empty—you can combine multiple conditions with a multiple-condition property trigger, as in Example 5-27.

Example 5-27. A multi-property trigger

```
<Style TargetType="{x:Type Button}">
  ...
  <Style.Triggers>
    <MultiTrigger>
      <MultiTrigger.Conditions>
        <Condition Property="IsMouseOver" Value="True" />
        <Condition Property="Content" Value="{x:Null}" />
      </MultiTrigger.Conditions>
      <Setter Property="Background" Value="Yellow" />
    </MultiTrigger>
  </Style.Triggers>
</Style>
```

Multi-condition property triggers check all of the properties' values to be set as specified, not just one of them. Here, we're watching for both a mouse hover and for the content to be null,* reflecting the game logic that only clicking on an empty cell will result in a move.

Figure 5-10 shows the yellow highlight on an empty cell when the mouse hovers, and Figure 5-11 shows the yellow highlight absent when the mouse hovers over a full cell.

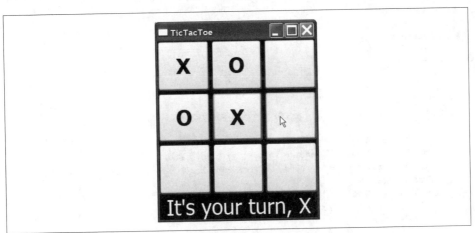

Figure 5-10. Multi-condition property trigger with hovering and null content

* The null value is set via a XAML markup extension, which you can read more about in Appendix A.

Figure 5-11. Multi-condition property trigger not triggering as content is not null

Property triggers are great for noticing when the user is interacting with a control displaying your program's state. However, we'd also like to be able to notice when the program's state itself changes, such as when a particular player makes a move, and update our style settings accordingly. For that, we have data triggers.

Data Triggers

Unlike property triggers, which check only WPF dependency properties, data triggers can check any old .NET object property. While property triggers are generally used to check WPF visual-element properties, data triggers are normally used to check the properties of non-visual objects used as content, such as our PlayerMove objects in Example 5-28.

Example 5-28. Two data triggers

```
<Window.Resources>
  <Style TargetType="{x:Type Button}">
    ...
  </Style>
  <Style x:Key="CellTextStyle" TargetType="{x:Type TextBlock}">
    ...
    <Style.Triggers>
      <DataTrigger Binding="{Binding Path=PlayerName}" Value="X">
        <Setter Property="Foreground" Value="Red" />
      </DataTrigger>
      <DataTrigger Binding="{Binding Path=PlayerName}" Value="O">
        <Setter Property="Foreground" Value="Green" />
      </DataTrigger>
    </Style.Triggers>
  </Style>
  <Style x:Key="MoveNumberStyle" TargetType="{x:Type TextBlock}">
    ...
```

Example 5-28. Two data triggers (continued)

```
    </Style>
    ...
    <DataTemplate DataType="{x:Type l:PlayerMove}">
      <Grid>
        <TextBlock
          TextContent="{Binding Path=PlayerName}"
          Style="{StaticResource CellTextStyle}" />
        <TextBlock
          TextContent="{Binding Path=MoveNumber}"
          Style="{StaticResource MoveNumberStyle}" />
      </Grid>
    </DataTemplate>
</Window.Resources>
```

DataTrigger elements go under the Style.Triggers element just like property triggers and, just like property triggers, there can be more than one of them active at any one time. While a property trigger operates on the properties of the visual elements displaying the content, a data trigger operates on the content itself. In our case, the content of each of the cells is a PlayerMove object. In both of our data triggers, we're binding to the PlayerName property. If the value is X, we're setting the foreground to red and if it's 0, we're setting it to green.

 Take care where you put the data trigger. In our example, we've got the Button-type style and the named CellTextStyle style as potential choices. I've written this chapter twice now and both times I've initially put the data trigger on the button style instead of on the content in the data template. Data triggers are based on content, so make sure you put them into your content styles, not your control styles.

We haven't had per-player colors since we moved to data templates after setting styles programmatically in Figure 5-5, but data triggers bring us that feature right back, along with all of the other features we've been building up, as shown in Figure 5-12.

Unlike property triggers, which rely on the change notification of dependency properties, data triggers rely on an implementation of the standard property-change notification patterns that are built into .NET and are discussed in Chapter 4—e.g., INotifyPropertyChanged. Since each PlayerMove object is constant, we don't need to implement this pattern, but if you're using data triggers, chances are that you will need to implement it on your custom content classes.

One other especially handy feature of data triggers is that there's no need for an explicit check for null content. If the content is null, the trigger condition is automatically false, which is why the application isn't crashing trying to dereference a null PlayerMove to get to the PlayerName property.

Figure 5-12. Data triggers in action

Multi-Condition Data Triggers

Just as property triggers can be combined into "and" conditions using the `MultiTrigger` element, data triggers can be combined using the `MultiDataTrigger` element. For example, if we wanted to watch for the 10th move of the game, make sure it's player "O," and do something special, we can do so as shown in Example 5-29.

Example 5-29. A multi-data trigger

```
<?Mapping XmlNamespace="sys" ClrNamespace="System" Assembly="mscorlib" ?>
...
<Window ... xmlns:sys="sys">
  <Style x:Key="MoveNumberStyle" TargetType="{x:Type TextBlock}">
    ...
    <Style.Triggers>
      <MultiDataTrigger>
        <MultiDataTrigger.Conditions>
          <Condition Binding="{Binding Path=PlayerName}" Value="O" />
          <Condition Binding="{Binding Path=MoveNumber}">
            <Condition.Value>
              <sys:Int32>10</sys:Int32>
            </Condition.Value>
          </Condition>
        </MultiDataTrigger.Conditions>
        <Setter Property="Background" Value="Yellow" />
      </MultiDataTrigger>
    </Style.Triggers>
  </Style>
  ...
</Window>
```

The only thing about Example 5-29 that may seem a little strange is the use of the mapping syntax to bring in the System namespace from the mscorlib .NET assembly. We do this so that we can pass 10 as an Int32 instead of as a string; otherwise, the multi-condition data trigger won't match our MoveNumber property correctly. The multi-condition data trigger in Example 5-29 sets the background of the move number to yellow to connote a cause for celebration for this special move that regular tic-tac-toe doesn't have, but you can use multi-condition data triggers for celebrations of your own kinds.

Event Triggers

While property triggers check for values on dependency properties and data triggers check for values on CLR properties, event triggers watch for events. When an event happens, such as a Click event, an event trigger responds by raising an animation-related action. While animation is challenging enough to deserve its own chapter (Chapter 8), Example 5-30 illustrates a simple animation that will transition a cell from solid yellow to white over five seconds when an empty cell is clicked.

Example 5-30. An event trigger

```
<Style TargetType="{x:Type Button}">
  ...
  <Setter Property="Background" Value="White" />
  <Style.Storyboards>
    <ParallelTimeline Name="CellClickedTimeline" BeginTime="{x:Null}">
      <SetterTimeline Path="(Button.Background).(SolidColorBrush.Color)">
        <ColorAnimation From="Yellow" To="White" Duration="0:0:5" />
      </SetterTimeline>
    </ParallelTimeline>
  </Style.Storyboards>
  <Style.Triggers>
    <EventTrigger RoutedEvent="Click">
      <EventTrigger.Actions>
        <BeginAction TargetName="CellClickedTimeline" />
      </EventTrigger.Actions>
    </EventTrigger>
  </Style.Triggers>
</Style>
```

Adding an animation to a style requires two things. The first is a storyboard with a named timeline that describes what you want to happen. In our case, we're animating the button's background brush color from yellow to white over five seconds.

 For any property being animated with a nested path, there needs to be an explicit property setting that creates the top level of the nesting. In Example 5-30, this means that we need a Setter element for the Background property. If the top level of the nesting isn't created, there won't be anything to animate at runtime.

The second thing you need is an event trigger to start the timeline. In our case, when the user clicks on a button with the CellButtonStyle style applied (all of them, in our case), we begin the action described by the named timeline in the storyboard.

 As of this writing, if you have an event trigger and a multi-condition property trigger animating the same property—e.g., the Background of a Button, make sure you put the multi-data trigger in the XAML file before the event trigger; otherwise, you'll get a nonsensical error at runtime.

The results of the animation, showing various shades of yellow, through past clicks can be seen in Figure 5-13.

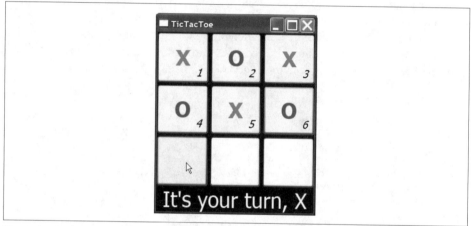

Figure 5-13. The event trigger and our fading yellow animation (Color Plate 10)

Property and data triggers let you set properties when properties change. Event triggers let you trigger events when events happen. While both are pretty different—e.g., you can't set a property with an event trigger or raise an event with a property or data trigger—both let you add a degree of interactivity to your applications in a wonderfully declarative way with little or no code.

For the full scoop on event triggers, you'll want to read Chapter 8.

Control Templates

If we take a closer look at our current tic-tac-toe game, we'll see that the Button objects aren't quite doing the job for us. What tic-tac-toe board has rounded inset corners (Figure 5-14)?

What we really want here is to be able to keep the behavior of the button—i.e., holding content and firing click events—but we want to take over the look of the

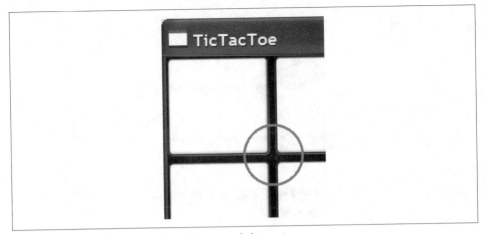

Figure 5-14. Tic-tac-toe boards don't have rounded insets!

button. WPF allows this kind of thing because the intrinsic controls are built to be *lookless*—i.e., they provide behavior, but the look can be swapped out completely by the client of the control.

Remember how we used data templates to provide the look of a non-visual object? We can do the same to a control using a *control template*, which is a set of storyboards, triggers, and, most importantly, elements that provide the look of a control.

To fix our buttons' looks, we'll build ourselves a control-template resource. Let's start things off in Example 5-31 with a simple rectangle and worry about showing the actual button content later.

Example 5-31. A minimal control template

```
<Window.Resources>
  <ControlTemplate x:Key="ButtonTemplate">
    <Rectangle />
  </ControlTemplate>
  ...
  <!-- let's just try one button for now... -->
  <Button Template="{StaticResource ButtonTemplate}" ... />
  ...
</Window.Resources>
```

Figure 5-15 shows the results of setting a single button's Template property.

Notice that no vestiges of what the button used to look like remain in Figure 5-15. Unfortunately, no vestige of our rectangles can be seen, either. The problem is that, without a fill explicitly set, the rectangle's fill defaults to transparent, showing the grid's black background. Let's set it to our other favorite Halloween color instead:

```
<ControlTemplate x:Key="ButtonTemplate">
  <Rectangle Fill="Orange" />
</ControlTemplate>
```

Figure 5-15. Replacing the control template with something less visual than we'd like…

Now we're getting somewhere, as Figure 5-16 shows.

Figure 5-16. Replacing the button's control template with an orange rectangle (Color Plate 11)

Notice how square the corners are? Also, if you click, you won't get the depression that normally happens with a button (and I don't mean "a sad feeling").

Control Templates and Styles

Now that we're making some progress on the control template, let's replicate it to the other buttons. We can do so by setting each button's Template property by hand or, as is most common, we can bundle the control template with the button's style, as in Example 5-32.

Example 5-32. Putting a control template into a style

```
<Window.Resources>
  <Style TargetType="{x:Type Button}">
    ...
    <Setter Property="Template">
      <Setter.Value>
        <ControlTemplate>
          <Rectangle Fill="Orange" />
        </ControlTemplate>
      </Setter.Value>
    </Setter>
  </Style>
  ...
</Window.Resources>
...
<!-- No need to set the Template property for each button -->
<Button ... x:Name="cell00" />
...
```

As Example 5-32 shows, the Template property is the same as any other and can be set with a style. Figure 5-17 shows the results.

Figure 5-17. Spreading the orange (Color Plate 12)

Still, the orange is kind of jarring, especially since the settings on the style call for a white background. We can solve this problem with template bindings.

Template Binding

To get back to our white buttons, we could hardcode the rectangle's fill to be white, but what happens when a style wants to change it (such as in the animation we've now broken)? Instead of hardcoding the fill of the rectangle, we can reach out of the template into the properties of the control using template binding, as in Example 5-33.

Example 5-33. Template binding to the Background property

```
<Style TargetType="{x:Type Button}">
  <Setter Property="Background" Value="White" />
  ...
  <Setter Property="Template">
    <Setter.Value>
      <ControlTemplate x:Key="ButtonTemplate">
        <Rectangle Fill="{TemplateBinding Property=Background}" />
      </ControlTemplate>
    </Setter.Value>
  </Setter>
  ...
</Style>
```

A *template binding* is like a data binding, except that the properties to bind come from the control whose template you're replacing (called the *templated parent*). In our case, things like Background, HorizontalContentAlignment, and so on, are fair game for template binding from the parent. And, like data binding, template bindings are smart enough to keep the properties of the items inside the template up to date with changing properties on the outside, as set by styles, animations, etc. For example, Figure 5-18 shows the effect of aliasing the rectangle's Fill property to the button's Background property with our click animation and mouse-over behavior still in place.

Figure 5-18. Setting the rectangle's fill using property aliasing (Color Plate 13)

We're not quite through yet, however. If we're going to change the paint swatch that Figure 5-18 has become into a playable game, we have to show the moves. To do so, we'll need a content presenter.

Content Presenters

If you've ever driven by a billboard or a bench at a bus stop that says "Your advertisement here!" then that's all you need to know to understand content presenters. A *content presenter* is the WPF equivalent of "your content here" that allows content held by a `ContentContainer` control to be plugged in at runtime.

In our case, the content is the visualization of our `PlayerMove` object. Instead of reproducing all of that work inside of the button's new control template, we'd just like to drop it in at the right spot. The job of the content presenter is to take the content provided by the templated parent and do all of the things necessary to get it to show up properly, including styles, triggers, etc. The content presenter itself can be dropped into your template wherever you'd like to see it (including multiple times, if it tickles your fancy—e.g., to produce a drop shadow). In our case, we'll compose a content presenter in Example 5-34 with the rectangle inside a grid using techniques from Chapter 2.

Example 5-34. A content presenter

```
<Style TargetType="{x:Type Button}">
  <Setter Property="Background" Value="White" />
  ...
  <Setter Property="Template">
    <Setter.Value>
      <ControlTemplate>
        <Grid>
          <Rectangle Fill="{TemplateBinding Property=Background}" />
          <ContentPresenter
            Content="{TemplateBinding Property=ContentControl.Content}" />
        </Grid>
      </ControlTemplate>
    </Setter.Value>
  </Setter>
  ...
</Style>
```

In Example 5-34, the content presenter's `Content` property is bound to the `ContentControl.Content` property so that content comes through. As with styles, we can avoid prefixing template binding property names with classes by setting the `TargetType` attribute on the `ContentTemplate` element:

```
<ControlTemplate TargetType="{x:Type Button}">
  <Grid>
    <Rectangle Fill="{TemplateBinding Property=Background}" />
    <ContentPresenter
      Content="{TemplateBinding Property=Content}" />
  </Grid>
</ControlTemplate>
```

Further, with the `TargetType` property in place, you can drop the explicit template binding on the `Content` property altogether, as it's now set automatically:

```
<ControlTemplate TargetType="{x:Type Button}">
  <Grid>
    <Rectangle Fill="{TemplateBinding Property=Background}" />
    <!-- with TargetType set, the template binding for the -->
```

```
    <!-- Content property is no longer required -->
    <ContentPresenter />
  </Grid>
</ControlTemplate>
```

The content presenter is all we need to get our game back to being functional, as shown in Figure 5-19.

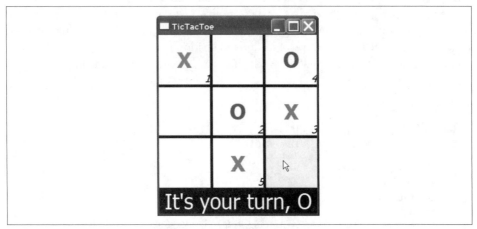

Figure 5-19. Adding a content presenter to our control template (Color Plate 14)

The Real Work

The last little bit of work is getting the padding right. Since the content presenter doesn't have its own Padding property, we can't bind the Padding property directly (it doesn't have a Background property, either, which is why we used Rectangle and its Fill property). For properties that don't have a match on the content presenter, you have to find mappings or compose the elements that provide the functionality that you're looking for. For example, Padding is an amount of space inside of a control. Margin, on the other hand, is the amount of space around the outside of a control. Since they're both of the same type, System.Windows.Thickness, if we could map the Padding from the inside of our button to the outside of the content control, our game would look very nice:

```
<Style TargetType="{x:Type Button}">
  <Setter Property="Background" Value="White" />
  <Setter Property="Padding" Value="10,5" />
  ...
  <Setter Property="Template">
    <Setter.Value>
      <ControlTemplate TargetType="{x:Type Button}">
        <Grid>
          <Rectangle Fill="{TemplateBinding Property=Background}" />
          <ContentPresenter
            Content="{TemplateBinding Property=Content}"
```

```
            Margin="{TemplateBinding Property=Padding}" />
          </Grid>
        </ControlTemplate>
      </Setter.Value>
    </Setter>
    ...
  </Style>
```

Figure 5-20 shows our completed tic-tac-toe variation.

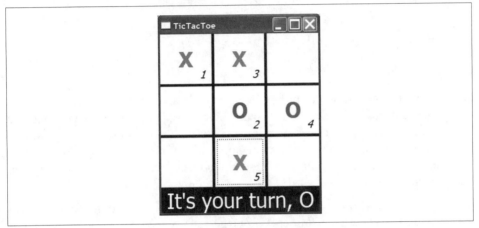

Figure 5-20. Binding the Padding property to the Margin property (Color Plate 15)

Like the mapping between `Padding` and `Margin`, building up the elements that give you the look you want and binding the appropriate properties from the templated parent is going to be a lot of the work of creating your own control templates.

Where Are We?

Styles enable you to define a policy for setting the dependency properties of visual elements. The sets of properties can be named and applied manually or programmatically by name, or applied automatically using element-typed styles. In addition to providing constant dependency-property values, styles can contain condition-based property values based on other dependency properties, data properties, or events. And, if setting properties isn't enough to get the look you're after, you can replace a lookless control's entire rendering behavior using a control template.

But that's not all there is to styles. For information about how animations work, you'll want to read Chapter 8, and for information about styles as related to resources, themes, and skins, you'll want to read Chapter 6.

Resources

WPF offers us great flexibility in how we construct an application's user interface. But with great power comes great responsibility—we must avoid bewildering the user with a garish and inconsistent frontend. An application's user interface should be internally consistent, and while some applications differentiate themselves visually, most should be consistent with the look and feel of the user's chosen operating system visual theme.

We've already seen how styling and templates allow us to take control of our application's visuals. These features depend on the resource system in WPF to make it easy to build visually consistent applications without sacrificing flexibility. If you want to build a graphically distinctive application, the resource system provides a straightforward way to *skin* your applications with customized yet consistent visuals. But, by default, the resource mechanism simply ensures consistency with the system-wide OS theme chosen by the user.

In this chapter, we will look at how the resource system lets us plug in visual features where they are needed. Not only will we see how to ensure that the right look and feel is applied to our application at runtime, we will also look at how the resource system lets you reuse objects or groups of objects such as drawings in multiple places in your application. Additionally, we'll look at how to use the resource facilities to manage binary streams and how to make our applications localizable.

Creating and Using Resources

The term *resource* has a very broad meaning—any object can be a resource. A brush or a color used in various parts of a user interface could be a resource. Snippets of graphics or text can be resources. There is nothing special an object has to do to qualify as a resource. The resource-handling infrastructure is entirely dedicated to making it possible to get hold of the resource you require, and it doesn't care what the resource is. It simply provides a mechanism for identifying and locating objects.

At the heart of resource management is the ResourceDictionary class. This is a fairly simple collection class. It behaves much like an ordinary Hashtable; it allows objects to be associated with keys, and provides an indexer that lets you retrieve those objects using these keys. So you could, in principle, use the ResourceDictionary like a Hashtable, as Example 6-1 shows.

Example 6-1. ResourceDictionary programming

```
ResourceDictionary myDictionary = new ResourceDictionary();
myDictionary.Add("Foo", "Bar");
myDictionary.Add("HW", "Hello, world");

Console.WriteLine(myDictionary["Foo"]);
Console.WriteLine(myDictionary["HW"]);
```

In practice, you will not often create your own ResourceDictionary like this. Instead, you will normally use ones provided by WPF. For example, the FrameworkElement base class, from which most user-interface elements derive, provides a resource dictionary in its Resources property. Moreover, this dictionary can be populated from markup, as Example 6-2 shows.

Example 6-2. Populating a ResourceDictionary from XAML

```
<?Mapping XmlNamespace="urn:System" ClrNamespace="System" Assembly="mscorlib" ?>

<Window x:Class="ResourcePlay.Window1" Text="ResourcePlay"
    xmlns="http://schemas.microsoft.com/winfx/avalon/2005"
    xmlns:x="http://schemas.microsoft.com/winfx/xaml/2005"
    xmlns:s="urn:System">

    <Window.Resources>
        <SolidColorBrush x:Key="Foo" Color="Green" />
        <s:String x:Key="HW">Hello, world</s:String>
    </Window.Resources>

    <Grid Name="myGrid">
    </Grid>
</Window>
```

The x:Key attribute specifies the key to be used for the resource in the dictionary. In principle, you can use anything as a key, but in practice, strings are the most common choice, although distinct object instances stored in public properties are used for system resources.

When you use XAML to populate a resource dictionary, WPF may choose to defer the creation of the resources. Under certain circumstances, it may choose to leave sections of the tree in their serialized form (known as BAML), and only expand this into real objects on demand. This can significantly improve the startup time for a user interface in cases where not all of the objects are needed as soon as the UI appears. For the most part, this optimization will not have any direct effect on your code's behavior other than speeding it up. However, if there is something wrong with your markup, this deferred creation can cause the resulting errors to emerge later than you might have expected.

Example 6-3 shows code retrieving the resources defined in Example 6-2.

Example 6-3. Retrieving resources from an element's ResourceDictionary

```
Brush b = (Brush) this.Resources["Foo"];
String s = (String) this.Resources["HW"];
```

Notice that this code accesses the ResourceDictionary using this.Resources. This is all very well for the code-behind for the markup that defined the resources. However it is not always this convenient to get hold of the right dictionary. What if we want to define resources accessible to all windows in the application? It would be both tedious and inefficient to copy the same resources into every window in the application. And what if we want a custom control to pick up resources specified by its parent window, rather than baking them into the control? To solve these problems, and to make it easy to achieve consistency across your user interface, FrameworkElement extends the basic ResourceDictionary facilities with a hierarchical resource scope.

Resource Scope

As well as offering a ResourceDictionary for every element that wants one, FrameworkElement also provides a FindResource method to retrieve resources. Example 6-4 shows the use of this method to retrieve the same resources as Example 6-3.

Example 6-4. Using FindResource

```
Brush b = (Brush) this.FindResource("Foo");
String s = (String) this.FindResource("HW");
```

This may seem rather pointless: why does this FindResource method exist when we could just use the dictionary's indexer as we did in Example 6-3? The reason is that FindResource doesn't give up if the resource is not in the specified element's resource dictionary. It will search elsewhere.

The code in Example 6-5 uses the myGrid element from Example 6-2 instead of this. The Grid does not have any resources, so this code will set the b1 variable to null. However, because b2 is set using FindResources instead of the resource dictionary indexer, WPF will consider all of the resources in scope, not just those directly set on the Grid. It will start at the Grid element, but will then examine the parent, the parent's parent, and so on, all the way to the root element. (In this case, the parent happens to be the root element, so this is a short search. But in general, it will search as many elements as it needs to.) The result is that the b2 variable is set to the same Brush object as was retrieved in Example 6-3 and Example 6-4.

Example 6-5. FrameworkElement.Resources versus FindResource

```
// Returns null
Brush b1 = (Brush) myGrid.Resources["Foo"];

// Returns SolidColorBrush from Window.Resources
Brush b2 = (Brush) myGrid.FindResource("Foo");
```

It doesn't stop here. If FindResource gets all the way to the root of the UI without finding the specified resource, it will then look in the application. Not only do all framework elements have a Resources property, so does the Application object. Example 6-6 shows how to define application-scope resources in markup. (If you are using the normal Visual Studio 2005 Avalon project template, you would put this in the *MyApp.xaml* file.)

Example 6-6. Resources at application scope

```
<Application x:Class="ResourcePlay.MyApp"
    xmlns="http://schemas.microsoft.com/winfx/avalon/2005"
    xmlns:x="http://schemas.microsoft.com/winfx/xaml/2005"
    StartingUp="AppStartingUp"
    >
    <Application.Resources>
        <LinearGradientBrush x:Key="shady" StartPoint="0,0" EndPoint="1,1">
            <LinearGradientBrush.GradientStops>
                <GradientStop Offset="0" Color="Red"/>
                <GradientStop Offset="1" Color="Black"/>
            </LinearGradientBrush.GradientStops>
        </LinearGradientBrush>
    </Application.Resources>
</Application>
```

The application scope is handy for anything used throughout your application. For example, if you use styles or control templates, you would typically put these in the application resources, to ensure that you get a consistent look across all the windows in your application.

Resource searching doesn't stop at the application level. If a resource is not present in the UI tree or the application, FindResource will finally consult the system scope, which contains resources that represent system-wide settings, such as the configured color for selected items or the scrollbar width.

Figure 6-1 shows a typical hierarchy of resource sources. Several applications are running, each application may have several windows, and each window has a tree consisting of multiple elements. If FindResource is called on the element labeled "1" in the figure, it will first look in that element's resource dictionary. If that fails, it will keep working its way up the hierarchy through the numbered items in order, until it reaches the system resources.

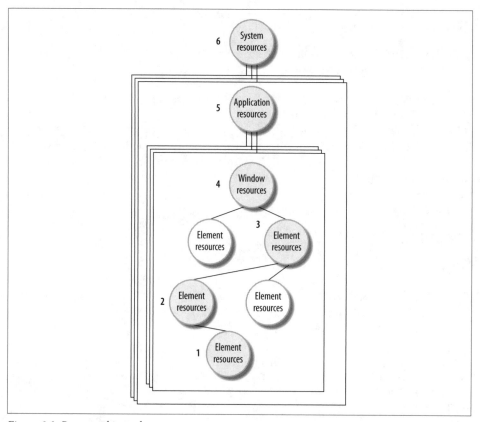

Figure 6-1. Resource hierarchy

WPF uses the system scope to define brushes, fonts, and metrics that the user can configure at a system-wide level. The keys for these are provided as static properties of the SystemColors, SystemFonts, and SystemParameters classes, respectively. (Between them, these classes define over 400 resources, so they are not listed here—consult the SDK documentation for each class to see the complete set.) Example 6-7 uses the system scope to retrieve a brush for the currently configured tool tip background color. (See Chapter 7 for more information on brushes.)

Example 6-7. Retrieving a system scope resource

```
Brush toolTipBackground = (Brush) myGrid.FindResource(SystemColors.InfoBrushKey);
```

 These system-resource classes use objects rather than strings as resource keys. This avoids the risk of naming collisions—because system resources are always identified by a specific object, there will never be any ambiguity between system resources and your own named resources.

The system-resource classes also define static properties that let you retrieve the relevant object directly rather than having to go via the resource system. For example, SystemColors defines an InfoBrush property, which returns the same value that FindResource returns when passed SystemColors.InfoBrushKey. So rather than writing the code in Example 6-7, we could have written the code in Example 6-8.

Example 6-8. Retrieving a system resource through its corresponding property

```
Brush toolTipBackground = SystemColors.InfoBrush;
```

When writing code, these properties are likely to be simpler to use than the resource system. However, using the resource-key properties offers three advantages. First, if you want to let the user change your application's color scheme away from the system-wide default, you can override these system settings by putting resources into the application scope. Example 6-9 shows an application resource section that defines a new application-wide value for the InfoBrushKey resource.

Example 6-9. Application overriding system colors

```
// (Hypothetical function for retrieving settings)
Color col = GetColorFromUserSettings( );

Application.Current.Resources[SystemColors.InfoBrushKey] =
    new SolidColorBrush(Colors.Red);
```

This replacement value would be returned in Example 6-7, but not in Example 6-8. This is because in Example 6-8, SystemColors has no way of knowing what scope you would like to use, so it always goes straight to the system scope.

The second advantage offered by resource keys is that they provide a straightforward way of using system-defined resources from markup. Third, you can make your application respond automatically to changes in system resources. Both of these last two benefits come from using resource references.

Resource References

So far, we have seen how to retrieve the current value of a named resource in code. Since we usually use resource values to set element properties, we will now look at how to set an element's property to the value of a resource. This may seem like a ridiculously trivial step. You might expect it to look like Example 6-10.

Example 6-10. How not to use a system resource value

```
this.Background = (Brush) this.FindResource(SystemColors.ControlBrushKey);
```

This will work up to a point—it will successfully set the Background property to a brush that paints with whatever the currently selected color for control backgrounds is at the moment when this line of code runs. However, if the user changes this setting using the Display Properties control panel applet, this Background property will not be updated automatically. The code in Example 6-10 effectively takes a snapshot of the resource value.

The code in Example 6-11 does not suffer from this problem. Instead of taking a snapshot, it associates the Background property with the resource.

Example 6-11. Self-updating system resource reference

```
this.SetResourceReference(Window.BackgroundProperty, SystemColors.ControlBrushKey);
```

Unlike Example 6-10, if the system resource value changes, the property will automatically receive the new value. The practical upshot of this is that if the user changes the color scheme using the Display Properties applet, Example 6-11 will ensure that your user interface is updated automatically.

WPF defines markup extensions that are the XAML equivalent of the code in the previous two examples. (See Appendix A for more information on markup extensions.) These are the StaticResource and DynamicResource extensions. If you are using a system resource, or any other resource that might change at runtime, choose DynamicResource. If you know the resource will never change, use StaticResource, which takes a snapshot, avoiding the cost associated with tracking the resource for changes. (The cost is small, but you may as well avoid it for resources that never change.) Example 6-12 shows the use of both resource reference types.

Example 6-12. Using resources from markup

```
<Window x:Class="ResourcePlay.Window1" Text="ResourcePlay"
    xmlns="http://schemas.microsoft.com/winfx/avalon/2005"
    xmlns:x="http://schemas.microsoft.com/winfx/xaml/2005">

    <Window.Resources>
        <SolidColorBrush x:Key="Foo" Color="LightGreen" />
    </Window.Resources>

    <Grid Background="{DynamicResource {x:Static SystemColors.ControlBrushKey}}">
```

Example 6-12. Using resources from markup (continued)

```
        <TextBlock FontSize="36" Width="200" Height="200"
                   Background="{StaticResource Foo}">Hello!</TextBlock>
    </Grid>
</Window>
```

The top-level Window defines a brush as a resource. The TextBlock uses this for its Background property via a StaticResource reference. This has a similar effect as the code in Example 6-10. It takes a snapshot and is appropriate for resources that will not change while the application runs.

The grid's Background has been set to the system "control" color. (This is typically battleship grey—the color often used as the background for dialogs.) Since this is a user-configurable color, and could therefore change at runtime, we've used a DynamicResource, which has the same effect as the call to SetResourceReference in Example 6-11.

The syntax here is a little more complex than for the StaticResource. This complexity is not because we are using DynamicResource. It is because the resource we wish to use is identified by an object, returned by the static SystemColors.ControlBrushKey property. We could have tried this:

```
<!-- This will not work as intended -->
<Grid Background="{DynamicResource SystemColors.ControlBrushKey}">
```

This is syntactically correct, but doesn't do what we want. It will be interpreted as a dynamic reference to a resource named by the *string* SystemColors.ControlBrushKey. However, there is no such resource, so the background will not be set. In order to retrieve the real resource key (the object returned by the ControlBrushKey static property) we have to use the x:Static markup extension as Example 6-12 does—this tells the XAML compiler that the text should be treated as the name of a static property, not as a string.

Reusing Drawings

It is often useful to put drawings and shapes into resources. There are two main reasons for doing so. One is that drawings can be quite complex, and putting them inline as part of the main markup for a user interface can make the XAML hard to read. By putting drawings into the resources section, the overall UI structure can be clearer. The other main reason is to enable reuse—you may want to use the same graphic in multiple places.

There are many different ways in which you can represent shapes and drawings, which are shown in Chapter 7. All of them can be used as resources, although there are some restrictions with using certain types. In particular, if you use any element that derives from FrameworkElement as a resource, you can only reference it once. The reason for this restriction is that FrameworkElement is the basis of the user-interface tree. An element knows what its parent is and what children it has, so it is not possible for it to be in more than one place in the tree. (When you use a resource, you are not using a copy of the object, you are using the object itself.)

So although you make an Ellipse a resource, or even a whole drawing in a Canvas, you should do this only if you intend to use the drawing exactly once, because Ellipse and Canvas both derive from FrameworkElement. This is sometimes a useful thing to do—you may want to turn a graphic into a resource just to move it out of the main part of your markup so as to reduce clutter. In this case, the single-use restriction isn't a big problem. Example 6-13 uses this to define an Ellipse resource called shape. It also shows how to use the resource.

Example 6-13. Using a FrameworkElement resource

```
<Window.Resources>
    <Ellipse x:Key="shape" Fill="Blue" Width="100" Height="80" />
</Window.Resources>

...

<StackPanel>
    <Button>Foo</Button>
    <StaticResource ResourceKey="shape" />
    <Button>Bar</Button>
</StackPanel>
```

The StaticResource element here will be replaced at runtime with the resource it names. The result will look like Figure 6-2.

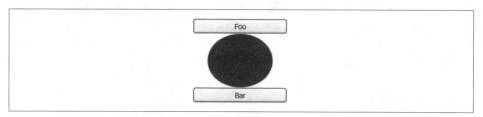

Figure 6-2. Reference to element resource

The Drawing classes, such as a GeometryDrawing or a DrawingGroup, are better candidates for storing drawings as resources. Since Drawing does not derive from FrameworkElement, you are free to use one instance in as many places as you like. DrawingGroup lets you put as many shapes and images into a single drawing as needed, and the various other types derived from Drawing provide access to all of WPF's graphics facilities. See Chapter 7 for more details.

Example 6-14 shows how to define and use a drawing resource—a Drawing is typically used in conjunction with a DrawingBrush. Figure 6-3 shows the result.

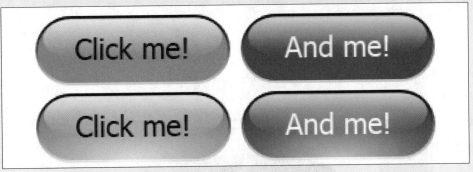

Color Plate 1 (Figures 1-20, 8-9). Buttons with animated glow

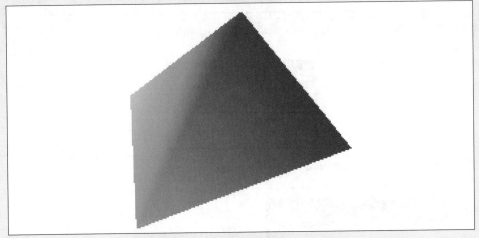

Color Plate 2 (Figures 1-22, 7-58). A very simple 3-D model

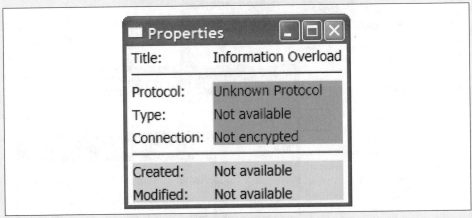

Color Plate 3 (Figure 2-19). Overlapping Grid items

Color Plate 4 (Figure 3-5). Buttons with nested content

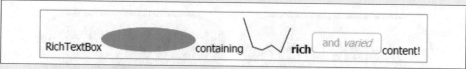

Color Plate 5 (Figure 3-12). RichTextBox with mixed content

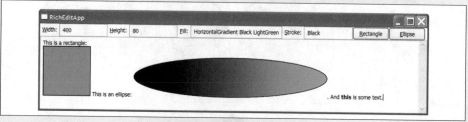

Color Plate 6 (Figure 3-13). Adding non-text elements to a RichTextBox

Color Plate 7 (Figure 3-21). Application with menu and toolbar

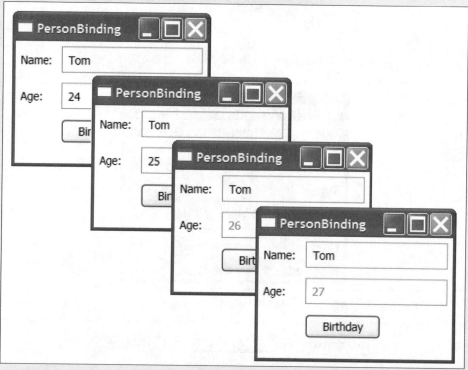

Color Plate 8 (Figure 4-10). A value converter in action

Color Plate 9 (Figure 5-5). Setting styles programmatically based on an object's content

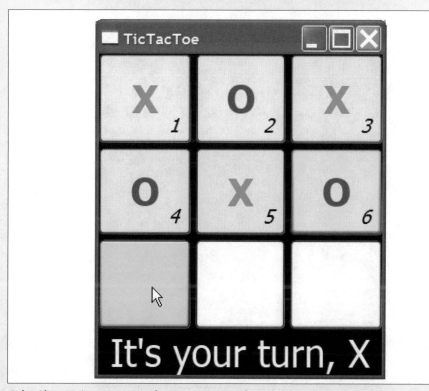

Color Plate 10 (Figure 5-13). The event trigger and our fading yellow animation

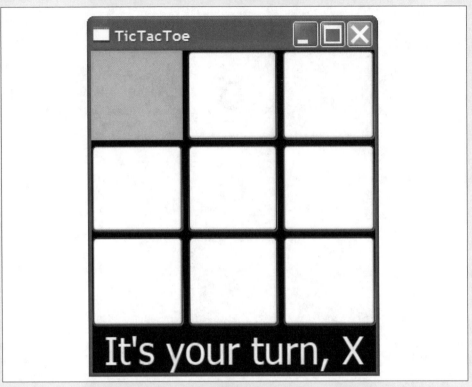

Color Plate 11 (Figure 5-16). Replacing the button's control template with an orange rectangle

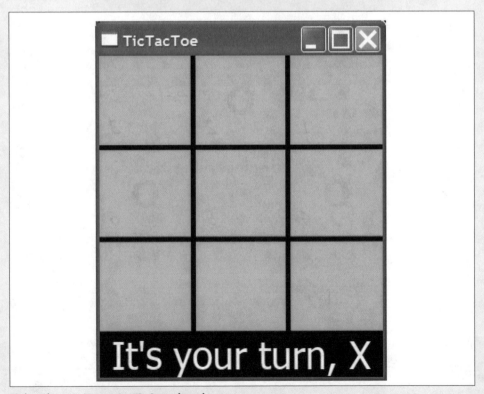

Color Plate 12 (Figure 5-17). Spreading the orange

Color Plate 13 (Figure 5-18). Setting the rectangle's fill using property aliasing

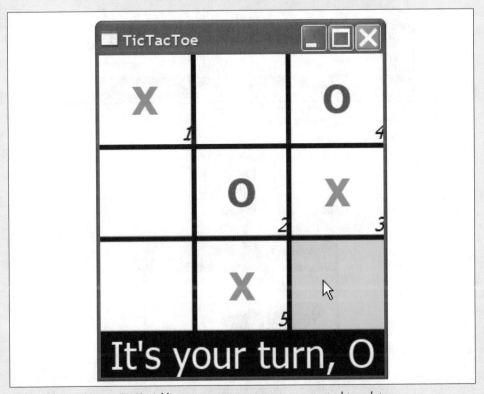

Color Plate 14 (Figure 5-19). Adding a content presenter to our control template

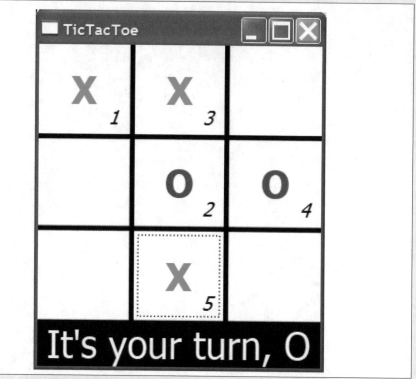

Color Plate 15 (Figure 5-20). Binding the Padding property to the Margin property

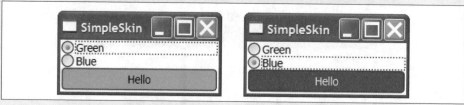

Color Plate 16 (Figure 6-5). Changing skins

Color Plate 17 (Figure 7-3). Button with Grid content

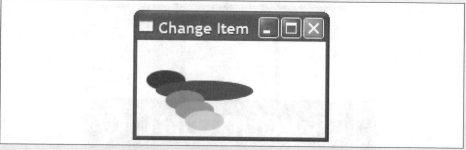

Color Plate 18 (Figure 7-4). Changing overlapping ellipses

Color Plate 19 (Figure 7-6). Enlarged button with graphics

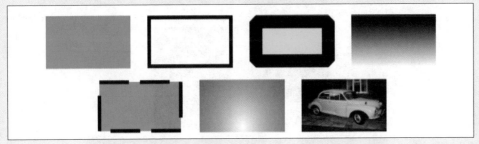

Color Plate 20 (Figure 7-9). Brushes and pens

Color Plate 21 (Figure 7-11). Rotated rectangles

Color Plate 22 (Figure 7-34). Multiple gradient stops

Color Plate 23 (Figure 7-35). Simple lighting effects with linear fills

Color Plate 24 (Figure 7-36). Simple radial fill

Color Plate 25 (Figure 7-37). Radial fills

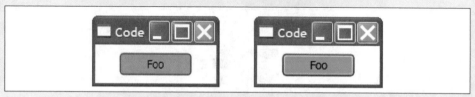

Color Plate 26 (Figure 8-8). Buttons at two points in an animation

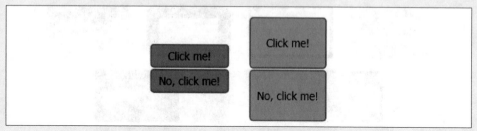

Color Plate 27 (Figure 8-10). Results of Example 8-19

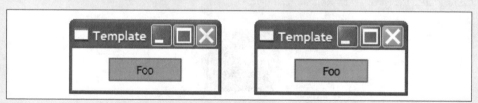

Color Plate 28 (Figure 8-11). Template animations in progress

Color Plate 29 (Figure A-1). Array of brushes provided by a ListBox

Example 6-14. Using a Drawing resource

```
<Window.Resources>
    <GeometryDrawing x:Key="drawing" Brush="Green">
        <GeometryDrawing.Geometry>
            <EllipseGeometry RadiusX="200" RadiusY="10" />
        </GeometryDrawing.Geometry>
    </GeometryDrawing>
</Window.Resources>

...

<Rectangle Width="250" Height="50">
    <Rectangle.Fill>
        <DrawingBrush Drawing="{StaticResource drawing}" />
    </Rectangle.Fill>
</Rectangle>
```

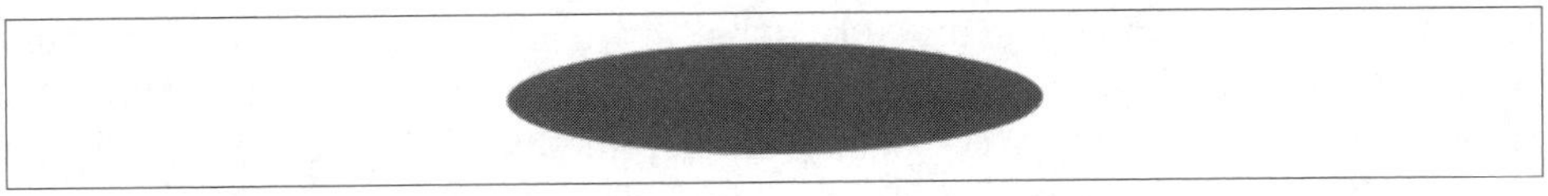

Figure 6-3. Reference to Drawing resource

Alternatively, you could just define a DrawingBrush resource. This moves some of the complexity into the Resources section, making the markup considerably simpler at the point at which you use the resource, as Example 6-15 shows. The results are the same as the previous example (Figure 6-3), but the markup that uses the resource is just one line long instead of five.

Example 6-15. Using a DrawingBrush resource

```
<Window.Resources>
    <DrawingBrush x:Key="dbrush" Drawing="{StaticResource drawing}" />
    <GeometryDrawing x:Key="drawing" Brush="Green">
        <GeometryDrawing.Geometry>
            <EllipseGeometry RadiusX="200" RadiusY="10" />
        </GeometryDrawing.Geometry>
    </GeometryDrawing>
</Window.Resources>

...

<Rectangle Width="250" Height="50" Fill="{StaticResource dbrush}" />
```

If you want the same shape to crop up in multiple drawings, you might want to drop down a level, and use individual geometry objects as resources. These can then be referred to from within drawings. Example 6-16 shows the use of a DrawingBrush with a GeometryDrawing that uses a Geometry resource. (Since this is yet another ellipse, we won't waste your time with another picture—it'll look much like Figure 6-3, only in cyan.)

Example 6-16. Using a Geometry resource

```
<Window.Resources>
    <EllipseGeometry x:Key="geom" RadiusX="200" RadiusY="30" />
</Window.Resources>

...

<Rectangle Width="250" Height="50">
    <Rectangle.Fill>
        <DrawingBrush>
            <DrawingBrush.Drawing>
                <GeometryDrawing Brush="Cyan" Geometry="{StaticResource geom}" />
            </DrawingBrush.Drawing>
        </DrawingBrush>
    </Rectangle.Fill>
</Rectangle>
```

In this particular example, the use of resources may seem a little extreme—it would probably have been less effort just to create a new geometry from scratch. However, some geometries, such as PathGeometry, can become quite complex, in which case this kind of reuse makes more sense.

While drawings and geometries are powerful, reusable, and lightweight, they have one disadvantage. Because they are not proper framework elements, they cannot take advantage of WPF's layout system. You can scale them using the brush scaling features described in Chapter 7, but you cannot make them adapt their layout intelligently using the panels described in Chapter 2, because panels are all framework elements. So you might think that you have to choose between the ability to use framework element features such as layout and the ability to be reuse the resource. However, you can get the best of both worlds by using a ControlTemplate.

Example 6-17 shows markup that uses a ControlTemplate resource. This uses the same Ellipse element multiple times, something we could not do by making the Ellipse element itself a resource. As you can see in Figure 6-4, each Ellipse has been positioned and sized individually by the Grid. Templates are discussed in more detail in Chapter 5.

Example 6-17. Reusing arbitrary markup with templates

```
<Window.Resources>
    <ControlTemplate x:Key="shapeTemplate">
        <Ellipse Fill="Blue" Margin="3" />
    </ControlTemplate>
</Window.Resources>

...

<Grid Width="300" Height="150">
    <Grid.RowDefinitions>
        <RowDefinition Height="2*" />
```

Example 6-17. Reusing arbitrary markup with templates (continued)

```
        <RowDefinition Height="*" />
    </Grid.RowDefinitions>
    <Grid.ColumnDefinitions>
        <ColumnDefinition Width="100" />
        <ColumnDefinition Width="*" />
    </Grid.ColumnDefinitions>

    <Control Template="{StaticResource shapeTemplate}"
             Grid.Row="0" Grid.Column="0" />
    <Control Template="{StaticResource shapeTemplate}"
             Grid.Row="0" Grid.Column="1" />
    <Control Template="{StaticResource shapeTemplate}"
             Grid.Row="1" Grid.Column="0" />
    <Control Template="{StaticResource shapeTemplate}"
             Grid.Row="1" Grid.Column="1" />
</StackPanel>
```

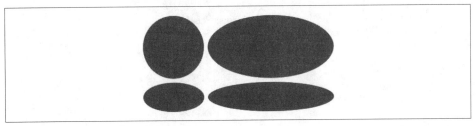

Figure 6-4. Reusing markup with templates

Control templates offer a good way of reusing arbitrary markup, but if you don't need to use `FrameworkElement`-based types in your drawing, using the more light-weight `DrawingBrush` class is more efficient. And if you are creating lots of drawings all containing similar shapes, you can even go as far as sharing individual geometry objects as resources. All of these drawing mechanisms are described in more detail in Chapter 7.

Resources and Styles

WPF's styling mechanism depends on the resource system to locate styles. As you already saw in Chapter 5, styles are defined in the Resources section of an element and can be referred to by name, as shown in Example 6-18.

Example 6-18. Referencing a Style resource

```
<Window x:Class="ResourcePlay.Window1" Text="ResourcePlay"
    xmlns="http://schemas.microsoft.com/winfx/avalon/2005"
    xmlns:x="http://schemas.microsoft.com/winfx/xaml/2005">

    <Window.Resources>
        <Style x:Key="myStyle">
```

Example 6-18. Referencing a Style resource (continued)

```
            <Setter Property="Button.FontSize" Value="36" />
        </Style>
    </Window.Resources>

    <Grid>
        <Button Style="{StaticResource myStyle}">Hello</Button>
    </Grid>
</Window>
```

However, it is also possible to define a style that is applied automatically to an element without the need for the explicit resource reference. This is useful if you want the style to be applied to all elements of a particular type without having to add resource references to every element. Example 6-19 shows a version of Example 6-18 modified to take advantage of this.

Example 6-19. Implicit use of a Style

```
<Window x:Class="ResourcePlay.Window1" Text="ResourcePlay"
    xmlns="http://schemas.microsoft.com/winfx/avalon/2005"
    xmlns:x="http://schemas.microsoft.com/winfx/xaml/2005">

    <Window.Resources>
        <Style TargetType="{x:Type Button}">
            <Setter Property="Button.FontSize" Value="36" />
        </Style>
    </Window.Resources>

    <Grid>
        <Button>Hello</Button>
    </Grid>
</Window>
```

Notice that the Button no longer has its Style property specified. However, the style will still be applied to the button because of its TargetType. Instead of defining a key, the style now has a TargetType set with the x:Type markup extension, which instructs XAML to provide a System.Type object for the named class.

If a FrameworkElement does not have an explicitly specified Style, it will always look for a Style resource using its own type as the target type.

 If you were to create some non-Style resource, such as a SolidColorBrush and set its x:Key to be the type of some UI element, an error would occur if you tried to use that element type. This is because when you create a Style with a TargetType and do not specify the x:Key, the x:Key is implicitly set to be the same as the TargetType. This key is used to locate the style. So, in general, you should avoid setting the x:Key to a Type object.

Because elements look for their styles in resources, you can take advantage of the resource scoping system. You can define a style resource at a local scope if you just wish to affect a small number of elements, or at a broader scope such as in `Window.Resources`, or at application scope. And styles may even be drawn from the system scope. This relationship between styling and resources is the key to both skinning and theming.

Skins and Themes

Skinning and theming are both techniques for controlling the look and feel of a UI. A theme is a system-wide look, such as the Classic Windows 2000 look, or the Windows XP "Luna" theme. A skin is a look specific to a particular application, such as the distinctive styles available for media programs like WinAmp and Windows Media Player.

Both skins and themes can be implemented in WPF as a set of resources that apply the required styles to controls. By using the convention that the resource name is the `Type` for the control to which it applies, styles will apply themselves consistently and automatically. These styles will usually set the `Template` property in order to manage the appearance of the control and may also set other properties, such as those for font handling. (Templates were discussed in Chapter 5.) The main difference between a skin and a theme is one of scope: a skin would typically be stored in the application's `Resources` property, while a theme lives at the system scope and is not directly associated with any one application.

 In the version of WPF available at the time of writing, there was no documented way in which to add a new theme. However, an understanding of how themes work is useful in order to understand how controls get their default appearance.

Since a skin's purpose is to control the appearance of a particular application, it may well provide more than just styles for standard controls; it might define various other named resources for use in specific parts of the application. For example, a music-player application might present a `ListBox` whose purpose is to present a list of songs. A skin might well want to provide a particular look for this list without necessarily affecting all listboxes in the application. So the application would probably set that `ListBox` to use a specific named style, enabling the skin to define a style for just that `ListBox`. In that particular case, the provision of such a specific style might be optional, but in other circumstances, the application might require the skin to provide certain resources. For example, if the application has a toolbar, the skin might be required to provide resources defining the graphics for that toolbar.

Also, a theme applies to all applications, so it must provide templates and styles for all control types. By contrast, a skin is application-specific, so it doesn't necessarily have to provide a comprehensive set of styles. If the application doesn't use every single control type, the skin needs to supply styles only for the controls the application uses. Examples 6-20 and 6-21 show the XAML and code-behind for an extremely simple skin.

Example 6-20. BlueSkin.xaml—a very simple skin

```
<ResourceDictionary x:Class="SimpleSkin.BlueSkin"
    xmlns="http://schemas.microsoft.com/winfx/avalon/2005"
    xmlns:x="http://schemas.microsoft.com/winfx/xaml/2005"
    >
    <Style TargetType="{x:Type Button}">
        <Setter Property="Background" Value="Blue" />
        <Setter Property="Foreground" Value="White" />
    </Style>
</ResourceDictionary>
```

Example 6-21. BlueSkin.xaml.cs—code-behind for a very simple skin

```
using System;
using System.Windows;

namespace SimpleSkin {

    public partial class BlueSkin : ResourceDictionary {

        public BlueSkin() {
            InitializeComponent();
        }
    }
}
```

This just sets the foreground and background for a Button. A more complex skin would target more element types and set more properties. Most skins include some Template property setters in order to customize the appearance of controls. But even in this simple example, the underlying principles remain the same. Example 6-22 shows a UI, and Example 6-23 shows the corresponding code-behind that allows skins to be switched. (This example assumes that two skin classes, BlueSkin and GreenSkin, have been defined using the technique shown in Example 6-20.)

Example 6-22. Window1.xaml—switching skins

```
<Window x:Class="SimpleSkin.Window1" Text="SimpleSkin"
    xmlns="http://schemas.microsoft.com/winfx/avalon/2005"
    xmlns:x="http://schemas.microsoft.com/winfx/xaml/2005">

    <Grid Margin="1">
        <Grid.RowDefinitions>
            <RowDefinition Height="Auto" />
            <RowDefinition Height="Auto" />
        </Grid.RowDefinitions>
```

Example 6-22. Window1.xaml—switching skins (continued)

```
        <RadioButtonList x:Name="radioSkins">
            <TextBlock>Green</TextBlock>
            <TextBlock>Blue</TextBlock>
        </RadioButtonList>

        <Button Grid.Row="1">Hello</Button>
    </Grid>
</Window>
```

Example 6-23. Window1.xaml.cs—switching skins code-behind

```
using System;
using System.Windows;
using System.Windows.Controls;

namespace SimpleSkin {

    public partial class Window1 : Window {

        public Window1() {
            InitializeComponent();

            EnsureSkins();

            radioSkins.SelectionChanged += SkinChanged;
        }

        static ResourceDictionary greenSkin;
        static ResourceDictionary blueSkin;
        static bool resourcesLoaded = false;

        private static void EnsureSkins() {
            if (!resourcesLoaded) {
                greenSkin = new GreenSkin();
                blueSkin = new BlueSkin();

                resourcesLoaded = true;
            }
        }

        private void SkinChanged(object o, SelectionChangedEventArgs e) {
            switch (radioSkins.SelectedIndex) {
                case 0:
                    Application.Current.Resources = greenSkin;
                    break;
                case 1:
                    Application.Current.Resources = blueSkin;
                    break;
            }
        }
    }
}
```

This `SimpleSkin` class contains some code to ensure that the skins get created just once. The code that changes skins simply sets the application resource dictionary to be the one for the selected skins. (The source for the second skin, `GreenSkin`, is not shown. It looks almost identical to Example 6-20, only using green instead of blue.) The styling and resource systems react automatically to the change in resources, updating all of the affected controls when you switch skins, so this is all the code that is required. Figure 6-5 shows the code in action.

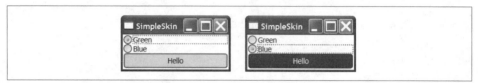

Figure 6-5. Changing skins (Color Plate 16)

There is one slight snag with switching skins this way. If you have any resources stored at the application scope other than the skin resources, they will be lost when switching skins. Currently, the only solution to this is to make sure each skin contains a copy of any non-skin-specific, application-scope resources. The best way to do this is to keep non-skin-specific resources in a separate class and merge them into the skin resources. The current build of WPF has no support for merging resource dictionaries automatically. WPF team members have indicated they are considering easier ways of doing this in a future release, but in the current preview, you must do this manually, as Example 6-24 shows.

Example 6-24. Merging resources

```
ResourceDictionary skinResources = new FooSkinResources();
ResourceDictionary nonSkinAppResources = new DrawingResources();

foreach (DictionaryEntry de in nonSkinAppResources) {
    skinResources.Add(de.Key, de.Value);
}
```

You would add code like this to the method in which you load the resources. In Example 6-23, you would perform this resource merging in the `EnsureSkins` method, merging the non-skin application resources into both the blue and the green skins.

Binary Resources

While `ResourceDictionary` and the resource-scope system are fine for data that can easily be contained in an object, not all resources fit comfortably into this model. Often it is useful to be able to deal with binary streams. For example, images, audio, and video have efficient binary representations, but they are not particularly at home in markup, and in the world of objects they are usually represented by wrappers for the underlying data. Markup itself also presents a challenge: XAML pages must somehow get built into our applications. So, a means of dealing with binary streams is needed.

WPF does not introduce any new technology for dealing with binary data. The .NET framework has always provided mechanisms for dealing with embedded binary streams, and WPF simply uses those.

The lowest level of stream support lets you embed resource streams into any assembly. This is a simple matter of supplying the files you would like to embed to the compiler. In Visual Studio 2005, you do this by setting a file's Build Action property to Embedded Resource. This copies the contents of the file into the assembly as an embedded stream. The stream can be retrieved at runtime using the Assembly class's GetManifestResourceStream method, as Example 6-25 shows.

Example 6-25. Retrieving assembly manifest resources

```
Assembly asm = Assembly.GetExecutingAssembly();
Stream s = asm.GetManifestResourceStream("StreamName");
```

Streams embedded in this way are called *assembly manifest resources*. Although WPF ultimately depends on this embedded-resource mechanism, it uses it indirectly through the ResourceManager class in the System.Resources namespace. This builds on the embedded-resource system, adding two features: localization, and the ability to store multiple named streams in a single low-level stream. The ResourceManager API allows you to ask for any resource by name, and it will attempt to locate the most appropriate resource based on the UI culture. This will be described in more detail in the next section.

By convention, a WPF application or component puts all of its resources into a single assembly manifest resource stream called *Appname*.g.resources, where *Appname* is the name of the component or executable without the file extension. This single resource stream contains binary resources that can be extracted using a ResourceManager. Example 6-26 shows how to retrieve a list of resource names.

Example 6-26. Listing binary resources

```
static List<string> GetResourceNames(Assembly asm,
                    System.Globalization.CultureInfo culture) {

    string resourceName = asm.GetName().Name + ".g";
    ResourceManager rm = new ResourceManager(resourceName, asm);
    ResourceSet resourceSet = rm.GetResourceSet(culture, true, true);
    List<string> resources = new List<string>();
    foreach (DictionaryEntry resource in resourceSet) {

        resources.Add((string) resource.Key);
    }
    rm.ReleaseAllResources();
    return resources;
}
```

Let's use this code to look at the resources found inside a typical application. Figure 6-6 shows the Visual Studio 2005 Solution Explorer view for a simple WPF project. It contains the usual `MyApp.xaml` file defining the application and a single `Window1.xaml` file defining the user interface. (In an application with more windows or pages, you would see more XAML files.) This application also has an Images directory, which contains two bitmap files. As you can see from the Properties panel in the bottom half of Figure 6-6, the Build Action of `Sunset.jpg` has been set to *Resource*. When you add a bitmap file to a project using Add → New Item... or Add → Existing Item... from the context menu in the Solution Explorer, its build action will be set to *Resource* automatically, so `Wheel.jpg` has the same setting.

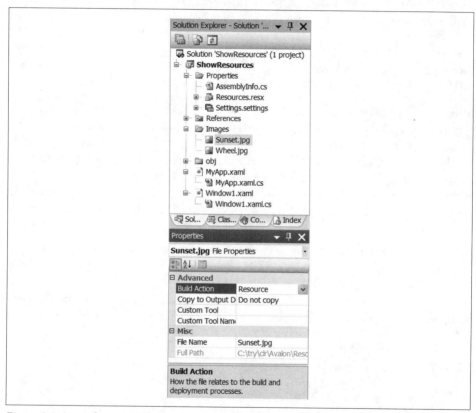

Figure 6-6. An application with resources

If we were to call the `GetResourceNames` function in Example 6-26 and print out each of the strings it returns, we would see the following output:

```
myapp.baml
window1.baml
images/wheel.jpg
images/sunset.jpg
```

As you can see, both of the bitmaps are present. You can use these embedded bitmaps from any element that accepts a URL for an image, as Example 6-27 shows. A relative URL such as this one indicates to the Image element that the resource is local—relative URLs can be used either when the bitmap file is in the same directory, or when it is embedded as a resource. Since the bitmap data is embedded inside the resource stream in the application binary, there is no need to ship a separate file containing bitmap data.

Example 6-27. Using a bitmap resource

```
<Image Source="images/wheel.jpg" />
```

The resource list also shows `myapp.baml` and `window1.baml` resources. These correspond to the two XAML files.

 BAML is a binary representation of an XAML file. XAML is compiled into BAML during the compilation process for two reasons. First, BAML is significantly more compact than XAML, so your executables are much smaller than they would be if XAML were built in. Second, BAML is designed to be very efficient to read, enabling the UI to load much faster than it would if it had to parse XAML.

In a WPF project, any file with a Build Action of *Page* is assumed to be XAML. It will be compiled into BAML and embedded as a resource.

Because bitmaps, BAML files, and any other embedded binary resource use the `ResourceManager` mechanism, this provides a way of making your application localizable.

Global Applications

If you plan to distribute your applications worldwide, you may need to prepare different versions of the user interface for different regions. At a minimum, this involves translating text into the appropriate language. It may also involve other UI changes. You might need to adapt certain visuals to local cultural conventions. Or you might find that the original layout doesn't quite work after translation, because the words are all different lengths (although WPF's layout system makes it easy to build flexible layouts that will avoid that last problem).

It is possible to build different versions of your software for different markets. However, a more common approach is to build a single version that can adapt to different locales, usually by selecting suitable resource files at runtime. The `ResourceManager` infrastructure that WPF uses makes this fairly straightforward.

Microsoft makes a distinction between localization and globalization. *Localization* is the process of enabling an application to be used in a particular locale, by creating culture-specific resources such as translated text. *Globalization* is the process of ensuring that an application can be localized without needing to be recompiled. Using ResourceManager helps to globalize your application, because its runtime resource selection enables a single build of the application to be localized by supplying suitable resources. For more information on recommended globalization and localization practices in Windows, see Microsoft's internationalization site: *http://msdn.microsoft.com/library/default.asp?url=/library/en-us/vbcon/html/vboriInternationalization.asp (http://shrinkster.com/6m9)*.

When a ResourceManager is asked to retrieve a named resource stream, the first thing it does is determine which culture it should use. A *culture* is the combination of a language and location, and is typically represented as a short string. For example, en-US means the English language, as spoken in the U.S. The en-GB culture represents English as spoken in Great Britain. The first two letters indicate the language and the last two the region. The reason both language and location are specified is that there are often variations in dialect and idiom even when two cultures ostensibly share a language. For example, one of the authors of this book hails from en-GB, and therefore prefers "color" to be spelled "colour."

The ResourceManager.GetStream method takes a CultureInfo object as a parameter. If you wish to use the end user's configured culture, you can retrieve a CultureInfo from the CurrentUICulture property of Thread.CurrentThread.

Although executables usually have resources compiled in, the ResourceManager will look for culture-specific resources before resorting to the built-in ones. It will look in the directory containing the application for a subdirectory named for the culture. So, if you are running in a French Canadian culture, it will look for an fr-CA subdirectory containing a file called *MyApp*.resources.dll, where *MyApp* is the name of your application or component. If that doesn't exist, it will then look for the same file in a directory called fr. This means that if your translation budget doesn't stretch to producing different versions for all of the various French-speaking regions of the world, you can instead provide a single set of French resources that will be used in any French-speaking region. Only if neither of these subdirectories exists will it resort to using the built-in resources.

The resource DLLs that the ResourceManager looks for are called *satellite resource assemblies*, so called because they are small assemblies associated with a larger assembly nearby.

Note that if you supply a satellite assembly, you are not required to provide localized versions of all of the resources. It might be that some of the resources you embed in your main assembly work just fine for all cultures. For example, the application shown in Figure 6-6 had an embedded bitmap called Sunset.jpg. The sun sets in most parts of the world, so while you might need to do something special for Arctic and Antarctic editions, the basic Sunset.jpg probably works for most cultures. It would be a bit of a waste of space for every satellite resource assembly to contain a copy of the same image. Fortunately, they don't have to—if a particular named resource is not present in a satellite resource assembly, the ResourceManager will fall back on the built-in resources.

You can think of satellite resource assemblies as containing just the differences between the built-in resources and those required for the target culture. Any common resources will live in the main assembly alone. An assembly in a language-specific but location-generic subdirectory (e.g., in the fr subdirectory) contains resources that need to be different for the specified language. And then the fully culture-specific subdirectories (e.g., fr-CA, fr-FR, fr-BE, etc.) contain only those resources that need to be adjusted to take into account local idioms. (In this context a "resource" is a single stream as retrieved by the ResourceManager, rather than an object retrieved from a ResourceDictionary.)

Building Localizable Applications with XAML

Because XAML is compiled into BAML resources that are retrieved using a ResourceManager, localizability is an intrinsic feature of any WPF application built using XAML. However, there is currently no built-in support for localizing WPF applications in Visual Studio 2005, so there are a few manual steps involved.

If you build a UI in XAML, localization effectively occurs one XAML file at a time—the ResourceManager cannot go more fine-grained than a single BAML resource, so each BAML resource is either localized or not. Since there is a close relationship between a XAML file and its code-behind file, however, it is important that the localized BAML resource has the same essential structure as the original. In principle, you could achieve this by writing a new XAML file for the localized version and trying to keep its structure the same. However, there is a more robust way of guaranteeing consistency.

Instead of authoring a set of XAML files for every culture, you can write one master set of XAML files—one for each window or page in your application. Then, for each culture you wish to support, you can use a tool to generate culture-specific satellite resource assemblies containing localized resources. You supply the tool with configuration files indicating how the resources should be modified in order to create the localized versions. Figure 6-7 illustrates the overall process.

 This is a slightly long-winded process. By the time the final release of WPF ships, this will no doubt be better streamlined and integrated into Visual Studio 2005. For now, welcome to the wonderful world of pre-release software.

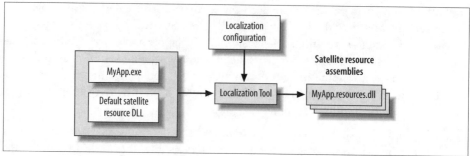

Figure 6-7. Localization process

First, you must make sure the project is set up to build a localizable application by specifying a default UI culture. At the time of writing, there was no way of doing this from within Visual Studio 2005, so you must edit the `.csproj` file using a text editor. Add a `UICulture` element inside the `PropertyGroup` element (it doesn't matter where the `UICulture` element appears within this section). Set it to the default culture for your application—the culture in which you will create the main resources. This will cause Visual Studio 2005 to put all of the binary resources into a satellite resource assembly for this default culture. Example 6-28 shows some sample markup that achieves this result.

Example 6-28. Specifying a UI culture for your project

```
<Project DefaultTargets="Build"
         xmlns="http://schemas.microsoft.com/developer/msbuild/2003">
  <PropertyGroup>
    ...
    <UICulture>en-US</UICulture>
    ...
  </PropertyGroup>
  ...
```

Next, you must add Uids to your XAML. A *Uid* is a special attribute on a XAML element indicating content that may require localization. The localization configuration file containing localization instructions will use Uids to indicate which elements are being changed. Example 6-29 shows a `TextBlock` with a Uid.

Example 6-29. A Uid

```
<TextBlock x:Uid="TextBlock_1">Hello, world</TextBlock>
```

You can add these by hand if you want. Or you can generate them automatically using `msbuild`. (`msbuild` is the command-line tool for building projects. Visual Studio 2005 uses the same build technology, but `msbuild` offers more control. For example, it lets you get at this Uid generation feature of the WPF build system.) To add Uids to your XAML automatically, run this command:

```
msbuild /t:updateuid MyProject.csproj
```

If you have done this already, and have subsequently edited your XAML, you may want to check that you've not ended up with any duplicated Uids. You can do this with the following command:

```
msbuild /t:checkuid MyProject.csproj
```

Now you can build the project, either by using VS 2005 or by running msbuild from the command line, passing just the project filename as a parameter. You should now find that as well as building an EXE or DLL, your project also adds a satellite resource assembly in a subdirectory. (The subdirectory will be the one you named when you added the UICulture element to the project file.)

The next step is to create the configuration file that will direct the localization process. This file will contain all localized items, such as translated strings. You can create the skeleton of this file using the LocBaml command-line tool. This tool examines resource assemblies for BAML streams and builds a file containing one line for each localizable piece of information in the file. You can then put your translated strings and whatever else is required into this file.

 In the current preview builds of WPF, LocBaml is supplied in source code form only, so you will need to build it before you can run it. You can find the code in the WinFX SDK documentation. In the Avalon → Globalization and Localization → How-to Topics section, find the "Localize an Application" topic. This provides the code for LocBaml.

Example 6-30 shows how to run LocBaml to generate the skeleton configuration file.

Example 6-30. Generating a CSV file with LocBaml

```
LocBaml bin\Debug\en-US\MyApp.resources.dll /out:MyAppResources.csv
```

This will create a CSV file. Table 6-1 describes each of the columns in the order in which they appear in the CSV file. To localize the resource, edit the Value column. (Note that the CSV file doesn't contain a heading line—it depends entirely on the column positions.)

Table 6-1. Columns generated by LocBaml

Column	Description
Baml Name	Identifies the BAML stream; the value will be of the form *AssemblyManifestStreamName:SubStream Name*.
Resource Key	Identifies the localizable resource; the value will be of the form *Uid:Element Type.$Property*.
Localization Category	An entry from the LocalizationCategory enumeration, indicating what kind of content this is.
Readable	Indicates whether the resource is visible for translation.
Modifiable	Indicates whether this value can be modified during translation.

Table 6-1. Columns generated by LocBaml (continued)

Column	Description
Comments	Localization comments.
Value	The value of this resource.

Example 6-31 shows a line from one of these configuration files. (It has been split across several lines here to make it fit. In a real file, this would be on a single line.)

Example 6-31. Example configuration file

```
HelloApp.g.fr-FR.resources:window1.baml,
TextBlock_1:System.Windows.Controls.TextBlock.$Content,
None,True,True,,Bonjour monde
```

Once you have translated all of the Values, you can then run LocBaml again to generate the new resource DLL. You must pass in the path of the original resource DLL, the path of the CSV file containing translations, a target directory, and the target culture, as shown in Example 6-32. (Note that this example has been split across multiple lines to fit into the book. It should be entered as a single line in practice.)

Example 6-32. Generating a resource DLL with LocBaml

```
LocBaml /generate bin\Debug\en-US\MyApp.resources.dll /trans:MyAppResource.csv
  /out:bin\Debug\en-GB /cul:en-GB
```

This will generate a new satellite resource assembly in the specified directory, targeting the chosen culture. (If you want to build several resource assemblies, create one CSV file for each culture and run LocBaml once for each file.) If you place the resulting resource assembly in a subdirectory of the application's directory named after the culture, it will automatically be picked up at runtime if the application is run with that particular culture selected.

Where Are We?

WPF provides resource facilities that let us plug bits of our user interface together dynamically but consistently. We can store any objects we like in resource dictionaries and then refer to these resources throughout our applications. WPF's styling mechanism relies on resource dictionaries to set properties and templates for our controls, based either on an application's skin or the currently configured system theme. And for binary resources, including the compiled BAML versions of our XAML files, WPF uses the localization-aware ResourceManager system, which chooses the most appropriate resources for the end user's chosen user-interface culture.

CHAPTER 7

Graphics

WPF makes it easy to build visually stunning applications. It offers a rich array of drawing capabilities and is built to exploit the full capability of modern graphics cards. This enables designers to create intricate designs and use animation to bring the UI to life much more easily than before.

WPF's graphics architecture is not just for designers. The key aspect of the graphics support in WPF is its deep integration with the rest of the programming model. It is easy to add graphical elements into any part of your application without the disconcerting change in programming techniques required with many user-interface technologies.

Since WPF is a presentation technology, graphics is an important and substantial part of the framework. It would be possible to fill a whole book on WPF's graphical capabilities alone, so we can only really scratch the surface here. In this chapter, we will look at the fundamental concepts behind using graphics in WPF applications. In the next chapter, we will look at animation.

Graphics Fundamentals

WPF makes it easy to use graphics in your application and to exploit the power of your graphics hardware. There are many aspects of the graphics architecture that contribute to this goal. This most important of these is *integration*.

Integration

Graphical elements can be integrated into any part of your user interface. Many GUI technologies tend to separate graphics off into a separate world. This requires a "gear shift" when moving from a world of buttons, text boxes, and other controls into a world of shapes and images, because in many systems, these two worlds have different programming models.

For example, Windows Forms and Mac OS X's Cocoa both provide the ability to arrange controls within a window and build a program that interacts through those controls. They also both provide APIs offering advanced, fully scalable two-dimensional drawing facilities. (GDI+ in the case of Windows Forms, and Quartz 2D on OS X.) But these drawing APIs are distinct from the control APIs. Drawing primitives are very different from controls in these systems—you cannot mix the two freely.

WPF, on the other hand, treats shapes as elements in the UI tree like any other. So, we are free to mix them in with any other kind of element. Example 7-1 shows various examples of this.

Example 7-1. Mixing graphics with other elements

```
<DockPanel>
    <StackPanel DockPanel.Dock="Top" Orientation="Horizontal">
        <TextBlock>Mix</TextBlock>
        <Rectangle Fill="Red" Width="20" />
        <TextBlock>text</TextBlock>
        <Ellipse Fill="Blue" Width="40" />
        <TextBlock>and</TextBlock>
        <Button>Controls</Button>
    </StackPanel>
    <Ellipse DockPanel.Dock="Left" Fill="Green" Width="100" />
    <Button DockPanel.Dock="Left">Foo</Button>
    <TextBlock FontSize="24" TextWrap="Wrap">
        And of course you can put graphics into
        your text: <Ellipse Fill="Cyan" Width="50" Height="20" />
    </TextBlock>
</DockPanel>
```

As you can see, graphical elements can be added seamlessly into the markup. Layout works with graphics exactly as it does for any other element. The results can be seen in Figure 7-1.

> Although this example is in XAML, you can also use code to create elements. Most of the examples in this chapter use XAML because the structure of the markup directly reflects the structure of the objects being created. However, whether you use markup or code will depend on what you are doing. If you are creating drawings, you will most likely use a design program to create the XAML for these drawings, but if you are building graphics from data, it might make more sense to do everything from code.
>
> Most of the techniques shown in this chapter can be used in either code or markup. See Appendix A for more information on the relationship between XAML and code.

Not only can graphics and the other content live side by side in the markup, they can even be intermingled. Notice how in Figure 7-1 the ellipse on the right-hand side has

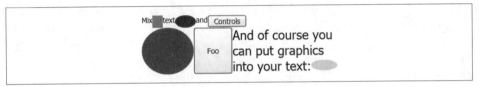

Figure 7-1. Mixed content

been arranged within the flow of the containing TextBlock. If you want to achieve this sort of effect in Windows Forms, it is not possible with its Label control—you would have to write a whole new control from scratch that draws both the text and the ellipse. This mixing goes both ways—not only can you mix controls into your graphics, you can also use graphical elements to customize the look of your control, as Chapter 5 showed.

This mixing isn't just about simple elements like text blocks—it also works for controls. For example, Figure 7-2 shows a button with mixed text and graphics as its caption.

Figure 7-2. Button with graphical content

Traditionally in Windows, you would get this effect by relying on the button being able to display a bitmap. But bitmaps are pretty inflexible—they are just a block of fixed graphics—so you can't easily make parts of a bitmap interactive or animate selected pieces in response to user input. So, in WPF, putting graphics in buttons works a little differently. The markup for this button is shown in Example 7-2.

Example 7-2. Adding graphics to a Button

```
<Button>
    <StackPanel Orientation="Horizontal">
        <Canvas Width="20" Height="18" VerticalAlignment="Center">
            <Ellipse Canvas.Left="1" Canvas.Top="1" Width="16" Height="16"
                     Fill="Yellow" Stroke="Black" />
            <Ellipse Canvas.Left="4.5" Canvas.Top="5" Width="2.5" Height="3"
                     Fill="Black" />
            <Ellipse Canvas.Left="11" Canvas.Top="5" Width="2.5" Height="3"
                     Fill="Black" />
            <Path Data="M 5,10 A 3,3 0 0 0 13,10" Stroke="Black" />
        </Canvas>
        <TextBlock VerticalAlignment="Center">Click!</TextBlock>
    </StackPanel>
</Button>
```

Of course, buttons with images are not a new idea, but traditionally, buttons enabled this by allowing an image to be set. For example, the Windows Forms Button has an Image property, and in Cocoa, NSButton has a setImage method. This implementation is pretty inflexible—these controls allow a single caption and a single image to be set. Compare this to Example 7-2, which uses a StackPanel to lay out the interior of the button and just adds the content it requires. You can use any layout panel inside the Button, with any kind of content. Example 7-3 uses a Grid to arrange text and some ellipses within a Button. The results are shown in Figure 7-3.

Example 7-3. Layout within a button

```
<Button HorizontalAlignment="Center" VerticalAlignment="Center">
    <Grid>
        <Grid.ColumnDefinitions>
            <ColumnDefinition />
            <ColumnDefinition />
            <ColumnDefinition />
        </Grid.ColumnDefinitions>
        <Grid.RowDefinitions>
            <RowDefinition />
            <RowDefinition />
            <RowDefinition />
        </Grid.RowDefinitions>

        <Ellipse Grid.Column="0" Grid.Row="0" Fill="Blue" Width="10" Height="10" />
        <Ellipse Grid.Column="2" Grid.Row="0" Fill="Blue" Width="10" Height="10" />
        <Ellipse Grid.Column="0" Grid.Row="2" Fill="Blue" Width="10" Height="10" />
        <Ellipse Grid.Column="2" Grid.Row="2" Fill="Blue" Width="10" Height="10" />

        <Ellipse Grid.ColumnSpan="3" Grid.RowSpan="3" Stroke="LightGreen"
StrokeThickness="3" />

        <TextBlock Grid.Column="1" Grid.Row="1" VerticalAlignment="Center">Click!</
TextBlock>
    </Grid>
</Button>
```

Figure 7-3. Button with Grid content (Color Plate 17)

In WPF, there is rarely any need for elements to provide inflexible properties such as Text or Image. If it makes sense for an element to present nested content, then it'll do just that—it will present whatever mixture of elements you choose to provide.

If you are familiar with two-dimensional drawing technologies such as Quartz 2D, GDI+, or good old GDI32, another advantage in the way drawing is done may well have struck you. We no longer need to write a function to respond to redraw requests—WPF can keep the screen repainted for us. This is because WPF lets us represent drawings as objects.

Drawing Object Model

With many GUI technologies, applications that want customized visuals are required to be able to re-create their appearance from scratch. The usual technique for showing a custom appearance was to write code that performed a series of drawing operations in order to construct the display. This code would run when the relevant graphics first needed to be displayed. In some systems, the OS did not retain a copy of what the application drew, so this method would end up running any time an area needed repainting—e.g., if a window was obscured and then uncovered.

When using this approach, where a rendering function constructs the whole image, updating individual elements is often problematic. Even where the OS does retain a copy of the drawing, it is often retained as a bitmap. This means that if you want to change one part of the drawing, you often need to repaint everything in the area that has changed.

WPF offers a different approach: you can add objects representing graphical shapes to the tree of user-interface elements. Shape elements are objects in the UI tree like any other, so your code can modify them at any time. If you change some property that has a visual impact—such as the size, location, or color—WPF will automatically update the display.

To illustrate this technique, Example 7-4 shows a simple window containing several ellipses. Each of these is represented by an Ellipse object, which we will use from the code-behind file to update the display.

Example 7-4. Changing graphical elements

```
<Window x:Class="ChangeItem.MainWindow"
    xmlns="http://schemas.microsoft.com/winfx/avalon/2005"
    xmlns:x="http://schemas.microsoft.com/winfx/xaml/2005"
    Text="Change Item"
    >
    <Canvas>
        <Ellipse Canvas.Left="10" Canvas.Top="30" Fill="Indigo"
                 Width="40" Height="20" MouseLeftButtonDown="OnClick" />
        <Ellipse Canvas.Left="20" Canvas.Top="40" Fill="Blue"
                 Width="40" Height="20" MouseLeftButtonDown="OnClick" />
        <Ellipse Canvas.Left="30" Canvas.Top="50" Fill="Cyan"
                 Width="40" Height="20" MouseLeftButtonDown="OnClick" />
        <Ellipse Canvas.Left="40" Canvas.Top="60" Fill="LightGreen"
                 Width="40" Height="20" MouseLeftButtonDown="OnClick" />
        <Ellipse Canvas.Left="50" Canvas.Top="70" Fill="Yellow"
                 Width="40" Height="20" MouseLeftButtonDown="OnClick" />
    </Canvas>
</Window>
```

Every ellipse's MouseLeftButtonDown event is handled by an OnClick method defined in the code-behind file for this window. As Example 7-5 shows, the OnClick method simply increases the Width property of whichever Ellipse raised the event. The result is that clicking on any ellipse will make it wider.

Example 7-5. Changing a shape at runtime.

```
using System.Windows;
using System.Windows.Shapes;

namespace ChangeItem
{
    public partial class MainWindow : Window
    {
        public MainWindow( ) : base( )
        {
            InitializeComponent( );
        }

        private void OnClick(object sender, RoutedEventArgs e)
        {
            Ellipse r = (Ellipse) sender;
            r.Width += 10;
        }
    }
}
```

If we were using the old approach of drawing everything in a single rendering function, this code would not be sufficient to update the display. It would normally be necessary to tell the OS that the screen is no longer valid, causing it to raise a repaint request. But in WPF, this is not necessary—when you set a property on an `Ellipse` object, WPF ensures that the screen is updated appropriately. Moreover, WPF is aware that the items all overlap, as shown in Figure 7-4, so it will also redraw the items beneath and above as necessary to get the right results. All you have to do is adjust the properties of the object.

Figure 7-4. Changing overlapping ellipses (Color Plate 18)

 Even though computer memory capacities have increased by orders of magnitude since GUIs first started to appear, there are still situations in which this object-model approach for drawing might be too expensive. In particular, for applications dealing with vast data sets, such as maps, having a complete set of objects in the UI tree mirroring the structure of the underlying data could use too much memory. Also, for certain kinds of graphics or data, it may be more convenient to use the old style of rendering code. Because of this, WPF also supports some lighter weight modes of operation. These are described later in this chapter, in the "Visual-Layer Programming" section.

You may have noticed that all of the drawing we've done so far has been with shapes and not bitmaps. WPF supports bitmaps, of course, but there is a good reason to use shapes—geometric shapes can be scaled and rotated without loss of image quality. This high-quality transformability is an important feature of drawing in WPF.

Resolution Independence

Not only have graphics cards improved dramatically since the first GUIs appeared, so have screens. For a long time, the only mainstream display technology was the Cathode Ray Tube (CRT). Color CRTs offered only limited resolution—they struggled to display images with higher definition than about 100 pixels per inch. However, flat-panel displays, which now outsell CRTs, can exceed this by a large margin.

One of the authors of this book has a two-year-old laptop whose display has a resolution of 150 pixels per inch. At the time of writing, displays are available with over 200 pixels per inch. It is possible to create even higher pixel densities. However, there is a problem with using these screens on current operating systems: everything ends up being so small that it becomes unusable. This is because of a pixel-based development culture—the vast majority of applications measure out their user interfaces in pixels.

This is not entirely the result of technical limitations. Ever since the first version of Windows NT shipped, it has been possible to draw things in a resolution-independent way, because the drawing API, GDI32, allows you to apply transformations to all of your drawings. GDI+, introduced in 2001, offers the same facility. But just because a feature is available doesn't mean applications will use it—most applications don't exploit this scalability.

Unfortunately, the split between graphics and other UI elements in Win32 means that even if an application does exploit the scalability of the drawing APIs, the rest of the UI won't automatically follow. Figure 7-5 shows a Windows Forms application that uses GDI+ to draw text and graphics scaled to an arbitrary size.

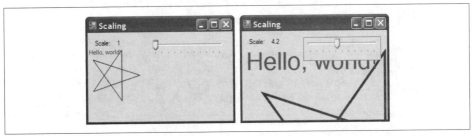

Figure 7-5. Incomplete UI Scaling in Windows Forms

Notice in Figure 7-5 that although the star and the "Hello, World" text have been scaled, the track bar and label controls have not. This is because drawing transformations affect only what you draw with GDI+—they do not affect the entire UI. And while Windows Forms offers some features to help with scaling the rest of the UI, it's not automatic—you have to take deliberate and nontrivial steps to build a resolution-independent UI in Windows Forms.

Scaling and rotation

WPF solves this problem by supporting transformations at a fundamental level. Instead of just providing scalability at the 2-D drawing level, WPF builds it into the underlying composition engine. The result is that everything in the UI can be transformed, not just the user-drawn graphics. Going back to our smiley-face button in Figure 7-2, we can exploit this scalability by modifying just the first line:

```
<Button LayoutTransform="scale 3 3">
```

The LayoutTransform property is available on all user-interface elements in WPF, so you can scale an entire window just as easily as a single button. Many kinds of transformation are available, and these will be discussed in more detail later. For now, we are simply asking to enlarge the button by a factor of 3 in both x- and y-dimensions. Figure 7-6 shows the enlarged button.

Figure 7-6. Enlarged button with graphics (Color Plate 19)

Comparing the original Figure 7-2 with Figure 7-6, the latter is obviously larger, as you would expect. More significantly, the details have become crisper. The rounded edges of the button are easier to see than they were in the small version. The shapes of the letters are much better defined. And our graphic is clearer. We get this clarity because WPF has rendered the button to look as good as it can at the specified size. Compare Figure 7-6 with the examples in Figure 7-7.

Figure 7-7. Enlarged bitmaps

Figure 7-7 shows what happens if you simply enlarge the original small-button bitmap. There are several different ways of enlarging bitmaps. The example on the left uses the simplest algorithm, known as *nearest neighbor*, or sometimes *pixel doubling*.

To make the image larger, pixels have simply been repeated. This lends a very square feel to the image. The example on the right uses a more sophisticated interpolation algorithm. It has done a better job of keeping rounded edges looking round, and doesn't suffer from the chunky pixel effect, but it ends up looking very blurred. Clearly, neither of these can hold a candle to Figure 7-6.

Resolution, coordinates, and "pixels"

This support for scaling graphics means that there is no fixed relationship between the coordinates your application uses and the pixels onscreen. This is true even if you do not use scaling transforms yourself—a transform may be applied automatically to your whole application if it is running on a high-DPI display.

What are the default units of measurement in a WPF application if not physical pixels? The answer is, somewhat confusingly, pixels! To be more precise, the real answer is device-independent pixels.

The official definition of a *device-independent pixel* in WPF is $1/96$th of an inch. If you specify the width of a shape as 96 pixels, this means that it should be exactly one inch wide. WPF will use as many physical pixels as are required to fill one inch. For example, high-resolution laptop screens have a resolution of 150 pixels per inch. So if you make a shape's width 96 "pixels," WPF will render it 150 physical pixels wide.

> WPF relies on the system-wide display settings to determine the physical pixel size. You can adjust them through the Windows Display Properties applet. Right-click on your desktop and select Properties to display the applet and then go to the Settings tab. Click on the Advanced button, and, in the dialog that opens, select the General tab. This lets you tell Windows your screen resolution.

You might be wondering why WPF uses the somewhat curious choice of $1/96$ inches, and why it calls this a "pixel." The reason is that 96dpi is the default display DPI in Windows when running with Normal Fonts, so this has long been considered the normal size for a pixel. This means that on screens with a normal pixel density, a device-independent pixel will correspond to a physical pixel, and on screens with a high pixel density, WPF will scale your drawings for you so that they remain at the correct physical size.

WPF's ability to optimize its rendering of graphical features for any scale means it is ideally placed to take advantage of increasing screen resolutions. For the first time, onscreen text and graphics will be able to compete with the crisp clarity we have come to expect from laser printers. Of course, for all of this to work in practice, we need a comprehensive suite of drawing primitives.

Shapes, Brushes and Pens

Most of the classes in WPF's drawing toolkit fall into one of three categories: shapes, brushes, and pens. There are many variations on these themes, and we will examine them in detail later. However, to get anywhere at all with graphics, a basic understanding of these classes is mandatory.

Shapes are objects in the user-interface tree that provide the basic building blocks for drawing. The Ellipse, Path, and Rectangle elements we have seen already are all examples of shape objects. There is also support for lines, both simple and multi-segment, using Line and Polyline, respectively. Arbitrary filled shapes can also be created. Polygon enables shapes whose edges are all straight, but if you want curved edges, the Path class supports filled shapes as well as curved lines. Figure 7-8 shows each of these shapes in action.

Figure 7-8. Rectangle, Ellipse, Line, Polyline, Polygon, and Path

Regardless of which shape you choose, you'll need to decide how it should be colored in. For this, you use a *brush*. There are many brush types available. The simplest is the single-color SolidColorBrush. You can achieve more interesting visual effects using the LinearGradientBrush or RadialGradientBrush. These allow the color to change over the surface of a shape, which can be a great way of providing an impression of depth. You can also create brushes based on images—the ImageBrush uses a bitmap, and the DrawingBrush uses a scalable drawing. Finally, the VisualBrush lets you take any visual tree—any chunk of user interface you like—and use that as a brush to paint some other shape. This makes it easy to achieve effects like reflections of whole sections of your user interface.

Finally, *pens* are used to draw the outline of a shape. A pen is really just an augmented brush. When you create a Pen object, you give it a Brush to tell it how it should paint onto the screen. The Pen class just adds information such as line thickness, dash patterns, and end-cap details. Figure 7-9 shows a few of the effects available using brushes and pens.

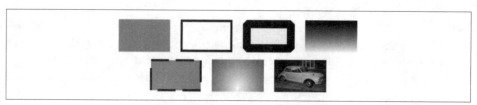

Figure 7-9. Brushes and pens (Color Plate 20)

Composition

The final key feature of the graphics architecture is composition. In computer graphics, the term *composition* refers to the process of combining multiple shapes or images together to form the final output. WPF's composition model is very different from the model on which Windows has traditionally worked, and it is crucial to enabling the creation of high-quality visuals.

In the classic Win32 model, each user-interface element (each HWND) has exclusive ownership of some region of the application's window. Within each top-level window, any given pixel in that window is controlled completely by exactly one element. This prevents elements from being partially transparent. It also precludes the use of anti-aliasing around the edges of elements, a technique that is particularly important when combining non-rectangular elements. Although various hacks have been devised to provide the illusion of transparency in Win32, they all have limitations and can be somewhat inconvenient to work with.

WPF's composition model supports elements of any shape and allows them to overlap. It also allows elements to have any mixture of partially and completely transparent areas. This means that any given pixel onscreen may have multiple contributing visible elements. Moreover, WPF uses anti-aliasing around the edges of all shapes. This reduces the jagged appearance that simpler drawing techniques can produce onscreen, resulting in a smooth-looking image. Finally, the composition engine allows any element to have a transformation applied before composition.

WPF's composition engine makes use of the capabilities of modern graphics cards to accelerate the drawing process. Internally, it is implemented on top of the Direct3D model. This may seem odd since the majority of WPF's drawing functionality is two-dimensional, but most of the 3-D-oriented functionality on a modern graphics card can also be used to draw 2-D shapes. For example, pixel shaders can be used to implement the advanced ClearType mechanism when composing text into a UI. WPF exploits the same ultra-fast polygon drawing facilities used by 3-D games to render primitive shapes. Moreover WPF caches portions of the visual tree on the graphics card, significantly improving the repainting performance when changing small details onscreen.

Now that we've seen the core concepts underpinning the WPF graphics system, let's take a closer look at the details.

Shapes

Shapes are drawing primitives, represented as elements in the user interface tree. WPF supports a variety of different shapes and provides element types for each of them.

Base Shape Class

All of the elements listed in this section derive from a common abstract base class, Shape. Although you cannot use this type directly, it is useful to know about it, because it defines a common set of features that you can use on all shapes. These common properties are all concerned with the way in which the interior and outline of the shape are painted.

The Fill property specifies the Brush that will be used to paint the interior. The Line and Polyline classes don't have interiors, so they will ignore this property. (This was simpler than complicating the inheritance hierarchy by having separate Shape and FilledShape base classes.) The Stroke property specifies the Brush that will be used to paint the outline of the shape.

If you do not specify either a Fill or a Stroke for your shape, it will be invisible, because both of these properties are transparent by default.

It may seem peculiar that the Stroke property is of type Brush. As we saw earlier, WPF defines a Pen class for specifying a line's thickness, dash patterns, and the like, so it would make more sense if the Stroke property were of type Pen. WPF does in fact use a Pen internally to draw the outline of a shape. The Stroke property is of type Brush mainly for convenience—all of the Pen features are exposed through separate properties on Shape, as shown in Table 7-1. This simplifies the markup in scenarios where you're happy to use the default pen settings—you don't need to provide a full Pen definition just to set the outline color.

Table 7-1. Shape Stroke properties and Pen equivalents

Shape property	Pen equivalent
Stroke	Brush
StrokeThickness	Thickness
StrokeLineJoin	LineJoin
StrokeMiterLimit	MiterLimit
StrokeDashArray	DashArray
StrokeDashCap	DashCap
StrokeDashOffset	DashOffset
StrokeStartLineCap	StartLineCap
StrokeEndLineCap	EndLineCap

Brushes and pens are described in detail in the "Brushes and Pens" section, later in this chapter.

Rectangle

Rectangle does what its name suggests. As with any shape, it can be drawn either filled in, as an outline, or both. As well as drawing a normal rectangle, it can also draw one with rounded corners.

Rectangle doesn't provide any properties for setting its size and location. It relies on the same layout mechanism as any other UI element. The location is determined by the containing panel. The width and height can either be set automatically by the parent, or they can be set explicitly using the standard layout properties, Width and Height.

Example 7-6 shows a Rectangle on a Canvas panel. Here, the Width and Height have been set explicitly, and the location has been specified using the attached Canvas.Left and Canvas.Top properties.

Example 7-6. Rectangle with explicit size and position

```
<Canvas>
    <Rectangle Fill="Yellow" Stroke="Black"
               Canvas.Left="30" Canvas.Top="10"
               Width="100" Height="20" />
</Canvas>
```

Example 7-7 shows the other approach. None of the rectangles have had their location or size set explicitly. They rely on the containing Grid, instead. Figure 7-10 shows the result.

Example 7-7. Rectangles with size and position controlled by parent

```
<Grid>
    <Grid.ColumnDefinitions>
        <ColumnDefinition />
        <ColumnDefinition />
    </Grid.ColumnDefinitions>

    <Grid.RowDefinitions>
        <RowDefinition />
        <RowDefinition />
    </Grid.RowDefinitions>

    <Rectangle Grid.Column="0" Grid.Row="0" Fill="LightGray" />
    <Rectangle Grid.Column="1" Grid.Row="0" Fill="Black" />
    <Rectangle Grid.Column="0" Grid.Row="1" Fill="DarkGray" />
    <Rectangle Grid.Column="1" Grid.Row="1" Fill="White" />
</Grid>
```

Figure 7-10. Rectangles arranged by a Grid

A Rectangle will usually be aligned with the coordinate system of its parent panel. This means that its edges will usually be horizontal and vertical, although if the parent panel has been rotated, the Rectangle will of course be rotated along with it. If you want to rotate a Rectangle relative to its containing panel, you can use the RenderTransform property available on all user-interface elements, as demonstrated in Example 7-8, which illustrates the use of RenderTransform to rotate a series of rectangles. The result is shown in Figure 7-11.

Example 7-8. Rotating rectangles

```
<Canvas>
    <Rectangle Canvas.Left="50" Canvas.Top="50" Width="40" Height="10"
      Fill="Indigo" />
    <Rectangle Canvas.Left="50" Canvas.Top="50" Width="40" Height="10"
      Fill="Violet" RenderTransform="rotate 45" />
    <Rectangle Canvas.Left="50" Canvas.Top="50" Width="40" Height="10"
      Fill="Blue" RenderTransform="rotate 90" />
    <Rectangle Canvas.Left="50" Canvas.Top="50" Width="40" Height="10"
      Fill="Cyan" RenderTransform="rotate 135" />
    <Rectangle Canvas.Left="50" Canvas.Top="50" Width="40" Height="10"
      Fill="Green" RenderTransform="rotate 180" />
    <Rectangle Canvas.Left="50" Canvas.Top="50" Width="40" Height="10"
      Fill="Yellow" RenderTransform="rotate 225" />
    <Rectangle Canvas.Left="50" Canvas.Top="50" Width="40" Height="10"
      Fill="Orange" RenderTransform="rotate 270" />
    <Rectangle Canvas.Left="50" Canvas.Top="50" Width="40" Height="10"
      Fill="Red" RenderTransform="rotate 315" />
</Canvas>
```

Figure 7-11. Rotated rectangles (Color Plate 21)

To draw a rectangle with rounded corners, use the RadiusX and RadiusY properties, as shown in Example 7-9. Figure 7-12 shows the result.

Example 7-9. Rounded rectangle

```
<Rectangle Width="100" Height="50" Fill="Black" RadiusX="30" RadiusY="40" />
```

Figure 7-12. Rectangle with rounded corners

Ellipse

Ellipse is similar to Rectangle. Obviously, it draws an ellipse rather than a rectangle, but the size, location, rotation, fill, and stroke of an Ellipse are controlled in exactly the same way as for a Rectangle, as Example 7-10 shows. The result is shown in Figure 7-13.

Example 7-10. Ellipse

```
<Ellipse Width="100" Height="50" Fill="Yellow" Stroke="Black" />
```

Figure 7-13. Ellipse

Line

The Line element draws a straight line from one point to another. It has four properties controlling the location of the start and end points: X1, Y1, X2, and Y2. These coordinates are relative to wherever the parent panel chooses to locate the Line. Consider Example 7-11.

Example 7-11. Two Lines in a StackPanel

```
<StackPanel Orientation="Vertical">
    <TextBlock Background="LightGray">Foo</TextBlock>
    <Line Stroke="Green" X1="20" Y1="10" X2="100" Y2="40" />
    <TextBlock Background="LightGray">Bar</TextBlock>
    <Line Stroke="Green" X1="0" Y1="10" X2="100" Y2="0" />
</StackPanel>
```

Example 7-11 uses a vertical StackPanel to arrange an alternating sequence of TextBlock and Line elements. The TextBlock elements have gray backgrounds to make it easier to see the vertical extent of each element. The results are shown in Figure 7-14.

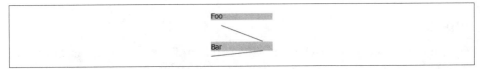

Figure 7-14. Two Lines in a StackPanel

As you can see from Figure 7-14, the Line elements have been placed in the stack just like any other element. The StackPanel has allocated enough height to hold the line. The first of the lines is interesting in that there is some space between the bottom of the TextBlock above it and the start of the line. This is because the line's Y1 property has been set to 10, indicating that the line should start slightly below the top of the location allocated for Line element. The second Line element goes all the way to the top because its Y2 property is set to 0, again illustrating that the coordinate system of the line endpoints is relative to the area allocated to the Line by the containing panel.

There is no way to set the line endpoints automatically as part of your layout. (The only reason you can rely on the layout system to position Ellipse and Rectangle elements is because their basic dimensions are determined by rectangles and the layout system essentially deals with rectangular arrangement.) For example, you cannot tell the Line to be exactly as wide as the space allocated by the parent panel. If you want to do this, just use the Rectangle instead—you can draw a line by creating a thin rectangle, rotating it if necessary. Or you could use a DrawingBrush or VisualBrush, as these can automatically scale drawings to fill the space available.

Polyline

A Polyline lets you draw a connected series of line segments. Instead of having properties for start and end points, Polyline has a Points property, containing a list of coordinate pairs, as shown in Example 7-12. WPF simply draws a line that goes through each of the points in turn, as shown in Figure 7-15.

Example 7-12. Polyline

```
<Polyline Stroke="Blue"
    Points="0,30 10,30 15,0 18,60 23,30 35,30 40,0 43,60 48,30 160,30" />
```

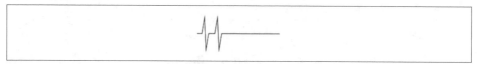

Figure 7-15. A Polyline

As with the Line class, the point coordinates in a Polyline are relative to wherever the containing panel chooses to locate the Polyline.

Polygon

Polygon is very similar to Polyline. It has a Points property that works in exactly the same way as Polyline's. The only difference is that while Polyline always draws an open shape, Polygon always draws a closed shape. To illustrate the difference, Example 7-13 contains a Polyline and a Polygon. All the same properties are set for both.

Example 7-13. A Polyline and a Polygon

```
<StackPanel Orientation="Horizontal">
  <Polyline Fill="Yellow" Stroke="Blue" Points="40,10 70,50 10,50" />
  <Polygon Fill="Yellow" Stroke="Blue" Points="40,10 70,50 10,50" />
</StackPanel>
```

As you can see in Figure 7-16, the `Polyline` has ignored the `Fill` property. The shape does not have an interior—it is left open. The `Polygon`, on the other hand, has closed the shape by drawing an extra line segment between the last and first points, and it has painted the interior of the shape.

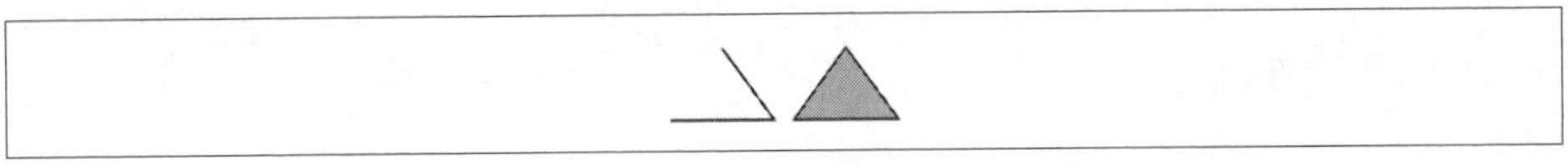

Figure 7-16. A Polyline and a Polygon

Because we are free to add points wherever we like to a `Polygon`, it is easy to end up with a self-intersecting shape, one whose edge crosses itself. With such shapes, there can be ambiguity about what counts as the interior of the shape. Figure 7-17 shows such a shape and two possible ways of filling it.

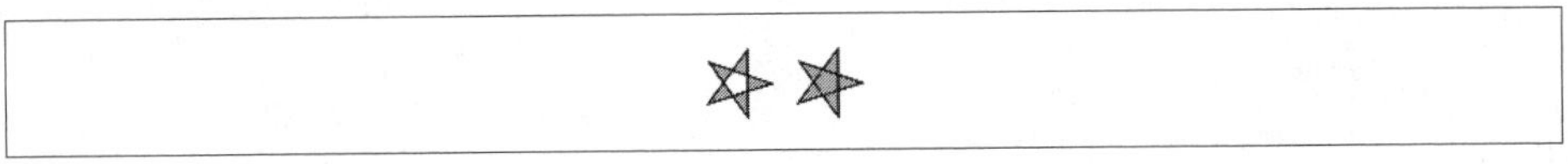

Figure 7-17. Two filling styles

The `Polygon` class provides a `FillRule` property to choose the way in which such potentially ambiguous regions are dealt with. (In some graphics systems, this is described as the *winding rule*.) WPF supports two fill rules. Example 7-14 is the markup for Figure 7-17 and shows both fill rules in use.

Example 7-14. Fill rules

```
<StackPanel Orientation="Horizontal">
  <Polygon Fill="Yellow" Stroke="Blue" FillRule="EvenOdd"
         Points="50,30 13,41 36,11 36,49 14,18" />
  <Polygon Fill="Yellow" Stroke="Blue" FillRule="Nonzero"
         Points="50,30 13,41 36,11 36,49 14,18" />
</StackPanel>
```

The default rule is `EvenOdd`, and this is used for the `Polygon` on the left of Figure 7-17. This is the simplest rule to understand. To determine whether a particular enclosed region is inside or outside the shape, the `EvenOdd` rule counts the number of lines you have to cross to get from that point to one completely outside of the shape. If this number is odd, the point is inside the shape. If it is even, the point is outside the shape.

The second fill rule, Nonzero, is more subtle. From Figure 7-17, you might have thought that any enclosed area was deemed to be inside the shape, but it's not quite that simple. The Nonzero rule performs a similar process to EvenOdd, but rather than simply counting the number of lines, it takes into account the direction in which the line is running. It either increments or decrements the count for each line it crosses, depending on the direction. If the sum total at the end is nonzero, the point is considered to be inside the shape.

In the Polygon on the right in Figure 7-17, the Nonzero rule has resulted in all enclosed regions being part of the interior. However, if the outline of the shape follows a slightly more convoluted path, the results can be a little more mixed, as Example 7-15 shows.

Example 7-15. Nonzero fill rule with more complex shape

```
<Polygon Fill="Yellow" Stroke="Blue" FillRule="Nonzero"
 Points="10,10 60,10 60,25 20,25 20,40 40,40 40,18 50,18 50,50 10,50" />
```

The results of Example 7-15 are shown in Figure 7-18. This illustrates that the Nonzero rule is not quite as straightforward as it may have first seemed.

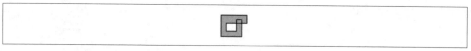

Figure 7-18. Nonzero rule in action

The Nonzero rule is a bit of an oddity. It was popularized by PostScript, so most drawing systems support it, but it's not always easy to get useful results from a Polygon with this fill rule. It makes more sense in the context of the Path element, which supports multiple figures in a single shape.

Path

Path is by far the most powerful shape. All of the shapes we have looked at up to now have been supplied for convenience, because it is possible to draw all of them with a Path. Path also makes it possible to draw considerably more complex shapes than is possible with the previous shapes we have seen.

Like Polygon, Path has a FillRule property to control the fill rule. In place of the Points property, Path has a Data property. Its type is Geometry, which is an abstract base class. A Geometry object represents a particular shape. There are various concrete classes for representing different kinds of shapes. Three of these will sound rather familiar: RectangleGeometry, EllipseGeometry, and LineGeometry. These represent the same shapes that we saw earlier. So this Rectangle:

```
<Rectangle Fill="Blue" Width="40" Height="80" />
```

is effectively shorthand for this Path:

```
<Path Fill="Blue">
  <Path.Data>
    <RectangleGeometry Rect="0, 0, 40, 80" />
  </Path.Data>
</Path>
```

At this point, you might be wondering when you would ever use RectangleGeometry, EllipseGeometry, or LineGeometry in a Path instead of the simpler Rectangle, Ellipse, and Line. The reason is that Path lets you use a special kind of geometry object called a GeometryGroup to create a shape with multiple geometries.

There is a significant difference between using multiple distinct shapes and having a single shape with multiple geometries. Let's look at an example (Example 7-16).

Example 7-16. Two Ellipses

```
<Canvas>
    <Ellipse Fill="Blue" Stroke="Black" Width="40" Height="80" />
    <Ellipse Canvas.Left="10" Canvas.Top="10" Fill="Blue" Stroke="Black"
            Width="20" Height="60" />
</Canvas>
```

This draws two ellipses, one on top of the other. They both have a black outline, so you can see the smaller one inside the larger one, as Figure 7-19 shows.

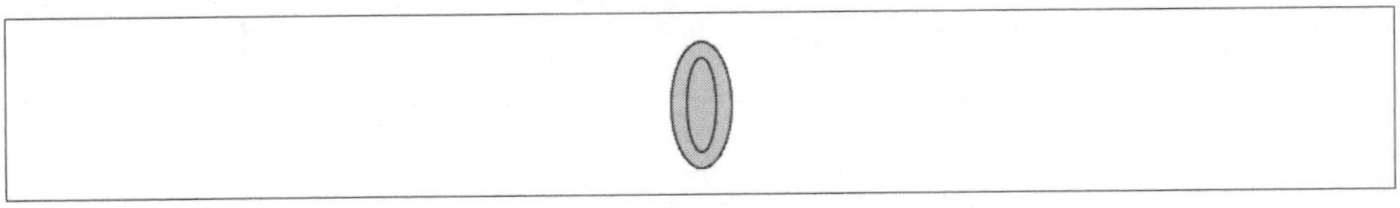

Figure 7-19. Two Ellipses

Since the Ellipse shape is just a simple way of creating an EllipseGeometry, the code in Example 7-16 is equivalent to the code in Example 7-17. (As you can see, using a Path is considerably more verbose. This is why the Ellipse and other simple shapes are provided.)

Example 7-17. Two Paths with EllipseGeometries

```
<Canvas>
    <Path Fill="Cyan" Stroke="Black">
        <Path.Data>
            <EllipseGeometry Center="20, 40" RadiusX="20" RadiusY="40" />
        </Path.Data>
    </Path>
    <Path Fill="Cyan" Stroke="Black">
        <Path.Data>
            <EllipseGeometry Center="20, 40" RadiusX="10" RadiusY="30" />
        </Path.Data>
    </Path>
</Canvas>
```

Because the code in Example 7-17 is equivalent to that in Example 7-16, it results in exactly the same output, as shown in Figure 7-19. So far, using geometries instead of shapes hasn't made a difference in the rendered results. This is because we are still using multiple shapes. So, we will now show how both ellipses can be put into a single Path and see how this affects the results. Example 7-18 shows the modified markup.

Example 7-18. One Path with two EllipseGeometries

```
<Canvas Canvas.Left="100">
    <Path Fill="Cyan" Stroke="Black">
        <Path.Data>
            <GeometryGroup>
                <EllipseGeometry Center="20, 40" RadiusX="20" RadiusY="40" />
                <EllipseGeometry Center="20, 40" RadiusX="10" RadiusY="30" />
            </GeometryGroup>
        </Path.Data>
    </Path>
</Canvas>
```

This version has just a single path. Its Data property contains a GeometryGroup. This allows any number of geometry objects to be added to the same path. Here we have added the two EllipseGeometry elements that were previously in two separate paths. The result, shown in Figure 7-20, is clearly different from the one in Figure 7-19—there is now a hole in the middle of the shape. Because the default even-odd fill rule was in play, the smaller ellipse makes a hole in the larger one.

Figure 7-20. Path with two geometries

Shapes with holes can be created only by combining multiple figures into a single shape. You could try to get a similar effect to that shown in Figure 7-20 by drawing the inner Ellipse with a Fill color of White, but that trick fails to work as soon as you draw the shape on top of something else, as Figure 7-21 shows.

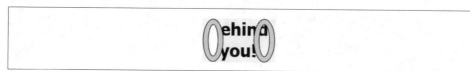

Figure 7-21. Spot the fake hole

You might be wondering if you could just draw the inner ellipse using the Transparent color, but that doesn't work either. Drawing something as totally transparent has the same effect as drawing nothing at all—that's what transparency means. Only by knocking a hole in the shape can we see through it.

To understand why, think about the drawing process. When it renders our elements to the screen, WPF draws the items one after the other. It starts with whatever's at the back—the text in this case. Then it draws the shape on top of the text—which will effectively obliterate the text that was underneath the shape. (It's still there in the element tree of course, so WPF can always redraw it later if you change or remove the shape.) Since you just drew over the text, you can't draw another shape on top to "undraw" a hole into the first shape. So if you want a hole in a shape, you'd better make sure that the hole is there before you draw the shape!

We have not yet looked at the most flexible geometry: PathGeometry. This can draw any shape that the Polyline or Polygon can represent, but it can draw many more besides.

A PathGeometry contains one or more PathFigure objects, and each PathFigure represents a single open or closed shape in the path. To define the shape of each figure's outline, you use a sequence of PathSegment objects.

PathGeometry's ability to contain multiple figures overlaps slightly with Path's ability to contain multiple geometries. This is just for convenience—if you need to make a shape where every piece will be a PathGeometry object, it is more compact to have a single PathGeometry with multiple PathFigures. If you just want to use simpler geometries like LineGeometry or RectangleGeometry, it is simpler to use a GeometryGroup and avoid PathGeometry altogether.

Example 7-19 shows a simple path. This contains just a single figure and draws a square.

Example 7-19. A square Path

```
<Path Fill="Cyan" Stroke="Black">
    <Path.Data>
        <PathGeometry>
            <PathGeometry.Figures>
                <PathFigure>
                    <PathFigure.Segments>
                        <StartSegment Point="0,0" />
                        <LineSegment Point="50,0" />
                        <LineSegment Point="50,50" />
                        <LineSegment Point="0,50" />
                        <CloseSegment />
                    </PathFigure.Segments>
```

Example 7-19. A square Path (continued)

```
            </PathFigure>
         </PathGeometry.Figures>
       </PathGeometry>
    </Path.Data>
</Path>
```

The result is shown in Figure 7-22. This seems like a vast amount of effort for such a simple result—we've used 17 lines of markup to achieve what could have been done with a single Rectangle element. This is why WPF supplies classes for the simpler shapes and geometries. You don't strictly need any of them because you can use Path and PathGeometry instead, but they require much less effort. Normally, you would use Path only for more complex shapes.

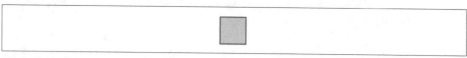

Figure 7-22. A square Path

Even though Example 7-19 produces a very simple result, it illustrates most of the important features of a Path with a PathGeometry. As with all the previous examples, the geometry is in the path's Data property. The PathGeometry is a collection of PathFigures, so all of the interesting data is inside its Figures property. This example contains just one PathFigure, but you can add as many as you like. The shape of the PathFigure is determined by the items in its Segments property.

The sequence of segments always begins with a StartSegment, which determines the starting point of the path. This is then followed by one or more segments that determine the shape of the figure. In Example 7-19, these are all LineSegments because the shape has only straight edges, but several types of curve are also on offer. Finally, this example ends with a CloseSegment, indicating that this is a closed shape. If we wanted to create an open shape (like a Polyline) we would simply omit the final CloseSegment.

You might be wondering why LineSegments don't work like the Line shape. With a Line, we specify start and end points, as in Example 7-11. This seems simpler than LineSegment, which needs us to begin with StartSegment.

However, line segments in a PathFigure can't work like that because there cannot be any gaps in the outline of a figure. With the Line element, each Line is a distinct shape in its own right, but with a PathFigure, each segment is a part of the shape's outline. To define a figure fully and unambiguously, each segment must start off from where the previous one finished. This is why the LineSegment specifies only an end point for the line. All of the segment types work this way. Of course, the figure needs to start somewhere, which is why we always begin with a StartSegment. It is illegal to use StartSegment anywhere other than at the start of a figure.

Example 7-19 isn't very exciting—it just uses straight line segments. We can create much more interesting shapes by using one of the curved segment types instead. Table 7-2 shows all of the segment types.

Table 7-2. Segment types

Segment type	Usage
StartSegment	Sets the starting point of the first segment of the figure.
CloseSegment	Indicates that this is a closed figure; where used, this must be the last segment.
LineSegment	Single straight line.
PolyLineSegment	Sequence of straight lines.
ArcSegment	Elliptical arc.
BezierSegment	Cubic Bézier curve.
QuadraticBezierSegment	Quadratic Bézier curve.
PolyBezierSegment	Sequence of cubic Bézier curves.
PolyQuadraticBezierSegment	Sequence of quadratic Bézier curves.

ArcSegment lets you add elliptical curves to the edge of a shape. ArcSegment is a little more complex to use than a simple LineSegment. As well as specifying the end point of the segment, we must also specify two radii for the ellipse with the Size property.

The ellipse size and the line start and end points don't provide enough information to define the curve unambiguously, because there are several ways to draw an elliptical arc given these constraints. Consider a segment with a particular start and end point, and a given size and orientation of ellipse. For this segment there will usually be two ways in which the ellipse can be positioned so that both the start and end point lie on the boundary of the ellipse, as Figure 7-23 shows. In other words, there will be two ways of "slicing" an ellipse with a particular line.

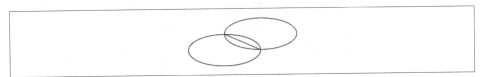

Figure 7-23. Potential ellipse positions

For each of these two ways of slicing the ellipse, there will be two resulting segments, a small one and a large one. This means that there are four ways in which the curve can be drawn between two points.

ArcSegment provides two flags enabling you to select which of the curves you require. LargeArc determines whether you get the larger or smaller slice size. SweepFlag chooses which side of the line the slice is drawn on. Example 7-20 shows markup illustrating all four combinations of these flags. It also shows the whole ellipse.

Example 7-20. ArcSegments

```
<Canvas>
    <Ellipse Fill="Cyan" Stroke="Black" Width="140" Height="60" />
    <Path Fill="Cyan" Stroke="Black" Canvas.Left="180">
        <Path.Data>
            <PathGeometry>
                <PathFigure>
                    <StartSegment Point="0,11" />
                    <ArcSegment Point="50,61" Size="70,30"
                                SweepFlag="False" LargeArc="False" />
                    <CloseSegment />
                </PathFigure>
                <PathFigure>
                    <StartSegment Point="30,11" />
                    <ArcSegment Point="80,61" Size="70,30"
                                SweepFlag="True" LargeArc="True" />
                    <CloseSegment />
                </PathFigure>
                <PathFigure>
                    <StartSegment Point="240,1" />
                    <ArcSegment Point="290,51" Size="70,30"
                                SweepFlag="False" LargeArc="True" />
                    <CloseSegment />
                </PathFigure>
                <PathFigure>
                    <StartSegment Point="280,1" />
                    <ArcSegment Point="330,51" Size="70,30"
                                SweepFlag="True" LargeArc="False" />
                    <CloseSegment />
                </PathFigure>
            </PathGeometry>
        </Path.Data>
    </Path>
</Canvas>
```

 You may be wondering why the Ellipse has a width of 140 and a height of 60, which is double the Size of each ArcSegment. This is because the ArcSegment interprets the Size as the two radii of the ellipse, while the Width and Height properties on the Ellipse indicate the total size.

Figure 7-24 shows the results, and, as you can see, each of the shapes has one straight diagonal line and one elliptical curve. The straight-line edge has the same length and orientation in all four cases. The curved edge is from different parts of the same ellipse.

In Figure 7-24, the ellipse's axes are horizontal and vertical. Sometimes you will want to use an ellipse where the axes are not aligned with your main drawing axes. ArcSegment provides an XRotation property, allowing you to specify the amount of rotation required in degrees.

Figure 7-24. An ellipse and four arcs from that ellipse

Figure 7-25 shows four elliptical arcs. These use the same start and end points as Figure 7-24 and the same ellipse size. The only difference is that an XRotation of 45 degrees has been specified, rotating the ellipse before slicing it.

Figure 7-25. Four arcs from a rotated ellipse

 There are two degenerate cases in which there will not be two ways of slicing the ellipse. The first is when the slice cuts the ellipse exactly in half. In this case, the LargeArc flag is irrelevant, because both slices are exactly the same size.

The other case is when the ellipse is too small—if the widest point at which the ellipse could be sliced is narrower than the segment is long, there is no way in which the segment can be drawn correctly. You should try to avoid this. (If you do make the ellipse too small, WPF seems to scale up the ellipse so that it is large enough, preserving the aspect ratio between the x- and y-axes.)

The remaining four curve types from Table 7-2—BezierSegment, PolyBezierSegment, QuadraticBezierSegment, and PolyQuadraticBezierSegment—are all variations on the same theme. They all draw Bézier curves.

Bézier curves

Bézier curves are curved line segments joining two points based on a particular mathematical formula. It is not necessary to understand the details of the formula in order to use Bézier curves. What makes Bézier curves useful is that they offer a fair amount of flexibility in the shape of the curve. This has made them very popular—most vector drawing programs offer them. (If you'd like to understand the formula, *http://mathworld.wolfram.com/BezierCurve.html* and *http://en.wikipedia.org/wiki/Bézier_curve* both provide good descriptions.) Figure 7-26 shows a variety of Bézier curve segments.

Figure 7-26. Bézier curve segments

Each of the five lines shown in Figure 7-26 is a single BezierSegment. Bézier curves have become very widely used in graphics systems because of the wide variation in shapes that even a single segment can offer. They are also fairly straightforward to use.

As with all of the segment types, a BezierSegment starts from where the previous segment left off and defines a new end point. It also requires two *control points* to be defined, and it is these that determine the shape of the curve. Figure 7-27 shows the same curves again, but with the control points drawn on. It also shows lines connecting the control points to the segment end points, because this makes it easier to see how the control points affect the curve shapes.

Figure 7-27. Bézier curves with control points shown

The most obvious way in which the control points are influencing the shapes of the curves is that they determine the tangent. At the start and end of each segment, the direction in which the curve runs at that point is exactly the same as the direction of the line joining the start point to the corresponding control point.

There is a second, less obvious way in which control points work. The distance between the start or end point and its corresponding control point (i.e., the length of the straight lines added on Figure 7-27) also has an effect. This essentially determines how extreme the curvature is.

Figure 7-28 shows a set of Bézier curves similar to those in Figure 7-27. The tangents of both ends of the lines remain the same, but, in each case, the distance between the start point and the first control point is reduced to one quarter of what it was before, while the other is the same as before. As you can see, this reduces the influence of the first control point. In all four cases, the shape of the curve is dominated by the control point that is further from its endpoint.

Figure 7-28. Bézier curves with less extreme control points

Example 7-21 shows the markup for the second curve segment in Figure 7-27. The Point1 property determines the location of the first control point—the one associated with the start point. Point2 positions the second control point. Point3 is the end point.

Example 7-21. BezierSegment

```
<StartSegment Point="0,50" />
<BezierSegment Point1="60,50" Point2="100,0" Point3="100,50" />
```

Flexible though Bézier curves are, you will rarely use just a single one. When defining shapes with curved edges, it is more common for a shape to have many Bézier curves defining its edge. WPF therefore supplies a `PolyBezierSegment` type, which allows multiple curves to be represented in a single segment. It defines a single `Points` property, which is an array of `Point` structures. Each Bézier curve requires three entries in this array: two control points and an end point. (As always, each curve starts from where the previous one left off.) Example 7-22 shows a sample segment with two curves. Figure 7-29 shows the results.

Example 7-22. PolyBezierSegment

```
<StartSegment Point="0,0" />
<PolyBezierSegment>
    <PolyBezierSegment.Points>
        <Point X="0" Y="10"/>
        <Point X="20" Y="10"/>
        <Point X="40" Y="10"/>
        <Point X="60" Y="10"/>
        <Point X="120" Y="15"/>
        <Point X="100" Y="50"/>
    </PolyBezierSegment.Points>
</PolyBezierSegment>
```

Figure 7-29. PolyBezierSegment

This markup is somewhat less convenient than simply using a sequence of `BezierSegment` elements. Fortunately, you can provide all of the point data in string form. This is equivalent to Example 7-22:

```
<PolyBezierSegment Points="0,10 20,10 40,10 60,10 120,15 100,50" />
```

Also, if you are generating coordinates from code, dealing with a single `PolyBezierSegment` and passing it an array of `Point` data is easier than working with lots of individual segments.

Cubic Bézier curves provide a lot of control over the shape of the curve. However, you might not always want that level of flexibility. The `QuadraticBezierSegment` uses a simpler equation that uses just one control point to define the shape of the curve. This does not offer the same range of curve shapes as a cubic Bézier curve, but if all you want is a simple shape, this reduces the number of coordinate pairs you need to provide by one third.

QuadraticBezierSegment is similar in use to the normal BezierSegment. The only difference is that it has no Point3 property—just Point1 and Point2. Point1 is the shared control point, and Point2 is the end point. PolyQuadraticBezierSegment is the multicurve equivalent. You use this in exactly the same way as PolyBezierSegment, except you only need to provide two points for each segment.

Combining shapes

Path has one more trick up its sleeve that we have not yet examined. It is capable of combining geometries to form new geometries. This is different from adding two geometries to a Path—it combines pairs of geometries in a way that forms a single geometry with a whole new shape.

Example 7-23 and Example 7-24 each define paths, both of which make use of the same RectangleGeometry and EllipseGeometry. The difference is that Example 7-23 puts both into a GeometryGroup, while Example 7-24 puts them into a CombinedGeometry.

Example 7-23. Multiple geometries

```
<Path Fill="Cyan" Stroke="Black">
    <Path.Data>
        <GeometryGroup>
            <RectangleGeometry Rect="0,0,50,50" />
            <EllipseGeometry Center="50,25" RadiusX="30" RadiusY="10" />
        </GeometryGroup>
    </Path.Data>
</Path>
```

Example 7-24. Combined geometries

```
<Path Fill="Cyan" Stroke="Black">
    <Path.Data>
        <CombinedGeometry CombineMode="Exclude">
            <CombinedGeometry.Geometry1>
                <RectangleGeometry Rect="0,0,50,50" />
            </CombinedGeometry.Geometry1>
            <CombinedGeometry.Geometry2>
                <EllipseGeometry Center="50,25" RadiusX="30" RadiusY="10" />
            </CombinedGeometry.Geometry2>
        </CombinedGeometry>
    </Path.Data>
</Path>
```

Figure 7-30 shows the results of Example 7-23 and Example 7-24. While the GeometryGroup has resulted in a shape with multiple figures, the CombinedGeometry has produced a single figure. The ellipse geometry has taken a bite out of the rectangle geometry. This is just one of the ways in which geometries can be combined. The CombineMode property determines which is used, and Figure 7-31 shows all five available modes.

Figure 7-30. Grouping and combining geometries

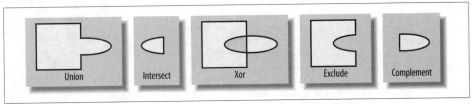

Figure 7-31. Combine modes: Union, Intersect, Xor, Exclude, and Complement

The combine modes have the following effects:

Union

Builds a shape where any point that was inside either of the two original shapes will also be inside the new shape.

Intersect

Creates a shape where only points that were inside both shapes will be in the new shape.

Xor

Creates a shape where points that were in one shape or the other but not both will be in the new shape.

Exclude

Creates a shape where points inside the first shape but not inside the second will be included.

Complement

Builds a shape where points inside the second but not inside the first shape will be included in the new shape.

Data property text format

We have now looked at all of the features that Path has to offer. As you have seen, we can end up with some pretty verbose markup. Fortunately, the Path element offers a shorthand mechanism that allows most of the features we have seen to be exploited without having to type quite so much.

So far, we have been setting the Data property using XAML's property-element syntax (see Appendix A for more details on this syntax). However, we can supply a string instead. Example 7-25 shows both techniques. As you can see, the string form is some 16 lines shorter.

Example 7-25. Path.Data as text

```
<!-- Longhand -->
<Path Fill="Cyan" Stroke="Black">
    <Path.Data>
        <PathGeometry>
            <PathGeometry.Figures>
                <PathFigure>
                    <PathFigure.Segments>
                        <StartSegment Point="0,0" />
                        <LineSegment Point="50,0" />
                        <LineSegment Point="50,50" />
                        <LineSegment Point="0,50" />
                        <CloseSegment />
                    </PathFigure.Segments>
                </PathFigure>
            </PathGeometry.Figures>
        </PathGeometry>
    </Path.Data>
</Path>

<!-- Shorthand -->
<Path Fill="Cyan" Stroke="Black" Data="M 0,0 L 50,0 50,50 0,50 Z" />
```

The syntax for the text form of the Path.Data property is simple. The string must contain a sequence of commands. A command is a letter followed by some numeric parameters. The number of parameters required is determined by the chosen command. Lines require just a coordinate pair. Curves require more data.

If you omit the letter, the same command will be used as last time. For example, Example 7-25 uses the L command—this is short for "Line" and represents a LineSegment. This requires only two numbers, the coordinates of the line end point. And yet in our example, there are six numbers. This simply indicates that there are three lines in a row. Table 7-3 lists the commands, their equivalent segment type, and their usage.

Table 7-3. Path.Data commands

Command	Command name	Segment type	Parameters
M (or m)	Move	StartSegment	Coordinate pair: start point
L (or l)	Line	LineSegment	Coordinate pair: end point
H (or h)	Horizontal Line	LineSegment	Single coordinate: end x-coordinate (y-coordinate will be the same as before)
V (or v)	Vertical Line	LineSegment	Single coordinate: end y-oordinate (x-coordinate will be the same as before)
C (or c)	Cubic Bézier Curve	BezierSegment	Three coordinate pairs: two control points and end point
Q (or q)	Quadratic Bézier Curve	QuadraticBezierSegment	Two coordinate pairs: control point and end point

Table 7-3. Path.Data commands (continued)

Command	Command name	Segment type	Parameters
S (or s)	Smooth Bézier Curve	BezierSegment	Two coordinates: second control point and end point (first control point generated automatically)
A (or a)	Elliptical Arc	ArcSegment	Seven numbers: Size pair, Rotation, LargeArc, SweepFlag, end point coordinate pair
Z (or z)	Close path	CloseSegment	None

The M command gets special treatment. It is illegal to use a StartSegment anywhere other than as the first segment of a PathFigure. If you use an M command in the middle of the data, this is taken to mean that you would like to start a new PathFigure. This enables multiple figures to be represented in this compact text format.

Notice that there are two ways of specifying a BezierSegment. The C command lets you provide all of the control points. The S command generates the first control point for you—it looks at the previous segment, and makes the first control point a mirror image of the previous one. This ensures that the segment's tangent aligns with the previous segment's tangent, resulting in a smooth join between the lines.

All of these commands can be used in two ways. You can specify the command in either uppercase or lowercase. In the uppercase form, coordinates are relative to the position of the Path element. If the command is lowercase, the coordinates are taken to be relative to the end point of the previous segment in the path.

We have now examined all of the shapes on offer, but so far, we have been rather unadventurous in our choice of fills and outlines for these shapes. We have used nothing but standard named colors and simple outline styles. WPF allows us a much greater variety of drawing styles through its brush and pen classes.

Brushes and Pens

In order to draw a shape onscreen, WPF needs to know how you would like that shape to be colored in and how its outline should be drawn. WPF provides several Brush types supporting a variety of painting styles. The Pen class augments this to provide information about stroke thickness, dash patterns, and the like.

In this section, we will look at all of the available brush types and the Pen class. However, since all brushes and pens are ultimately about deciding what colors to use where, and how they are combined, we must first look at how colors are represented.

Color

WPF uses the Color structure in the System.Windows.Media namespace to represent a color. Note that if you have worked with Windows Forms, ASP.NET, or GDI+ in the past, this is not the same structure those technologies use. They use the Color structure in the System.Drawing namespace. WPF introduces this new Color structure because it can work with floating-point color values, enabling much higher color precision, and greater flexibility.

The Color structure uses four numbers, or *channels*, to represent a color. These channels are red, green, blue, and alpha. Red, green, and blue channels are the traditional way of representing color in computer graphics. (This is because color screens work by mixing together these three primary colors.) A value of zero indicates that the color component is not present at all; zero on all three channels corresponds to black. The alpha channel represents the level of opacity—a Color can be opaque, completely transparent, or anywhere in between these two extremes. WPF's composition engine supports transparency fully, so anything can be drawn with any level of transparency. Zero is used to represent complete transparency.

Windows has traditionally used 24 bits of color information, 8 bits per channel, to represent "true" or "full" color, and 32 bits for full color with transparency. This is just about sufficient for the average computer screen—the color and brightness range of normal computer displays is such that 24 bits of color has always been adequate for most purposes. However, for many imaging applications, this is not sufficient. For example, film can accommodate a much wider range of brightness than a computer screen, and 24-bit color is simply not adequate for graphics work with film as its output medium. The same is true for many medical imaging applications. And even for computer or video images, 24-bit color can cause problems—if images are going through many stages of processing, these can amplify the limitations of 24-bit source material.

WPF therefore supports a much higher level of detail in its representation of color. Each color channel uses 16 bits instead of 8. The Color structure still supports the use of 8-bit channels where required, because a lot of imaging software depends on such a representation. Color exposes the 8-bit channels through the A, R, G, and B properties, which accept values in the range 0 to 255.* The higher definition representations are available through the ScA, ScR, ScG, and ScB properties, which present the channels as single-precision floating-point values ranging from 0 to 1.

---

* The old GDI+ Color structure exposed 8-bit properties of the same names, which may be useful if you need to port code.

The "Sc" in the ScA, ScR, ScG, and ScB properties refers to the fact that they support the standard "Extended RGB colour space—scRGB" color space defined in the IEC 61966-2-2 specification. (This is an international specification, hence the "u" in "colour.") The "sc" is short for "scene" because this is nominally a *scene-referred* color space. This means that color values in the scRGB space represent the colors of the original image. This is different from how computer images are often stored—traditionally we have used *output-referred* color spaces, where the color values do not need to be mapped before being displayed on the target device.

Output-referred color spaces are efficient to work with, as long as they happen to target the output device type you are working with. However, scene-referred color spaces preserve all of the information that was available at the point at which the image was generated or captured. For highly accurate color representation, scene-referred models are therefore clearly better, even though they are slightly less efficient to work with.

There is also a Colors class. This provides a set of standard named colors, with all the old favorites such as PapayaWhip, BurlyWood, LightGoldenrodYellow, and Brown.

You cannot use a Color directly for drawing. To draw, you need either a Brush or a Pen.

SolidColorBrush

SolidColorBrush is the simplest brush. It uses one color across the whole area being painted. It has just one property, Color. Note that this color is allowed to use transparency, despite what the word "solid" suggests.

We have already been using the SolidColorBrush extensively even though we have not yet referred to it by name. This is because WPF creates this kind of brush if you specify the name of a color in markup—if you work mostly with markup, you very rarely need to specify that you require a SolidColorBrush, because you'll get one by default. (The only reason you would normally specify it in full is if you want to use data binding with the brush's properties.) Consider this example:

```
<Rectangle Fill="Yellow" Width="100" Height="20" />
```

The XAML compiler will recognize Yellow as one of the standard named colors from the Colors class, and will supply a suitable SolidColorBrush. (See Appendix A for more information on how XAML maps from strings to property values.) It does not need to create the brush, because there is a Brushes class, providing a set of brushes for each of the named colors in Colors.

You will also be provided with a SolidColorBrush if your markup uses a numeric color value. Example 7-26 shows various examples of numeric colors. They all begin with a # symbol and contain hexadecimal digits. A three-digit number is taken to be one digit each of red, green, and blue. A four-digit number is interpreted as alpha, red, green, and blue. These are compact formats, but provide just four bits per channel. Six- or eight-digit numbers allow eight bits per channel for RGB or ARGB, respectively. (To exploit the full 16-bit accuracy of scRGB, you would need to set the property using property-element syntax—there is no text shorthand. See Appendix A for more information on XAML's property-element syntax.)

Example 7-26. Numeric color values

```
<Rectangle Fill="#8f8"      Width="100" Height="20" />
<Rectangle Fill="#1168ff"   Width="50" Height="40" />
<Rectangle Fill="#8ff0"     Width="130" Height="10" />
<Rectangle Fill="#72ff8890" Width="70" Height="30" />
```

The SolidColorBrush is lightweight and straightforward. However, it makes for fairly flat-looking visuals. WPF offers some more interesting brushes if you want to make your user interface look a little more appealing.

LinearGradientBrush

With a LinearGradientBrush, the painted area transitions from one color to another, or even through a sequence of colors. Figure 7-32 shows a simple example.

Figure 7-32. LinearGradientBrush

This brush fades from black to white, starting at the top-left corner and finishing at the bottom-right corner. The fade always runs in a straight line—you cannot do curved transitions, hence the name "linear." Example 7-27 shows the markup for Figure 7-32.

Example 7-27. Using a LinearGradientBrush

```
<Rectangle Width="80" Height="60">
    <Rectangle.Fill>
        <LinearGradientBrush StartPoint="0,0" EndPoint="1,1">
            <LinearGradientBrush.GradientStops>
                <GradientStop Color="Black" Offset="0" />
                <GradientStop Color="White" Offset="1" />
            </LinearGradientBrush.GradientStops>
        </LinearGradientBrush>
    </Rectangle.Fill>
</Rectangle>
```

The StartPoint and EndPoint properties indicate where the color transition begins and ends. These coordinates are relative to the area being filled, so 0,0 is the top left and 1,1 is the bottom right, as shown in Figure 7-33. (Note that if the brush is painting an area that is narrow or wide, the coordinate system is squashed accordingly.)

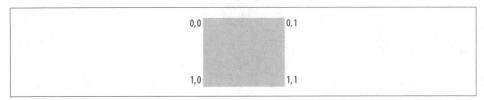

Figure 7-33. Fill coordinate system

Example 7-27 uses the property-element syntax to initialize the brush. In this particular example, this wasn't strictly necessary, because XAML supports a more compact syntax. This is exactly equivalent to Example 7-27:

```
<Rectangle Width="80" Height="60" Fill="LinearGradient 0,0 1,1 Black White" />
```

This compact syntax allows the most important aspects to be set. The two pairs of numbers correspond to the StartPoint and EndPoint properties, and the remaining two items are color names. If you want the gradient to be vertical or horizontal, you can use an even simpler syntax:

```
<Rectangle Width="80" Height="60" Fill="VerticalGradient Black White" />
<Rectangle Width="80" Height="60" Fill="HorizontalGradient Black White" />
```

In all of these string representations, the start and end color are specified. These correspond to the GradientStop elements in Example 7-27. Notice that in the fully expanded compound-property version, each GradientStop has an Offset property as well as a Color. This enables the more verbose style to achieve something that the string representations cannot. It allows the fill to pass through multiple colors. Example 7-28 shows a LinearGradientBrush with multiple colors.

Example 7-28. Multiple gradient stops

```
<Rectangle Width="80" Height="60">
  <Rectangle.Fill>
    <LinearGradientBrush StartPoint="0,0" EndPoint="1,1">
      <LinearGradientBrush.GradientStops>
        <GradientStop Color="Black" Offset="0" />
        <GradientStop Color="Orange" Offset="0.2" />
        <GradientStop Color="Red" Offset="0.4" />
        <GradientStop Color="Black" Offset="0.6" />
        <GradientStop Color="Blue" Offset="0.8" />
        <GradientStop Color="White" Offset="1" />
      </LinearGradientBrush.GradientStops>
    </LinearGradientBrush>
  </Rectangle.Fill>
</Rectangle>
```

The result is shown in Figure 7-34. Note that the shorthand string syntaxes shown earlier do not support multiple color values—you have to use the full property-element syntax if you want this effect.

Figure 7-34. Multiple gradient stops (Color Plate 22)

LinearGradientBrush is often used to add a feeling of depth to a user interface. Example 7-29 shows a typical example. It uses just two shapes—a pair of rounded Rectangle elements. (The Grid doesn't contribute directly to the appearance. It is there to make it easy to resize the graphic—changing the grid's Width and Height will cause both rectangles to resize appropriately.) The second rectangle's gradient fill fades from a partially transparent shade of white to a completely transparent color, which provides an interesting visual effect.

Example 7-29. Simulating lighting effects with linear fills

```
<Grid Width="80" Height="26">
    <Grid.RowDefinitions>
        <RowDefinition Height="2*" />
        <RowDefinition Height="*" />
    </Grid.RowDefinitions>

    <Rectangle Grid.RowSpan="2" RadiusX="13" RadiusY="13"
            Fill="VerticalGradient Green DarkGreen"
            Stroke="VerticalGradient Black LightGray" />
    <Rectangle Margin="3,2" RadiusX="8" RadiusY="12"
            Fill="VerticalGradient #dfff #0fff" />
</Grid>
```

Figure 7-35 shows the result. This is an extremely simple graphic, containing just two shapes. The use of gradient fills has added an impression of depth that these shapes would otherwise not have conveyed.

Figure 7-35. Simple lighting effects with linear fills (Color Plate 23)

RadialGradientBrush

RadialGradientBrush is very similar to LinearGradientBrush. Both allow transitions through a series of colors. But while LinearGradientBrush paints these transitions in a straight line, the RadialGradientBrush fades from a starting point out to an elliptical boundary. This opens up more opportunities for making your user interface appear less flat, as shown in Example 7-30.

Example 7-30. Using a RadialGradientBrush

```
<Rectangle Width="200" Height="150">
    <Rectangle.Fill>
        <RadialGradientBrush Center="0.5,0.4" RadiusX="0.3" RadiusY="0.5"
                             GradientOrigin="0.25,0.4">
            <RadialGradientBrush.GradientStops>
                <GradientStop Color="White" Offset="0" />
                <GradientStop Color="DarkBlue" Offset="1" />
            </RadialGradientBrush.GradientStops>
        </RadialGradientBrush>
    </Rectangle.Fill>
</Rectangle>
```

The RadialGradientBrush takes a list of GradientStop objects to determine the colors that the fill runs through, just like LinearGradientBrush. This example uses the RadiusX and RadiusY properties to determine the size of the elliptical boundary, and the Center property to set the position of the ellipse. The values chosen here make the fill boundary fit entirely into the shape, as Figure 7-36 shows. The area of the shape that falls outside of this boundary is filled with the color of the final GradientStop. Notice that the focal point of the fill is to the left. This is because the GradientOrigin has been set. (By default, the focal point is in the center of the ellipse.)

Figure 7-36. Simple radial fill (Color Plate 24)

Example 7-30 makes it easy to see the effects of the properties of the RadialGradientBrush, but it's not a very exciting example. Example 7-31 shows something a little more adventurous. It is similar to Example 7-29—it uses a small number of shapes with gradient fills to convey a feeling of depth and reflection, but this time using radial fills.

Example 7-31. Radial gradient fills

```
<Grid Width="16" Height="16" Margin="0,0,5,0" >
    <Grid.ColumnDefinitions>
        <ColumnDefinition Width="*" />
        <ColumnDefinition Width="10*" />
        <ColumnDefinition Width="*" />
    </Grid.ColumnDefinitions>

    <Grid.RowDefinitions>
        <RowDefinition Height="*" />
        <RowDefinition Height="20*" />
```

Example 7-31. Radial gradient fills (continued)

```
        <RowDefinition Height="6*" />
    </Grid.RowDefinitions>



    <Ellipse Grid.RowSpan="3" Grid.ColumnSpan="3" Margin="0.5">
        <Ellipse.Fill>
            <RadialGradientBrush Center="0.5,0.9" RadiusX="0.7" RadiusY="0.5">
                <RadialGradientBrush.GradientStops>
                    <GradientStop Color="PaleGreen" Offset="0" />
                    <GradientStop Color="Green" Offset="1" />
                </RadialGradientBrush.GradientStops>
            </RadialGradientBrush>
        </Ellipse.Fill>
    </Ellipse>
    <Ellipse Grid.Row="1" Grid.Column="1">
        <Ellipse.Fill>
            <RadialGradientBrush Center="0.5,0.1" RadiusX="0.7" RadiusY="0.5">
                <RadialGradientBrush.GradientStops>
                    <GradientStop Color="#efff" Offset="0" />
                    <GradientStop Color="Transparent" Offset="1" />
                </RadialGradientBrush.GradientStops>
            </RadialGradientBrush>
        </Ellipse.Fill>
    </Ellipse>
    <Ellipse Grid.RowSpan="3" Grid.ColumnSpan="3"
            Stroke="VerticalGradient Gray LightGray" />

</Grid>
```

This time, three ellipses have been used, two with `RadialGradientBrush` fills and one with a `LinearGradientBrush` stroke. The fill in the first ellipse creates the glow at the bottom of the drawing. The second adds the reflective highlight at the top. The third draws a bezel around the outside. The result is shown in Figure 7-37. The radial fills suggest a curved surface and give the graphic a slightly translucent look.

Figure 7-37. Radial fills (Color Plate 25)

ImageBrush, DrawingBrush, and VisualBrush

It is often useful to fill shapes with a pattern or image of some kind. WPF provides three brushes that allow us to use whatever graphics we choose as a brush. The `ImageBrush` lets us paint with a bitmap. With `DrawingBrush` we use a scalable drawing.

VisualBrush allows us to use any markup at all as the brush image—we can, in effect, use one piece of our user interface to paint another.

All of these brushes have a certain amount in common, so they all derive from the same base class, TileBrush.

TileBrush

ImageBrush, DrawingBrush, and VisualBrush all paint using some form of source picture. Their base class, TileBrush, decides how to stretch the source image to fill the available space, whether to repeat ("tile") the image, and how to position the image within the shape. (TileBrush is an abstract base class, so you cannot use it directly. It exists to define the API common to the ImageBrush, DrawingBrush, and VisualBrush.)

Figure 7-38 shows the default TileBrush behavior. This figure shows three rectangles so that you can see what happens when the brush is made narrow or wide, as well as the effect when the brush shape matches the target-area shape. All three are rectangles painted with an ImageBrush specifying nothing more than the image.

Figure 7-38. Default stretching and placement (Stretch.Fill)

While Figure 7-38 was drawn with an ImageBrush, the behavior would be exactly the same for any of the tile brushes. We'll look at the ImageBrush in more detail shortly, but for now Example 7-32 shows the basic usage.

Example 7-32. Using an ImageBrush

```
<Rectangle>
    <Rectangle.Fill>
        <ImageBrush ImageSource="Images\Moggie.jpg" />
    </Rectangle.Fill>
</Rectangle>
```

The brush has stretched the source image to fill the available space. We can change this behavior by modifying the brush's Stretch property. It defaults to Fill, but we can show the image at its native size by specifying None, as Example 7-33 shows.

Example 7-33. Specifying a Stretch of None

```
<Rectangle>
    <Rectangle.Fill>
        <ImageBrush ImageSource="Images\Moggie.jpg" Stretch="None" />
    </Rectangle.Fill>
</Rectangle>
```

This preserves the aspect ratio, but if the image is large, it will simply be cropped to fit the space available, as Figure 7-39 shows.

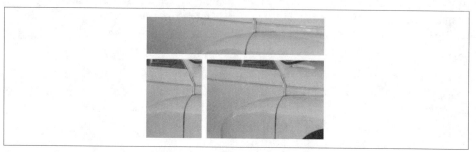

Figure 7-39. Stretch.None

For displaying images, you may be more likely to want to stretch the image to match the available space without distorting the aspect ratio. TileBrush supports this with the Uniform stretch mode, shown in Figure 7-40. This scales the source image down so that it fits entirely within the space available.

Figure 7-40. Stretch.Uniform

The Uniform stretch mode typically results in the image being made smaller than the area being filled. The default behavior is to paint the image wherever the alignment properties specify and to leave the remainder of the shape transparent. However, you can choose other behaviors for the spare space with the TileMode property. The default is None, but if you specify Tile, as in Example 7-34, the image will be repeated to fill the space available.

Example 7-34. Specifying a Stretch and a TileMode

```
<Rectangle>
    <Rectangle.Fill>
        <ImageBrush ImageSource="Images\Moggie.jpg"
                    Stretch="Uniform" TileMode="Tile" />
    </Rectangle.Fill>
</Rectangle>
```

Figure 7-41 shows the effect of the Uniform stretch mode and the Tile tile mode combined. There is one potential problem with tiling. It can often be very obvious where each repeated tile starts. If your goal was simply to fill in an area with a texture, these discontinuities can jar somewhat. To alleviate this, TileBrush supports three other modes of tiling: FlipX, FlipY, and FlipXY. These alternate mirror images, as shown in Figure 7-42. Although mirroring can reduce the discontinuity between tiles, for some source images it can change the look of the brush quite substantially.

Figure 7-41. Stretch="Uniform" and TileMode="Tile"

Figure 7-42. TileMode="FlipXY"

An alternative to tiling is to scale the image so that it completely fills the space available while preserving the aspect ratio, cropping in one dimension if necessary. The UniformToFill stretch mode does this and is shown in Figure 7-43.

UniformToFill is most appropriate if you are filling an area with some non-repeating textured pattern, because it guarantees it will paint the whole area. It is probably less appropriate if your goal is simply to display a picture—as Figure 7-43 shows, this stretch mode will crop images where necessary. If you want to show the whole picture, Uniform is the best choice.

Figure 7-43. Stretch.UniformToFill

All of the stretch modes except for `Fill` present an extra question: how should the image be positioned? With `None` and `UniformToFill`, cropping occurs, so WPF needs to decide which part of the image to show. With `Uniform`, the image may be smaller than the space being filled, so WPF needs to decide where to put it.

Images are centered by default. In the examples where the image has been cropped (Figures 7-39 and 7-43) the most central parts are shown. In the case of `Uniform`, where the image is smaller than the area being painted, it has been placed in the middle of that area (Figure 7-40). You can change this with the `AlignmentX` and `AlignmentY` properties. These can be set to `Left`, `Middle`, or `Right`, and `Top`, `Middle`, or `Bottom`, respectively. Example 7-35 shows the `UniformToFill` stretch mode again, but this time with alignments of `Left` and `Bottom`. Figure 7-44 shows the results

Example 7-35. Specifying a stretch and alignment

```
<Rectangle>
    <Rectangle.Fill>
        <ImageBrush ImageSource="Images\Moggie.jpg" Stretch="UniformToFill"
                    AlignmentX="Left" AlignmentY="Bottom" />
    </Rectangle.Fill>
</Rectangle>
```

Figure 7-44. Stretch.UniformToFill, bottom-left aligned

The stretch and alignment properties are convenient to use, but they do not allow you to choose to focus on any arbitrary part of the image or choose specific scale factors. `TileBrush` supports these features through the `Viewbox`, `Viewport`, and `ViewportUnits` properties.

The Viewbox property chooses the portion of the image to be displayed. By default, this property is set to encompass the whole image, but you can change it to focus on a particular part. Figure 7-45 shows the UniformToFill stretch mode, but with a Viewbox set to zoom in on the front of the car.

Figure 7-45. Stretch.UniformToFill with Viewbox

As Example 7-36 shows, the Viewbox is specified as four numbers. The first two are the coordinates of the upper-left-hand corner of the Viewbox, and the second two are the width and height of the box. These coordinates are relative to the source image. In this case, because an ImageBrush is being used, these are coordinates in the source bitmap. In the case of a DrawingBrush or VisualBrush, the Viewbox would use the coordinate system of the source drawing.

Example 7-36. Specifying a Viewbox

```
<ImageBrush Stretch="UniformToFill" Viewbox="593,250,200,200"
            ImageSource="Images\Moggie.jpg" />
```

While Viewbox lets you choose which portion of the source image you would like to focus on, Viewport lets you choose where that image should end up in the brush. Its functionality overlaps with the alignment properties, but Viewport allows much more control.

Figure 7-46 illustrates the relationship between Viewbox and Viewport. On the left, we see the source image—a bitmap in this case, but it could also be a drawing or visual tree. The Viewbox specifies an area of this source image. On the right, we see the brush. The Viewport specifies an area within this brush. WPF will scale and position the source image so that the area specified in Viewbox ends up being painted into the area specified by Viewport.

The Viewport does not specify the extent of the brush. As Figure 7-46 shows, the brush does not need to be the same size as the Viewport. Nor will the brush be clipped to be the size of the Viewport. All the Viewport and Viewbox do is establish the scale and position at which the source image will be drawn in the target brush. Example 7-37 shows Viewport and Viewbox settings that correspond to the areas highlighted in Figure 7-46.

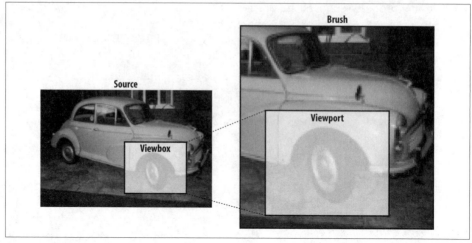

Figure 7-46. Meaning of Viewbox and Viewport

Example 7-37. Using Viewbox and Viewport

```
<ImageBrush Viewbox="380,285,308,243"
            Viewport="0.1,0.321,0.7, 0.557"
            ImageSource="Images\Moggie.jpg" />
```

Notice in Example 7-37 that while the Viewbox coordinates are relative to the source image, the Viewport uses numbers between 0 and 1. By default, the Viewport coordinate system is based on the full size of the brush, with 0,0 being at the top left and 1,1 being at the bottom right. This means that the area of the image shown by the brush will always be the same, regardless of the brush size. This results in a distorting behavior similar to the default StretchMode of Fill, as shown in Figure 7-47. (In fact the Fill stretch mode is equivalent to setting the Viewbox to be the size of the source image, and the Viewport to be "0,0,1,1".)

You can specify different units for the Viewport with the ViewportUnits property. The default is RelativeToBoundingBox, but if you change it to Absolute, the Viewport is measured using the user interface's coordinate system.

Remember that all of this scaling and positioning functionality is common to all of the brushes derived from TileBrush. We will now look at the features specific to the individual brushes.

ImageBrush

ImageBrush paints areas of the screen using a bitmap. The ImageBrush was used to create all of the pictures in the previous section. This brush is straightforward—you simply need to tell it what bitmap to use with the ImageSource property, as Example 7-38 shows.

Figure 7-47. Viewbox and Viewport in use

Example 7-38. Using an ImageBrush

```
<Rectangle>
    <Rectangle.Fill>
        <ImageBrush ImageSource="Images\Moggie.jpg" />
    </Rectangle.Fill>
</Rectangle>
```

To make a bitmap file available to the ImageBrush, simply add one to your project in Visual Studio 2005. The file in Example 7-38 was in a subdirectory of the project called Images. The bitmap must be built into the project as a resource. To do this, select the bitmap file in Visual Studio 2005's Solution Explorer and then in the Properties panel, make sure the Build Action property is set to Resource. This embeds the bitmap into the executable, enabling the ImageBrush to find it at runtime. (See Chapter 6 for more information on how binary resources are managed.) Alternatively, you can specify an absolute URL for this property—you could, for example, display an image from a web site.

ImageBrush is quite happy to deal with images with a transparency channel (also known as an "alpha" channel). Not all image formats support partial transparency, but some, such as the PNG and BMP formats, can. (And to a lesser extent, GIF can do so as well. It only supports fully transparent or fully opaque pixels. This is effectively a 1-bit alpha channel.) Where an alpha channel is present, the ImageBrush will honor it.

DrawingBrush

The ImageBrush is convenient if you have a bitmap you need to paint with. However, bitmaps do not fit in well with resolution independence. The ImageBrush will scale bitmaps correctly for your screen's resolution, but bitmaps tend to become blurred when scaled. DrawingBrush does not suffer from this problem, because you usually provide a scalable vector image as its source. This enables a DrawingBrush to remain clear and sharp at any size and resolution.

The vector image is represented by a Drawing object. This is an abstract base class. Shapes can be drawn with a GeometryDrawing—this allows you to construct drawings using all of the same geometry elements supported by Path. You can also use bitmaps and video with ImageDrawing and VideoDrawing. Text is supported with GlyphRunDrawing. Finally, you can combine these together using the DrawingGroup.

Even if you use nothing but shapes, you will still probably want to group the shapes together with a DrawingGroup. Each GeometryDrawing is effectively equivalent to a single Path, so if you want to draw using different pens and brushes, or if you want your shapes to overlap rather than combine, you will need to use multiple GeometryDrawing elements. Example 7-39 shows a Rectangle using a DrawingBrush for its Fill.

Example 7-39. Using DrawingBrush

```
<Rectangle Width="80" Height="30">
    <Rectangle.Fill>
        <DrawingBrush>
            <DrawingBrush.Drawing>
                <DrawingGroup>
                    <DrawingGroup.Children>
                        <GeometryDrawing Brush="VerticalGradient Green DarkGreen">
                            <GeometryDrawing.Pen>
                                <Pen Thickness="0.02"
                                     Brush="VerticalGradient Black LightGray" />
                            </GeometryDrawing.Pen>
                            <GeometryDrawing.Geometry>
                                <RectangleGeometry RadiusX="0.2" RadiusY="0.5"
                                                   Rect="0.02,0.02,0.96,0.96" />
                            </GeometryDrawing.Geometry>
                        </GeometryDrawing>
                        <GeometryDrawing Brush="VerticalGradient #dfff #0fff">
                            <GeometryDrawing.Geometry>
                                <RectangleGeometry RadiusX="0.1" RadiusY="0.5"
                                                   Rect="0.1,0.07,0.8,0.5" />
                            </GeometryDrawing.Geometry>
                        </GeometryDrawing>
                    </DrawingGroup.Children>
                </DrawingGroup>
            </DrawingBrush.Drawing>
        </DrawingBrush>
    </Rectangle.Fill>
</Rectangle>
```

The brush in Example 7-39 paints the same visuals seen earlier in Figure 7-35. Because each of the rectangular elements that make up the drawing uses different linear gradient fills, they both get their own GeometryDrawing, nested inside a DrawingGroup.

With a DrawingBrush, the Viewbox defaults to 0,0,1,1. All of the coordinates and sizes in Example 7-39 are relative to this coordinate system. If you would prefer to work with coordinates over a wider range, you can simply set the Viewbox to the range you require. We already saw how to use the Viewbox in Example 7-36. The only difference with DrawingBrush is that you're using it to indicate an area of the drawing, rather than a bitmap.

Note that we can use the Viewbox to focus on some subsection of the picture, just as we did earlier with the ImageBrush. We can modify the DrawingBrush in Example 7-39 to use a smaller Viewbox, as shown in Example 7-40.

Example 7-40. Viewbox and DrawingBrush

```
<DrawingBrush Viewbox="0.5,0,0.5,0.25">
```

The result is that most of the drawing is now outside of the Viewbox, so the brush only shows a part of the whole drawing, as Figure 7-48 shows.

Figure 7-48. DrawingBrush with small Viewbox

DrawingBrush is extremely powerful, as it lets you use more or less any graphics you like as a brush, and because it is vector based, the results remains crisp at any scale. It does have one drawback if you are using it from markup, though: it is somewhat cumbersome to use from XAML. Consider that Example 7-39 produces the same appearance as Example 7-29, but these examples are 28 lines and 10 lines long, respectively.

The DrawingBrush is much more verbose because it requires us to work with geometry objects rather than higher-level constructs such as the Grid or Rectangle used in Example 7-29. (Note that this problem is less acute when using this brush from code, where the higher-level objects are no more convenient to use than geometries. So this is really only a XAML issue.) Fortunately, VisualBrush allows us to paint with these higher-level elements.

VisualBrush

The VisualBrush can paint with the contents of any element derived from Visual. Since Visual is the base class of all WPF user-interface elements, this means that in practice you can plug any markup you like into a VisualBrush. Example 7-41 shows a Rectangle filled using a VisualBrush.

Example 7-41. Using a VisualBrush

```
<Rectangle Width="80" Height="30">
    <Rectangle.Fill>
        <VisualBrush Viewbox="0,0,80,26">
            <VisualBrush.Visual>
                <Grid Width="80" Height="26">
                    <Grid.RowDefinitions>
                        <RowDefinition Height="2*" />
                        <RowDefinition Height="*" />
                    </Grid.RowDefinitions>
                    <Rectangle Grid.RowSpan="2" RadiusX="13" RadiusY="13"
                               Fill="VerticalGradient Green DarkGreen"
                               Stroke="VerticalGradient Black LightGray" />
                    <Rectangle Margin="3,2" RadiusX="8" RadiusY="12"
                               Fill="VerticalGradient #dfff #0fff" />
                </Grid>
            </VisualBrush.Visual>
        </VisualBrush>
    </Rectangle.Fill>
</Rectangle>
```

The brush's visuals in Example 7-41 have been copied directly from Example 7-29, resulting in a much simpler brush than the equivalent DrawingBrush. (The results look exactly the same as Figure 7-35—the whole point of the VisualBrush is that it paints areas to look just like the visuals it wraps.)

You might be wondering why on earth you would ever use a DrawingBrush when VisualBrush is so much simpler. One reason we have both is that DrawingBrush is more efficient—a drawing doesn't carry the overhead of a full FrameworkElement for every drawing primitive. Although it takes more effort to create a DrawingBrush, it consumes fewer resources at runtime. If you want your user interface to have particularly intricate visuals, the DrawingBrush will enable you to do so with lower overheads. If you plan to use animation, this low overhead may translate to smoother-looking animations.

VisualBrush makes it very easy to create a brush that looks exactly like some part of your user interface. You could use this to create effects such as reflections, or to make the user interface appear to rotate in 3-D. (This goes beyond the scope of this book.)

Pen

Brushes are used to fill the interior of a shape. To draw the outline of a shape, WPF needs a little more information—not only does it need a brush in order to color in areas of the screen, it also needs to know how thick you would like the line to be drawn and whether you want a dash pattern and/or end caps. The Pen class provides these.

A Pen is always based on a brush, meaning that all of the drawing effects we've seen so far can be used when drawing outlines. The brush is set using the Brush property.

Remember that if you are working with any of the high-level shape elements, you will not work with a Pen directly. A Pen is used under the covers, but you set all of the properties indirectly. Table 7-1 shows how Shape properties correspond to Pen properties.

You will typically deal directly with a Pen only if you work at a lower level, such as with the GeometryDrawing in a DrawingBrush.

The line width is set with the Thickness property. For simple outlines, this and Brush may be the only properties you set. However, Pen has more to offer. For example, you can set a dash pattern with the DashArray property. This is simply an array of numbers. Each number corresponds to the length of a particular segment in the dash pattern. Example 7-42 illustrates the simplest possible pattern.

Example 7-42. DashArray

```
<Rectangle Stroke="Black" StrokeThickness="5" StrokeDashArray="1" />
```

This indicates that the first segment in the dash pattern is of length one. The dash pattern repeats, and since only one segment length has been specified, every segment will be of length 1. Figure 7-49 shows the result.

Figure 7-49. Simple dash pattern

Example 7-43 shows two slightly more interesting pattern sequences. Note that the second case supplies an odd number of segments. This means that the first time around, the solid segments will be of size 6 and the gap will be of size 1, but when the sequence repeats, the solid segment will be of length 1 and the gaps of size 6. So, the effective length of the dash pattern is doubled. The results of both patterns are shown in Figure 7-50.

Example 7-43. Dash patterns

```
<Rectangle Stroke="Black" StrokeThickness="5" StrokeDashArray="10 1 3 1" />
<Rectangle Stroke="Black" StrokeThickness="5" StrokeDashArray="6 1 6" />
```

Figure 7-50. Longer dash patterns

Corners can be drawn in three different ways. The LineJoin property can be set to Miter, Bevel, or Round, shown from left to right in Figure 7-51.

Figure 7-51. LineJoin types: Miter, Bevel, and Round

For open shapes such as Line or PolyLine, you can specify the shape of the starts and ends of lines with the StartLineCap and EndLineCap properties. The DashCap property specifies the shape that dashes start and end with. These properties support four styles of cap: Round, Triangle, Flat, and Square, shown from top to bottom in Figure 7-52. Flat and Square both square off the ends of lines. The distinction is that with Flat, the flat end intersects the end point of the line, but with Square, it extends beyond it. The amount by which it overshoots the line is equal to half the line thickness.

Figure 7-52. Line cap styles: Round, Triangle, Flat, and Square

Transformations

Support for high-resolution displays is an important feature of WPF. This is enabled in part by the emphasis on the use of scalable vector graphics rather than bitmaps. But, as experience with GDI+ and GDI32 has shown, if scalability is not integrated completely into the graphics architecture, resolution independence is very hard to achieve consistently in practice.

WPF's support for scaling is built in at a fundamental level. Any element in the user interface can have a transformation applied, making it easy to scale or rotate anything.

All user-interface elements have a RenderTransform property of type Transform. This is an abstract base class, from which there are derived classes implementing various affine transformations:[*] rotation, scaling, translation, and shearing. All of these are just convenience classes—all supported transformations can be represented by the

---

[*] An affine transformation is one in which features arranged in a straight line before the transform continue to be in a straight line after the transform. Note that 3-D perspective transformations do not preserve straight lines.

`MatrixTransform` class. This contains a 3×3 matrix, allowing any affine transformation to be used.

Example 7-44 shows the use of the `RenderTransform` property.

Example 7-44. Using RenderTransform

```
<StackPanel Orientation="Horizontal">
    <TextBlock>
        <TextBlock.RenderTransform>
            <TransformGroup>
                <ScaleTransform ScaleX="2" ScaleY="2" />
                <RotateTransform Angle="10" />
            </TransformGroup>
        </TextBlock.RenderTransform>
        Hello,
    </TextBlock>
    <TextBlock>world</TextBlock>
</StackPanel>
```

Notice that a `TransformGroup` has been used here to combine the effects of two transforms. (Note that the rotation angle is specified in degrees here.) The results are shown in Figure 7-53.

Hello, world

Figure 7-53. RenderTransform

In markup, you would not normally write transforms out in full as Example 7-44 does, because you can use the abbreviated string syntax shown in Example 7-45.

Example 7-45. Using abbreviated transform syntax

```
<StackPanel Orientation="Horizontal">
    <TextBlock RenderTransform="scale 2,2 rotate 10">Hello,</TextBlock>
    <TextBlock>world</TextBlock>
</StackPanel>
```

The `RenderTransform` property allows you to specify a sequence of transforms, which will be converted into suitable `Transform` objects for you.

`RenderTransform` changes the appearance of an element but has no effect on layout. Notice how in Figure 7-53 the "Hello" `TextBlock` runs underneath the "world" block. These elements are both in a horizontal `StackPanel`, so you would normally expect the second element to be completely to the right of the first element, instead of overlapping. However, `RenderTransform` is effectively invisible to the layout logic, so `StackPanel` has arranged the elements as though the transform were not in place.

In practice, you will often want the transformation to be taken into account by the layout system. In this case, you should not use the `RenderTransform` property. Instead, you should use the `LayoutTransform` property, as Example 7-46 shows.

Example 7-46. Using LayoutTransform

```
<StackPanel Orientation="Horizontal" Margin="10">
    <TextBlock LayoutTransform="scale 2,2 rotate 10">Hello,</TextBlock>
    <TextBlock>world</TextBlock>
</StackPanel>
```

The LayoutTransform property applies the transformation in a way that is visible to the layout system. As Figure 7-54 shows, this means that the StackPanel now allocates enough space for the transformed text, and the two elements no longer overlap.

Hello,ᵂᵒʳˡᵈ

Figure 7-54. LayoutTransform

You can apply any number of transforms at any place in the visual tree. Figure 7-55 shows a user interface where the main area has been rotated and slightly enlarged, but part of its contents have been rotated in the opposite direction and reduced. Obviously this particular example isn't terribly useful, but it does show that transformations can be added at arbitrary places. Moreover, layout continues to work correctly—the main user interface is arranged using a Grid, and the rotated inner contents are in a nested Grid. If the main window is resized, both of these grids rearrange their contents correctly, unfazed by the presence of the transforms.

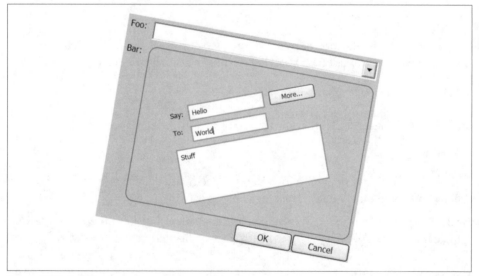

Figure 7-55. Pointless use of transformations

This thorough support for transformations is important, not because it enables wacky layouts like Figure 7-55, but because you can depend on transformations to work consistently and reliably.

Visual-Layer Programming

The shape elements can provide a convenient way to work with graphics. However, in some situations, adding elements representing a drawing to the UI tree may be more trouble than it's worth. Your data may be structured in such a way that it's easier to write code that simply performs a series of drawing operations based on the data, rather than constructing a tree of objects.

WPF provides a "visual layer" API as a lower-level alternative to shape elements. (In fact the shape elements are all implemented on top of this visual layer.) This API lets us write code that renders content on demand.

 A *visual* is a visible object. A WPF application's appearance is formed by composing all of its visuals onto the screen. Since WPF builds on top of the visual layer, every element is a visual—the FrameworkElement base class derives indirectly from Visual. Programming at the visual layer simply involves creating a visual and writing code that tells WPF what we'd like to appear in that visual.

Even at this low level, WPF behaves very differently from Win32. The way in which graphics acceleration is managed means that your on-demand rendering code is called much less often than it would be in a classic Windows application.

Rendering On Demand

The key to custom on-demand rendering is the OnRender method. This method is called by WPF when it needs your component to generate its appearance. (This is how the built-in shape classes render themselves.)

 The virtual OnRender method is defined by the OnDemandVisual class. Most elements derive from this indirectly via FrameworkElement, which adds core features such as layout and input handling.

Example 7-47 shows a custom element that overrides OnRender.

Example 7-47. A custom OnRender implementation

```
public class CustomRender : FrameworkElement
{
    protected override void OnRender(DrawingContext drawingContext)
    {
        Debug.WriteLine("OnRender");

        base.OnRender(drawingContext);

        drawingContext.DrawRectangle(Brushes.Red, null, new Rect(0, 0, 100, 50));
```

Example 7-47. A custom OnRender implementation (continued)

```
        FormattedText text = new FormattedText("Hello, world",
            CultureInfo.CurrentUICulture, FlowDirection.LeftToRightThenTopToBottom,
            new Typeface("Verdana"), 24, Brushes.Black);
        drawingContext.DrawText(text, new Point(3, 3));
    }

}
```

The `OnRender` method is passed a single parameter of type `DrawingContext`. This is the low-level drawing API in WPF. It provides a set of primitive drawing operations, which are listed in Table 7-4. Example 7-47 uses the `DrawRectangle` and `DrawText` methods.

Note that the `DrawingContext` uses the `Brush` and `Pen` classes to indicate how shapes should be filled and outlined, just like the higher-level shape objects we saw earlier. We can also pass in the same `Geometry` and `Drawing` objects we saw earlier in the chapter.

Table 7-4. DrawingContext drawing operations

Operation	Usage
DrawDrawing	Draws a Drawing object.
DrawEllipse	Draws an ellipse.
DrawGeometry	Draws any Geometry object.
DrawGlyphRun	Draws a series of glyphs (i.e., text elements) offering detailed control over typography.
DrawImage	Draws a bitmap image.
DrawLine	Draws a line (a single segment).
DrawRectangle	Draws a rectangle.
DrawRoundedRectangle	Draws a rectangle with rounded corners.
DrawText	Draws text.
DrawVideo	Draws a rectangular region that can display video.
PushTransform	Sets a transform that will be applied to all subsequent drawing operations until Pop is called; if a transform is already in place, the net effect will be the combination of all the transforms currently pushed.
PushClip	Sets a clip region that will be applied to all subsequent drawing operations until Pop is called; as with PushTransform, multiple active clip regions will combine.
PushOpacity	Sets a level of opacity that will be applied to all subsequent drawing operations until Pop is called; as with transforms and clips, multiple opacities are combined.
Pop	Removes the transform, clip region, or opacity added most recently by PushTransform, PushClip, or PushOpacity. If those methods have been called multiple times, calls to Pop remove their effects in reverse order. (The transforms, clip regions, and opacities behave like a stack.)

Because our custom element derives from `FrameworkElement`, it integrates naturally into any WPF application. Example 7-48 shows markup for a window that uses this custom element—we can use it just like we'd use any custom element. This window is shown in Figure 7-56.

Example 7-48. Loading a custom visual into a window

```
<?Mapping XmlNamespace="controls" ClrNamespace="VisualRender" ?>
<Window x:Class="VisualRender.Window1"
    xmlns="http://schemas.microsoft.com/winfx/avalon/2005"
    xmlns:x="http://schemas.microsoft.com/winfx/xaml/2005"
    xmlns:cc="controls"
    Text="Visual Layer Rendering"
    >
    <Canvas>
        <cc:CustomRender Canvas.Top="10" Canvas.Left="10" x:Name="customRender" />
    </Canvas>
</Window>
```

Figure 7-56. Visual layer rendering in action

Notice that the `OnRender` function in Example 7-47 calls `Debug.WriteLine`. If the program is run inside the VS 2005 debugger, this will print a message to the Output window each time `OnRender` is called. This enables us to see how often WPF asks our custom visual to render itself. If you are used to how the standard on-demand painting in Win32 and Windows Forms works, you might expect to see this called regularly whenever the window is resized or partially obscured and uncovered. In fact it is called just once!

It turns out that on-demand rendering is not as similar to old-style Win32 rendering as you might think. WPF will call your `OnRender` function when it needs to know what content your visual displays, but the way graphics acceleration works in WPF means that this happens far less often than the equivalent repaints in Win32. WPF caches the rendering instructions. The extent and form of this caching is not documented, but it clearly occurs. Moreover, it is more subtle than simple bitmap-based caching. We can add this code to the host window in Example 7-48 (this would go in the code-behind file):

```
protected override void OnMouseLeftButtonDown(MouseButtonEventArgs e)
{
    VisualOperations.SetTransform(customRender, new ScaleTransform(6, 6));
}
```

The preceding snippet applies a transform to our element, scaling it up by a factor of 6. When clicking on the user interface, the custom visual expands as you would expect, and yet OnRender is not called. Moreover, the enlarged visual does not show any of the pixelation or blurring artifacts you would see with a simple bitmap scale—it continues to be sharp, as you can see in Figure 7-57.

Figure 7-57. Scaled custom rendering

This indicates that WPF is retaining scalable information about the contents of the visual. It is able to redraw our visual's onscreen appearance without bothering our OnRender method, even when the transformation has changed. This is in part due to the acceleration architecture, but also because transformation support is built into WPF at the most fundamental levels.

WPF's ability to redraw without calling OnRender allows the user interface to remain intact onscreen even if our application is busy. It also enables the animation system to work without much intervention from the application—because all of the primitive drawing operations are retained, WPF can rebuild any part of the UI that it needs to even when individual elements change.

If the state of our object should change in a way that needs the appearance to be updated, we can call the InvalidateVisual method. This will cause WPF to call our OnRender method, allowing us to rebuild the appearance.

Note that when you override OnRender, you should typically also override the MeasureOverride and ArrangeOverride methods. Otherwise, WPF's layout system will have no idea how large your element is. The only reason we got away without doing this here is that we used the element on a Canvas, which doesn't care how large its children are. To work in other panels, it is essential to let the layout system know your size. Chapter 2 described the MeasureOverride and ArrangeOverride methods.

Video and 3-D

Although it is beyond the scope of this book to talk about media and 3-D in detail, it is worth being aware of the support for these features.

Video is supported with the MediaElement type. This element can be added anywhere in the UI tree. Simply set its Source property to refer to the video stream it should play, as Example 7-49 shows.

Example 7-49. Using MediaElement

```
<MediaElement Source="C:\WINDOWS\system32\oobe\images\intro.wmv" Stretch="Fill" />
```

3-D content is supported through the Viewport3D control. As far as WPF's layout system is concerned, the Viewport3D is just a rectangular control, and it will be sized and positioned like any other control. However, you provide the control with 3-D model, lighting, and camera position information, and it will render that model. The control acts as a window onto a 3-D scene, as shown in Example 7-50.

Example 7-50. Viewport3D

```
<Viewport3D ClipToBounds="true">
    <Viewport3D.Camera>
        <PerspectiveCamera NearPlaneDistance="1" FarPlaneDistance="100"
                           LookAtPoint="0,0,0" Position="30, -2, 20" Up="0, 0, 1"
                           FieldOfView="45" />
    </Viewport3D.Camera>

    <Viewport3D.Models>
        <Model3DGroup>
            <DirectionalLight Color="#FFFFFFFF" Direction="10,25,-1" />
            <AmbientLight Color="#66666666" />

            <GeometryModel3D>
                <GeometryModel3D.Geometry>
                    <MeshGeometry3D
                        TriangleIndices="0 1 2  1 2 3  2 3 0  0 1 3"
                        Normals="-1,-1,0 1,-1,0 1,0,0 0,0,1"
                        Positions="-2,-2,-2  2,-2,-2  0,2,-2  0,0,1"/>
                </GeometryModel3D.Geometry>
                <GeometryModel3D.Material>
                    <MaterialGroup>
                        <DiffuseMaterial Brush="LightGreen" />
                        <SpecularMaterial Brush="White" />
                    </MaterialGroup>
                </GeometryModel3D.Material>
            </GeometryModel3D >
        </Model3DGroup>
    </Viewport3D.Models>
</Viewport3D>
```

This sets up a very simple 3-D model containing a single square-based pyramid. Figure 7-58 shows the result. The model also contains some light sources to make sure the model is visible. And the Viewport3D also has a camera position specified.

Figure 7-58. Viewport3D (Color Plate 2)

In practice, you would normally use some kind of 3-D design tool to create 3-D models, so you would not typically expect to be working with model markup such as that shown in Example 7-50. The Viewport3D just provides a convenient way of integrating the results into your visual tree.

Where Are We?

WPF provides a range of high-quality rendering and composition services. A set of shape elements support various drawing primitives. Several brush types are available for determining how shapes are painted, and pens augment brushes to define how outlines are drawn. Transformability is supported at all levels, making it easy to scale a user interface to any resolution or size. You can integrate video and 3-D content into your applications. And a low-level API is available for working at the *visual* layer when necessary.

CHAPTER 8

Animation

Imagine an application with a completely static appearance, which offers no visible reaction to mouse clicks or other input—it would sometimes be hard to tell whether that application was functioning or had frozen up. We depend on visual feedback to assure us that applications are responding to our input. Adding movement to your user interface can bring it to life and enhance the interactive feel of your application. Controls often mimic physical behavior—buttons become visibly pushed in when clicked, for example. However, if the button transitions instantaneously between its normal and pushed-in states, it can look artificial. With animation we can make such transitions look more realistic and provide a more natural feel to the application.

Animation is also useful for dealing with transitions from one view to another. In the real world, we are not used to seeing items materialize instantaneously out of nowhere, but computer programs often use such abrupt transitions. In the very early days of cinema, editing shots to make objects or people appear suddenly was an effective way of scaring the audience, since it was such an unnatural thing to see. These days we are accustomed to unreal imagery, and are not so easily shocked, but sudden transitions can still jar. Careful and subtle use of animation can make it much easier for a user to follow visual transitions, such as a move from one page to another or the appearance and disappearance of windows and other UI features.

For many years, Windows has been able to play video clips, but this just provides isolated islands of moving content. Animating features of ordinary controls has typically been much harder. WPF makes it easy to add animation to your application by providing comprehensive support for the animation of almost any visible aspect of any user-interface element.

Animation Fundamentals

Animation involves changing some visible characteristic of a user interface, such as its size, position, or color, over some time period. You could do this the hard way, by creating a timer and modifying the user interface's appearance on each timer tick.

Indeed, this is how animation is typically done in Win32 or Windows Forms. Fortunately, WPF takes care of these low-level details. Animation, like many features of WPF, simply requires us to declare what we would like done. The system takes care of doing it for us.

All of WPF's animation support boils down to changing one or more properties over time. This means that there are some limitations on what WPF's animation system can do for you. For example, the structure of the visual tree remains the same throughout. An animation will not add and remove elements for you (although it is possible for animation to set properties that will make elements invisible). There is no way of providing a "before" and "after" scene, or of getting WPF to interpolate between the two. This means there is no automatic way of animating a transition from one layout to another in such a way that the elements all slide from their start positions to their end positions.

The key to knowing what animation can or cannot do is to understand its property-focused nature—it just changes whichever properties you tell it to. When deciding how to animate a UI, ask yourself what you would expect to see exactly halfway through the animation, and work out how the properties would need to be set in order to capture that halfway point. If you apply this thought process to animating from a horizontal to a vertical StackPanel, it's obvious that there's a problem. You can't set a property on a StackPanel to make it display something halfway between horizontal and vertical. And if you can't, neither can the animation system! (If you wanted to achieve this kind of effect, you would probably use a Canvas, as that allows arbitrary placement of elements. You would need to animate each element's position and size manually.)

Before we look at any of the parts of the animation framework in detail, let's examine a simple example. Example 8-1 shows the markup for a window containing a single red ellipse. The Ellipse element's Height is set to 100, but it does not declare a Width directly. Instead, the Width property is determined by an animation—the ellipse will change its width over time.

Example 8-1. A simple animation

```
<Window Text="Simple Animation" Width="320" Height="150"
    xmlns:x="http://schemas.microsoft.com/winfx/xaml/2005"
    xmlns="http://schemas.microsoft.com/winfx/avalon/2005">

    <Window.Storyboards>
        <SetterTimeline TargetName="myEllipse" Path="(Ellipse.Width)">
            <DoubleAnimation From="10" To="300" Duration="0:0:5"
                             RepeatBehavior="Forever" />
        </SetterTimeline>
    </Window.Storyboards>

    <Ellipse x:Name="myEllipse" Fill="Red" Height="100" />

</Window>
```

The animation is declared inside the `Window.Storyboards` property. A *storyboard* is a collection of animations and is used to coordinate multiple animations. When animations are defined in markup, they always appear inside storyboards, even in simple examples like this one where there is just one animation.

The animation in this example consists of two pieces, a `SetterTimeline` and a `DoubleAnimation`. The `SetterTimeline` determines what is to be animated through its `TargetName` property, which refers to the ellipse's `x:Name` property. Its `Path` property indicates that the ellipse's `Width` is to be animated.

The `Path` property needs the name of both the property to be animated and the class that defines the property. This is because properties do not always have to be defined by the class they are applied to—you might want to animate attached properties such as `Canvas.Left`. For consistency, you are required always to specify both class and property, even when the property is a member of the target object.

The `DoubleAnimation` nested inside the `SetterTimeline` determines how the animated property is to be changed over time. The significance of the "Double" in `DoubleAnimation` is that the property being animated is of type `Double`, as opposed to `Int32`, `Point`, `Size`, or some other type. Not all types are animated in the same way. For example, `Point` is a two-dimensional value, meaning we may want control over aspects of its animation that wouldn't make sense for a one-dimensional type like `Double`. The `Ellipse.Width` property we are animating here is of type `Double`, so we must use a `DoubleAnimation`.

Example 8-1 sets the `From` property to 10, the `To` property to 300, and the `Duration` property to 0:0:5. As you might guess, this means that the width will start at the value 10 and will gradually change to 300 over the course of 5 seconds. The `RepeatBehavior` property has been set to `Forever`, indicating that once the animation reaches the end, it should go back to the start and repeat indefinitely. Figure 8-1 shows how the ellipse appears at various stages during the animation.

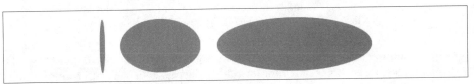

Figure 8-1. Animation at start, after 2.5 seconds, and after 5 seconds

Make sure you specify all three parts of any duration value in an animation. The value 2 would be interpreted as 2 hours! If you meant 2 seconds, you must use 0:0:2, meaning 0 hours, 0 minutes, and 2 seconds.

As we will see, there are a number of ways of choosing exactly how the properties change, making it straightforward to support curved motion and changes in speed, but these are all just ways of getting WPF to set properties to the right value at the right time.

Animatable Properties

The majority of properties that have an impact on an element's appearance can be animated. There are just three requirements to be able to animate a property: the property must be a dependency property, a suitable animation type must be available, and the target element must derive from FrameworkElement.

The animation system relies on the dependency-property system to be able to update property values automatically. Chapter 9 describes dependency properties in detail. The majority of properties of WPF elements are dependency properties.

The second requirement, that the property's type must have a corresponding animation type, refers to types such as DoubleAnimation or PointAnimation. WPF supplies animation types for the majority of types used by properties that affect appearance. The main exceptions are enumeration types. For example, the Orientation type used by StackPanel has no corresponding animation type. This makes sense when you consider that this enumeration supports just two values, Horizontal and Vertical. There is no way to represent some intermediate value between these choices, so animation is not supported.

 You can write your own animation types. This can be useful if you write a control that has properties of some custom type that you would like to animate. Technically, there is nothing stopping you writing an animation type for system types that do not support animation. For example, you could in theory write an OrientationAnimation. However, it would be of limited use, because at any given moment during the animation, it would be required to set the property to one of the two supported values: Horizontal or Vertical. There is no way of animating smoothly between these two values, so the best you could do is flip from one to the other partway through an animation.

The final requirement listed above is that the target element for animation must be a FrameworkElement. This is usually not a problem, because all WPF user-interface elements derive from this class. However, there will sometimes be quantities you may wish to animate that are not in fact properties of FrameworkElements, but which are nested properties of properties. For example, the ellipse in Example 8-1 is red, but we might want to animate this color. The Fill property's type is Brush, and the XAML compiler interprets the value of Red as shorthand for a SolidColorBrush property. (Brushes are discussed in detail in Chapter 7. The way that XAML converts strings to objects is discussed in Appendix A.) Example 8-2 shows the markup for the full version—this is exactly equivalent to the one-line Ellipse declaration in Example 8-1.

Example 8-2. Ellipse with explicit SolidColorBrush

```
<Ellipse x:Name="myEllipse" Height="100">
    <Ellipse.Fill>
        <SolidColorBrush Color="Red" />
    </Ellipse.Fill>
</Ellipse>
```

This fully expanded version makes it clear that to change the ellipse's color over time, we need to animate the `SolidColorBrush.Color` property. But there's a problem. `SolidColorBrush` is not a `FrameworkElement`, because brushes are not a part of the user-interface tree. Brushes are very lightweight objects that describe how elements look, rather than being visible elements in their own right. You cannot assign an `x:Name` to a brush, and it cannot be the direct target of an animation.

This may seem like a rather severe restriction. Fortunately, a solution exists. An animation can target nested properties—the `Path` of a `SetterTimeline` can drill into subobjects inside a property, and we can use that to animate properties of brushes and other similar lightweight types.

Example 8-3 shows how to animate the color of the ellipse.

Example 8-3. Animating nested properties

```
...
<Window.Storyboards>
    <SetterTimeline TargetName="myEllipse"
                    Path="(Ellipse.Fill).(SolidColorBrush.Color)">
        <ColorAnimation Duration="0:0:7" From="Red" To="Purple"
                        RepeatBehavior="Forever" AutoReverse="True" />
    </SetterTimeline>
</Window.Storyboards>
...
```

The animation needs a `FrameworkElement` as its target, so its `TargetName` refers to the ellipse again. The `SetterTimeline.Path` property first identifies the `Ellipse.Fill` property and then indicates that it wants to drill into that property, which is a `SolidColorBrush`, and set the nested `Color` property. The `ColorAnimation` then specifies that the color should fade between red and purple every seven seconds.

> If you are using the low-level geometry types described in Chapter 7 to build drawings, you will need to use the technique shown in Example 8-3, because `Geometry` does not derive from `FrameworkElement`. You can animate geometries inside the `Data` property of a `Path` by making the `Path` element the animation target and using the `Path` property of the `SetterTimeline` to specify properties on the geometry nested inside the `Path`. The same technique is also used to animate 3-D primitives.

`SetterTimeline` and the various animation types are all examples of timelines. Timelines are fundamental to animation, so we will now look at them in detail.

Timelines

A timeline represents a stretch of time. It usually also describes one or more things that happen during that time. For example, the animation types described in the previous section are timelines. Consider this `DoubleAnimation`:

```
<DoubleAnimation From="10" To="300" Duration="0:0:5" />
```

As the `Duration` property indicates, this represents a stint of time five seconds long. Timelines of all kinds always have a start time and a duration. If the start time is not specified, it defaults to 0:0:0, but it can be set using the `BeginTime` property. The start time can be relative to various frames of reference, such as when the page is parsed, or to another timeline, depending on where the timeline is defined.

 You can also set `BeginTime` to null. (In XAML this is done with the `{x:Null}` markup extension.) This indicates that the timeline doesn't have a fixed start time but is triggered by some event. We will see how to trigger such timelines later.

As well as representing a particular stretch of time, this particular timeline also represents a change of some value over that time. At the start of the timeline, the value is 10, and at the end, the value is 300. `DoubleAnimation` is one of the many built-in animation types.

Animation Timeline Types

WPF provides a set of animation classes that all conform to the same basic pattern. So while you must choose an animation type that matches the type of the property being animated, the behavior of the animation types is pretty consistent.

For example, properties of type `Double` can be animated using a `DoubleAnimation`, while for a `Color` property, you can use `ColorAnimation`. These types all follow the same naming convention of *Type*Animation, as you can see from the list in Table 8-1.

Table 8-1. Animation types

BooleanAnimation	Int64Animation	SingleAnimation
ByteAnimation	MatrixAnimation	Size3DAnimation
CharAnimation	Point3DAnimation	SizeAnimation
ColorAnimation	PointAnimation	StringAnimation
DecimalAnimation	Rect3DAnimation	ThicknessAnimation
DoubleAnimation	RectAnimation	Vector3DAnimation
Int16Animation	Rotation3DAnimation	VectorAnimation
Int32Animation		

All of the built-in classes provide To and From properties to set the start and end values. As an alternative, many also offer a By property, which lets you modify the property without needing to know its current value. If Example 8-4 were to be applied to an object's Width, it would make it 100 logical pixels wider, regardless of the starting Width.

Example 8-4. Animating "by"

```
<DoubleAnimation By="100" Duration="0:0:5" />
```

 You can make animations overlap by starting one before another has finished. You can even do this with animations that target the same property. If the animations are using To and From, the last animation overrides the others. But if the animations use By, their effects are accumulated—the net result is the sum of the effect of the individual animations.

The To and From properties are available on all the animation types in Table 8-1. (The By property is not available on all types, because there are some, such as Color, for which it makes no sense.) Of course, the types of these properties match the target type—on a ColorAnimation, these properties would be of type Color, while on a DoubleAnimation they are of type Double. The essential behavior is the same in all cases. The animation simply interpolates from one value to another over the animation's duration.

By default, this interpolation is linear—the value changes with constant speed over the duration of the whole animation. However, you can change this with the AccelerationRatio and DecelerationRatio properties. These allow you to provide a "soft" start and finish to the animation. If you set AccelerationRatio to 0.2, the animation's rate of change will start at zero, and it will gradually accelerate up to full speed over the first fifth of the timeline's duration. If you were to set DecelerationRatio to 0.1, the animation would slow to a halt over the last tenth of the timeline's duration.

It is fairly unusual to want to use just one animation in isolation. You will often want to group together multiple related animations that work in concert to produce the required visual effect. To support this, timelines can be grouped and nested.

Hierarchy

Timelines are usually arranged in a hierarchy. We've already seen the SetterTimeline as a parent of a DoubleAnimation, but it is common to have deeper nesting than this to manage more complex animations. We do this using ParallelTimeline, a type of timeline intended for grouping other timelines.

Child timelines' start times are relative to their parent. So a BeginTime of 0:1:0 does not necessarily mean one minute into the execution of the application. For a child timeline, it means one minute after the time at which the parent starts.

Example 8-5 uses a ParallelTimeline to group several animations together.

Example 8-5. A hierarchy of timelines

```
<Window Text="TimelineHierarchy" Width="320" Height="100"
    xmlns="http://schemas.microsoft.com/winfx/avalon/2005"
    xmlns:x="http://schemas.microsoft.com/winfx/xaml/2005">

    <Window.Storyboards>

        <ParallelTimeline RepeatBehavior="Forever">

            <SetterTimeline BeginTime="0:0:0" TargetName="button1"
                            Path="(Button.Height)">
                <DoubleAnimation Duration="0:0:0.2"
                                 By="30" AutoReverse="True" />
            </SetterTimeline>

            <SetterTimeline BeginTime="0:0:1" TargetName="button2"
                            Path="(Button.Height)">
                <DoubleAnimation Duration="0:0:0.2"
                                 By="30" AutoReverse="True" />
            </SetterTimeline>


            <ParallelTimeline BeginTime="0:0:2">
                <SetterTimeline BeginTime="0:0:0" TargetName="button3"
                                Path="(Button.Height)">
                    <DoubleAnimation Duration="0:0:0.2"
                                     By="30" AutoReverse="True" />
                </SetterTimeline>
                <SetterTimeline BeginTime="0:0:1" TargetName="button4"
                                Path="(Button.Height)">
                    <DoubleAnimation Duration="0:0:0.2"
                                     By="30" AutoReverse="True" />
                </SetterTimeline>
            </ParallelTimeline>

        </ParallelTimeline>

    </Window.Storyboards>

    <StackPanel Orientation="Horizontal" VerticalAlignment="Center">
        <Button x:Name="button1" Height="25">One</Button>
        <Button x:Name="button2" Height="25">Two</Button>
        <Button x:Name="button3" Height="25">Three</Button>
        <Button x:Name="button4" Height="25">Four</Button>
    </StackPanel>
</Window>
```

The animation modifies each button's height in sequence, enlarging the button and then shrinking it back to its initial size. Figure 8-2 shows the animation part way through the sequence.

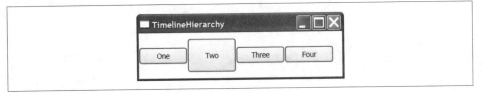

Figure 8-2. Hierarchical animation in action

The storyboard's structure is not as straightforward as this simple sequence suggests—it has a somewhat contrived structure in order to show the effects of a timeline hierarchy. Each of the buttons has a SetterTimeline and DoubleAnimation animating its height. The first two of these are simple enough—they are both children of the parent ParallelTimeline, and the SetterTimeline.BeginTime properties are set to 0:0:0 and 0:0:1 respectively. This means that the second button expands and contracts one second after the first button. However, the third and fourth buttons are slightly surprising—they also have their BeginTime properties set to 0:0:0 and 0:0:1. Despite this, they do not expand and contract at the same time as the first two buttons—if they did, Figure 8-2 would show the fourth button at the same size as the second one.

The buttons animate one after the other from left to right. The reason this works even though the third and fourth buttons have the same BeginTime as the first and second is that they are nested inside another ParallelTimeline, which is in turn nested inside the top-level ParallelTimeline. The third and fourth animations' BeginTime properties are relative to this nested ParallelTimeline, rather than the top level ParallelTimeline. This nested ParallelTimeline has a BeginTime of 0:0:2, meaning that it will not start to run until two seconds into the top-level timeline, after the first two buttons have been animated. This in turn means that the animations for the nested buttons will not start to run until then.

Figure 8-3 illustrates the structure of the storyboard in Example 8-5. Each timeline (including the SetterTimeline and DoubleAnimation timelines) is represented as a horizontal line, with a dot at the start and end. Its horizontal position indicates when the timeline runs—as the scale along the top shows, the further to the right a timeline appears, the later it runs. (This scale is relative to when the application started.)

This hierarchical structure makes it easy to change when an animation sequence starts, without having to edit any of the details of that sequence. Because each BeginTime property refers to its parent, we can move sequences around by adjusting a single BeginTime. For example, we can change when the third and fourth button are animated by changing only the BeginTime of their parent. One way to picture this is to imagine picking up part of the structure in Figure 8-3 by one of the vertical arrows

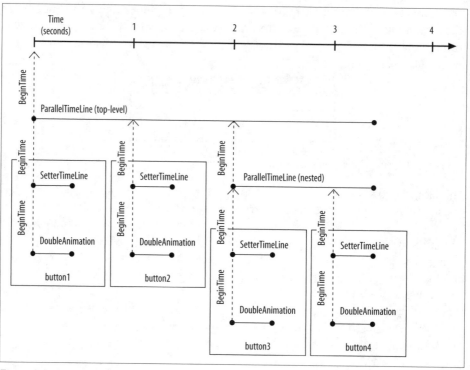

Figure 8-3. Animation hierarchy structure

labeled BeginTime—if you move the line from side to side, everything beneath the line moves with it.

The only BeginTime in this example that is relative to elapsed time is the top-level ParallelTimeline with no parent. By default, a top-level ParallelTimeline will use the *global application clock* as its reference. The global application clock starts running as soon as the application first parses markup or loads BAML, so the BeginTime of any such timeline is relative to when the application first loads your UI.

> The global application clock does not wait for the first window to open—it starts running when the UI initializes. This means that it is possible for your animation start times to precede the appearance of the window. In extreme cases, the animations may even be finished before the window appears! If you want animations to start only once the window has appeared, you could give them a null BeginTime and use the techniques discussed later in this chapter to start them from the code-behind. We hope that a future version will make it easier to set animation start times relative to the appearance of the UI.

Notice in Figure 8-3 that to the right-hand side of the diagram, all four active timelines come to an end at exactly the same moment. This is not mere coincidence. It's not even the result of careful coding. If you look at Example 8-5, you'll see that the only timelines with a specified duration are the DoubleAnimation elements. All of the other timelines have their durations determined automatically.

Duration

If you do not provide a Duration property, a timeline will attempt to work out what its duration should be. It will base this on the duration of its children, setting its own duration to be just long enough to contain whichever child timeline finishes last.

Consider Example 8-6.

Example 8-6. Implicit duration of parent timeline

```
<ParallelTimeline>

    <SetterTimeline BeginTime="0:0:0" TargetName="button1"
                        Path="(Button.Height)">
        <DoubleAnimation Duration="0:0:0.2" By="30" />
    </SetterTimeline>

    <SetterTimeline BeginTime="0:0:1" TargetName="button2"
                        Path="(Button.Height)">
        <DoubleAnimation Duration="0:0:0.2" By="30" />
    </SetterTimeline>

</ParallelTimeline>
```

Each DoubleAnimation has an explicit Duration, but the two SetterTimeline elements do not. They will both have an implicit duration determined by when their child DoubleAnimation finishes. In this example, that means both SetterTimeline elements have a duration of 0.2 seconds.

The parent ParallelTimeline is interesting, because it contains two SetterTimeline elements, both with an implicit duration of 0.2 seconds. However, this timeline's effective duration is not 0.2 seconds; it is 1.2 seconds. Remember that an implicit duration is not simply the length of the longest child timeline, but is determined by when the last child timeline finishes. The second of the two SetterTimeline objects has a BeginTime of 0:0:1—i.e., 1 second after its parent ParallelTimeline begins. Since this child's duration is 0.2 seconds, it will not finish until 1.2 seconds after its parent begins, meaning its parent has an implicit duration of 1.2.

All timelines offer an AutoReverse property. If this is set to true, the timeline will run in reverse when it reaches the end. This doubles its duration. This can be slightly confusing when used in conjunction with an explicit Duration. An element with an explicit Duration of 0:0:0.2 and AutoReverse set to True has an effective duration of 0.4 seconds. This is why the timelines in Figure 8-3 are all slightly longer than you might have expected.

In general, the implicit-duration mechanism works well and can save you a lot of effort. However, there are situations in which it can cause surprises. Indeed, it causes a slight glitch in one of the earlier examples. If you try out Example 8-5, you will notice that there is a gap of just over half a second between each of the buttons expanding and contracting, except for when the sequence repeats. There is no gap between when the fourth button finishes contracting and the first button starts to expand. This glitch is visible in Figure 8-3—you can see that each DoubleAnimation starts a whole number of seconds into the sequence. The first button animates immediately, the second after one second, the third after two, and the fourth after three. But because the animation repeats after 3.4 seconds, this causes a slightly lopsided feel—it would be better if it repeated after 4 seconds.

There are two easy ways of fixing this. We could just set the duration of the top-level ParallelTimeline to be four seconds. More subtly, we could set the duration of the fourth SetterTimeline to be one second. This would implicitly extend its parent ParallelTimeline to be two seconds long, making the top-level ParallelTimeline four seconds long. While this second approach looks less straightforward, it avoids hardcoding the duration of the top-level timeline, meaning that if you were to add more child animations later, you wouldn't need to go back and adjust the top-level duration.

Repetition

By default, a timeline starts at the offset specified by its BeginTime and then stops when it reaches the end of its Duration. However, all timelines have a RepeatBehavior property, enabling them to repeat one or more times after reaching their end.

We have seen this already in Example 8-5, where the top-level ParallelTimeline had a RepeatBehavior of Forever. This has a straightforward enough meaning for top-level elements: they will repeat for as long as the UI is running. For nested timelines, it is not quite this simple. When a nested timeline with a RepeatBehavior of Forever reaches the end of its duration, it goes back to the start and continues to repeat until the end of time, but only for small values of "the end of time."

Remember that any nested timeline's BeginTime is relative to its parent. In fact, its whole view of time is determined by its parent. So for a nested timeline, "the end of time" means the end of its parent's duration. Example 8-7 shows how a RepeatBehavior of Forever can be cut off after only a short time.

Example 8-7. When Forever isn't

```
<Window Text="The End Of The World As We Know It" Width="330" Height="100"
    xmlns:x="http://schemas.microsoft.com/winfx/xaml/2005"
    xmlns="http://schemas.microsoft.com/winfx/avalon/2005">

    <Window.Storyboards>
        <ParallelTimeline Duration="0:0:5">
```

Example 8-7. When Forever isn't (continued)

```
            <SetterTimeline BeginTime="0:0:2" TargetName="button1"
                            Path="(Button.Background).(SolidColorBrush.Color)">
                <ColorAnimation From="Red" To="Yellow" Duration="0:0:1"
                                AutoReverse="True"
                                RepeatBehavior="Forever" />
            </SetterTimeline>
        </ParallelTimeline>
    </Window.Storyboards>

    <Button x:Name="button1" Background="Red" VerticalAlignment="Center"
            HorizontalAlignment="Center">
        I feel fine
    </Button>
</Window>
```

In this example, a button's background is animated to fade between red and yellow. It uses a ColorAnimation with a RepeatBehavior of Forever. Running this shows a button that is red for two seconds, fades to yellow and back once, fades to yellow one more time, and then abruptly goes back to red and stays that way forever. The two-second delay is caused by the SetterTimeline.BeginTime of 0:0:2. The animation is cut off after only one-and-a-half cycles (three seconds) because the top-level ParallelTimeline has an explicit duration of 0:0:5. Once this is reached, the timeline and all of its descendants are finished, the animation is disabled, and the button reverts to its original color.

Figure 8-4 shows the structure of the timeline in Example 8-7. As you can see, the SetterTimeline starts after two seconds because its BeginTime is 0:0:2. The ColorAnimation.Duration property is set to 0:0:1, but this is not the effective duration. First, the AutoReverse property is set to True, doubling the effective length. Moreover, because its RepeatBehavior is Forever, its will run for as long as it is allowed to, so its effective duration is only constrained by its context.

The containing SetterTimeline does not have an explicit duration, so it picks up the indefinite effective duration of the ColorAnimation. But both of these are cut off by the parent ParallelTimeline, with its explicit five-second duration.

> If you use a RepeatBehavior of Forever and do not cut it off with an explicit duration in the parent, the implicit duration of the parent element will be indefinite. Removing the Duration property from the ParallelTimeline in Example 8-7 allows the color animation to run indefinitely.

The RepeatBehavior property also supports finite repetition. You can instruct a timeline to repeat either for a particular length of time or for a fixed number of iterations. Example 8-8 shows examples of both techniques.

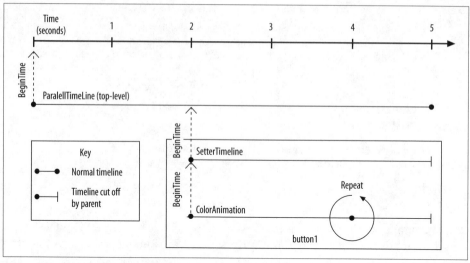

Figure 8-4. Cutting off RepeatBehavior.Forever

Example 8-8. Repetition count and duration

```
<ColorAnimation From="Red" To="Yellow" Duration="0:0:1"
                RepeatBehavior="3x" />
...
<DoubleAnimation By="20"  Duration="0:0:0.25"
                RepeatBehavior="0:0:2" />
```

The `ColorAnimation` in Example 8-8 has a `RepeatBehavior` of `3x`. This indicates that the animation should repeat three times and then stop. The effective duration of the animation ends up being three seconds—three times longer than it would be without repetition. The `DoubleAnimation` has a `RepeatBehavior` of `0:0:2`. This means the animation will repeat until two seconds have elapsed.

Filling

Many animations have finite duration. This raises a question: what happens to the animated property when the animation finishes? The examples presented so far have been slightly sneaky—all the animations we've seen either repeat forever or put the property back to its original value before they end. Example 8-9 uses neither of these tricks.

Example 8-9. A simple, finite animation

```
<Window x:Class="Holding.Window1" Text="Holding"
    xmlns="http://schemas.microsoft.com/winfx/avalon/2005"
    xmlns:x="http://schemas.microsoft.com/winfx/xaml/2005"
    Width="320" Height="150">

    <Window.Storyboards>
```

Example 8-9. A simple, finite animation (continued)

```
        <SetterTimeline BeginTime="0:0:2" TargetName="myEllipse"
                        Path="(Ellipse.Width)">
            <DoubleAnimation From="10" To="300" Duration="0:0:5" />
        </SetterTimeline>
    </Window.Storyboards>

    <StackPanel Orientation="Horizontal">
        <Ellipse x:Name="myEllipse" Height="100" Fill="Red" />
    </StackPanel>

</Window>
```

Example 8-9 is very similar to Example 8-1. Both examples animate the size of an ellipse from 10 to 300 over five seconds. There only two differences. Example 8-9 runs the animation just once—it omits the RepeatBehavior from Example 8-1. It also waits two seconds before starting.

When you run this program, the ellipse will initially be invisible. After two seconds, it appears and then gradually expands as before. At the end of the five-second animation, the ellipse stays at its final size. We can add some code to look at this in a little more detail, as shown in Example 8-10.

Example 8-10. Code-behind for Example 8-9

```
using System;
using System.Windows;
using System.Windows.Threading;
using System.Diagnostics;

namespace Holding
{
    public partial class Window1 : Window
    {
        public Window1()
        {
            InitializeComponent();

            t = new DispatcherTimer();
            t.Tick += new EventHandler(OnTimerTick);
            t.Interval = TimeSpan.FromSeconds(0.5);
            t.Start();
            start = DateTime.Now;
        }
        private DispatcherTimer t;
        private DateTime start;

        void OnTimerTick(object sender, EventArgs e)
        {
            TimeSpan elapsedTime = DateTime.Now - start;
            Debug.WriteLine(elapsedTime.ToString() + ": " +
                myEllipse.Width);
```

Example 8-10. Code-behind for Example 8-9 (continued)

```
        }
    }
}
```

Example 8-10 sets up a timer to call our `OnTimerTick` function twice a second. (The `DispatcherTimer` is a special WPF timer and guarantees to call our timer function in a context in which it is safe to do UI work. This means we don't need to worry about whether we're on the right thread. See Appendix C for more information on threading in WPF.) On each timer tick, the ellipse's width is printed with the `Debug` class. Running the program in Visual Studio 2005 lets us see these messages in the Output panel. Here's the output I get:

```
00:00:00.5007200: NaN
00:00:01.1917136: NaN
00:00:01.6924336: 19.4539942
00:00:02.1931536: 48.57
00:00:02.6938736: 77.512
00:00:03.1945936: 106.628
00:00:03.6953136: 135.57
00:00:04.1960336: 164.628
00:00:04.6967536: 193.686
00:00:05.1974736: 222.686
00:00:05.6981936: 251.744
00:00:06.1989136: 280.802
00:00:06.6996336: 300
00:00:07.2003536: 300
```

This illustrates two points. First, don't rely on a `DispatcherTimer` to be especially precise about when it calls you back, particularly if you're running in the debugger. Second, before the animation runs, the actual width reported by the ellipse is `NaN`. This is short for *Not a Number* and indicates that the `Width` property doesn't have a value.

> NaN is one of a few special values supported by the `Double` floating-point type. This is not peculiar to WPF—the IEEE standard for floating-point defines special values for positive and negative infinities, and this "not a number" value. NaN usually arises from questionable operations, such as attempting to divide zero by zero or subtracting infinity from infinity.
>
> Although NaN is a standard value, WPF's use of it here is slightly unusual. It is acting as a kind of sentinel value, indicating that a property is not set.

We shouldn't be surprised that the ellipse initially has no width, since we haven't set the ellipse's `Width` property directly in the markup. We set it indirectly using the animation, so the `Width` property only has a meaningful value once that animation starts. We can fix this by setting the ellipse's `Width`:

```
<Ellipse x:Name="myEllipse" Height="100" Fill="Red" Width="42" />
```

Having made this change, the ellipse is visible before the animation starts—it is initially 42 pixels wide. (As before, it is 300 pixels wide once the animation has finished.) The debug output reflects this, showing the value 42 for the width at the start of the animation, instead of NaN:

```
00:00:00.5007300: 42
00:00:01.0415184: 42
00:00:01.5422484: 42
00:00:02.0429784: 21.4259942
00:00:02.5537230: 50.948
00:00:03.0544530: 79.948
00:00:03.5551830: 109.006
00:00:04.0659276: 138.644
00:00:04.5666576: 167.7019942
00:00:05.0673876: 196.76
00:00:05.5781322: 226.34
00:00:06.0788622: 255.398
00:00:06.5795922: 284.398
00:00:07.0803222: 300
00:00:07.5810522: 300
```

This is the default behavior of animations—when they reach their end, their final value continues to apply for as long as their parent timeline continues to be active. This may not always be the behavior you require—in some circumstances, you might want to be sure that the property returns to its original value. Even when it is the behavior you require, it's not quite as straightforward as it may seem.

When an animation reaches the end of its duration, the animation isn't quite finished yet. The reason that we see the animation's final value applied in the example above is that the animation is still active, even though it has reached the end of its duration. This twilight zone between the end of the animation's duration and its final deactivation is called the *fill period*.

All timelines have a `FillBehavior` property that specifies what happens after the timeline reaches the end of its effective duration. The default value is `HoldEnd`, meaning the animation will continue to apply its final value until the UI closes, unless something causes it to be deactivated. The alternative `FillBehavior`, shown in Example 8-11, is `Deactivate`. This deactivates the animation as soon as it reaches the end of its duration, meaning the relevant property will revert to the value it had before the animation began.

Example 8-11. Deactivate in fill period

```
<Ellipse x:Name="myEllipse" Height="100" Fill="Red" FillBehavior="Deactivate" />
```

Note that unlike `RepeatBehavior`, the `FillBehavior` property has no impact on the effective duration of a timeline. `FillBehavior.HoldEnd` only does anything if the parent timeline runs for longer than the duration of the timeline in question. Example 8-12 shows such a scenario—the parent `SetterTimeline` has a duration of

10 seconds, while the child has a duration of 5 seconds, leaving it a fill period of 5 seconds. The child's FillBehavior has not been set, so it will default to HoldEnd.

Example 8-12. A child with a fill period

```
<SetterTimeline TargetName="myEllipse" Path="(Ellipse.Width)"
                Duration="0:0:10" HoldEnd="Deactivate">
    <DoubleAnimation From="10" To="300" Duration="0:0:5" />
</SetterTimeline>
```

Figure 8-5 illustrates this pair of timelines. Since the parent timeline's FillBehavior is Deactivate, it deactivates at the end of its natural duration. When a parent deactivates, all its children are deactivated, so this causes the child's fill period to come to an end, meaning that the corresponding properties will all revert to the values they had before the animation started.

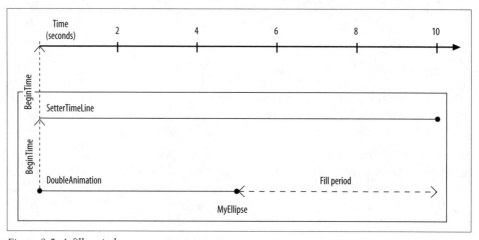

Figure 8-5. A fill period

If a top-level timeline has the default FillBehavior of HoldEnd, its fill period will be indefinite. This in turn means its children's fill periods will also be indefinite. Example 8-13 shows such a timeline hierarchy. (This is the same set of timelines we saw in Example 8-9.)

Example 8-13. Top-level HoldEnd FillBehavior

```
<Window.Storyboards>
    <SetterTimeline BeginTime="0:0:2" TargetName="myEllipse"
                    Path="(Ellipse.Width)">
        <DoubleAnimation From="10" To="300" Duration="0:0:5" />
    </SetterTimeline>
</Window.Storyboards>
```

Here, neither the DoubleAnimation nor the SetterTimeline have an explicit FillBehavior, so they default to HoldEnd. Since the SetterTimeline is a top-level timeline (it has no parent) this means its fill period is effectively indefinite. This in turn means that the `DoubleAnimation` also gets an indefinite fill period, as indicated by the double-headed arrows in Figure 8-6. The upshot is that with the storyboard in Example 8-13, the ellipse's width grows from 10 to 300 and then stays at 300.

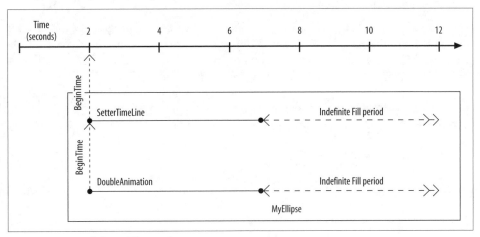

Figure 8-6. An indefinite fill period

The default fill behavior means animations typically end up with an indefinite fill period. This usually results in the desired behavior: an animation's final value is the value that remains in place once the animation's duration is over. However, it has one potentially surprising result if you apply multiple animations to the same property one after the other and those animations use the `By` property. For example, you might have an animation that moves an object to the right for a few seconds and then another animation that moves it to the left a few seconds later. When the second animation starts, the first animation will be in its fill period. This means both animations are active simultaneously. If the second animation were to use `From` and `To`, it would override the first animation. But if it uses the `By` property, the animations will accumulate—the animation system will add the effect of the second animation to the first one.

Fortunately, in this case, the end result of this behavior is likely to be the one you want when using the `By` property: the second animation's starting point will be the final value of the first animation.

Speed

You may sometimes find that you want to change the speed at which some part of an animation runs. For a simple animation consisting of a single element, you can just change the duration. For a more complex animation, consisting of many timelines, it would become tedious to adjust each of the durations by hand. A simpler solution is to warp time, using the `SpeedRatio` property available on any timeline.

SpeedRatio allows you to change the rate at which a timeline is played back. Its default value is 1, meaning that all timelines advance by one second for each second of real time that elapses. However, if you modify one of your timelines to have a SpeedRatio of 2, that timeline and all its children will be advanced by two seconds for each second of real time that elapses.

SpeedRatio is relative to the rate at which the parent timeline progresses, rather than absolute elapsed time. This becomes important if you specify speed in multiple places. Example 8-14 shows a modified version of the animations from Example 8-5, with a SpeedRatio attribute added to some of the timelines.

Example 8-14. Using SpeedRatio in a hierarchy

```
<ParallelTimeline RepeatBehavior="Forever">

    <SetterTimeline BeginTime="0:0:0" TargetName="button1"
                    Path="(Button.Height)">
        <DoubleAnimation Duration="0:0:0.2" By="30" AutoReverse="True" />
    </SetterTimeline>

    <SetterTimeline SpeedRatio="2" BeginTime="0:0:1" TargetName="button2"
                    Path="(Button.Height)">
        <DoubleAnimation Duration="0:0:0.2" By="30" AutoReverse="True" />
    </SetterTimeline>

    <ParallelTimeline BeginTime="0:0:2" SpeedRatio="4">
        <SetterTimeline SpeedRatio="0.25" BeginTime="0:0:0" TargetName="button3"
                        Path="(Button.Height)">
            <DoubleAnimation Duration="0:0:0.2"
                             By="30" AutoReverse="True" />
        </SetterTimeline>
        <SetterTimeline SpeedRatio="0.5" BeginTime="0:0:1" TargetName="button4"
                        Path="(Button.Height)">
            <DoubleAnimation SpeedRatio="0.125"  Duration="0:0:0.2"
                             By="30" AutoReverse="True" />
        </SetterTimeline>
    </ParallelTimeline>
</ParallelTimeline>
```

Figure 8-7 shows the effect of these changes. The top-level timeline's speed is not specified, so it will default to 1 and progress at a normal rate. So will its first SetterTimeline child. The second SetterTimeline has a SpeedRatio of 2. This does not affect the time at which this timeline starts—its BeginTime is relative to its parent and therefore depends on its parent's speed. But the contents of this timeline, a DoubleAnimation, will run twice as fast as normal, so it will be as though this animation's duration is set to 0.1 rather than 0.2 seconds. The result is that the second button expands and contracts in half the time that the first one expands and contracts.

The third and final child of the top-level timeline is a ParallelTimeline element with a SpeedRatio of 4. This quadruples the rate at which it works through its child

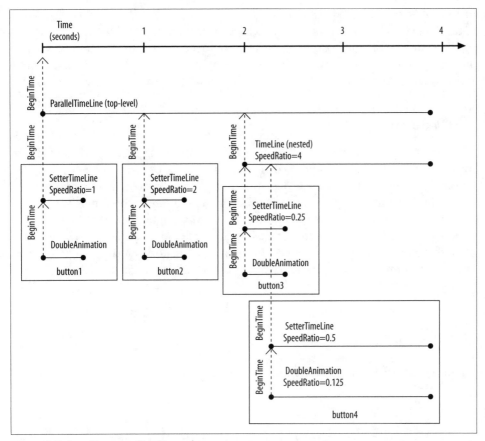

Figure 8-7. Speed in a timeline hierarchy

timelines. However its first child is a `SetterTimeline` with a `SpeedRatio` of 0.25. Consequently, this timeline, which animates the third button, will run at normal speed. The next nested `SetterTimeline`, which controls the fourth button, has a `BeginTime` of 0:0:1, but because its parent's `SpeedRatio` is 4, it will start only a quarter of a second into that timeline, causing it to overlap slightly with the previous animation, as Figure 8-7 shows. Its speed is 0.5, but that is relative to its parent's speed of 4, meaning that this timeline runs at double speed. However, its child is a `DoubleAnimation` with a speed of 0.125. There are three `SpeedRatio` values in play here—the nested `ParallelTimeline`, the `SetterTimeline`, and the `DoubleAnimation` have speeds of 4, 0.5, and 0.125, respectively. Combining these, we get 0.25, so the final result is that the fourth button animates at one quarter of the normal speed and therefore has four times the duration.

With all of the examples in this chapter so far, you might have been wondering why the animations are all in storyboards. It would arguably be simpler for the `ColorAnimation` to be nested directly inside the `SolidColorBrush` in Example 8-2, instead of being separated out into the `Window.Storyboard` property, where it needs a `SetterTimeline` element to indicate which element it applies to. For very simple animations, the use of storyboards can be a bit cumbersome, but as soon as you want to animate multiple properties simultaneously, the challenge of keeping these animations synchronized arises. Storyboards exist to solve this problem.

Storyboards

A storyboard is a collection of animations. If you are using markup, all animations must be defined inside a storyboard. (It is possible to create isolated animation objects in code, as shown in the "Creating Animations Procedurally" section, at the end of this chapter.) The structure of an animation is often very different from the structure of the UI being animated. For example, you might want two separate user-interface elements to be animated at exactly the same time. Because storyboards separate the animations from the objects being animated, storyboards are free to reflect such connections even though the elements being animated may be defined in completely different parts of the file.

Example 8-15 shows markup for a user interface containing two ellipses:

Example 8-15. Two related animations

```
<Window Text="Two Animations" Width="420" Height="150"
    xmlns="http://schemas.microsoft.com/winfx/avalon/2005"
    xmlns:x="http://schemas.microsoft.com/winfx/xaml/2005">

    <Window.Storyboards>
        <ParallelTimeline>
            <SetterTimeline TargetName="myEllipse" Path="(Ellipse.Width)">
                <DoubleAnimation From="10" To="300" Duration="0:0:5"
                                RepeatBehavior="Forever" />
            </SetterTimeline>
            <SetterTimeline TargetName="myOtherEllipse" Path="(Ellipse.Width)">
                <DoubleAnimation From="300" To="10" Duration="0:0:5"
                                RepeatBehavior="Forever" />
            </SetterTimeline>
        </ParallelTimeline>
    </Window.Storyboards>

    <StackPanel Orientation="Horizontal">
        <Ellipse x:Name="myEllipse" Height="100" Fill="Red" />
        <TextBlock>This is some text</TextBlock>
        <Ellipse x:Name="myOtherEllipse" Height="100" Fill="Blue" />
    </StackPanel>
</Window>
```

The ellipses are not adjacent to each other, but their widths are both animated in a synchronized way. This synchronization is reflected in the structure of the storyboard: both animations are nested inside the same `ParallelTimeline` element, indicating that the animations are both to be run at the same time. One animates from 10 to 300 while the other animates from 300 to 10, so the total width of the three items in the StackPanel will remain constant.

Storyboards must go in one of three places. They can live inside a Style, a ContentTemplate, or a top-level element. Top-level elements are Window and Page, or classes derived from these. (Styles and templates are discussed in Chapter 5.)

 All user-interface elements have a Storyboards property, inherited from the base FrameworkElement type. You might think this means you could add a storyboard to any element. This is not currently supported. A storyboard will work only if it is either in a Style, a ControlTemplate, or the top-level element.

The ability to put animations into a style's storyboards lets you apply animations via the styling system. This can be useful if you want to use the same animations in several places. By putting animations in a style rather than the window or page, you avoid duplication and eliminate the possibility of accidental inconsistency. Example 8-16 shows a style with storyboards.

Example 8-16. A storyboard in a Style

```
<Window Text="StyleAnimations" Width="220" Height="200"
    xmlns="http://schemas.microsoft.com/winfx/avalon/2005"
    xmlns:x="http://schemas.microsoft.com/winfx/xaml/2005">

    <Window.Resources>
        <Style TargetType="{x:Type Button}">
            <Setter Property="Height" Value="25" />
            <Setter Property="Background" Value="Green" />

            <Style.Storyboards>
                <SetterTimeline
                        Path="(Button.Background).(SolidColorBrush.Color)">
                    <ColorAnimation To="LimeGreen" Duration="0:0:0.3"
                        AutoReverse="True" RepeatBehavior="Forever" />
                </SetterTimeline>
                <ParallelTimeline RepeatBehavior="Forever" Duration="0:0:2">
                    <SetterTimeline Path="(Button.Width)">
                        <DoubleAnimation From="80" To="90" Duration="0:0:0.1"
                                        AutoReverse="True" />
                    </SetterTimeline>
                    <SetterTimeline Path="(Button.Height)"
                                BeginTime="0:0:0.4">
                        <DoubleAnimation By="30" Duration="0:0:0.5"
                                        AutoReverse="True"/>
                    </SetterTimeline>
                </ParallelTimeline>
            </Style.Storyboards>
        </Style>
```

Example 8-16. A storyboard in a Style (continued)

```
    </Window.Resources>

    <StackPanel Orientation="Vertical">
        <Button HorizontalAlignment="Center">Click me!</Button>
        <Button HorizontalAlignment="Center">No, click me!</Button>
    </StackPanel>

</Window>
```

These animations don't do anything particularly unusual. They just change the size and color of a couple of buttons, as shown in Figure 8-8. However, notice that the SetterTimeline elements do not specify a TargetName. This is because with a style storyboard, there is an implicit target: the element to which the style has been applied (a Button in this case). Also, as Figure 8-8 shows, since this is a style, the animations it defines apply to all of the buttons.

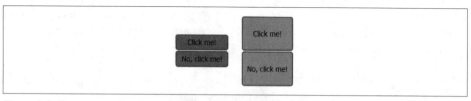

Figure 8-8. Buttons at two points in an animation (Color Plate 26)

If you define a template for a control, it might contain features that do not correspond directly to properties on the element but that you may want to animate nonetheless. For example, Figure 8-9 shows two pairs of buttons. On the top row, the buttons are shown with custom visuals with a rounded, reflective look. The bottom row is similar, but a radial fill has been added to suggest an inner glow to the button. We might want to animate that glow to make the button pulsate gradually.

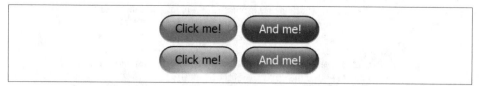

Figure 8-9. Buttons with animated glow (Color Plate 1)

The Button type does not provide a property we can use to represent the glow color, so in order to animate the glow, the animation would need to target that specific element within the control template. In this case, we would put the animations in the template's storyboards rather than the style's storyboards. If you set a x:Name attribute on the relevant element in the template, you can then refer to this in the animation with TargetName. Example 8-17 shows the markup for Figure 8-9.

Example 8-17. VisualTree and animation targets

```
<Window xmlns="http://schemas.microsoft.com/winfx/avalon/2005"
    xmlns:x="http://schemas.microsoft.com/winfx/xaml/2005"
    Text="Style VisualTree Animation" Width="400" Height="150"
    >

    <Window.Resources>
        <Style TargetType="{x:Type Button}">
            <Setter Property="Background" Value="CornflowerBlue" />
            <Setter Property="Height" Value="26" />
            <Setter Property="Template">
                <Setter.Value>

                    <ControlTemplate TargetType="{x:Type Button}">
                        <Grid Height="{TemplateBinding Height}">
                            <RowDefinition Height="1.8*" />
                            <RowDefinition Height="*" />

                            <Rectangle Grid.RowSpan="2" RadiusX="13" RadiusY="13"
                                    Fill="{TemplateBinding Background}"
                                    Stroke="VerticalGradient Black LightGray" />


                            <!-- Glow -->

                            <Rectangle Grid.RowSpan="2" RadiusX="13" RadiusY="13"
                                    x:Name="glow">
                                <Rectangle.Fill>
                                    <RadialGradientBrush Center="0.5, 1"
                                            RadiusX="0.7" RadiusY="0.8">
                                        <RadialGradientBrush.GradientStops>
                                            <GradientStop Offset="0"
                                                            Color="White" />
                                            <GradientStop Offset="1"
                                                            Color="Transparent" />
                                        </RadialGradientBrush.GradientStops>
                                    </RadialGradientBrush>
                                </Rectangle.Fill>
                            </Rectangle>


                            <Rectangle Margin="3,1.1" RadiusX="11" RadiusY="12"
                                    Fill="VerticalGradient #dfff #0fff" />
                            <ContentPresenter Grid.RowSpan="3" Margin="13,2,13,4"
                                            HorizontalAlignment="Center"
                                            VerticalAlignment="Center" />

                        </Grid>

                        <ControlTemplate.Storyboards>
                            <SetterTimeline TargetName="glow"
Path="(Rectangle.Fill).(LinearGradientBrush.GradientStops)[0].(GradientStop.Color)">
```

Example 8-17. VisualTree and animation targets (continued)

```
                              <ColorAnimation From="#1fff" To="#cfff"
                                  Duration="0:0:1"
                                  AutoReverse="True" RepeatBehavior="Forever"
                                  AccelerationRatio="0.4"
                                  DecelerationRatio="0.6"/>
                        </SetterTimeline>
                      </ControlTemplate.Storyboards>
                    </ControlTemplate>
                  </Setter.Value>
              </Setter>

        </Style>
    </Window.Resources>

    <StackPanel VerticalAlignment="Center"
              Orientation="Horizontal">
        <Button Margin="4,0">Click me!</Button>
        <Button Background="DarkRed" Foreground="White">And me!</Button>
    </StackPanel>

</Window>
```

Most of the template is static, but the glow is animated. Note the x:Name attribute
with a value of glow on the relevant shape. The animation is in the template's
Storyboards, as you would expect, and it contains a single SetterTimeline with a
TargetName also set to glow. The Path is somewhat complex, simply because we are
animating a particular GradientStop within a brush. Remember that lightweight
objects such as brushes or gradient stops cannot be animated directly. Instead, we
have to make the relevant full UI element the animation target and then use the Path
property to navigate down to the property we wish to modify.

> This particular Path introduces a new feature we've not seen before:
> the [0] part. This [*index*] syntax is used to indicate an item at a partic-
> ular offset inside a collection.

As we saw in Chapter 5, styles and templates can both define triggers that allow
properties to be set automatically according to certain stimuli. For example, you can
trigger any animation in the storyboard when a particular event occurs.

Example 8-18 shows a style for a button with a very simple template—it just draws a
rectangle around the button's contents. The template's storyboards contain two animations. The first fades the color to PeachPuff and back again, while the other oscil-
lates the thickness of the rectangle's outline. Note that both of these have a
BeginTime of {x:Null}. This prevents them from running automatically as soon as the
application starts.

Example 8-18. Triggering animations in a ContentTemplate

```
<Style TargetType="{x:Type Button}">
    <Setter Property="Template">
        <Setter.Value>
            <ControlTemplate TargetType="{x:Type Button}">
                <Grid>
                    <Rectangle x:Name="mainRect"  Fill="Aqua" Stroke="Blue" />
                    <ContentPresenter
                        HorizontalAlignment=
                                    "{TemplateBinding HorizontalContentAlignment}"
                        VerticalAlignment=
                                    "{TemplateBinding VerticalContentAlignment}" />
                </Grid>

                <ControlTemplate.Storyboards>

                    <!-- Click animation -->

                    <SetterTimeline x:Name="clickTimeline" BeginTime="{x:Null}"
                                TargetName="mainRect"
                                Path="(Rectangle.Fill).(SolidColorBrush.Color)">
                        <ColorAnimation To="PeachPuff" Duration="0:0:0.2"
                                    AutoReverse="True" />
                    </SetterTimeline>


                    <!-- Mouse over animation -->

                    <SetterTimeline x:Name="enterTimeline" BeginTime="{x:Null}"
                                TargetName="mainRect" Duration="1"
                                Path="(Rectangle.StrokeThickness)" >
                        <DoubleAnimation To="3" Duration="0:0:0.2"
                                    AutoReverse="True"
                                    RepeatBehavior="Forever" />
                    </SetterTimeline>

                </ControlTemplate.Storyboards>

                <ControlTemplate.Triggers>
                    <EventTrigger RoutedEvent="ButtonBase.Click">
                        <EventTrigger.Actions>
                            <BeginAction TargetName="clickTimeline" />
                        </EventTrigger.Actions>
                    </EventTrigger>

                    <EventTrigger RoutedEvent="Mouse.MouseEnter">
                        <EventTrigger.Actions>
                            <BeginAction TargetName="enterTimeline" />
                        </EventTrigger.Actions>
                    </EventTrigger>

                    <EventTrigger RoutedEvent="Mouse.MouseLeave">
                        <EventTrigger.Actions>
```

Example 8-18. Triggering animations in a ContentTemplate (continued)

```
                    <StopAction TargetName="enterTimeline" />
                </EventTrigger.Actions>
            </EventTrigger>
        </ControlTemplate.Triggers>

        </ControlTemplate>
      </Setter.Value>
    </Setter>
</Style>
```

The animations are all triggered by `EventTrigger` elements in the template's `Triggers` section. The first of these responds to the button's `Click` event. (This event is defined by the button's base class, hence `ButtonBase.Click`.) Whenever the button is clicked, this will cause the `clickTimeline` animation to be run, making the button fade to PeachPuff and back when clicked.

The other animation gets two `EventTrigger` elements, one for when the mouse enters the control and one for when it leaves. This is because the line-thickness animation repeats forever. If there were just one trigger, starting the animation when the mouse enters the button, the animation would start and then never stop, since it is a top-level timeline. So we need a second `EventTrigger`, responding to the `MouseLeave` event that uses a `StopAction` to stop the animation.

The mouse events in this example are named `Mouse.MouseEnter` and `Mouse.MouseLeave`. This is slightly unusual, as events are named for the elements that define them. These events are inherited from the `UIElement` base class, so you might expect them to be called `UIElement.MouseEnter` and `UIElement.MouseLeave`. However, these events provided by `UIElement` are just wrappers around some underlying attached events. (Attached events are much like attached properties—they allow an element to raise events defined by some other class entirely. See Chapter 9 for more details.) The underlying events are defined by the `Mouse` class in the `System.Windows.Input` namespace, which is why the event names start with `Mouse`. `UIElement` simply wraps these attached events as normal .NET events for convenience.

Each `EventTrigger` can have as many actions as you like, so you can kick off or deactivate several animations at once.

It is usually very convenient to get WPF to start and stop your animations automatically when events occur, as it means you don't need to write any code. However, there will not always be a suitable event to use as a trigger, so it is sometimes useful to be able to start animations programmatically.

Launching Animations with Code

In order to start an animation from code, it is necessary to understand the distinction between timelines and clocks. As we have already seen, a timeline hierarchy is a description of one or more things happening over some stretch of time. But it is just a description. The existence of a timeline hierarchy with a `SetterTimeline` and a `DoubleAnimation` is not enough to cause animation to occur. The work of performing the animation is done by one or more clocks.

A *clock* is an object created at runtime that keeps track of the current position in a timeline and executes whatever actions the timeline defines. If you refer back to one of the timeline diagrams, such as Figure 8-7, the clock is the thing that knows where we are on the time scale at the top of the diagram.

 The relationship between timelines and clocks is not unlike the relationship between code and threads. Executable code defines what operations are to be performed, but a thread is required to execute the code. Likewise, a timeline describes what happens over a particular length of time, but a clock is required to run the timeline.

WPF creates clocks automatically. When creating a user interface, it looks in the relevant `Storyboards` properties and creates clocks for any timelines. If a style or template with storyboards is used in multiple places, each instance gets its own set of clocks, enabling the animations to run independently. This is just as well—otherwise, if you have an animation that runs when the mouse enters a button, it would run for all the buttons on the screen simultaneously, which wouldn't be terribly useful.

Usually, top-level timelines' clocks are started automatically, based on their `BeginTime`. However, if you specify a `BeginTime` of `{x:Null}`, the clock will not be started, so the animation will not run. We saw in the previous section how to use triggers to launch animation—a `BeginAction` in a trigger just tells WPF to start the relevant timeline's clock when the trigger occurs. You can also write code to start the animation yourself.

To start an animation ourselves, we need to get hold of its clock. The code required to find a timeline's clock looks slightly different depending on whether you are dealing with timelines in a style, a template, or a top-level element.

Example 8-19 animates a button using the top-level `Window.Storyboards` collection.

Example 8-19. Timeline in top-level element to be started in code

```
<Window x:Class="StartAnimationWithCode.Window1"
    xmlns="http://schemas.microsoft.com/winfx/avalon/2005"
    xmlns:x="http://schemas.microsoft.com/winfx/xaml/2005"
    Text="Code" Width="150" Height="100">
```

```
    <Window.Storyboards>
        <SetterTimeline BeginTime="{x:Null}" TargetName="myButton"
                x:Name="clickTimeline"
                Path="(Button.Background).(SolidColorBrush.Color)">
            <ColorAnimation To="Red" Duration="0:0:0.2" AutoReverse="True" />
        </SetterTimeline>
    </Window.Storyboards>

    <StackPanel HorizontalAlignment="Left" VerticalAlignment="Top">
        <Button x:Name="myButton" Background="Aqua">Foo</Button>
    </StackPanel>
</Window>
```

This animation changes the color of the button to red and back. Since the animation has its `BeginTime` set to `{x:Null}` and does not have any automated triggers, we will need to write some code to run them. We will do this by adding a click handler to the button in Example 8-19. Example 8-20 shows the code containing this click handler.

Example 8-20. Launching top-level animation from code

```
using System;
using System.Windows;
using System.Windows.Media.Animation;

namespace StartAnimationWithCode
{
    public partial class Window1 : Window
    {
        public Window1() : base()
        {
            InitializeComponent();

            myButton.Click += ButtonClick;
        }

        private void ButtonClick(object sender, RoutedEventArgs e)
        {
            Clock clock;
            Timeline clickTimeline = FindName("clickTimeline") as Timeline;
            clock = this.FindStoryboardClock(clickTimeline);

            clock.ClockController.Begin();
        }
    }
}
```

The handler obtains the animation timeline and then retrieves its Clock. It uses the clock's controller to run the animation. Figure 8-10 shows the animation in progress.

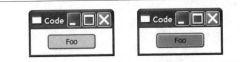

Figure 8-10. Results of Example 8-19 (Color Plate 27)

If the animation lives in a style, the code has to work a little differently. Example 8-21 shows a style with an animation. (This animation has exactly the same effect as the previous example; it is merely being applied in a different way.)

Example 8-21. Timeline in style to be started in code

```
<Window x:Class="StartAnimationWithCode.StyleAnimationFromCode"
    xmlns="http://schemas.microsoft.com/winfx/avalon/2005"
    xmlns:x="http://schemas.microsoft.com/winfx/xaml/2005"
    Text="Style" Width="150" Height="100">

    <Window.Resources>
        <Style TargetType="{x:Type Button}">
            <Style.Storyboards>
                <SetterTimeline BeginTime="{x:Null}" x:Name="clickTimeline"
                                Path="(Button.Background).(SolidColorBrush.Color)">
                    <ColorAnimation To="Red" Duration="0:0:0.2"
                                    AutoReverse="True" />
                </SetterTimeline>
            </Style.Storyboards>
        </Style>
    </Window.Resources>

    <Button x:Name="myButton" Background="Aqua"
            HorizontalAlignment="Center" VerticalAlignment="Center">
        Foo
    </Button>
</Window>
```

The click handler has to be modified, because the animation is now defined in the style. Example 8-22 shows the new handler.

Example 8-22. Launching style animation from code

```
private void ButtonClick(object sender, RoutedEventArgs e)
{
    Clock clock;
    clock = Style.FindStoryboardClock(myButton, "clickTimeline");

    clock.ClockController.Begin( );
}
```

Of course, if the style defines a template, we might wish to animate parts of the template directly, in which case the animations would live in the template storyboards rather than the style storyboards. Example 8-23 shows a style containing a template with storyboards.

Example 8-23. Template with storyboards

```
<Style TargetType="{x:Type Button}">
    <Setter Property="Template">
        <Setter.Value>
            <ControlTemplate TargetType="{x:Type Button}">
                <Grid>
                    <Rectangle x:Name="mainRect"  Fill="Aqua" Stroke="Blue" />
                    <ContentPresenter HorizontalAlignment="{TemplateBinding
                                         HorizontalContentAlignment}"
                                      VerticalAlignment="{TemplateBinding
                                         VerticalContentAlignment}" />
                </Grid>

                <ControlTemplate.Storyboards>
                    <SetterTimeline BeginTime="{x:Null}" TargetName="mainRect"
                            x:Name="clickTimeline"
                            Path="(Rectangle.Fill).(SolidColorBrush.Color)">
                        <ColorAnimation To="Red" Duration="0:0:0.2"
                                        AutoReverse="True" />
                    </SetterTimeline>
                </ControlTemplate.Storyboards>
            </ControlTemplate>
        </Setter.Value>
    </Setter>
</Style>
```

Despite the fact that the animations are now nested inside the styles template rather than the style, we can still launch this animation in the same way as before, using the code shown in Example 8-22. Figure 8-11 shows the results.

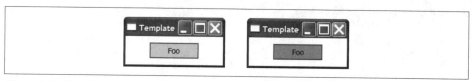

Figure 8-11. Template animations in progress (Color Plate 28)

In all of these examples, we use the clock's ClockController. This provides a programming interface for control operations such as starting, pausing, stopping, rewinding, and so on. Here we use Begin, which starts the animation immediately. Note that we need to start the clock only for the top-level timeline—child clocks will be started at the appropriate times as a result of running the parent.

Key Frame Animations

So far, we have only looked at simple point-to-point animations. We've used either the To and From properties or the By property to animate relative to the current property value. This is fine for simple animations, but while we could create more complex animations by building sequences of simple animations, this would be very cumbersome. Fortunately, there is no need. WPF provides animation objects that allow us to specify a series of times and values.

In traditional animation in television and the cinema, it is common to start by drawing the most important steps of the animation. These *key frames* define the basic flow of the scene, capturing its most important points. Only once these key frames are satisfactory are the remaining frames drawn. The drawings in between the key frames do not require much creative input—they are simply meant to interpolate from one key frame to the next. WPF utilizes the same concept. You could consider the simple From and To approach to be equivalent to providing just two key frames, a "before" frame and an "after" frame where WPF interpolates between the two for you. Key-frame animations simply extend this concept to multiple frames.

 As with the simpler animation types, key-frame animations still target one property at a time. So they are not quite the same as key frames in traditional animation, where each frame would consist of a whole drawing. You cannot provide two drawings and tell WPF to morph from one to the other.

Key-frame animation types use the naming convention of *Type*AnimationUsingKeyFrames. Example 8-24 shows a simple animation of a bouncing rectangle that makes use of DoubleAnimationUsingKeyFrames.

Example 8-24. Key-frame animation

```
<Window Text="Key Frames" Width="850" Height="300"
    xmlns="http://schemas.microsoft.com/winfx/avalon/2005"
    xmlns:x="http://schemas.microsoft.com/winfx/xaml/2005">



    <Window.Storyboards>
        <SetterTimeline TargetName="rect" Path="(Canvas.Left)"
                        RepeatBehavior="Forever" AutoReverse="True">
            <DoubleAnimation From="0" To="800" Duration="0:0:10" />
        </SetterTimeline>

        <SetterTimeline TargetName="rect" Path="(Canvas.Top)">
            <DoubleAnimationUsingKeyFrames Duration="0:0:2"
                                           RepeatBehavior="Forever">
                <DoubleAnimationUsingKeyFrames.KeyFrames>
                    <LinearDoubleKeyFrame Value="0" KeyTime="0:0:0" />
                    <LinearDoubleKeyFrame Value="50" KeyTime="0:0:0.5" />
                    <LinearDoubleKeyFrame Value="200" KeyTime="0:0:1" />
                    <LinearDoubleKeyFrame Value="50" KeyTime="0:0:1.5" />
                    <LinearDoubleKeyFrame Value="0" KeyTime="0:0:2" />
                </DoubleAnimationUsingKeyFrames.KeyFrames>
            </DoubleAnimationUsingKeyFrames>
        </SetterTimeline>
    </Window.Storyboards>
```

Example 8-24. Key-frame animation (continued)

```
    <Canvas>
        <Rectangle x:Name="rect" Fill="Red" Width="20" Height="20" />
    </Canvas>
</Window>
```

There are two timelines here. The first moves the rectangle from left to right, using a normal DoubleAnimation. The second controls the vertical position using a DoubleAnimationUsingKeyFrames. This contains five key frames, specifying the required vertical position of the rectangle at half-second intervals. As Figure 8-12 shows, the key frames show the rectangle at the top and bottom of its bounce, with the midway point being slightly higher than halfway up to indicate the gradual change in speed over time. WPF interpolates between these positions for us.

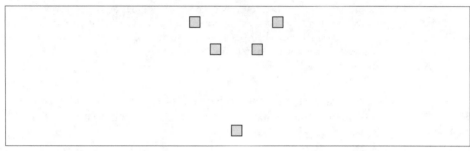

Figure 8-12. Key frames

Each key-frame value in Example 8-24 is specified with a LinearDoubleKeyFrame. This indicates that linear interpolation should be used—the rate of change will be constant between any two frames. This results in motion that is not especially smooth. The rectangle speeds up as it falls, but the changes in speed take place in visible "steps" moving from one stage of the animation to the next. We could reduce this effect by adding more key frames, but there is an easier way. Rather than the simple linear interpolation shown on the left of Figure 8-13, it is possible to get a curved interpolation like that shown on the right, improving the smoothness without needing to add more key frames.

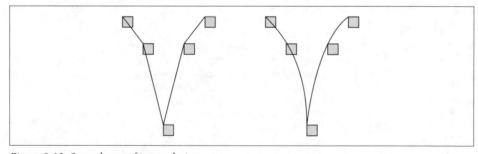

Figure 8-13. Smoothness of interpolation

To get the smoother changes in animation speed we want, we can use `SplineDoubleKeyFrame`. With a spline key frame, a Bézier curve specifies how the animation value should change. However, the way in which the curve is used is not completely straightforward. As we saw in Chapter 7, Bézier curves can be used to define curved shapes. However, with animations, we cannot simply define the path a point will follow as a Bézier curve in this example—the curve is a two-dimensional shape, but the animation object is only modifying the y-coordinate, meaning it is effectively just one-dimensional. (Remember that Example 8-24 uses two `SetterTimeline` elements, one for each dimension.)

Instead of defining the path of a point, the Bézier curve in a spline key frame defines the shape of a mathematical function. This function takes as its input the proportion of the key frame's time that has elapsed. As its output, it provides a number indicating the proportion in which the previous and current values should be mixed. The curve always moves from 0,0 to 1,1, but you position the two control points that determine its shape in between these extremes. These are set using the `KeySpline` property of the key frame.

Figure 8-14 shows three sample animation splines, with the control points marked on as small squares. Remember that these curves simply determine the rate at which the animation progresses. The first "curve" is a straight line, meaning that the animation progresses at a constant rate. This is equivalent to a `LinearDoubleKeyFrame`. The second indicates that the animation should start slowly and then speed up. The third shows that the animation should start quickly and then gradually slow to a halt.

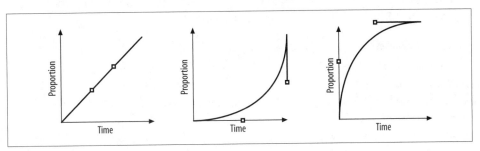

Figure 8-14. Spline animation curves

Example 8-25 is a modified version of the key-frame animation in Example 8-24. The animation passes through the same key-frame values but uses splines to indicate that the rate of animation should gradually change. This makes the animation feel much smoother without needing to add more key frames.

Example 8-25. Key-frame spline animation

```
<SetterTimeline TargetName="rect" Path="(Canvas.Top)">
    <DoubleAnimationUsingKeyFrames Duration="0:0:2" RepeatBehavior="Forever">
        <DoubleAnimationUsingKeyFrames.KeyFrames>
            <LinearDoubleKeyFrame Value="0" KeyTime="0:0:0" />
```

Example 8-25. Key-frame spline animation (continued)

```
        <SplineDoubleKeyFrame Value="50" KeyTime="0:0:0.5"
                              KeySpline="0.4,0 0.75,0.75" />
        <SplineDoubleKeyFrame Value="200" KeyTime="0:0:1"
                              KeySpline="0.2,0.2 1,0.4" />
        <SplineDoubleKeyFrame Value="50" KeyTime="0:0:1.5"
                              KeySpline="0,0.3 0.75,0.75" />
        <SplineDoubleKeyFrame Value="0" KeyTime="0:0:2"
                              KeySpline="0.25,0.25 0.6,1" />
      </DoubleAnimationUsingKeyFrames.KeyFrames>
    </DoubleAnimationUsingKeyFrames>
</SetterTimeline>
```

The first frame still uses a `LinearDoubleKeyFrame`, because there is no "before" frame from which to interpolate. The two "downward" key frames use curve shapes similar to the one in the middle of Figure 8-14. This causes the animation to start slowly and then speed up, as you would expect in an animation of a falling object. The two "upward" key frames use curve shapes similar to the one on the right of Figure 8-14, causing the animation to slow gradually as the object rises to the top. This provides a more convincing visual approximation of how a real object would move.

There is one more interpolation style available: *discrete interpolation*. If you use a discrete key frame, WPF doesn't really "interpolate" at all—it jumps instantaneously to the specified value. This makes it easy to introduce discontinuities into your animation if necessary.

Note that WPF provides key-frame versions of most of the animation types it supports, not just `Double`. Table 8-2 lists these types.

Table 8-2. Key-frame animation types

BooleanAnimationUsingKeyFrames	PointAnimationUsingKeyFrames
ByteAnimationUsingKeyFrames	Rect3DAnimationUsingKeyFrames
CharAnimationUsingKeyFrames	RectAnimationUsingKeyFrames
ColorAnimationUsingKeyFrames	Rotation3DAnimationUsingKeyFrames
DecimalAnimationUsingKeyFrames	SingleAnimationUsingKeyFrames
DoubleAnimationUsingKeyFrames	Size3DAnimationUsingKeyFrames
Int16AnimationUsingKeyFrames	SizeAnimationUsingKeyFrames
Int32AnimationUsingKeyFrames	StringAnimationUsingKeyFrames
Int64AnimationUsingKeyFrames	ThicknessAnimationUsingKeyFrames
MatrixAnimationUsingKeyFrames	Vector3DAnimationUsingKeyFrames
Point3DAnimationUsingKeyFrames	VectorAnimationUsingKeyFrames

Creating Animations Procedurally

All of the techniques illustrated with XAML in this chapter can also be used from code, as you would expect. (See Appendix A for more information on the relationship

---

between XAML and code.) However, code can use animation in a way that is not possible from markup.

Creating animations in code requires slightly more effort than using markup. However, code offers more flexibility. You can calculate properties at runtime rather than hardcoding them into XAML, enabling your animation to be adapted to circumstances. For example, it might be useful to base the parameters of the animation on the current size of the window.

One extra benefit of using code is that we don't have to use a storyboard. Instead, we can create something called a local animation. A *local animation* is one applied directly to a particular property, and which is not part of a storyboard. For single animations, local animations can be simpler to use than storyboards. Suppose your markup contains the following ellipse:

```
<Ellipse x:Name="theEllipse" Width="50" Height="100" Fill="Red" />
```

You could create and launch a local animation for this using the code shown in Example 8-26.

Example 8-26. Local animation

```
DoubleAnimation widthAnimation = new DoubleAnimation();
widthAnimation.By = 100;
widthAnimation.Duration = new Duration(TimeSpan.FromSeconds(2));
theEllipse.PersistentAnimations[Ellipse.WidthProperty] =
    widthAnimation;

Clock clock = theEllipse.PersistentAnimations.GetClock(Ellipse.WidthProperty);
clock.ClockController.Begin();
```

Not only did we not need to put this into a storyboards collection, we also didn't need a SetterTimeline. With a storyboard, the SetterTimeline is required to indicate which object and property are being animated. With a local animation, you add the animation directly to the target object's PersistentAnimations collection, specifying the property as the index to the collection.

Where Are We?

Animation can enhance an application's interactive feel. It can make for smoother transitions when items appear and disappear. It should, of course, be used with taste and restraint—if you animate everything in your application, it will be a bewildering mess. You should also take care not to frustrate your users by forcing them to wait for animations to finish before proceeding. Fortunately, WPF makes it easy to tweak animations, and all user-interface elements remain active while animations are in progress.

The key concept in animation is the *timeline*. Timelines are objects that describe what happens over some particular stretch of time. They form a hierarchy, allowing the relationships between different parts of an animation to be expressed. The execution of animations is controlled by *clocks*, which provide us with a means of starting and stopping animations. Animations can be built into top-level elements, and they can also be added to styles and templates. In styles and templates, animations can be triggered automatically by events. If you create animations in code, you can configure them at runtime, offering greater flexibility, and you also have the option to apply them directly to target elements as *local animations*.

CHAPTER 9

Custom Controls

One of the benefits of WPF is that you don't need to write custom controls as often as you would have to in many user-interface frameworks. If you need to customize the appearance of an existing control or adjust its superficial interactive behavior, WPF provides various tools that can let you do this. In earlier chapters, we've seen features such as composability, the content model, styling, templates, animation, and integrated graphics support. These let you customize existing controls extensively without having to write a new control type.

Custom controls still have a place, of course. As we saw in Chapter 3, the role of a control is to define essential behavior. While you can customize and animate the visuals of a button to your heart's content, it still retains its essence—it is just something clickable. If the behavior you require is not provided by any existing controls and cannot be created by bolting a few controls together, you will need to write a custom control.

If you want your control to be reusable, you will want it to have the same kind of flexibility that the built-in controls offer, such as support for rich content, styling, and templates. In this chapter, we will see how to make your custom controls take advantage of the same powerful flexibility as the built-in controls.

Custom Control Basics

Before you write a custom control, the first question you should ask is *do I really need a custom control?* One of the main reasons for writing custom controls in older user-interface technologies is to modify the appearance of a control, but as we've seen in earlier chapters, the content model and templates mean this is often unnecessary. WPF offers a progressive scale of customization techniques that you should bear in mind when considering writing a custom control:

1. Use properties to modify the appearance or behavior an of existing control.

2. Compose existing controls.

3. Nest content in an existing control.

4. Replace the template of an existing control.

5. Create a custom control or other custom element.

This sequence offers increasing levels of power in exchange for slightly more effort at each step. In the simplest cases, you might be able to adjust a built-in control's behavior or appearance to meet your needs just by setting properties. The next step is to combine controls together to form a more powerful whole. You can take composition a step further by nesting content inside of another control. You can replace the appearance completely with a template, as described in Chapter 5. But if techniques 1–4 don't meet your needs, writing some kind of custom element such as a custom control is likely to be the answer.

An important indicator of whether you need to write a new visual element type is whether you plan to add new API features. Even in this case, you should consider carefully what type of custom element to write—controls are not the only kind of element. You might get more flexibility by writing a lower-level component that can be integrated into the visuals of an existing control. For example, a lot of the elements that make WPF so flexible, such as layout classes and shapes, derive from FrameworkElement, but are not in fact controls—i.e., they do not derive from the Control base class.

If you are certain that a custom element is the best way to proceed, you need to work through a number of design steps. First, you must pick the base class—will it derive from FrameworkElement, Control, or one of the other base types provided by WPF? Then you must define the API, deciding which properties, events, and commands your component will provide. Finally, if your new element is to provide the same flexibility that built-in components offer, you need to pay careful attention to the interface between the element and its template.

Choosing a Base Class

WPF provides many classes from which you can derive when creating custom elements. Figure 9-1 shows a set of classes that are most likely to be suitable base classes and illustrates the inheritance relationship between them. Note that this is by no means a complete inheritance diagram—it simply shows the classes you should consider as possible base classes.

Whichever base class you choose, your element will derive directly or indirectly from FrameworkElement. This offers event routing, advanced property handling, animation, data binding, layout support, styling, and logical-tree integration.

 It is not an absolute requirement to derive from FrameworkElement. Chapter 7 discussed the low-level *visual layer* graphics API, and although the example in that chapter derived from FrameworkElement, you can derive directly from Visual when using the low-level drawing API. However, if you do so, you will lose all of the services offered by FrameworkElement. Deriving from low-level elements is something you would do only in very specialized circumstances.

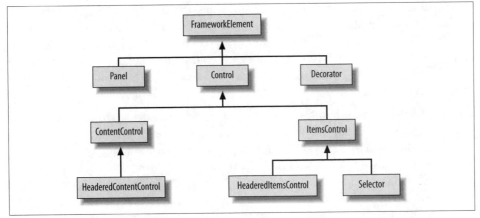

Figure 9-1. Partial class hierarchy, showing candidate base classes for custom elements

Deriving directly from `FrameworkElement` might be appropriate for an element designed to be composed into other elements. For example, consider an element that binds to a data source and renders the data as a graph. You might be tempted to make it derive from `Control`. However, the raw graph-drawing element would usually be used in conjunction with other elements such as `TextBlock` to provide labels for the graph and its axes. It might therefore make more sense to separate the graph drawing into a low-level element, which could then be incorporated into the visuals of any number of different controls.

 It is possible to use controls inside the template of another controls. But if you find yourself writing a custom control purely to be used in the template of another custom control, you probably need to review your choice of base class.

If you are writing an element that performs custom layout logic, you should derive from `Panel` to be consistent with the built-in layout elements.

If you are writing an element that wraps around another element, augmenting it in some way, consider deriving from `Decorator`. Many built-in elements derive from `Decorator`. For example, there is `Border`, which adds a border around an element. There is also `Viewbox`, which automatically scales the element it wraps to fill the available space. If you wish to provide some kind of wrapper that adds functionality around other content, consider deriving from `Decorator`.

If your element provides behavior or supports user interactions not available from built-in components, it is appropriate to derive from `Control`, either directly or indirectly. For example, if you want to make an interactive graphing component, where the user can click on items in the graph to inspect them, or zoom around, this would typically be written as a control. (And it might use the lower-level graph-rendering element you wrote earlier.)

`Control` offers several derived classes, augmenting the basic control functionality. If you are writing a control that provides a space in which the user can place some content (e.g., a caption) you should derive from `ContentControl`—this provides your control with support for the content model. If your control supports content in both a header caption and also the main area (such as a tab page), consider deriving from `HeaderedContentControl`.

If you need to present multiple child items, first of all consider whether the combination of `ListBox`, data binding, and data styling will meet your requirements. Data binding and styling enable WPF's `ListBox` to handle a wide range of scenarios for which the Win32 and Windows Forms listboxes are unsuited. But if you need extra functionality not provided by the built-in list controls, you should consider deriving your custom element type from either `Selector` or its base class, `ItemsControl`. `ItemsControl` provides the basic support for controls containing lists of items, including optional data-binding functionality. `Selector` augments this with the ability to track a currently selected item or set of items.

Custom Functionality

Once you have picked a base class, you will need to devise an API for your control. Most WPF elements expose the majority of their functionality through properties, events, and commands, because these get extensive support from the framework and are easily used from XAML. The WPF framework can provide automatic support for routing of events and commands, and its dependency-property system provides data binding and animation support. You can, of course, write methods as well, and for certain kinds of functionality, methods will be the best approach. (For example, the `ListBox` has a `ScrollIntoView` method that ensures a particular item is visible. This is a convenient thing to be able to do from code.) But you should prefer properties, events, and commands where they are a reasonable fit.

Properties

The .NET type system provides a standard way of defining properties for an object. It prescribes a convention for supplying get and set accessor methods, but the implementation of these, and the way in which the property value is stored, is left up to the developer. In WPF, elements normally use the dependency-property system. NET-style property accessors are typically provided, but these are just wrappers around dependency properties (DPs), added for convenience.

The DP system adds a number of features not offered by standard .NET properties. For example, a DP can *inherit* its value from a parent element. This is not the same as inheritance in the OO sense, where a derived class inherits features from its base class (although DPs also support inheritance in that sense). Property-value inheritance is a more dynamic feature, allowing a property to be set on a single element and automatically propagate to all of its children. For example, all elements have a Cursor property to control the mouse cursor. This property uses value inheritance, meaning that if you set the Cursor on an element, all of the child elements will automatically get the same Cursor property value. (You will be familiar with this idea if you've used Windows Forms, in which *ambient properties* offered the same feature.)

DPs can also pick up their values automatically from elsewhere. DPs support data binding and styling, and they provide a mechanism for defining a default value. The animation system also relies on DPs—it uses the DP infrastructure to adjust property values over time.

By implementing your element's properties as DPs, not only do you get all of these features automatically, but the DP system also manages the storage of the value for you—you do not need to define any instance fields to hold property values.

> Storage management may seem like a small thing—after all, how hard is it to add a field to a class? However, this feature can offer surprisingly significant memory savings.
>
> Simply by inheriting from Control, your element will support over 40 properties (plus any attached properties) of varying complexity, most of which are likely to be left at their default values on most objects. If each element had its own set of fields to hold these values, this would take hundreds of bytes per element. A complex user interface may have thousands of elements. (Even if the UI has a fairly simple structure, the visual tree can multiply the number of elements greatly.)
>
> If most of the properties on these many elements are either inheriting values from their parents or are set to their default values, then using per-element fields to hold these values could waste hundreds of kilobytes of memory. A more sophisticated storage approach that exploits the fact that most properties are left unset can be far more efficient. And while memory is cheap, moving data into and out of the CPU is expensive. The CPU can execute code far faster than data can be transferred from main memory. Only cache memory is fast enough to keep up with the processor, and most modern processors typically have only a few hundred kilobytes of cache. Even high-end systems have only a couple of megabytes of cache. Saving a few hundred kilobytes can improve performance dramatically.
>
> By deferring to the DP system, we can let it handle the information more efficiently by storing just the property values that have been set explicitly.

Finally, the DP system tracks changes to values. This means that if any interested party wants to know when a property value changes, it can register for notifications with the DP system. (Data binding relies on this.) We do not need to write any special code to make this happen—the DP system manages storage of our property values so it knows whenever a property changes.

Any custom WPF element you create will automatically have everything it requires to support DPs, because FrameworkElement derives indirectly from the DependencyObject base class. To define a new property on our custom element, we must create a new DependencyProperty object in the element's static constructor. By convention, we expose the property object by storing it in a public static field of our class, as Example 9-1 shows.

Example 9-1. Defining a dependency property

```
public class MyCustomControl : ContentControl {

    public static DependencyProperty FooProperty;

    static MyCustomControl() {
        PropertyMetadata fooMetadata = new PropertyMetadata(Brushes.Green);
        FooProperty = DependencyProperty.Register("Foo", typeof(Brush),
            typeof(MyCustomControl), fooMetadata);
    }

    public Brush Foo {
        get { return (Brush) GetValueBase(FooProperty); }
        set { SetValueBase(FooProperty, value); }
    }
}
```

This custom control defines a single DP called Foo, of type Brush. A default value of Brushes.Green is supplied by passing in a PropertyMetadata object when registering the property.

> You might be wondering why WPF invents new types to represent properties and associated metadata when the Reflection API already provides the PropertyInfo class and an extension mechanism in the form of custom attributes. Unfortunately, the Reflection API was unable to provide the combination of flexibility and performance WPF requires. This is why there is some overlap between the DP metadata system and reflection.

Example 9-1 also provides a normal .NET property get and set pair. These are not strictly necessary—you could access the properties using the public GetValue and SetValue methods inherited from DependencyObject like so:

```
myControl.SetValue(MyCustomControl.FooProperty, Brushes.Red);
```

However, in most .NET languages, it is easier to use a normal CLR property, so you would normally provide a property wrapper, as Example 9-1 does. As you can see, the accessors simply defer to the GetValueBase and SetValueBase methods inherited from the DependencyObject base class. These methods are defined specifically to be called from property accessors.

Example 9-2 shows how to use this custom property from XAML. (This assumes that the namespace containing this control has been associated with the XML namespace prefix local. See Appendix A for more information on the relationship between .NET namespaces and XML namespaces.)

Example 9-2. Using properties from XAML

```
<local:MyCustomControl Foo="VerticalGradient Black Red" />
```

Note that because our property's type is Brush, we can use the same shorthand text format for representing the brush as we saw in Chapter 7. Example 9-2 exploits this to create a vertical gradient brush.

Attached properties

If you wish to define an *attached property*—one that can be applied to elements other than the defining element—you register it with the DP system with a different call: RegisterAttached. As Example 9-3 shows, this is called in much the same way as the normal Register method.

Example 9-3. Registering attached properties

```
public class ControlWithAttachedProp : Control {

    public static DependencyProperty IsBarProperty;

    static ControlWithAttachedProp () {
        PropertyMetadata isbarMetadata = new PropertyMetadata(false);
        IsBarProperty = DependencyProperty.RegisterAttached("IsBar", typeof(bool),
            typeof(ControlWithAttachedProp), isbarMetadata);
    }

    public static bool GetIsBar(DependencyObject target) {
        return (bool) target.GetValueBase(IsBarProperty);
    }

    public static void SetIsBar(DependencyObject target, bool value) {
        target.SetValueBase(IsBarProperty, value);
    }

}
```

Note that the accessors look different. .NET does not define a standard way of exposing properties that are defined by one type but that can be applied to another. XAML and WPF recognize the idiom used in Example 9-3, in which we define a pair of static methods called Get*Propname* and Set*Propname*. These methods are both passed the target object to which the property is to be applied.

Example 9-4 shows how to apply this custom attached property to a Button element in XAML.

Example 9-4. Using an attached property from XAML

```
<Button local:ControlWithAttachedProp.IsBar="true" />
```

Value-change notification

Your properties will not always be set using the accessor methods. For example, data binding and animation use the DP system to modify property values directly. If you need to know when a property value is changed, you should not depend on your accessors being called, because they often won't. Instead, you should register for invalidation notifications. You do this by passing a callback to the `PropertyMetadata` during property registration. It works the same way for both normal and attached properties. Example 9-5 shows the modifications you would make to Example 9-3 in order to be notified when the property value changes.

Example 9-5. Handling property changes

```
...
static ControlWithAttachedProp () {
    PropertyInvalidatedCallback isBarInvalidated =
        new PropertyInvalidatedCallback(OnIsBarChanged);
    PropertyMetadata isbarMetadata = new PropertyMetadata(false, isBarInvalidated);
    IsBarProperty = DependencyProperty.RegisterAttached("IsBar", typeof(bool),
        typeof(ControlWithAttachedProp), isbarMetadata);
}

static void OnIsBarChanged(DependencyObject target) {
    Debug.WriteLine("IsBar just changed: " + GetIsBar(target));
}
...
```

The change handler function will be called whenever the property is changed, whether it is altered by a call to the static `SetIsBar` method shown in Example 9-3 or by code that uses the DP system to change the value directly.

Events

We looked at the handling of routed events in Chapter 3. If you wish to define custom events for your control, it makes sense to implement them as routed events. Not only will this make your element consistent with other WPF elements, but you can also take advantage of the same bubbling and tunneling routing strategies where appropriate.

Creating custom routed events is similar to creating custom properties. You simply create them in your class's static constructor. For convenience, you can also add a .NET style event to wrap the underlying routed event handling. These techniques are demonstrated in Example 9-6.

Example 9-6. Defining a custom RoutedEvent

```
public class MyCustomControl : ContentControl {

    public static RoutedEvent BarEvent;
    public static RoutedEvent PreviewBarEvent;

    static MyCustomControl() {
        BarEvent = EventManager.RegisterRoutedEvent("Bar",
            RoutingStrategy.Bubble, typeof(EventHandler), typeof(MyCustomControl));
        PreviewBarEvent = EventManager.RegisterRoutedEvent("PreviewBar",
            RoutingStrategy.Tunnel, typeof(RoutedEventHandler),
            typeof(MyCustomControl));
    }

    public event RoutedEventHandler Bar {
        add { AddHandler(BarEvent, value); }
        remove { RemoveHandler(BarEvent, value); }
    }
    public event RoutedEventHandler PreviewBar {
        add { AddHandler(PreviewBarEvent, value); }
        remove { RemoveHandler(PreviewBarEvent, value); }
    }

    protected virtual void OnBar() {
        RoutedEventArgs args = new RoutedEventArgs();
        args.RoutedEvent = PreviewBarEvent;
        RaiseEvent(args);
        if (!args.Handled) {
            args = new RoutedEventArgs();
            args.RoutedEvent = BarEvent;
            RaiseEvent(args);
        }
    }
    ...
}
```

Example 9-6 shows the definition of a pair of events: a tunneling `PreviewBar` and a bubbling `Bar`. It provides .NET event members for convenience—these just defer to the `AddHandler` and `RemoveHandler` methods built into the base class.

This example also provides an `OnBar` method to raise the event. This raises the preview event, and if that isn't marked as handled, it goes on to raise the main `Bar` event. The `RaiseEvent` method provided by the base class does the work of event routing and calling any registered handlers. Note that just as with normal CLR events, routed events are raised synchronously—`RaiseEvent` will call the event handlers sequentially and will not return until they have all run.

Attached events

Just as some properties can be attached to types other than their defining types, so can events. Unlike dependency properties, routed events do not need to be registered in a different way in order to work as attached events. For example, you could attach a handler for the `MyCustomControl.Bar` event defined in Example 9-6 to a `Button` using the code shown in Example 9-7.

Example 9-7. Attached event handler

```
RoutedEventHandler handler = MyBarHandlerMethod;
myButton.AddHandler(MyCustomControl.BarEvent, handler);
```

The `MyBarHandlerMethod` referred to in this example is the event-handler method that will get called when the `Bar` event is raised on this button. Of course, the button knows nothing about the `Bar` event, so we need to write the code to raise the event. This is shown in Example 9-8.

Example 9-8. Raising an attached event

```
RoutedEventArgs re = new RoutedEventArgs();
re.RoutedEvent = MyCustomControl.BarQuuxEvent;
myButton.RaiseEvent(re);
```

Attached events enable you to introduce your own events into the UI tree without needing to worry whether the elements in the tree understand them.

Commands

We saw in Chapter 3 that WPF's `RoutedCommand` class represents a particular user action, which may be invoked through any number of different inputs. There are two ways in which a custom control might want to interact with the command system. It might define new command types, or it might handle commands defined elsewhere.

Example 9-9 shows how to register a custom command.

Example 9-9. Registering a custom command

```
public class MyControl : Control {
    public static RoutedCommand FooCommand;

    static MyControl() {
        InputGestureCollection fooInputs = new InputGestureCollection();
        fooInputs.Add(new KeyGesture(Key.F,
                                 ModifierKeys.Control|ModifierKeys.Shift));
        FooCommand = new RoutedCommand("Foo", typeof(MyControl), fooInputs);
    }
    ...
}
```

You will typically want to make your control handle any custom commands it defines. You might also want it to handle an existing command. For example, you might wish to respond to some of the standard commands provided by `CommandLibrary`. In Chapter 3, we saw how to achieve this by adding a `CommandBinding` to your custom control's `CommandBindings` collection. However, this is usually not an appropriate technique for a custom control. You will normally want all instances of your control to respond to the command in the same way, and while you could set up command bindings for every instance, it would be better to register a *class handler*. This lets you set up a command-handling association just once in your static constructor, and it will work for all instances of your custom element. Example 9-10 shows how.

Example 9-10. Adding a class-level command handler

```
public class MyCustomControl : ContentControl {

    static MyCustomControl( ) {
        CommandBinding copyCommandBinding = new CommandBinding(
            CommandLibrary.Copy,
            HandleCopyCommand);
        CommandManager.RegisterClassCommandBinding(typeof(MyCustomControl),
            copyCommandBinding);
    }

    private static void HandleCopyCommand(object target, ExecuteEventArgs e) {
        MyCustomControl myControl = (MyCustomControl) target;
        ...
    }
}
```

Note that the handler must be a static method—when your static constructor runs there will not yet be any instances of your custom element. Besides, this handler will be registered once on behalf of all instances, so it would not make sense for it to be an instance method. When the command is invoked, the handler will be passed a reference to the target element as its first parameter.

Example 9-11 shows XAML that configures a `Button` to invoke this custom command when clicked.

Example 9-11. Invoke a command from XAML

```
<Button Command="local:MyControl.FooCommand">Click me</Button>
```

Templates

The final design consideration for any custom element is how it will connect with its visuals. If the element derives directly from `FrameworkElement`, it might be appropriate for it to generate its own visuals. (Chapter 7 describes how to create a graphical appearance.) In particular, if you are creating an element whose purpose is to provide a particular visual representation, the element should take complete control of how this is managed. However, if you are writing a control, you would not normally hardwire the graphics into it.

Remember that a control's job is to provide behavior. The visuals are provided by the control template. A control may provide a default set of visuals, but it should allow these to be replaced in order to offer the same flexibility as the built-in controls. (Chapter 5 described how to replace a control's visuals with a template.) Controls that conform to this approach, where the visuals are separated from the control, are often referred to as *lookless* controls. All of the controls built into WPF are lookless.

Of course, it is not possible for the control to be entirely independent of its visuals. Any control will impose some requirements that the template must satisfy if the control is to operate correctly. The extent of these requirements varies from one control to another. For example, Button has fairly simple requirements: it needs nothing more than a placeholder in which to inject the caption or content. The slider control has much more extensive requirements: the visuals must supply two buttons (increase and decrease), the "thumb," and a track for the thumb to run in. Moreover, it needs to be able to respond to clicks or drags on any of these elements and to be able to position the thumb.

There is an implied contract between any control type and the style or template. The control allows its appearance to be customized by replacing the visual tree, but the tree must in turn provide certain features on behalf of the control. The nature of the contract will depend on the control—the built-in controls use several different styles depending on how tightly they depend on the structure of their visuals. The following sections describe the various ways in which a control and its template can be related.

Property Aliasing

The loosest form of contract between control and template is where the control simply defines public properties and allows the template to decide which of these properties to make visible through aliasing. (See Chapter 5 for more information on property aliasing.) The control does not care what is in the template.

This is effectively a one-way contract: the control provides properties and demands nothing in return. Despite this, such a control can still respond to user input if necessary—event routing allows events to bubble up from the visuals to the control. The control can handle these events without needing to know anything about the nature of the visuals from which they originated.

To support this model, all you need to do is implement properties using the dependency-property mechanism described earlier in this chapter. Example 9-1 showed a custom control that defined a single dependency property called Foo, of type Brush. The dependency property enables users of this control to refer to it in a template, as Example 9-12 shows.

Example 9-12. Using property aliasing

```
<ControlTemplate TargetType="{x:Type local:MyCustomControl}">
    <Grid>
        <Rectangle Fill="{TemplateBinding Foo}" />
    </Grid>
</ControlTemplate>
```

All dependency properties automatically support property aliasing. The "contract" in this case is implied by the set of dependency properties your control offers.

Placeholders

Some controls expect to find a certain placeholder element in the template. This can either take the form of an element of a prescribed type, or it can be an element marked with a certain property.

Controls that support the content model by deriving from `ContentControl` use the element-type approach. They expect to find a `ContentPresenter` element in the template. This is a special-purpose element whose job is to act as a placeholder for other content.

 In practice, this is a loosely enforced contract. A `ContentControl` will not usually complain if there is no `ContentPresenter` in the template. The control doesn't absolutely depend on the content being presented in order to function. Or you can go to the other extreme and put several `ContentPresenter`s into your template, causing the child content to appear several times.

You do not need to do anything special to enable the use of a `ContentPresenter`—as long as you derive from `ContentControl`, it will just work. Users of your control will be able to write templates such as that shown in Example 9-13.

Example 9-13. Using a ContentPresenter

```
<ControlTemplate TargetType="{x:Type local:MyContentControl}">
    <Grid>
        <Rectangle Fill="White" />
        <ContentPresenter />
    </Grid>
</ControlTemplate>
```

Placeholders Indicated by Properties

Some controls look for elements marked with a particular property. For example, controls derived from `ItemsControl`, such as `ListBox` and `MenuItem`, expect the template to contain an element with the `Panel.IsItemsHost` property set to true. This identifies the panel that will act as the host for the items in the control. The reason ItemsControl uses an attached property instead of a placeholder is to allow you to decide what type of panel to use to host the items. (ItemsControl also supports the use of the ItemsPresenter placeholder element. This is used when the style does not wish to impose a particular panel type and wants to use whatever the control's default panel is.)

To implement a control that uses this technique, you will need to define a custom attached dependency property to be applied to the placeholder. This should be a Boolean property. Example 9-14 registers such an attached property and defines the usual accessor functions.

Example 9-14. Registering the attached placeholder property

```
public class ControlWithPlaceholder : Control {
    public static DependencyProperty IsMyPlaceholderProperty;

    static ControlWithPlaceholder( ) {

        PropertyMetadata isMyPlaceholderMetadata = new PropertyMetadata(false,
            new PropertyInvalidatedCallback(OnIsMyPlaceholderChanged));

        IsMyPlaceholderProperty = DependencyProperty.RegisterAttached(
            "IsMyPlaceholder", typeof(bool),
            typeof(ControlWithPlaceholder), isMyPlaceholderMetadata);
    }

    public static bool GetIsMyPlaceholder(DependencyObject target) {
        return (bool) target.GetValue(IsMyPlaceholderProperty);
    }
    public static void SetIsMyPlaceholder(DependencyObject target, bool value) {
        target.SetValue(IsMyPlaceholderProperty, value);
    }
...
```

Notice that Example 9-14 supplies a PropertyInvalidatedCallback to PropertyMetadata. This denotes a method that is to be called any time this attached property is set or modified on any element. It is in this method that our control will discover which element was set as the placeholder. Example 9-15 shows the method.

Example 9-15. Discovering when the placeholder property is applied

```
...
    private static void OnIsMyPlaceholderChanged(DependencyObject target) {

        FrameworkElement targetElement = target as FrameworkElement;
        if (targetElement != null && GetIsMyPlaceholder(targetElement)) {
            ControlWithPlaceholder containingControl =
                targetElement.TemplatedParent as ControlWithPlaceholder;
            if (containingControl != null) {
                containingControl.placeholder = targetElement;
```

Example 9-15. Discovering when the placeholder property is applied (continued)

```
            }
        }
    }
    private FrameworkElement placeholder;

    ...
}
```

This example starts by checking that the property was applied to an object derived from FrameworkElement. Remember that we're expecting this to be applied to a particular UI element inside the control template, so if it is applied to something other than a FrameworkElement, there's nothing useful we can do with it.

Next, we check the value of the property by calling the GetIsMyPlaceholder accessor method we defined for the attached property in Example 9-14. It would be slightly odd if someone explicitly set this property to false, but if they do, we definitely shouldn't treat the element as the placeholder!

If the property was set to true, we go on to retrieve the target element's TemplatedParent property. For elements that are part of a control's template, this returns the control to whose visuals they belong. (It returns null if the element is not a member of a control. Since this property has meaning only for elements inside a template, we just do nothing when there is no templated parent.) We also check that the parent is an instance of our control type and ignore the property if it is applied to an element in the template of some other kind of control.

If the target element was a member of a template for an instance of this custom control type, we know we've found the placeholder. This example stores a reference to the placeholder in a private field of the control, so that the control can then go on to do whatever it needs to do with the placeholder, such as add child elements or set its size.

Example 9-16 shows how you would make use of this property in a control template to indicate which element is the placeholder.

Example 9-16. Specifying a placeholder with a property

```
<ControlTemplate TargetType="{x:Type local:ControlWithPlaceholder}">
    <Grid local:ControlWithPlaceholder.IsMyPlaceholder="true" />
</ControlTemplate>
```

Some controls expect the template to provide a specific set of elements that fulfill certain roles in the control's makeup. For example, the HorizontalSlider control will expect the template to contain elements to represent the draggable thumb, the clickable track on either side of the thumb, and so on. The template needs to indicate which element is which. This can be done by defining multiple attached properties using the technique shown above.

When you write a control that uses placeholders, you may choose not to enforce the contract. For example, the slider controls do not complain if any parts of the template are missing. If you provide only some of the elements it is looking for, it will work with those without complaining.

Default Visuals

Although the ability to provide a custom look for a control is useful, developers should be able to use a control without having to supply custom visuals. The control should just work when used in its most straightforward way. This means that a control should supply a default set of visuals.

These default visuals are stored in binary resource in your component, the source file for which is *themes\generic.xaml*. If you create an Avalon Control Library project in Visual Studio 2005, it automatically adds this file to your project and sets its build action to embed the file as a resource. (See Chapter 6 for more information on how compiled XAML resources are embedded in components.)

Inside this *themes\generic.xaml* file, define a style with a `TargetType` specifying your control. This style should set the `Template` property with a `ControlTemplate` defining the default visuals for your control, such as the one shown in Example 9-17. See Chapter 5 for more information on how to define a style that supplies a template.

Example 9-17. Default visuals

```
<?Mapping XmlNamespace="Local" ClrNamespace="CustomControlLib" ?>
<ResourceDictionary
    xmlns="http://schemas.microsoft.com/winfx/avalon/2005"
    xmlns:x="http://schemas.microsoft.com/winfx/xaml/2005"
    xmlns:local="Local"
    >
    <Style TargetType="{x:Type local:MyCustomControl}">
        <Setter Property="Template">
            <Setter.Value>
                <ControlTemplate TargetType="{x:Type local:MyCustomControl}">
                    <Border Background="{TemplateBinding Background}"
                            BorderBrush="{TemplateBinding BorderBrush}"
                            BorderThickness="{TemplateBinding BorderThickness}">
                        <ContentPresenter />
                    </Border>
                </ControlTemplate>
            </Setter.Value>
        </Setter>
    </Style>
</ResourceDictionary>
```

In order to make sure your control picks up this default theme, you need to let the dependency-property system know that the style is there. If you don't, you will just pick up the default style for your chosen base class. Example 9-18 shows how to do so.

Example 9-18. Ensuring your default style is used

```
public class MyCustomControl : ContentControl {
    static MyCustomControl() {
        ThemeStyleKeyProperty.OverrideMetadata(typeof(MyCustomControl),
                new FrameworkPropertyMetadata(typeof(MyCustomControl)));
    }
    ...
}
```

Note that Visual Studio 2005 puts this code in for you when you add a new Custom Control to a Control Library project.

Where Are We?

You will write a custom control only if the underlying behavior you require is not offered by any of the built-in controls. When you write a custom control, you will make use of the dependency property system to provide properties that support data binding and animation. You will use the routed-event infrastructure to expose events. If you want to write a *lookless* control that allows its visuals to be replaced just like the built-in controls, you must consider how your control and template will interact with one another. You will also most likely want to supply a default style with a template that provides a default set of visuals.

CHAPTER 10

ClickOnce Deployment

In this chapter, we'll take a look at the basics of ClickOnce deployment, focusing on what you need to know as a WPF programmer. For more details on ClickOnce in general, I recommend the SDK documentation and the book *Smart Client Deployment with ClickOnce* by Brian Noyes and Duncan Mackenzie (still being written as this book heads into production).

A Brief History of Windows Deployment

The problem of getting software to users' machines has been with us since we moved away from 3270 terminals to personal computers. The solution we adopted was one based on the distribution medium that was available at the time we made the decision: floppy disks. With a disk, you provide your application either for the user to run directly or, as applications got more complicated and hard disks provided more space, for the user to decompress onto their computers. As computer operating systems became more complicated and shell integration became the rule of the day, applications weren't simply decompressed but "installed," which was the act of decompressing the application files plus running the necessary instructions to put the application onto the computer in such a way that it was integrated with other applications already installed, including but not limited to the shell.

As installation options and updates become more prevalent, Windows itself came to support installation via Microsoft Installation (MSI) files. By this time, the marketing, support, and usability folks had gotten their hands into the game, and setup for even the simplest applications became a multiple-step affair that included a welcome message, instructions on what to install, how to install, where to install, and who was installing, a thank-you message, and a query as to whether you'd actually like to run the application you'd just spent all this effort installing (as if the answer would ever be "no"). That's not to say that full-blown setups aren't useful, especially when you've got a bunch of optional functionality and you want a high degree of integration, but the level of effort to install, let alone update, the typical Windows application is often perceived as overblown, especially when compared with other deployment options.

One of the most popular deployment options is the Web, which provides a whole new distribution medium. However, because of limited bandwidth, we continued to treat the Web as a floppy disk for deploying Windows applications, compressing them into setups for download and install. In the meantime, a whole other means of application deployment sprang up to take advantage of the low-bandwidth, cross-platform nature of the Web: the Hypertext Transfer Protocol (HTTP). In a very 3270-terminal kind of way, HTTP provides users with applications a screen at a time (although now we call them "pages"). HTTP-based applications are deployed to the web server by an administrator and then deployed to each user's machine on demand. As features are added and bugs are fixed, the administrator has only to update one web server (or one web farm), letting the users pull the updated pages the next time the application is run. This vastly simplified means of application deployment was much loved by users because the multi-screen installation was gone, and much loved by administrators because the need to get users' machines updated with the new application was handled automatically by HTTP's protocol for clients to detect updated content. It was also much loved by developers because of the ability of their applications to cross operating systems with a reach that OS-specific applications have never been able to achieve.

On the other hand, the reach of OS-independent applications is not without its price. HTTP, and its primary presentation framework, Hypertext Markup Language (HTML), do not come close to encompassing the full functionality of Windows, nor can they hope to keep up as Windows evolves. In an effort to leverage the functionality of Windows and keep the deployment characteristics of HTTP, developers have employed Windows-specific techniques such as ActiveX and Windows Forms controls or specific versions of specific browsers that expose more functionality. These techniques can absolutely provide richer functionality while keeping the deployment characteristics of HTTP, but they fall short of providing complete control over the user experience by the very thing that's providing the deployment functionality: the browser. For a long time, if you wanted the browser to deploy your applications, you put up with how it did things, which included the frame and page-at-a-time deployment. The former required a whole navigation infrastructure to be built into every web page, while the latter requires a connection to the web server to provide each page.

Microsoft's first attempt to keep the benefits of HTTP-based deployment was .NET 1.x's No-Touch Deployment (NTD). In NTD, if you launched a managed *.exe* file using an URL, it was downloaded into a client-side cache and launched immediately. There was no messy installation process, the application had full control over the user experience, and as the application was updated on the web server, the users' machines were automatically updated on the next run. However, NTD was not without its problems, including lack of tool support, a confusing user experience (e.g., no download progress UI), no good means to distribute files that weren't .NET assemblies (e.g., Access database files, COM components, or even help files), no integrated way to ask the user for more permissions, and no offline support. These last two restrictions were the real problem because they took away the ability for a NTD application to really take advantage of the features of the operating system.

Microsoft's latest attempt, .NET 2.0's ClickOnce technology, is meant to provide the benefits of HTTP-based application deployment while addressing the issues with NTD. ClickOnce provides for HTTP-based application deployment of both *locally installed applications* that appear on the Start menu and in the Add or Remove Programs Control Panel and *online-only applications* that feel like web applications in that they are only available inside the browser. ClickOnce applications have extensive tool support in Visual Studio 2005 and in the freely available SDK, and they support non-assembly files (including COM components and datafiles), the ability to prompt the user for additional permissions, and, in the case of locally installed applications, the ability to launch the application with no network connection within 30,000 feet.

This brings us back around to the subject of this book. WPF has been engineered to integrate with ClickOnce, supporting both full-blown locally installed applications and a limited form of online-only applications called express applications. A WPF *express application* has low impact on the system—i.e., no Start menu item, no entry in the Add or Remove Programs Control Panel, temporarily cached, etc.—but has two further restrictions: it runs only hosted in the browser, and it cannot ask the user for additional permissions. Unlike locally installed WPF applications, express applications are meant to be deployed like a web page (although still look like the insides of a WPF application).

 ClickOnce is built as a custom MIME handler into Internet Explorer that recognizes ClickOnce-related files by their MIME types (listed later in this chapter). ClickOnce requires Internet Explorer on the client to do its magic.

ClickOnce: Local Install

For the purposes of demonstration, let's build something vital for procrastinators the world over: an application to generate excuses. This application was started with the Avalon Application project template in Visual Studio and implemented with some very simple code. When you run it, it gives you an excuse from its vast database, as shown in Figure 10-1.

Figure 10-1. A WPF excuse generator

Simple Publishing

The simplest way to publish your WPF application is by right-clicking on the project in the Visual Studio Solution Explorer and choosing the Publish option, which will bring up the first page of the Publish Wizard, as shown in Figure 10-2.

Figure 10-2. Publication location in the Publish Wizard

Figure 10-2 is asking you to choose where you'd like to deploy your application: options include deploying to the disk, to a network share, to an FTP server, or to a web site. By default, the Publish Wizard will assume you want to publish to your local machine's web server for testing and that's what we'll assume for the purposes of this demonstration. Pressing the Next button shows Figure 10-3.

For WPF applications, Figure 10-3 lets us choose whether we'd like to publish this application as a locally installed application (which Visual Studio calls "online or offline") or an express application (which Visual Studio calls "only online").

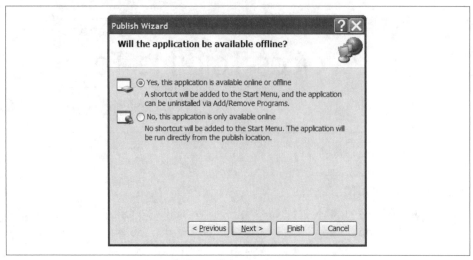

Figure 10-3. Install mode in the Publish Wizard

Visual Studio calls the two ClickOnce installation modes "online or offline" and "online only."

The ClickOnce team calls them "locally installed" and "online only."

The WPF team calls them "locally installed" and "express application."

Hopefully by the time that WPF 1.0 ships and is integrated with Visual Studio, the names will be aligned, but if that doesn't happen, you'll always have this book as your magic decoder ring.

We'll discuss express applications later, so assume the default local install and press the Finish button to yield Figure 10-4.

Figure 10-4 reminds us what we get with a locally installed ClickOnce application; i.e., the application will appear in the Start menu and in the Add or Remove Programs Control Panel. Pressing Finish causes Visual Studio to publish the application to your local web server and to yield an HTML file for testing it, as shown in Figure 10-5.

If you like the default publication settings that Visual Studio provides, this is the complete experience for publishing a WPF ClickOnce locally installed application.

The User Experience

The user experience for running a ClickOnce locally installed application begins with a web page, like Figure 10-5, that includes a link to install the ClickOnce application. Clicking the link for the first time shows a download progress dialog like Figure 10-6.

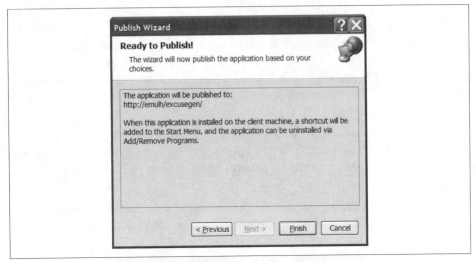

Figure 10-4. A summary of the default Publish options

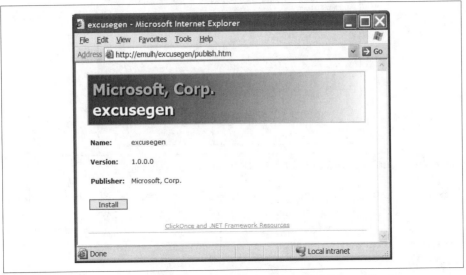

Figure 10-5. The Visual Studio–generated HTML file for testing ClickOnce applications

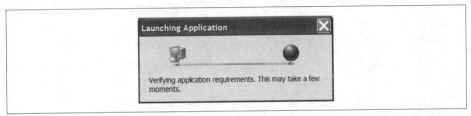

Figure 10-6. Progress dialog for checking the application manifest

Once the metadata file describing the application deployment settings has been downloaded (this file is called the *application manifest*), it will be checked for a *certificate*, which is extra information attached to the application that identifies a validated publisher name. We'll discuss using certificates to sign your ClickOnce applications later in this chapter, but as Visual Studio requires all ClickOnce applications to be signed, it will generate a certificate file for us as part of the initial publication process.

If the certificate used to sign the application manifest identifies a publisher that is already "known" and trusted to run the application, the application will be run without further ado, as shown at the beginning of this chapter in Figure 10-1 ("known" means that you can see who they are, not that you recognize them).

If, on the other hand, the publisher is unknown or is known but not trusted enough to run the application, a dialog like Figure 10-7 will be presented.

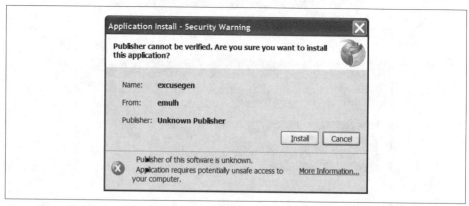

Figure 10-7. The Application Install dialog with an unknown publisher

Figure 10-7 displays the name, source, and publisher of the application. It also lists a summary of the reasons that this dialog is being shown along with a link to more detailed warning information. However, such information will likely be ignored by the user who will choose between the Install and Cancel buttons based on the level of trust they have for the publisher they see in Figure 10-7.

If the user chooses Cancel, no application code will be downloaded or executed. If the user chooses Install, the application is downloaded, added to the Start menu, and added to the Add or Remove Programs Control Panel, all under the umbrella of the progress dialog shown in Figure 10-8, after which the application is executed.

Subsequent runs of the same version of the application, either as launched from a web site or from the Start menu, will not show Figure 10-7 or 10-8 but launch the installed application directly, yielding the "one click" experience after which ClickOnce is named.

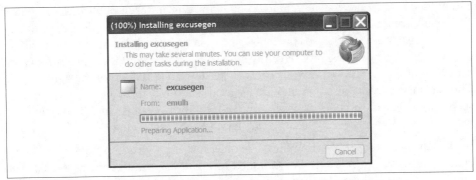

Figure 10-8. Progress dialog for installing a locally installed ClickOnce application

The Pieces of ClickOnce

To produce the user experience we've discussed, Visual Studio generates a set of files and folders wherever it's told to publish the application. Table 10-1 lists the files in the *excusegen* folder that Visual Studio created for us under the Internet Information Server's (IIS's) *wwwroot* folder.

Table 10-1. The files generated by the Visual Studio publication process

Folder	Files
...\excusegen	excusegen.application excusegen_1_0_0_0.application publish.htm setup.exe
...\excusegen\excusegen_1_0_0_0	excusegen.exe.deploy excusegen.exe.manifest

You're already familiar with the *publish.htm* file. The *setup.exe* file is for bootstrapping the .NET Framework 2.0 (required for ClickOnce) if it's not already installed. You can also use Visual Studio to augment this installation to add standard packages, such as Crystal Reports or SQL Server Express, or custom packages specific to your application.

The *.application* files at the root of the application deployment, called *deployment manifests*, are XML files that describe the deployment and update settings for the application. The *.application* file is what the user clicks on to launch a locally installed ClickOnce application.

Each *.application* file references a version-specific specific *.exe.manifest* file, called an *application manifest*, which is an XML file that lists the security-permission requirements and the files associated with a specific version of the application.

Visual Studio generates a *.application/.exe.manifest* pair for each published version of the application, naming each with the version number (either in the file or the folder name). Visual Studio also keeps the *.application* file without the version number up to date with a reference to the most recently published *.exe.manifest* file. This *.application* file is useful if you want all of your users to get the latest version of the application. The version-named *.application* files are useful if you'd like to add code on your web server to do staged roll-outs, satisfying the request for the latest *.application* file with one of the version-specific *.application* files based on the requesting user.

By default, the actual application files, like the application's assemblies or other associated files, have a *.deploy* extension added to guard against security problems that prevent web administrators from allowing files with *.exe* and *.dll* extensions on the web server. The *.deploy* extensions are stripped after the files are downloaded.

Figure 10-9 shows how the deployment manifests reference the application manifest, which in turn references the application's files.

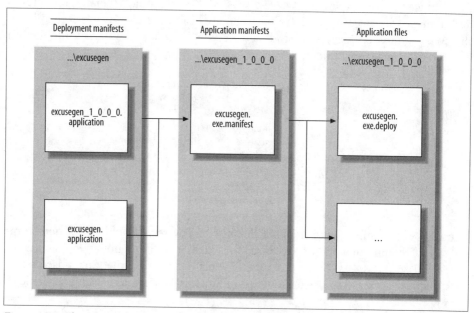

Figure 10-9. The relationship between manifests and files for a single version

While *excusegen* has only a single file, if it had others, the application manifest would reference them as well.

Publish Properties

To manage the settings that control the publication process, including the settings in the manifest files, what extra files to include, how applications should be updated, whether the *.deploy* extension should be added, what belongs in the prerequisite setup, and so on, you can open your project's properties and choose the Publish tab, as shown in Figure 10-10.

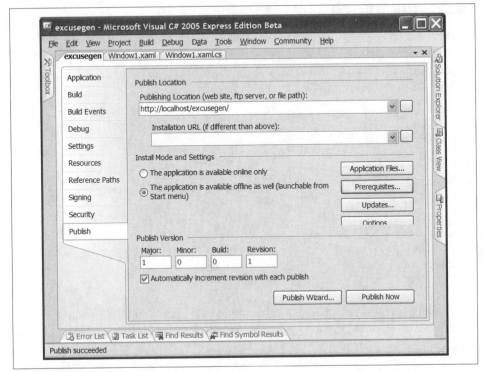

Figure 10-10. Visual Studio project Security settings

Notice that the Publish tab shows the publish location and installation mode settings that we saw in the Publish Wizard before. Notice also the Publish Wizard button, which shows the Publish Wizard, and the Publish Now button, which uses the settings on this tab (as well as the Signing and Security tabs that we'll discuss presently), to publish your application without invoking the wizard.

The numbers in the Publish Version fields are used to version the deployments and are the source of the version numbers in the deployment-manifest filename (*.application* files) and the application-manifest folder name (to hold the *.exe.manifest* and application files). By default, the version number is automatically incremented on each publication, so for every minor change, you can simply press the Publish Now button, getting a new revision number each time. You can also change the Major and Minor version numbers manually when you're ready to publish a major change in the application.

The Application Files, Prerequisites, Updates, and Options buttons let you set detailed publishing options, such as the publisher and product name, whether to add the *.deploy* extension, what non-assembly files to add to the ClickOnce deployment, and lots of other fun things you might want to explore.

Deploying Updates

When you change your application, perhaps to display excuses in italics to emphasize their importance, replace the *.application* file with a new file referencing the new version of the application. After publishing, the folder will be updated as shown in Table 10-2.

Table 10-2. The files generated by the Visual Studio update publication process

Folder	Files
...\excusegen	*excusegen.application* *excusegen_1_0_0_0.application* **excusegen_1_0_0_1.application** *publish.htm* *setup.exe*
...\excusegen\excusegen_1_0_0_0	*excusegen.exe.deploy* *excusegen.exe.manifest*
...\excusegen\excusegen_1_0_0_1	*excusegen.exe.deploy* *excusegen.exe.manifest*

In addition to creating a new folder for the application manifest (*.exe.manifest*), which includes all of the files necessary for that new version, there's a new *.application* file with the new version number, and the other *.application* file has been updated to point at the most current version. Figure 10-11 shows the relationship with two versions in place.

With the new version of the application in place, the user could choose to execute it from the web page, as they did initially, or from the Start menu. With the default update settings in Visual Studio, if they choose to launch the application from the web page, the application will be automatically updated without asking the user, just like surfing to a new version of a web page. However, if the user launches the application from the Start menu, they'll be greeted with a dialog like Figure 10-12.

If the user presses Skip, they will not be bothered by this version again.

If the user presses OK, the updated version will be downloaded and launched just as if it were the newly installed application.

As I mentioned, in addition to the entry in the Start menu, a locally installed Click-Once application has an entry in the Add or Remove Programs Control Panel, as shown in Figure 10-13.

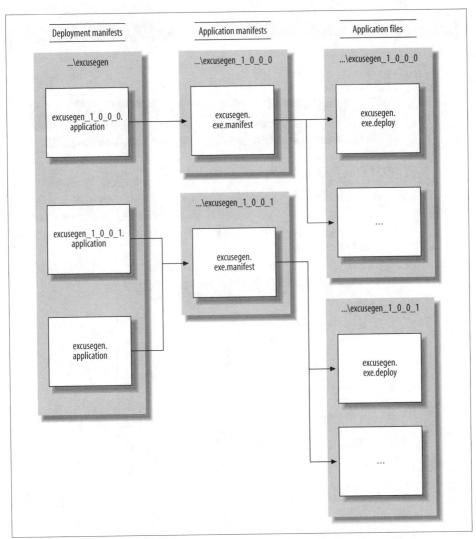

Figure 10-11. The relationship between manifests and files for multiple versions

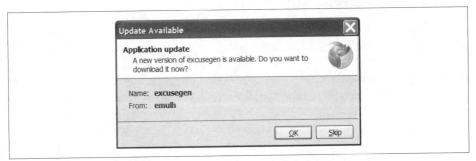

Figure 10-12. "Application update" dialog for locally installed applications

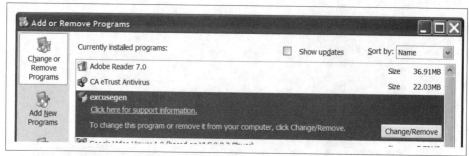

Figure 10-13. Add or Remove Programs entry for locally installed applications

The Change/Remove button allows you to remove the locally installed ClickOnce application. Further, if there's been an update to the application, the Change/Remove button also lets you roll back the application from its current version to the previous version, as shown in Figure 10-14.

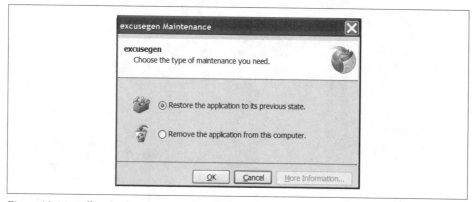

Figure 10-14. Rolling back or removing locally installed applications

If the user chooses to roll back the application to the previous version, it will be as if they'd pressed the Skip button when the latest version was made available.

ClickOnce: Express Applications

A WPF *express application* is an application (most often a navigation application) that is hosted in the browser and runs under a set of restricted permissions that cannot be elevated by the user. Getting a new express application started is most easily accomplished by creating a new Visual Studio project using the Avalon Express Application project template. The generated project will be a navigation application hosted in the browser (as described in Chapter 1), have an install mode of "online only," and will request Internet permissions.

If you'd like to change an existing WPF locally installed application into an express application in the version of Visual Studio available as of this writing, you'll have to set the Install Mode to "online only" on the Publish tab of the project's properties, change the ClickOnce Security Settings to "partial trust" on the Security tab and add a HostInBrowser property set to True under a PropertyGroup element in the project's *.csproj* file using Notepad (or some similarly advanced text editor).

These are all things that are handled for you when you create a new project using the Avalon Express Application project template and will hopefully be handled more holistically in a future version of WPF.

Partial Trust

By default, a locally installed ClickOnce application will be set to *full trust*, as you can see in the Security tab of a project's properties. This means that there will be no use of .NET's Code Access Security permission checking; with full trust, an application can do whatever the executing user is allowed to do. While you are allowed to crank down the set of permissions required to run a locally installed ClickOnce application (in fact, you're encouraged to do so), you are required to request fewer permissions in the case of an express application. The reason is that an express application is not allowed to request increased permissions from the user; either the express application has sufficient permissions by default, or it's not allowed to run at all.

You can set the permissions your ClickOnce application needs in the Security tab of your project's properties, as shown in Figure 10-15.

By default, a new express application project has Internet permissions, which are the maximum your express application can be awarded by default when deployed over the Internet—e.g., from a site with a dot in the name, such as *http://example.com*. If the plan is to deploy the express application in an intranet environment—e.g., *http://hrapps*, you can set the requested security permissions to Intranet instead of Internet.

Programming for partial trust using .NET's Code Access Security is beyond the scope of this book, but one of this book's reviewers, Brian Noyes, recommends *Programming .NET Components* by Juval Lowy (O'Reilly) for a good description.

Publishing Express Applications

Once you've established your express application's publication settings, you can publish it just as you'd publish a locally installed ClickOnce application. The

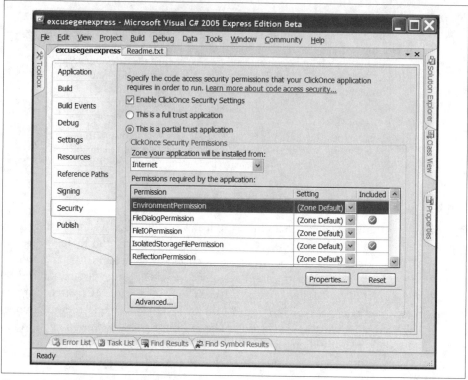

Figure 10-15. Project Security settings

publication process and the generated files will be the same, except that the generated deployment manifest will have a *.xapp* extension instead of a *.application* extension, as shown in Table 10-3.

Table 10-3. Files generated by the Visual Studio publication process for express applications

Folder	Files
...\excusegenexpress	excusegenexpress.xapp
	excusegenexpress_1_0_0_0.xapp
	publish.htm
	setup.exe
...\excusegenexpress\excusegenexpress_1_0_0_0	excusegenexpress.exe.deploy
	excusegenexcuse.exe.manifest

As of this writing, publishing an express application doesn't work so well. For one thing, publication will fail if you use the Publish Wizard; to do as much as Visual Studio will do, you have to press the Publish Now button, and even that won't succeed completely because of the lack of a generated *.application* file. Most of the work will be done, however, and you can finish the job by manually copying the generated *.xapp* file from your project's publish folder into the root of the target of the publication—e.g., *c:\inetpub\wwwroot\excusegenexpress*. If you want both the file with the version number and the one without, you'll have to create both. Also, you'll have to edit the generated *.xapp* application to point to the appropriate *.exe.manifest* file—e.g., change the following:

```
<dependentAssembly ...
  codebase="excusegenexpress.exe.manifest">
```

to include the relative path information:

```
<dependentAssembly ...
  codebase=
    "excusegenexpress_1_0_0_0/excusegenexpress.exe.manifest">
```

Finally, while Visual Studio will create the *publish.htm* file for you, it will contain a link to the nonexistent *.application* file, so you'll either have to edit the *publish.htm* file and launch it yourself, or you can launch the the *.xapp* file for testing yourself—e.g., *http://localhost/ excusegenexpress/excusegenexpress.xapp*

The *.xapp* extension signifies a WPF application that is to be hosted in Internet Explorer.

Browser Hosting

The Avalon Navigation Application project template adds a HostInBrowser property set to True to the project's *.csproj* file. This setting is what causes the *.xapp* file to be generated ("xapp" stands for "Express Application" and is pronounced "zap," as if pulled straight from the world of Flash Gordon). The generated *publish.htm* will show the application links with a Run button instead of an Install button, as shown in Figure 10-16.

Pressing the Run button launches the *.xapp* file, causing the express application to be checked for appropriately limited permissions, downloaded, and hosted in the browser, as shown in Figure 10-17.

As described in Chapter 1, a WPF application hosted in the browser will have its frame provided by Internet Explorer; each Page will be able to set the caption title via its Text property; and you can establish navigation via hyperlinks, which populate the history shown in the Forward and Back buttons.

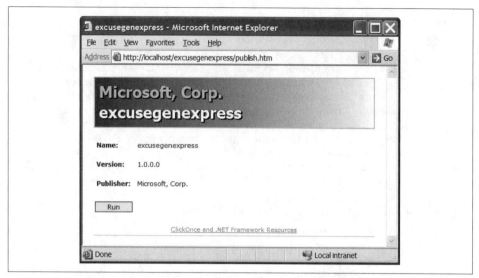

Figure 10-16. Visual Studio–generated HTML file for testing express applications

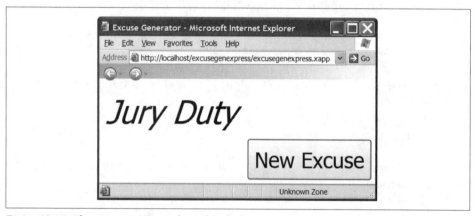

Figure 10-17. The excuses generator hosted in the browser

 Figure 10-17 demonstrates an interesting consequence of pre-release software. In spite of the hosting of the application in the browser, it still has its own Forward and Back buttons that are separate from the browser's Forward and Back buttons, which makes browser hosting a somewhat quirky feature. It's my understanding that the combination of WPF 1.0 and Internet Explorer 7 will eliminate the redundant toolbar and allow the user to navigate back and forth between an express application and HTML.

Choosing Local Install versus Express

Unlike locally installed ClickOnce applications, which are meant to expose the full function of the Windows platform (permissions permitting), an express application is meant to have the same experience of a web page, but with much richer presentation capabilities than HTML allows. A summary of the differences between the two types of ClickOnce WPF applications is shown in Table 10-4.

Table 10-4. Summary of differences between express and locally installed applications

Feature	Express application	Locally installed
Deployed via ClickOnce	✓	✓
Updated when new version is available	✓	✓
Shown in the Start menu		✓
Shown in Add or Remove Programs		✓
Prompted when updates are available		✓
Roll-back to previous version		✓

Signing ClickOnce Applications

In the case of an express application, the publisher will never be shown to the user (even the Visual Studio–generated *publish.htm* file uses the publisher entered in the Publish settings, not the one from the certificate). Either the publisher has sufficient permissions or they don't, but in neither case will the user be shown a dialog to increase the permissions, because that's not allowed for express applications.

However, in the case of ClickOnce applications, a publisher is shown in the Application Install dialog if the application has been signed with a certificate issued by a trusted certificate authority. This changes the Publisher from "Unknown Publisher," as shown in Figure 10-7, into something that helps the user make their installation decision, as shown in Figure 10-18.

Showing a publisher in Figure 10-18 requires the ClickOnce application to be signed with more than the temporary certificate that Visual Studio generates on the fly the first time you publish a ClickOnce application, shown in Figure 10-19.

In addition to putting the publisher name into Figure 10-18, signing your ClickOnce applications (and keeping the certificate files away from prying eyes) prevents someone from breaking onto your web server and changing the manifests—e.g., to sneak in an extra file or ask for full trust.

Even so, there's still the issue of how you prevent bad men from signing the manifests with their own certificates. If they're already messing around with files on your server, you can't stop this. However, the client machine will no longer implicitly trust the files, because the certificate will be different, and therefore the publisher

Figure 10-18. *The Application Install dialog with a known publisher*

Figure 10-19. *The Visual Studio–generated certificate*

will be different. This is why getting your users involved in the trust decision is so important. If they surf to *goodcode.com* and see a ClickOnce dialog asking for permission on behalf of Good Code, Inc., they can have confidence that things are as they seem. If, on the other hand, they see a ClickOnce dialog asking for permission on behalf of "Unknown Publisher," they have the opportunity to stop the code before it's downloaded, let alone executed.

Obtaining a Certificate

If you're going to be publishing code using ClickOnce, you should purchase a code-signing certificate from a signature authority like thawte (*www.thawte.com*) or VeriSign (*www.verisign.com*). You can expect to pay something less than $500 to get started. For this money, the signature authority will verify your identity before issuing your certificate and provide you with a certificate signed with their certificate. This is how ClickOnce knows that, even if you as a publisher may not be trusted on a specific machine, your identity has been verified by a trusted third party.

For testing or internal purposes, however, you may choose to generate a certificate yourself, either manually or using Visual Studio 2005.

If you go the manual route, you can use the makecert tool:

```
C:\>makecert.exe -n "CN=csells" -r -sv excusegen.pvk excusegen.cer
```

After prompting for a password (which you'll need to remember), the makecert tool creates two files, a private key (*excusegen.pvk*) and an X.509 certificate (*excusegen.cer*), embedding the subject name you pass using X.500 notation and marking the certificate as *self-signed*. A self-signed certificate can be used as its own trusted root, which will come in handy later. Also, I've chosen to make an application-specific certificate, but you could also choose to make a department or company-wide certificate.

Keep in mind that since you're making this certificate yourself, it will be really useful only for internal tools when you have some means of pushing a trust decision to the client's machine—e.g., Active Directory or a developer-specific command-line tool (which I'll discuss shortly). Otherwise, the user will surf to some internal web site to use your tool, but get a scary "Unknown Publisher" message, which will be indistinguishable from bad men hijacking your intranet web server.

Once you've created your private key and certificate, it's useful to package them together into a single file for use by other tools using the cert2spc and pvk2pfx* tools:

```
C:\>cert2spc.exe excusegen.cer excusegen.spc
C:\>pvk2pfx.exe -pvk excusegen.pvk -spc excusegen.spc
   -pfx excusegen.pfx -pi pw1 -po pw2
```

The cert2spc tool converts the X.509 certificate to the PKCS #7 format suitable for use by the pvk2pfx tool, which combines the PCKS #7 certificate with the private key into a single file of the Personal Information Exchange format (a.k.a. PKCS #12) with a *.pfx* file extension. In generating the pfx file, you'll need to provide two passwords. The input password is specified via -pi and must match the password you used to generate the X.509 certificate. The output password, specified via -po, is the password associated with the PKCS #12 certificate and will be used to sign applications.

 Be careful how you manage any file that contains a private key, such as a *.pvk* or *.pfx* file, whether you create it yourself or get it from a certificate authority. The private key is meant to be kept private so that it can't be used to sign files by someone else as if you had done it. Keeping these files secure is the cornerstone of the security of asymmetric public/private key signatures.

If, on the other hand, you'd like to let Visual Studio generate your certificate, it can do all of the magic of makecert, cert2spc, and pvk2pfx with a click of a Create Test Certificate button from the Signing tab of the project properties (without the self-signing).

---

* If you don't have pvk2pfx, you can download it from the latest Platform SDK from *http://msdn.microsoft.com/ library/default.asp?url=/library/en-us/sdkintro/sdkintro/devdoc_platform_software_development_kit_start_ page.asp* (*http://shrinkster.com/6jr*).

In fact, that's exactly what happens to create the temporary key on the initial Click-Once publication, although no passwords are used.

Signing with a Certificate

Once you've obtained a PKCS #12 certificate, you can use it to sign your ClickOnce application by pressing the Select from File button on the Signing tab. Or, you can install the certification into the machine's certification store by right-clicking on the file and choosing Install PFX. Once you've done that, you use it to sign applications by clicking the Select from Store button.

If you have Visual Studio generate a certificate for you, it will create the file, place it in the certificate store, and select it to sign your application.

Debugging a Certificate

Once you've generated the certificate, you can explore it using the certutil tool,* as illustrated in Example 10-1.

Example 10-1. Exploring a certificate with certutil

```
c:\>certutil.exe excusegen.pfx
402.203.0: 0x80070057 (WIN32: 87): ..CertCli Version
Enter PFX password:
================ Begin Nesting Level 1 ================
Element 0:
X509 Certificate:
Version: 3
Serial Number: df22bf4b6b58ac9f42a2131171584a84
Signature Algorithm:
    Algorithm ObjectId: 1.2.840.113549.1.1.4 md5RSA
    Algorithm Parameters:
    05 00
Issuer:
    CN=Root Agency

NotBefore: 4/9/2005 4:41 PM
NotAfter: 12/31/2039 4:59 PM

Subject:
    CN=csells

Public Key Algorithm:
    Algorithm ObjectId: 1.2.840.113549.1.1.1 RSA
    Algorithm Parameters:
```

---

* The certutil tool is available with Windows Server 2003 or can be found in the Windows Server 2003 Admin-istration Tools Pack (*http://www.microsoft.com/downloads/details.aspx?familyid=c16ae515-c8f4-47ef-a1e4-a8dcbacff8e3&displaylang=en*) (*http://shrinkster.com/4of*), which can be installed on Windows XP.

Example 10-1. Exploring a certificate with certutil (continued)

```
    05 00
Public Key Length: 1024 bits
Public Key: UnusedBits = 0
    0000   30 81 89 02 81 81 00 dc   8a b5 c5 91 4b 3a 19 1d
...
```

For example, when I was experimenting with the command-line code-signing tools, I found that if I didn't pass a subject name to makecert, the default was "Joe's-Software-Emporium." That's something you'd like to know before passing a certificate out to 10,000 desktops...

Awarding Publisher Trust

If you sign your ClickOnce manifests with a certificate and that publisher is sufficiently trusted on the user's machine, the user will not see a prompt. If you want to maintain the literal meaning of ClickOnce—i.e., not require an extra click to get through the "Application Install" dialog—then you, as a publisher, already need to be trusted on the user's machine with the appropriate permissions.

If an administrator would like to trust a publisher on a set of machines, he can add the publisher's certificate to the user's machine via Active Directory's group policy management. This is useful for adding a certificate from a signature authority or from makecert to a set of client machines in an intranet scenario.

If, on the other hand, you'd like to trust a publisher on your own machine for developer testing, you can do so with the certmgr tool (the same tool that gets launched when you choose Install Certificate on a *.cer* file's context menu). Adding the certificate to the list of trusted publishers makes ClickOnce aware of the publisher so long as the certificate is trusted by a trusted root authority. Adding the same certificate to the list of trusted root authorities will cause a giant warning dialog and cause the trusted publisher to be trusted. Note that adding the certificate to the list of roots works only if the certificate is self-signed or contains your private key (You'll want to avoid the latter, except for you own developer testing.)

As a certmgr shortcut, you can add a self-signed X.509 certificate (*.cer* file) as a root and a trusted publisher from the command line:

```
c:\>certmgr /add excusegen.cer /s TrustedPublisher
c:\>certmgr /add excusegen.cer /s Root
```

If you prefer, you can do the same thing from within Visual Studio with the PKCS #12 certificate (*.pfx* file) by pressing the More Details button on the Signing tab of the project's properties and then pressing the Install Certificate button, which shows the Certificate Import Wizard. You'll need to run through this wizard twice, once for Trusted Publishers and once for Trusted Root Certification Authorities.

Make sure to install the X.509 certificate (*.cer* file) or the PKCS #12 certificate (*.pfx* file) without a private key into the certificate store. The certificate store needs only the public parts of your certificate to identify you as a publisher; the private key should be kept private.

Whether you choose Install Certificate, certmgr, or Visual Studio, once you're done, the publisher described in your certificate will be trusted on the machine in question, which will skip the Application Install Security Warning dialog. Of course, that still leaves it to you to actually be trustworthy...

Programming for ClickOnce

Given the focus on developers for this book, I feel kind of guilty to have gotten this far into this chapter without showing any code. As a programmer targeting ClickOnce, one important constraint is going to be partial trust, where you'll need to know how to code against .NET's Code Access Security (CAS). I've already mentioned *Programming .NET Components* by Juval Lowy (O'Reilly), but feel free to look into your own favorite .NET security resource for the details.

Debugging ClickOnce Applications

No matter which book you pick, when building your ClickOnce applications, you're likely to run into security errors that don't pop up until runtime (often because you didn't request quite the right permissions), along with other kinds of errors. In many cases—e.g., security, communication to another machine, etc.—the errors are going to be specific to the environment into which they're deployed. While an exception dialog is better than nothing, it doesn't hold a candle to a real debugging session. However, if you do nothing and debug as you would normally, you're going to be running in the context of an assembly that's been installed normally, having been awarded full trust by default. To debug your application in partial trust, you'll want to use the Advanced Security Settings dialog (shown in Figure 10-20), accessible via the Advanced button on the Security tab of your Visual Studio project's settings.

By choosing "Debug this application with the selected permission set," you're choosing to enable a CAS environment just like the set of permissions that you're using to deploy your application. Also, by checking "Grant the application access to its site of origin" and filling in the "Debug this application as if it were downloaded from the following URL" field, you've allowed your partially trusted application to "phone home" using web service calls. (By default, partially trusted applications can only communicate off the machine by using web services, and then only to the server from which they were deployed.)

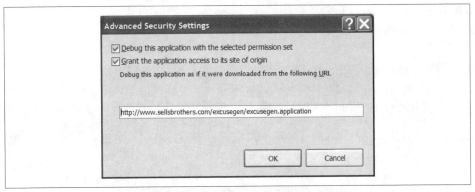

Figure 10-20. Visual Studio ClickOnce debug security settings

In addition to debugging security issues, you're also going to want to see what has gone wrong with deployment itself, or maybe you'd just like to see some of the inner guts of ClickOnce deployment. To see what's going on, under *HKEY_CURRENT_USER\Software\Microsoft\Windows\CurrentVersion\Deployment* in the Registry, add a LogFilePath value with a filename like *c:\clickoncelog.txt*. This logfile will grow as ClickOnce activity happens, so feel free to clear it out to reset it. When something bad happens while running a ClickOnce, you may be offered a dialog to show error details; this will provide access to the same information as is generated into this file.

Command-Line Arguments

As you know, Windows programs, both console and GUI, support the passing of command-line arguments:

```
c:\>excusegen.exe /favorite "land shark" bob
```

In a WPF application, you're most likely to access command-line arguments in the StartingUp application event, as shown in Example 10-2.

Example 10-2. Accessing command-line arguments in the application StartingUp event

```
public partial class MyApp : Application {
  // Usage: excusegen.exe [/favorite excuse] [target]
  void MyApp_StartingUp(object sender, StartingUpCancelEventArgs e) {
    string favorite = "dog ate it";
    string target = "";
    if( e.Args.Length == 1 ) target = e.Args[0];
    if( e.Args.Length > 1 && e.Args[0].ToLower() == "/favorite" ) {
      favorite = e.Args[1];
      if( e.Args.Length == 3 ) target = e.Args[2];
    }
    ...
  }
}
```

However, when launching a ClickOnce application, the application isn't launched directly, it's launched using an URL to a deployment manifest. Based on this, you might like to be able to pass arguments to a ClickOnce applications like so:

```
http://localhost/excusegen.application?favorite=land%20shark&bob
```

This syntax is supported by ClickOnce (actually, you can pass any legal URL past the question mark—it doesn't have to use the standard URL query-string argument format). However, passing arguments to ClickOnce applications is turned off by default. To turn it on, you have to enable parameter passing, which you can do in the Publish Options dialog in Visual Studio, as shown in Figure 10-21.

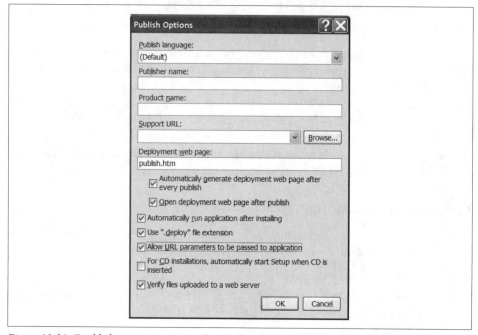

Figure 10-21. Enabled parameter passing for ClickOnce applications in Visual Studio

Once parameter passing is enabled, you still need to handle them. While the StartingUp event is still a fine place to get at them, the ClickOnce arguments are not going to come in via the event arguments. Instead, you'll need to access the current instance of the ApplicationDeployment class from the System.Deployment.Application namespace. The ApplicationDeployment class allows you to do several interesting things, including checking for a network deployment (handy when writing code that works when deployed via ClickOnce and when being run directly from the local computer), getting the current version (handy for About boxes), and the ability to check for update availability and start an update (handy when implementing the Check For Updates menu item).

To access the URL query string holding ClickOnce argument parameters, use `ApplicationDeployment` to access the `ActivationUri` property (see Example 10-3).

Example 10-3. Accessing the ActivationURI property

```
...
using System.Deployment.Application; // ApplicationDeployment

public partial class MyApp : Application {
  void MyApp_StartingUp(object sender, StartingUpCancelEventArgs e) {
    if( ApplicationDeployment.IsNetworkDeployed ) {
      Uri uri = ApplicationDeployment.CurrentDeployment.ActivationUri;

      // The whole thing, e.g.
      // http://localhost/excusegen.application?favorite=land%20shark&bob
      string url = uri.ToString();
      MessageBox.Show(url, "Launch URL:");

      // Just the args, e.g. ?favorite=land%20shark&bob
      string query = uri.Query;
      MessageBox.Show(query, "Query String (Args):");
    }
    ...
  }
}
```

One thing the `ApplicationDeployment` class doesn't do is decode and split an URL-style query string for you. To solve this problem, your instinct may to be reach for the `ParseQueryString` method on the `HttpUtility` class in the `System.Web` assembly, but there are two downsides in doing so. The first is that ASP.NET is not meant to be used from partial trust, so unless your ClickOnce application is running under full trust, you won't be allowed to call the `ParseQueryString` method at all. Even if you were allowed, the second downside is having to load ASP.NET into your ClickOnce application process just to parse a string.

Security Considerations

When building a ClickOnce application, you may have some security questions:

How do I prevent file tampering? Signing your ClickOnce applications, as discussed earlier in this chapter, is the best way to prevent your ClickOnce application users from getting code on their machines that they don't want.

How can I program for partial trust? I've already listed Juval's book twice, so let's make it an even three: *Programming .NET Components* (O'Reilly).

Who can run ClickOnce applications? Any regular user may execute both locally installed ClickOnce and express applications, but only members of the Administrator group can install ClickOnce prerequisites.

How can I keep executable code off of my web server?   Many web sites, including *microsoft.com* itself, prohibit executable code on the web server that has not undergone rigorous testing and security checks for execution in that environment. Since ClickOnce applications aren't meant to run on the web server at all, such testing is inappropriate for this environment. However, since ClickOnce files are not packed into any kind of archive, any executable files associated with a ClickOnce deployment will be loose and therefore a cause for concern. It's for this case that ClickOnce supports the option to append every file in a Click-Once deployment with the *.deploy* extension—e.g., *excusegen.exe* and *readme. txt* become *excusegen.exe.deploy* and *readme.txt.deploy*, respectively. These files are no longer "executable" on the web server, but when downloaded, the files will be renamed transparently.

What MIME types should the web server enable?   In restrictive environments, only a limited set of file extensions are made available for download—e.g., no *.exe* or *.dll* files. This is enabled by restricting the web server to serve up known file extensions using known MIME types. For ClickOnce to function properly, the file extensions and MIME types in Table 10-5 must be enabled.

Table 10-5. Web server MIME types required to enable ClickOnce

File extension	MIME type
.application	application/x-ms-application
.manifest	application/x-ms-manifest
.deploy	application/octet-stream
.xapp	application/x-ms-xapp
.baml	application/baml+xml
.container	application/avalon+progressive
.deploy	application/deployment
.xaml	application/xaml+xml

While these are the special ClickOnce security considerations, these are by no means all of the security considerations you should take into account when writing .NET applications in general. You'll also need to make sure that you're applying the advice of your favorite .NET security books. For these kinds of general-purpose issues, I recommend *The .NET Developer's Guide to Windows Security* by Keith Brown (Addison Wesley). (You thought I was going to mention Juval again, didn't you?)

Where Are We?

WPF application deployment via ClickOnce is managed with two manifest files, an application manifest (*.exe.manifest*) for each new version of the application and a deployment manifest (*.application*) that points at the current version of the application and that the user clicks on to deploy the application. Manifests (and assemblies) should be signed with a trusted certificate so that users can make trust decisions about the publisher of the ClickOnce application. WPF ClickOnce applications can be express or locally installed application. *Express applications* are hosted in the browser with limited permissions and are gone when they're closed, just like web applications. *Locally installed applications* can be executed from the Start menu and managed from the Add or Remove Programs Control Panel, and the user is informed of updates, just like with Windows applications. If there are prerequisites that need installation before your ClickOnce application is installed, Visual Studio can help you prepare them, and, in fact, Visual Studio is an all-around good tool for managing, deploying, signing, and debugging ClickOnce applications. In nearly all ways, ClickOnce is superior to .NET 1.x's No-Touch Deployment; ClickOnce should be your new friend.

XAML

XAML—the eXtensible Application Markup Language—is an XML-based language for creating trees of .NET objects. XAML provides a convenient way of constructing WPF user interfaces. This appendix explores the syntax of XAML and its relationship to .NET code.

Although XAML is seen as being strongly associated with WPF, the two are, strictly speaking, separate. You do not have to use XAML in order to write a WPF application, and it is possible to use XAML for technologies other than WPF. WPF is designed to be convenient to use from XAML, but to understand XAML fully, it is important to realize that it has no special connection with the WPF framework. XAML is essentially just a language for constructing trees of .NET objects.

XAML Essentials

In order to examine the relationship between XAML and .NET, we will work through a very simple XAML file, shown in Example A-1.

Example A-1. Simple XAML file

```
<Window
    xmlns="http://schemas.microsoft.com/winfx/avalon/2005"
    xmlns:x="http://schemas.microsoft.com/winfx/xaml/2005"
    x:Class="XamlProj.Window1"
    Text="Main Window">

    <Grid>
    </Grid>
</Window>
```

Example A-1 is a typical XAML file, such as you would find in a newly created WPF project. Let's look at it in detail to understand what the XAML compiler will do with it.

Namespaces

The first things to examine are the XML namespaces the file uses. There are two here:

```
<Window
    xmlns="http://schemas.microsoft.com/winfx/avalon/2005"
    xmlns:x="http://schemas.microsoft.com/winfx/xaml/2005"
    x:Class="XamlProj.Window1"
    Text="Main Window">
```

XAML relies on XML namespaces to determine the meaning of elements. For example, the root element of this file is a `Window`, but WPF needs to know what .NET type this corresponds to. Many class names are ambiguous—the same name crops up in multiple places in the class libraries. The .NET Framework has a namespace mechanism that is used for disambiguation. Standard XML also has a namespace system that is used for the same purpose. XAML uses XML namespaces to represent .NET namespaces.

There is not a one-to-one correspondence between XML namespaces in XAML and .NET namespaces. One XML namespace can encompass several .NET namespaces. This makes XAML less verbose—WPF's types are spread across a number of namespaces, so a one-to-one mapping would require XAML to contain a lot more XML namespace boilerplate. This one-to-many mapping is workable because no naming collisions result from merging these particular .NET namespaces into a single XML namespace.

The WPF build environment predefines the meaning of certain XML namespaces, including the two in Example A-1. The first indicates types that are part of the WPF framework. (This particular XML namespace encompasses several .NET namespaces, including `System.Windows` and many of its children.) Since this is declared as the default namespace here (there is no colon after the `xmlns`), this indicates that, unless specified otherwise, all elements in this file are WPF elements.

The second namespace, associated here with the "x" prefix, represents various XAML utility features not specific to WPF. This is a special namespace, in that not everything in it corresponds to a type—some features in this namespace are used to control the XAML compiler's behavior.

 There is no particular significance to XML namespace prefixes—you are free to associate any prefix with any namespace. Prefixes are local to the XML within the element that declares the prefix, and there is no requirement that you use the same prefixes from one file to the next. However, the usual convention in XAML is to associate "x" with the XAML namespace. Nothing depends on this convention, but it makes it easier for others to understand your XAML.

Since the root `Window` element is qualified by the WPF XML namespace, the XAML compiler knows that this refers to the `System.Windows.Window` class. The XAML compiler imposes no restrictions on the type of the top-level element, although in WPF applications, the most common choices are `Window`, `Page`, and `Application`.

Generating Classes

Our example has an `x:Class` attribute on the root element:

```
<Window
    xmlns="http://schemas.microsoft.com/winfx/avalon/2005"
    xmlns:x="http://schemas.microsoft.com/winfx/xaml/2005"
    x:Class="XamlProj.Window1"
    Text="Main Window">
```

The `x:` prefix is standard XML shorthand to indicate that this particular attribute is in the namespace specified by the `xmlns:x` attribute. As explained earlier, this is the XAML namespace. The `x:Class` attribute is a signal to the XAML compiler that it should generate a class definition based on this XAML file. The `x:Class` attribute determines the name of the generated class, and it will derive from the type of the root element.

You do not have to specify a `x:Class` attribute. If we were to omit the attribute from this example, the root object's type would be `Window`, rather than the generated `Window1` class.

Opting to generate a class provides an easy way to build the tree of objects represented by the XAML. Each `Window1` instance we generated will contain a set of objects as specified by the XAML, so we can just use normal object construction syntax:

```
Window1 myWindow = new Window1();
```

If you do not provide an `x:Class` attribute, creating the object tree is a little more involved. There are several ways of doing this, and they are discussed at the end of the chapter in the "Loading XAML" section.

Properties

Next, consider the `Text` attribute on the `Window` element:

```
<Window
    xmlns="http://schemas.microsoft.com/winfx/avalon/2005"
    xmlns:x="http://schemas.microsoft.com/winfx/xaml/2005"
    x:Class="XamlProj.Window1"
    Text="Main Window">
```

This attribute has no namespace qualifier. In XAML, unqualified attributes usually correspond to properties on the .NET object to which the element refers. (They can also refer to events, as we'll see later.) The `Text` attribute indicates that when an instance of this generated `XamlProj.Window1` class is constructed, it should set its own Text property to "Main Window". This is equivalent to the following code:

```
myWindow.Text = "Main Window";
```

Children

Next, consider the contents of the Window element:

```
<Grid>
</Grid>
```

The default XML namespace specified by the xmlns attribute in the Window element is the scope for the whole of the XML file, so this element is also in the WPF XML namespace. This therefore corresponds to the System.Windows.Controls.Grid class. But what does it mean for this to be "inside" the window? There isn't any single model for nesting one object inside another in .NET, so there are potentially many different interpretations. XAML does not impose a model—instead, it lets the parent object decide how to deal with child elements.

The XAML compiler will require the parent type (Window in this case) to implement either the IAddChild interface in the System.Windows.Serialization namespace or the standard collection interface ICollection. (The compiler will report an error if you try to add children to an element type that does not implement either of these interfaces.) The IAddChild interface defines two methods: AddChild and AddText. The compiler simply calls these methods for each piece of child content. AddChild is used for elements, and AddText is used for plain text content.

In our example, there is just a single Grid element, so it will arrange for a Grid object to be created and passed to AddChild. Example A-2 shows the code equivalent.

Example A-2. AddChild

```
myWindow.AddChild(new Grid());
```

The Window element implements AddChild by putting the child it in its Content property. (The Window will check that it doesn't already have a child—it only supports a single child and will throw an exception if you try to add more.) This approach is used by all classes derived from ContentControl. So while Example A-2 shows how the child will be added, the effect is as though we had written this:

```
myWindow.Content = new Grid();
```

In the case where the element does not implement IAddChild but implements ICollection, the child elements will simply be added to the collection.

The steps we've just seen illustrate more or less all of what XAML does. The XAML file causes a type to be defined, and the contents cause objects to be created, properties to be set, and methods on the IAddChild interface to be called. Everything else is just a refinement of these basics.

Properties

In Example A-1, the only property we set was the Window element's Text property. This property's type was String. Pure text properties are a natural fit with XML, since XML is a text-based format. But what about other property types? Example A-3 uses a slightly wider range of types.

Example A-3. Non-string properties

```
<Rectangle Width="100"
           Height="20"
           Stroke="Black"
           Fill="VerticalGradient Black Red" />
```

None of the properties set here is a string. Width and Height are both of type Double, while Stroke and Fill both require a Brush. In order to support diverse property types, XAML relies on .NET's TypeConverter system. This has been around since v1.0 of .NET and is used in design-time scenarios. A TypeConverter maps between different representations of a value, most commonly between String and a property's native type.

The Width and Height properties are converted using the LengthConverter type. (WPF knows to use this type because the FrameworkElement class's WidthProperty and HeightProperty fields are marked with a TypeConverterAttribute indicating which converter to use.) The BrushConverter class is used for the other two properties, because while they do not have a TypeConverterAttribute, they are of type Brush, and the Brush type has a TypeConverterAttribute indicating that BrushConverter should be used. The Stroke is set to a standard named color, so this will cause the relevant SolidColorBrush to be fetched from the Brushes class. The Fill in this example is a little more complex—its syntax indicates to the BrushConverter that a linear gradient brush should be created. Here is the equivalent code:

```
Rectangle r = new Rectangle();
r.Width = 100.0;
r.Height = 20.0;
r.Stroke = Brushes.Red;
r.Fill = new LinearGradientBrush(Colors.Black, Colors.Red, 90.0);
```

Custom components can provide their own type converters if they wish to allow properties with nonstandard types to be set easily from XAML.

Property-Element Syntax

Although the type converter system often makes it possible to specify property values using attributes in your XAML, it sometimes falls short; either a suitable converter is not available, or you need to do something too complex to fit into a string. For example, the BrushConverter does not provide a way of specifying multiple

GradientStops in a gradient fill. For these situations, XAML supports the *property-element* syntax.

With the property-element syntax, you set the property using a nested element instead of an attribute. The nested element's name will be of the form *Parent.PropertyName*, where *Parent* is the name of the element whose property is being set and *PropertyName* is the name of the property, as Example A-4 shows. This dotted syntax marks the element as being a property value rather than child content.

Example A-4. Property element syntax

```
<Button>
    <Button.Background>
        <SolidColorBrush Color="Blue" />
    </Button.Background>
    Click me
</Button>
```

Example A-4 uses the property-element syntax to set a Button element's Background property. It is equivalent to this code:

```
Button btn = new Button();
SolidColorBrush brush = new SolidColorBrush();
brush.Color = Colors.Blue;
btn.Background = brush;
btn.AddText("Click me");
```

This particular example has the same effect as a simple Background="Blue" attribute would—if you specify a named color as a brush, the BrushConverter converts it into a SolidColorBrush. While this property-element version is a lot more verbose, it is also more explicit—we can see exactly what kind of a brush will be created here.

Although this more verbose syntax can help demystify some of the magic that type converters do behind the scenes, this is not the normal reason for using the property element syntax. It is typically necessary because we need to nest more complex definitions inside the property. Example A-5 uses property-element syntax for a Button element's Background in order to use a relatively complex brush. The brush itself also uses property-element syntax for a list of GradientStops.

Example A-5. Nested property elements

```
<Button VerticalAlignment="Center" HorizontalAlignment="Center">
    <Button.Background>
        <LinearGradientBrush StartPoint="0,0" EndPoint="0,1">
            <LinearGradientBrush.GradientStops>
                <GradientStop Offset="0"    Color="#800" />
                <GradientStop Offset="0.35" Color="Red" />
                <GradientStop Offset="1"    Color="#500" />
            </LinearGradientBrush.GradientStops>
        </LinearGradientBrush>
    </Button.Background>
```

Example A-5. Nested property elements (continued)

```
    Click me
</Button>
```

Here is the equivalent C# code:

```
Button b = new Button();
b.VerticalAlignment = VerticalAlignment.Center;
b.HorizontalAlignment = HorizontalAlignment.Center;
LinearGradientBrush brush = new LinearGradientBrush();
brush.StartPoint = new Point(0,0);
brush.EndPoint = new Point(0,1);
GradientStop gs = new GradientStop();
gs.Offset = 0;
gs.Color = Color.FromRgb(0x80, 0, 0);
brush.GradientStops.AddChild(gs);
gs = new GradientStop();
gs.Offset = 0.35;
gs.Color = Colors.Red;
brush.GradientStops.AddChild(gs);
gs = new GradientStop();
gs.Offset = 0.35;
gs.Color = Color.FromRgb(0x50, 0, 0);
brush.GradientStops.AddChild(gs);
b.Background = brush;
b.AddText("Click me");
```

Attached Properties

In addition to allowing normal .NET style properties to be set, XAML also supports *attached properties*. An attached property is one where the property is defined by a different type than the element to which the property is applied. Most of WPF's layout elements exploit this to allow attributes specific to the layout type to be applied to child elements, as Example A-6 shows.

Example A-6. Attached properties

```
<Button Grid.Row="1" x:Name="myButton" />
```

The syntax for attached properties is straightforward—they are always of the form *DefiningType.PropertyName*, where *DefiningType* is the name of the type that defines the property and *PropertyName* is the name of the property. XAML interprets this as a call to the static *DefiningType.SetPropertyName* method, passing in the target object and value. Example A-7 shows the code for setting the same attached property set in markup in Example A-6.

Example A-7. Setting an attached property in code

```
Grid.SetRow(myButton, 1);
```

Attached properties are not a standard .NET feature—they are really nothing more than a useful idiom supported by XAML. Attached properties are used extensively in WPF and make an important contribution to its flexibility.

For example, the use of attached properties helps keep the layout system open to extension. Properties specific to a particular layout style are always attached properties. Otherwise, properties such as Grid.Row, DockPanel.Dock, and Canvas.Left would all have to be built into the base FrameworkElement class, making it difficult to add new layout types. With attached properties, you can define your own new layout systems with a corresponding set of attachable properties. All you need to do is provide a static SetPropertyName method on the defining class for each attached property.

Markup Extensions

Type converters and property elements let us initialize most properties to constant values or fixed structures. However, there are certain situations where a little more flexibility is required. For example, we might want to set a property to be equal to the value of some particular static property, but we don't know at compile time what that value will be (for example, setting properties representing user-configured colors). XAML provides a powerful solution in the form of *markup extensions*. A markup extension is a class that decides what the value of a property should be.

Markup-extension classes derive from MarkupExtension, the public members of which are shown in Example A-8.

Example A-8. MarkupExtension class

```
public abstract class MarkupExtension {
    public MarkupExtension () { }

    public abstract object ProvideValue(object targetObject,
                                        object targetProperty);
}
```

Example A-9 shows an example of a markup extension in use.

Example A-9. Using a markup extension

```
...
<Style TargetType="{x:Type Button}">
...
```

The TargetType property of the Style has a value enclosed in braces. This indicates to the XAML compiler that a markup extension is being used. The first string inside the braces is the name of the markup extension class, and the remaining contents are passed to the markup extension during initialization.

We are using x:Type in Example A-9. There is no class called Type in any of the .NET namespaces represented by the XAML namespace, but when the XAML compiler fails to find the markup-extension class, it tries appending Extension to the name. There is a TypeExtension class, so the XAML compiler will use that, passing the string Button to its constructor. Then it will call the extension's ProvideValue method, to obtain the real value to be used for the property. The TypeExtension will return the Type object for the Button class.

The XAML compiler singles out certain markup-extension classes for special treatment, evaluating them at compile time, because the compiler developers know those extensions will always return the same value for a particular input. (Most extensions are evaluated at runtime, including any custom extensions you write.) TypeExtension is one of these special cases. So at compile time, the compiler will do the equivalent of the code in Example A-10.

Example A-10. Compile-time effect of TypeExtension

```
TypeExtension te = new TypeExtension("Button");
object val = te.ProvideValue(s, Style.TargetTypeProperty);
```

The runtime effect of using the TypeExtension in Example A-9 is equivalent to the code in Example A-11.

Example A-11. Runtime effect of TypeExtension

```
Style s = new Style();
s.TargetType = typeof(Button);
```

There are two ways of passing data into a markup extension. One is to provide constructor parameters, as Example A-9 shows. (You can pass multiple parameters, separating each one with a comma.) The other is to set properties on the extension, which you can do by putting *PropertyName=Value* pairs into the list, as Example A-12 shows.

Example A-12. Using Name=Value pairs with a markup extension

```
<TextBlock TextContent="{Binding Path=SimpleProperty, Mode=OneTime}"/>
```

Properties passed to a type extension are parsed using type converters, just like all other properties. Example A-12 is equivalent to the following code in Example A-13.

Example A-13. Setting properties on a Binding

```
Binding b = new Binding();
b.Path = new PropertyPath("SimpleProperty");
b.Mode = BindingMode.OneTime;
```

You can create your own markup-extension type by writing a class that derives from MarkupExtension. (Use the techniques described in the "Using Custom Types" section, later in this chapter, to make sure the XAML compiler can find your extension type.) To enable data to be passed to your extension, either provide one or more constructors that take strings or define suitable properties. Your extension will be instantiated and its ProvideValue method called when the object tree corresponding to the relevant XAML is instantiated at runtime.

WPF supplies a number of useful built-in markup extensions. Most of them are defined in the XAML XML namespace, so by convention they are accessed using the x: prefix. A few are specific to WPF and are in the WPF namespace. The most commonly used built-in extensions are listed in Table A-1 and are in described in the following sections.

Table A-1. Commonly used markup extensions

Type	XAML	Usage
NullExtension	x:Null	Used to indicate null (evaluated at compile time).
TypeExtension	x:Type	Retrieves type object (evaluated at compile time).
StaticExtension	x:Static	Retrieves static property value.
StaticResource	StaticResource	Performs one-shot resource lookup.
DynamicResource	DynamicResource	Sets up resource binding.
ArrayExtension	x:Array	Creates array.
Binding	Binding	Creates a data binding.
TemplateBinding	TemplateBinding	Establishes a property alias.

NullExtension

The NullExtension provides a way of setting a property to null. In some cases, the distinction between not setting a property and setting it explicitly to null is important. For example, a Style might be setting the Background property on all elements of a particular value, and you might want to disable this on a specific element. If you wanted to remove the background entirely rather than setting it to some other color, you would do so by setting that element's Background explicitly to null.

This extension always evaluates to null, so it does not require any parameters. Example A-14 shows the NullExtension being used to set a button's background— this prevents the button from filling in its background.

Example A-14. Using the NullExtension

```
<Button Background="{x:Null}">Click</Button>
```

Example A-14 is equivalent to the code in Example A-15.

Example A-15. Effect of NullExtension

```
Button b = new Button();
b.Background = null;
b.AddText("Click");
```

TypeExtension

TypeExtension returns a System.Type object for the named type. It always takes a single parameter: the type name. The TypeExtension has access to information about the XAML parsing context in which it appears, enabling it to resolve type names in the same way that the XAML compiler does. This means that you do not need to provide a fully qualified type name including the .NET namespace extension. Instead, you use it like this:

```
<Style TargetType="{x:Type Button}">...
```

The TypeExtension will resolve the string "Button" to a type in the same way the XAML compiler will—it will take into account the default XML namespace and any namespace mappings that are present. (See the "Using Custom Types" section, later in this chapter, for more information on namespace mappings.) The effect of this extension is equivalent to the code in Example A-16.

Example A-16. Effect of TypeExtension

```
Style s = new Style();
s.TargetType = typeof(Button);
```

StaticExtension

StaticExtension sets the target property to the value of a specified static property. This markup extension always takes a single parameter, which identifies the source property. The parameter is of the form *ClassName.PropertyName*. Example A-17 uses this extension to retrieve the value of one of the SystemColors properties.

Example A-17. Retrieving a static property

```
<TextBlock Background="{x:Static SystemColors.ActiveCaptionBrush}">Foo</TextBlock>
```

Note that in practice you would not normally use the markup shown in this example. It does not integrate properly with the resource system, so if the application resources contained a brush overriding this system brush, this example would bypass that application-level resource. Also, Example A-17 does not update the property automatically when the property changes—StaticExtension takes a snapshot of the property value. Its effect is equivalent to the following code:

```
TextBlock tb = ne w TextBlock();
tb.Background = SystemColors.ActiveCaptionBrush;
tb.AddText("Foo");
```

However, the StaticExtension is typically used in conjunction with the resource markup extensions described in the next two sections in order to overcome one or both of these issues.

StaticResource

StaticResource returns the value of the specified resource. It is equivalent to calling the FindResource method on the element with which you use the extension. (See Chapter 6 for more information on resource lookup.)

Example A-18 shows how to use this element to retrieve a named resource. Note that StaticResource does not need to be qualified with an x: prefix. This is because resource management is a WPF feature, rather than a generic XAML feature, so the resource markup extensions are in the WPF namespace.

Example A-18. Using a resource with StaticResource

```
<Grid>
    <Grid.Resources>
        <SolidBrush x:Key="fooBrush" Color="Yellow" />
    </Grid.Resources>

    <Button Background="{StaticResource fooBrush}" Name="myButton" />
</Grid>
```

The use of StaticResource in this markup is effectively equivalent to the following code:

```
myButton.Background = (Brush) myButton.FindResource("fooBrush");
```

This is a one-shot resource lookup. The property value will be set to the resource value during initialization and then never changed. If the value associated with the resource name changes, the property will not be updated automatically. For Example A-18 that might not be a problem, but consider Example A-19.

Example A-19. Using a system resource with StaticResource

```
<TextBlock
    Name="myText"
    Background="{StaticResource
        {x:Static SystemColors.ActiveCaptionBrushKey}}" />
```

This markup is similar to Example A-17, except that it performs a resource lookup, enabling this resource's value to be overridden by an application skin. It is equivalent to the following code:

```
myText.Background = (Brush)
            myText.FindResource(SystemColors.ActiveCaptionBrushKey);
```

While this uses the resource-lookup system to retrieve the value, it still takes a snapshot—if the user changes the OS color scheme, this element's background will not be updated automatically. When using resources whose values might change, the DynamicResource extension is a better choice.

DynamicResource

DynamicResource associates the value of the property with the specified resource. This extension is similar to the StaticResource extension, except it tracks changes. Example A-20 shows the dynamic equivalent of Example A-19.

Example A-20. Using a system resource with DynamicResource

```
<TextBlock Name="myText" Background="{DynamicResource
    {x:Static SystemColors.ActiveCaptionBrushKey}}" />
```

This is equivalent to the following code:

```
myText.SetResourceReference(TextBlock.Background,
    SystemColors.ActiveCaptionBrushKey);
```

Instead of taking a snapshot of the resource, this tracks the value of the resource and will update the text block's background automatically if the value changes. The resource system tracks changes made by the user to the OS color scheme, so this will automatically update if the user changes the relevant color.

ArrayExtension

ArrayExtension allows you to set a property to be an array of elements. This is a slightly unusual markup extension in that you do not use the brace syntax—you usually use the property-element syntax instead. This is because an array can contain multiple items, and with the ArrayExtension, these are represented as children of the extension. (You could use the brace syntax if you wanted an empty array, though.)

Example A-21 uses ArrayExtension to create an array as a resource. It then uses this array as the data source for a ListBox. The ArrayExtension requires the array type to be specified through its Type property, for which we use the TypeExtension discussed previously. Here we are creating an array of type Brush.

Example A-21. Creating an array resource with ArrayExtension

```
<Grid>
    <Grid.Resources>
        <x:ArrayExtension Type="{x:Type Brush}" x:Key="brushes">
            <SolidColorBrush Color="Blue" />
            <LinearGradientBrush StartPoint="0,0" EndPoint="0.8,1.5">
                <LinearGradientBrush.GradientStops>
                    <GradientStop Color="Green" Offset="0" />
                    <GradientStop Color="Cyan" Offset="1" />
                </LinearGradientBrush.GradientStops>
            </LinearGradientBrush>
            <LinearGradientBrush StartPoint="0,0" EndPoint="0,1">
                <LinearGradientBrush.GradientStops>
                    <GradientStop Color="Black" Offset="0" />
                    <GradientStop Color="Red" Offset="1" />
                </LinearGradientBrush.GradientStops>
```

Example A-21. Creating an array resource with ArrayExtension (continued)

```
                </LinearGradientBrush>
            </x:ArrayExtension>
        </Grid.Resources>

        <ListBox ItemsSource="{StaticResource brushes}" Name="myListBox">
            <ListBox.ItemTemplate>
                <DataTemplate>
                    <Rectangle Fill="{Binding}" Width="100" Height="40" Margin="2" />
                </DataTemplate>
            </ListBox.ItemTemplate>
        </ListBox>
    </Grid>
```

This is effectively equivalent to the code in Example A-22.

Example A-22. Effect of ArrayExtension

```
Brush[] brushes = new Brush[3];
SolidColorBrush scb = new new SolidColorBrush();
scb.Color = Colors.Blue;
brushes[0] = scb;

LinearGradientBrush lgb = new LinearGradientBrush();
lgb.StartPoint = new Point(0,0);
lgb.EndPoint = new Point(0.8, 1.5);
GradientStop gs = new GradientStop();
gs.Offset = 0;
gs.Color = Colors.Green;
lgb.GradientStops.AddChild(gs);
gs = new GradientStop();
gs.Offset = 1;
gs.Color = Colors.Cyan;
lgb.GradientStops.AddChild(gs);
brushes[1] = lgb;

lgb = new LinearGradientBrush();
lgb.StartPoint = new Point(0,0);
lgb.EndPoint = new Point(0, 1);
gs = new GradientStop();
gs.Offset = 0;
gs.Color = Colors.Black;
lgb.GradientStops.AddChild(gs);
gs = new GradientStop();
gs.Offset = 1;
gs.Color = Colors.Red;
lgb.GradientStops.AddChild(gs);
brushes[2] = lgb;

myGrid.Resources["brushes"] = brushes;
...
myListBox.ItemsSource = myListBox.Resources["brushes"];
```

The results are shown in Figure A-1.

Figure A-1. Array of brushes presented by a ListBox (Color Plate 29)

Note that this is an example where markup may not be the best choice. Example A-22 is a literal translation of the markup in Example A-21. However, it is possible to write much more succinct code to build an equivalent array:

```
Brush[] brushes = new Brush[3];
brushes[0] = Brushes.Blue;
brushes[1] = new LinearGradientBrush(Colors.Green, Colors.Cyan,
                          new Point(0, 0), new Point(0.8, 1.5));
brushes[2] = new LinearGradientBrush(Colors.Black, Colors.Red,
                          new Point(0, 0), new Point(0, 1));
```

If you have a choice between putting something in markup and putting it in code, code can often offer a more compact representation. The main reason ArrayExtension exists is for the benefit of XAML-based tools. It enables such tools to create an array without needing to be able to generate code.

Binding

The Binding markup extension is used for data binding. Example A-23 shows a very simple example.

Example A-23. Binding markup extension

```
<TextBlock TextContent="{Binding Foo}" x:Name="txt" />
```

This binds the TextContent property to the Foo property on whatever object is in the data context. It is effectively equivalent to the following code:

```
Binding b = new Binding("Foo");
BindingOperations.SetBinding(txt, TextBlock.TextContentProperty, b);
```

Chapter 4 provides a full explanation of how data binding works and describes the use of the Binding extension.

TemplateBinding

TemplateBinding is used in control templates to indicate where properties from the source object are to be mapped into properties of objects in the template. Example A-24 shows a simple example.

Example A-24. TemplateBinding markup extension

```
<Rectangle Width="100" Height="200" Fill="{TemplateBinding Background}" />
```

This causes the `Rectangle` element's `Fill` property to alias the underlying control's `Background` property. It is equivalent to the following:

```
FrameworkElementFactory factory = new FrameworkElementFactory(typeof(Rectangle));
factory.SetValue(Rectangle.WidthProperty, 100);
factory.SetValue(Rectangle.HeightProperty, 200);
TemplateBindingExtension tb =
                        new TemplateBindingExtension(Button.BackgroundProperty);
factory.SetValue(Rectangle.FillProperty, tb);
```

This code looks rather different from everything else because template bindings are used in the context of a template. A template element handles its child content differently from other elements—it generates a `FrameworkElementFactory` that is capable of building the content, rather than simply building the content. This is because a template may be instantiated any number of times. The use of property aliasing in control templates is explained in Chapter 5.

Code-Behind

Separate handling of appearance and behavior is an important design principle for keeping UI code manageable. In order to help with this separation, XAML supports the concept of *code-behind*, where a XAML file has a corresponding source file containing executable code. The idea is that the XAML file defines the structure of the user interface, while the code-behind file provides its behavior.

The exact definition of *behavior* can look a little different in WPF applications compared with what you may be used to. It is possible use styling and event triggers to make a UI respond automatically to simple stimuli. In older UI technologies, you would typically have used code to achieve this, but in WPF we normally use markup. Although this is behavior in the sense that it is something the application does in response to input, it is essentially superficial behavior—part of the look and feel of the application, rather than the functionality. This superficial behavior usually lives in the control template, and can therefore be replaced without altering the underlying behavior of the control, as described in Chapter 5.

In the context of code-behind, behavior usually means the application functionality invoked when you click a button, rather than what the button looks like when it is clicked.

Of course you won't want to put much application logic in your code-behind if you care about maintainability and testability. In practice, the code-behind is likely to act as the glue between the UI and the code that implements the bulk of the application logic.

XAML supports code-behind through the use of *partial classes*. Partial classes allow a class definition to be spread across multiple source files—each individual file contains only a partial definition of the class. At compile time, the compiler combines these to form the full class definition. The main purpose of partial classes is to allow generated code and handwritten code to share a class without having to share a source file.

When you add the x:Class attribute to the root element, the XAML compiler generates a partial class definition from the markup. You can then put your code-behind in another partial definition for the same class. At compile time, the compiler will merge these two partial definitions into a single, complete class. This lets the XAML compiler add members into the class. These are private members, making them inaccessible to anyone who uses the class, but because these members are added to your class, they are directly accessible to your code-behind.

If you have defined an element in XAML that you wish to use from the code-behind, just set an x:Name attribute:

```
<Button x:Name="myButton">Click</Button>
```

The XAML compiler will add a myButton field to the class and will set this to refer to the button during initialization. This enables you to write code in the code-behind that uses the element directly:

```
myButton.Background = Brushes.Green;
```

 If you are using Visual Studio, you will need to compile your project after adding an x:Name attribute to an element in XAML before IntelliSense will work in the current WPF preview. This is because IntelliSense depends on being able to see the code that the XAML compiler generates in order to know that the field is present.

The main job of the code-behind is to enact application functionality in response to user input. So you will often need to attach event handlers to elements in the XAML. The preferred approach is to write code that attaches handlers during initialization in your code-behind. (Chapter 3 discussed why this is the preferred technique.) However, XAML can attach event handlers for you, and for a simple UI where both the code and the XAML are maintained by the same individual, this can be slightly more convenient. The syntax is similar to that for properties—we use attributes in the XAML:

```
<Button Click="ButtonClicked">Click</Button>
```

Although this looks similar to the property syntax, the XAML compiler will detect that the Click member is an event, not a property. It will expect your code-behind to provide a function called ButtonClicked and will add that function as a handler for the button's `Click` event. You must make sure that the function has the correct signature—all .NET events expect a particular kind of function signature. Example A-25 shows a suitable method declaration for the `Click` event handler. Many event handlers will look something like this, but you should consult the documentation for the event you wish to handle to determine the exact signature required.

Example A-25. Event handler

```
private void ButtonClicked(object sender, RoutedEventArgs e) { ... }
```

 WPF's command-handling architecture can often provide a more elegant and flexible way of responding to user input than handling events directly from elements, so you should consider using commands where possible. Chapter 3 describes handling input with events and commands in more detail.

The class generated by the XAML compiler clearly has a fair amount of work to do during initialization. It needs to create the tree of objects specified by elements in the XAML. It needs to assign values to properties. It needs to populate fields for named elements. It must attach any specified event handlers. All of this work is done by a method called `InitializeComponent`, which gets generated at compile time as a result of specifying the x:Class attribute. This is why when you create a new XAML page in Visual Studio, the class in the code-behind always looks something like Example A-26.

Example A-26. Code-behind and initialization

```
public partial class Window1 : Window {
    public Window1() {
        InitializeComponent();
    }
}
```

You must not delete the call to `InitializeComponent`. This does all of the work specified by the XAML document. All of the fields referring to elements on the page will be null until you call this function, so you will normally want to leave it as the very first thing your constructor does. If you add overloaded constructors in order to allow parameters to be passed, make sure you call `InitializeComponent` from these, too.

Code in XAML

You will normally keep all of your source code in the code-behind. This separation of code from UI structure usually makes code maintenance easier, and there is rarely any reason to put code onto the XAML page. However, while the authors of this book aren't fans of this technique, it is supported.

You can embed source into the XAML file by adding a Code element in the XAML XML namespace, as shown in Example A-27.

Example A-27. Inline code

```
<Window x:Class="XamlProj.Window1"
    xmlns="http://schemas.microsoft.com/winfx/avalon/2005"
    xmlns:x="http://schemas.microsoft.com/winfx/xaml/2005"
    Text="XamlProj">

    <Grid>
        <Button Name="myButton" Click="InlineClickHandler">Click!</Button>

    </Grid>
    <x:Code><![CDATA[
    private void InlineClickHandler(object sender, RoutedEventArgs e) {
        myButton.Background = Brushes.Blue;
    }
    ]]></x:Code>
</Window>
```

The XAML compiler takes any such Code elements and simply adds the content directly to the class it generates.

> The XML CDATA section tells the XML reader that a section of non-XML content follows and saves us from adding escape sequences to prevent the code from being misinterpreted. You are not obliged to use CDATA—you could instead manually escape any characters that would otherwise be misinterpreted. But CDATA is usually easier—it allows blocks of non-XML text to be inserted verbatim.

If you try this yourself in Visual Studio, you will find this to be an unsatisfactory way of working. Because the file type is *.xaml*, the editor offers no syntax highlighting or IntelliSense for embedded C# code. And since the code in question is simply injected into the partial class that the XAML compiler creates, it is equivalent to putting the exact same code into your code-behind. So it offers no compelling benefits and some considerable disadvantages.

Why does this feature exist if it is so useless? Its only attractive feature is that it allows the UI structure and functionality to be combined into a single source file rather than split across two. For very short example code, this simple packaging might look more attractive than splitting the code across two files. But in general, you should avoid this style of coding—for anything nontrivial, it will just cause pain.

Using Custom Types

XAML is not restricted to using types defined by WPF. You are free to use your own types, too. Suppose we wanted to use the following custom element in Example A-28.

Example A-28. A (very) simple custom element

```
public class CustomElement : ContentControl {

}
```

Obviously that's not a terribly exciting custom element, but the steps required to use a boring custom type are exactly the same as those required for more useful examples. So let's look at how we would make use of this type in XAML.

Recall that XAML relies on XML namespaces to determine which .NET class an element represents, so all you need to do is introduce a new XML namespace of your own.

In XAML, we use a *processing instruction* to establish the relationship between an XML namespace used in a XAML file and a .NET namespace. Processing instructions (or PIs for short) are a standard feature of XML, allowing XML files to pass extra information that is "out of band" of the main tree of elements. A PI is similar to #pragma in C++ and C#—it lets you control how the compiler deals with some aspect of the code, but it is not treated as part of the code.

A processing instruction is a sequence of characters starting with <?*Name* and ending with ?>, where *Name* indicates the type of PI. (Slightly confusingly, this syntax is also used for the optional <?xml ... ?> declaration at the start of the file, which is not treated as a PI, despite having the same syntax.) The XML specification allows any *Name* other than xml to be used in a PI. The XAML compiler looks for a Mapping PI, such as that shown in Example A-29.

Example A-29. Mapping processing instruction

```
<?Mapping XmlNamespace="http://example.com/foo" ClrNamespace="MyNamespace" ?>
```

 Do not put a space between <? and Mapping. It might look nicer, but it won't work.

Example A-29 simply tells the XAML compiler that whenever it finds an element defined in the http://example.com/foo XML namespace, it should look for the corresponding class in the MyNamespace .NET namespace.

There is no particular significance to the text used for the XML namespace. The XML Namespace specification requires that the string be a valid URI. It is therefore common to use a URL—if you own a domain name, you implicitly own any URLs under that domain, which makes this a convenient way of defining globally unique identifiers. If you prefer the inscrutability of GUIDs, feel free to use a UUID URN instead, such as `urn:uuid:6b2c8a2f-29cb-4dbe-b118-8fd23be27145`.

The use of URLs often confuses people unfamiliar with XML namespaces, because it appears to imply that something will be downloaded from that URL. In fact this is not the case—the URL is being used as nothing more than a unique name. The XAML compiler will not attempt to download anything. In fact, it won't do anything at all with the name—you could specify `foo` as a namespace, and it would be perfectly happy, as it just treats the string as an opaque identifier.

Syntactically, a simple string like `foo` is a relative URI, and as such is valid. Such a URI is unlikely to be globally unique of course, but it can be useful when introducing a namespace for types defined within the project. Some examples in this book use `local` as a namespace to refer to custom types defined within the local project.

Having established a mapping, we can now use the XML namespace in our XAML. Because URIs are designed to be globally unique, they tend to be somewhat cumbersome to work with, so it's much more convenient to define a shortcut to refer to the namespace. So we usually add an XML namespace prefix in the root element, as Example A-30 shows.

Example A-30. Defining and using a custom XML namespace

```
<?Mapping XmlNamespace="http://example.com/foo" ClrNamespace="MyNamespace" ?>

<Window
    xmlns="http://schemas.microsoft.com/winfx/avalon/2005"
    xmlns:x="http://schemas.microsoft.com/winfx/xaml/2005"
    xmlns:my="http://example.com/foo">

    <my:CustomElement />

</Window>
```

This example refers to three XML namespaces. The default namespace here—the namespace to which elements will be presumed to belong unless otherwise specified—is the WPF namespace. We have also defined the usual x prefix for the XAML namespace. Finally, we have chosen to use my as shorthand for the namespace introduced with the Mapping PI at the top of the file.

When the XAML compiler sees the my:CustomElement element, it will know that my refers to the http://example.com/foo XML namespace. The processing instruction tells it that this refers to the MyNamespace .NET namespace. So it will look for a type called MyNamespace.CustomElement.

With Example A-30, the XAML compiler will expect the CustomElement type to be defined in the same project as the XAML file itself. But what if we want to use an element type defined in some external library? In this case, we can provide an extra parameter to the Mapping processing instruction. As well as specifying the XmlNamespace and ClrNamespace, we can also supply an Assembly, specifying the name of the assembly that contains the type, as Example A-31 shows.

Example A-31. Referring to external components

```
<?Mapping XmlNamespace="urn:whatever" ClrNamespace="MyLib.Controls"
    Assembly="mycustomlibrary"?>
```

This works in much the same way as the mapping shown in Example A-30—it associates a particular XML namespace with a specific .NET namespace, but this time, the XAML compiler will look for an assembly called mycustomlibrary, rather than looking for the type in the same project as the XAML file.

Custom Attached Properties

Earlier in this appendix, we looked at the syntax for attached properties. As we saw, you indicate the use of an attached property with an attribute of the form *TypeName.PropertyName*, as shown here:

```
<Button Grid.Row="1" x:Name="myButton">Click me</Button>
```

You can define custom attached properties. You simple need to provide a pair of Get and Set static methods. Example A-32 defines an attached property called Foo.Bar, of type Brush. (The XAML compiler doesn't care how you implement these accessors, so the details have not been shown.)

Example A-32. Defining a custom attached property

```
public class Foo {
    public void SetBar(DependencyObject target, Brush b) { ... }
    public Brush GetBar(DependencyObject target) { ... }
}
```

To use such a property, you would need to define an XML namespace with a mapping instruction in exactly the same way as you would to use a custom element. Example A-33 shows this syntax.

Example A-33. Using a custom attached property

```
<?Mapping XmlNamespace="http://example.com/foo" ClrNamespace="MyNamespace" ?>

<Window
```

Example A-33. Using a custom attached property (continued)

```
    xmlns="http://schemas.microsoft.com/winfx/avalon/2005"
    xmlns:x="http://schemas.microsoft.com/winfx/xaml/2005"
    xmlns:my="http://example.com/foo">

    <Button my:Foo.Bar="Blue" />

</Window>
```

This example illustrates the syntax required to use a custom attached property. As with any attached property, it follows the *TypeName.PropertyName* pattern. But since the defining type is not in the default namespace, the *TypeName* has to be qualified by a namespace prefix. So the syntax is in effect *xmlNamespacePrefix:TypeName.PropertyName*.

Common Child-Content Patterns

Earlier in this appendix, we saw that XAML has no preconceived notions of how elements deal with child content—it defers to the parent's implementation of the `IAddChild` interface or, in the case of collections, its `ICollection` interface. However, although in theory each element type could handle child content differently, in practice WPF uses one of a few common handling patterns for most elements. This section describes these patterns.

 These patterns are not built into the XAML compiler. These are just common ways in which `IAddChild` is implemented in WPF.

Panels

As we saw in Chapter 2, most of WPF's layout containers derive from the `Panel` base class. They all inherit the same behavior for child content. Child elements in XAML are added to the `Children` property. Consider this markup:

```
<StackPanel>
    <Button>Foo</Button>
    <Button>Bar</Button>
</StackPanel>
```

This is effectively shorthand for this:

```
<StackPanel>
    <StackPanel.Children>
        <Button>Foo</Button>
        <Button>Bar</Button>
    <StackPanel.Children>
</StackPanel>
```

Singular Content

Some controls can accept only a single child element. All controls derived from ContentControl fall into this category, and they all use the same approach. (ContentControl enables the rich content model shown in Chapter 3.) They use their child element as the value of the Content property. If you supply more than one child, they throw an exception. For example, consider this markup:

```
<Button>
    <Ellipse Fill="Red" Height="20" Width="70"/>
</Button>
```

This is shorthand for the following:

```
<Button>
    <Button.Content>
        <Ellipse Fill="Red" Height="20" Width="70"/>
    </Button.Content>
</Button>
```

If you supply just text rather than an element, content controls will automatically wrap the text in a TextBlock element for you.

Items Collection

Some controls present a collection of children in a uniform manner. For example, in a RadioButtonList, every child item is a radio button. ListBox and ComboBox both present each child as an item in the list. A TabControl presents each child as a tab page.

When you add a child to one of these elements, the IAddChild implementation adds the child to the Items collection. So the following markup is just shorthand:

```
<ListBox>
    <TextBlock>Foo</TextBlock>
    <TextBlock>Bar</TextBlock>
    <TextBlock>Quux</TextBlock>
    <TextBlock>Spong</TextBlock>
</ListBox>
```

The equivalent full version is:

```
<ListBox>
    <ListBox.Items>
        <TextBlock>Foo</TextBlock>
        <TextBlock>Bar</TextBlock>
        <TextBlock>Quux</TextBlock>
        <TextBlock>Spong</TextBlock>
    </ListBox.Items>
</ListBox>
```

Collections

The XAML compiler recognizes the ICollection interface. Since most collections implement ICollection, when a property is of a collection type, you typically do not need to supply an element for the collection itself. This example shows the normal way to populate the GradientStops property of a LinearGradientBrush:

```
<LinearGradientBrush StartPoint="0,0" EndPoint="0,1">
    <LinearGradientBrush.GradientStops>
        <GradientStop Color="Black" Offset="0" />
        <GradientStop Color="Red" Offset="1" />
    </LinearGradientBrush.GradientStops>
</LinearGradientBrush>
```

It is equivalent to the following:

```
<LinearGradientBrush StartPoint="0,0" EndPoint="0,1">
    <LinearGradientBrush.GradientStops>
        <GradientStopCollection>
            <GradientStop Color="Black" Offset="0" />
            <GradientStop Color="Red" Offset="1" />
        </GradientStopCollection>
    </LinearGradientBrush.GradientStops>
</LinearGradientBrush>
```

Some classes take this a step further and allow you to omit both the element for the collection, as well as the name of the property that holds the collection. This is common for elements that have only one viable property for holding children, such as the GeometryGroup. The only children you could meaningfully add to this element are child geometry elements. So you can write this:

```
<GeometryGroup>
    <PathGeometry>...</PathGeometry>
    <PathGeometry>...</PathGeometry>
</GeometryGroup>
```

The preceding markup is equivalent to this more verbose markup:

```
<GeometryGroup>
    <GeometryGroup.Children>
        <GeometryCollection>
            <PathGeometry>...</PathGeometry>
            <PathGeometry>...</PathGeometry>
        </GeometryCollection>
    </GeometryGroup.Children>
</GeometryGroup>
```

Loading XAML

If you use the x:Class attribute to generate a class from your XAML file, you can instantiate the tree of objects defined in the XAML by creating an instance of the relevant class. However, you are not required to generate a class.

If you do not generate a class, there are two ways you can get from XAML to a tree of objects. You can either compile the XAML at runtime, or you can precompile it into a binary form called BAML and load that.

In either case, we use the `Parser` class in the `System.Windows.Serialization` namespace to create the tree of objects.

Parsing XAML at Runtime

The `Parser` class defines a static `LoadXml` method. You can pass this a `Stream` or an `XmlReader`. Example A-34 passes an `XmlTextReader`, which derives from `XmlReader`.

Example A-34. Parsing XAML at runtime

```
StringReader sr = new StringReader(@"
    <Canvas xmlns='http://schemas.microsoft.com/winfx/avalon/2005'>
        <Rectangle Width='30' Height='100' Fill='Red' />
    </Canvas>");
XmlTextReader xr = new XmlTextReader(sr);

Canvas tree = (Canvas) Parser.LoadXml(xr);
```

This is a slightly contrived example, as it loads the XAML as a string constant. It would have been simpler just to create the relevant objects from code. But you could load the XAML from elsewhere, at which point this becomes a much more powerful technique. For example, you could generate the XML dynamically, perhaps using an XSLT. This would be one way of generating your user interface dynamically (although, depending on what you want to achieve, data binding might be a better alternative).

Note that if you put an `x:Class` attribute into XAML loaded in this way, you will get an error. You can only generate a class for a XAML file as part of a build process.

Loading BAML

The `Parser.LoadXml` has to parse your XAML at runtime. This makes it flexible, but it is also expensive. If your XAML is not being dynamically generated, this overhead is serving no useful purpose. Fortunately, you can precompile the XAML into a binary form called BAML. By doing this at compile time, you can minimize the runtime costs.

 As we saw in Chapter 6, this is exactly what happens by default when you add a XAML file to a project—VS 2005 runs the XAML compiler on it and adds the resulting BAML to your executable as an embedded resource.

You can retrieve this resource stream using the resource APIs shown in Chapter 6. Once you have a BAML stream, you can call `Parser.LoadBaml`. This works just like `Parser.LoadXml`—it will build a tree of objects corresponding to the original XAML.

Interoperability

A few lucky souls have the luxury of building their applications using only WPF, ignoring the long history of Windows presentation frameworks that have come before. Unfortunately, the rest of us have presentation logic built up in Win32, MFC, Windows Forms, ActiveX, and HTML that we'd like to keep, whether that means bringing new WPF-based controls into our existing application or bringing existing controls built with other frameworks into our new WPF applications.

There are two gaps of interoperability that we have to worry about. The first is the core abstraction that defines the regions of functionality we'd like to use as a host or as a control: the HWND versus the WPF element. Raw Win32 applications are built in terms of HWNDs, as are MFC-, Windows Forms–, and ActiveX-based applications. HTML applications are built in terms of pages, which are served up with an instance of the Web Browser ActiveX control and which host other ActiveX controls as content. On the other side of this gap, we have the WPF element, which is a new thing that breaks the long tradition of Windows-based presentation stacks by not being HWND-based.

The second interoperability gap is characterized as native versus managed code. Raw Win32, MFC, and even HTML applications and controls are native, whereas both Windows Forms and WPF are managed. Bridging the native/managed gap requires the Platform/Invoke (P/Invoke) capabilities of .NET.

Whether you have to cross one or both of these bridges depends on what techniques you need to bring to bear in hosting or being hosted. For example, moving between Windows Forms and WPF requires us to worry about HWNDs versus WPF elements, but the code for both of these presentation stacks is managed, which eases the journey. On the other hand, hosting a WPF control in an MFC dialog requires P/Invoke of some form to be able to build call chains back and forth between native and managed code.

WPF and HWNDs

Whether the existing code you're integrating with WPF is managed or not, it's going to be HWND-based if it was built on Windows. If you run a normal Windows application, such as Calc, it will be composed of a parent window and several child windows. If you run the developer tool Spy++ and examine Calc, you'll see that the buttons and the calculation display are all windows, as shown in Figure B-1.

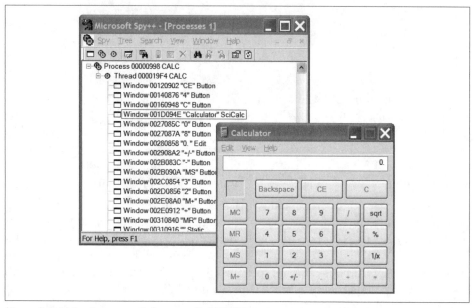

Figure B-1. Using Spy++ on Calc to see the HWNDs

Each of the windows in Figure B-1 is an HWND instance exposed by the User API, which is what has put the "Windows" in Windows since 1985 (when Microsoft Windows 1.0 was released). The top-level window, 001D094E, is the parent window for the child-button and edit-box windows that make up the calculator UI.

If you run Spy++ against the WPF calculator sample in the SDK, you'll see a very different picture, as shown in Figure B-2.

In Figure B-2, notice that there's a top-level window (00430326), but no child windows for calculator-related UI elements, because there are none. In fact, the only visible HWND in the entire application is the one provided for the main window. Every child on the main window is a Visual, not an HWND, and is managed directly by WPF. By default, only top-level Window elements get HWNDs. (This includes menus, tool tips and combo box drop-downs so that they can extend past the main window's borders if necessary.)

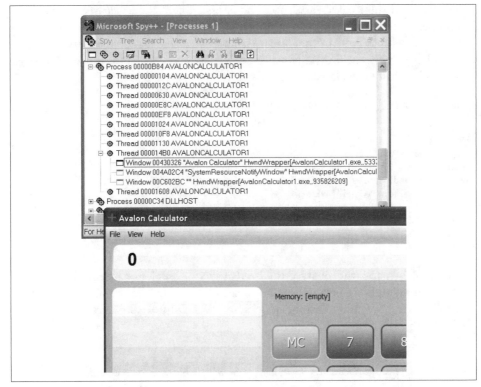

Figure B-2. Exposing the single HWND in a WPF version of Calc

The lack of HWNDs in WPF leads to somewhat of a problem for interoperability between WPF and the Windows applications that have come before it. If you want to host an HWND, whether it's the edit control provided by Win32 or the TextBox class provided by Windows Forms, you're going to first need to introduce an HWND into the WPF tree to serve as the control's parent, which is exactly what the HwndHost is for.

The HwndHost class is an abstract class that provides much of the functionality required to interop with HWND-based windowing, including message hooks, measuring, positioning, keyboard handling, and, of course, the ever-important window procedure (WndProc), into which all windowing messages come.

Hosting a Windows Form Control in WPF

On top of this core functionality of the HwndHost class, deriving classes handle details germane to their specific framework. As of this writing, WPF exposes only one such specialization: the WindowsFormsHost class from the System.Windows.Forms.Integration namespace and the WindowsFormsIntegration assembly.* The WindowsFormsHost class has properties for background, font, and tab index properties to provide integration at those points with WPF. Also, the WindowsFormsHost element is able to serve as a parent of other elements in XAML. However, before we get to using the WindowsFormsHost as a host, let's just take a look at one on its own in Example B-1.

Example B-1. Adding an HWND host to a WPF tree

```
<!-- Window1.xaml -->
<?Mapping
  XmlNamespace="wfi"
  ClrNamespace="System.Windows.Forms.Integration"
  Assembly="WindowsFormsIntegration" ?>
<Window ... xmlns:wfi="wfi" xmlns:wf="wf">
  <Grid>
    <wfi:WindowsFormsHost Width="100" Height="100" />
  </Grid>
</Window>
```

Example B-1 maps the System.Windows.Forms.Integration namespace from the WindowsFormsIntegration assembly and creates an instance of the WindowsFormsHost control of size 100×100. This introduces an HWND into WPF's tree, as shown in Figure B-3.

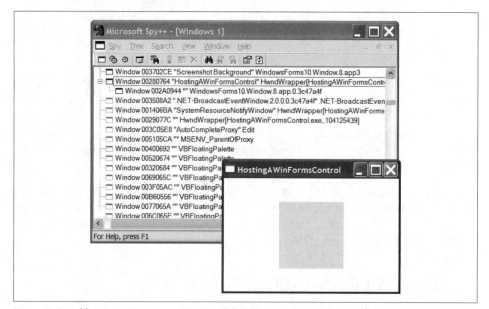

Figure B-3. Adding an HWND to a WPF application using the WindowsFormsHost

---

* Available in the *C:\Program Files\Reference Assemblies\Microsoft\Avalon\v2.0.50215* folder on my machine.

With an HWND injected into the WPF tree, we can now host a control from the HWND-based UI framework that WPF integrates best with: Windows Forms. For example, after adding a reference to the System.Windows.Forms assembly to the project, we can host a DataGridView control, as shown in Example B-2.

Example B-2. Hosting a Windows Forms DataGridView in WPF

```
<!-- Window1.xaml -->
<?Mapping
  XmlNamespace="wfi"
  ClrNamespace="System.Windows.Forms.Integration"
  Assembly="WindowsFormsIntegration" ?>
<?Mapping
  XmlNamespace="wf"
  ClrNamespace="System.Windows.Forms"
  Assembly="System.Windows.Forms" ?>
<Window ... xmlns:wfi="wfi" xmlns:wf="wf" >
  <Grid>
    <wfi:WindowsFormsHost>
      <wfi:WindowsFormsHost.Controls>
        <wf:DataGridView x:Name="gridView" />
      </wfi:WindowsFormsHost.Controls>
    </wfi:WindowsFormsHost>
  </Grid>
</Window>
```

Here, we've mapped in the System.Windows.Forms namespace so that we have access to the DataGridView control. We've also named the control in the same way that you would any element in WPF, which gives us programmatic access to the DataGridView from our code in Example B-3.

Example B-3. Populating the DataGridView from code

```
// Window1.xaml.cs
...
namespace HostingAWinFormsControl {
  public class Person {...}
  public class People : System.Collections.Generic.List<Person> { }

  public partial class Window1 : Window {
    public Window1( ) {
      InitializeComponent( );

      People family = new People( );
      family.Add(new Person("Tom", 9));
      family.Add(new Person("John", 11));
      family.Add(new Person("Melissa", 36));
      gridView.DataSource = family;
    }
  }
}
```

In Example B-3, we're using normal Windows Forms data binding by setting the data source to a collection of Person objects. Since both WPF and Windows Forms are managed, we can call from one to the other without any special considerations. Figure B-4 shows the hosted DataGridView control in action.

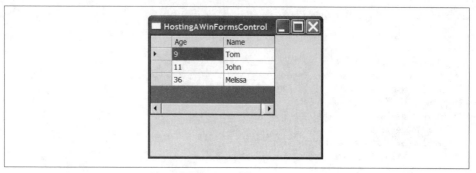

Figure B-4. Hosting a Windows Forms DataGridView in a WPF application

In the case of the DataGridView control, we can go even further when taking advantage of XAML, as in Example B-4.

Example B-4. Hosting and populating the DataGridView from XAML

```
<!-- Window1.xaml -->
<?Mapping
  XmlNamespace="wfi"
  ClrNamespace="System.Windows.Forms.Integration"
  Assembly="WindowsFormsIntegration" ?>
<?Mapping
  XmlNamespace="wf"
  ClrNamespace="System.Windows.Forms"
  Assembly="System.Windows.Forms" ?>
<?Mapping
  XmlNamespace="local"
  ClrNamespace="HostingAWinFormsControl" ?>
<Window ... xmlns:wfi="wfi" xmlns:wf="wf" xmlns:local="local" >
  <Grid>
    <Grid.Resources>
      <local:People x:Key="Family">
        <local:Person Name="Tom" Age="9" />
        <local:Person Name="John" Age="11" />
        <local:Person Name="Melissa" Age="36" />
      </local:People>
    </Grid.Resources>
    <wfi:WindowsFormsHost>
      <wfi:WindowsFormsHost.Controls>
        <wf:DataGridView x:Name="gridView"
          DataSource="{StaticResource Family}" />
      </wfi:WindowsFormsHost.Controls>
    </wfi:WindowsFormsHost>
  </Grid>
</Window>
```

Notice that in Example B-4, we've mapped our local assembly and namespace into the XAML so that we could create our collection declaratively. With this in place, we can set the DataSource property of the DataGridView to this named resource with no special consideration for Windows Forms. In fact, as far as the DataSource property is concerned, it's just being handed a pre-initialized collection, which is what it needs to drive its data-binding implementation; it has no idea that the collection was declared in XAML and couldn't care less. It's not the case that every Windows Forms control "won't care" that it's being created in XAML, but sometimes you can get lucky.

 In general, you may want to avoid using the WindowsFormsHost for hosting Windows Forms controls directly. Instead, you'll want to create a custom Windows Forms User Control and use that as a container for your Windows Forms controls. This allows you the benefits of the Windows Forms Designer for visual layout of the Windows Forms controls inside the User Control and separates you from some of the limitations of XAML—e.g., its inability to set the value of a nested property (such as the SplitterPanel.BackColor property on each SplitterPanel in a SplitContainer control).

Limitations of Hosting Windows Forms in WPF

Not everything is as seamless when hosting a Windows Forms control in a WPF host, however. Here are some limitations you may experience[*] with the version of WPF available as of this writing (only time will tell if the WPF team is able to remove any of these limitations):

- WindowsFormsHost cannot be rotated, scaled, or skewed by a transform.

- WindowsFormsHost supports only Opacity = 100% and can be contained only within other elements that are Opacity = 100%.

- WindowsFormsHost will appear on top of other WPF elements in the same top-level window, although menus, ToolTips, and combo-box drop-downs are separate top-level windows and should work fine with WindowsFormsHost.

- WindowsFormsHost does not respect the clipping region of its parent UIElement.

- While the mouse is over the WindowsFormsHost, you won't receive WPF mouse events, and WPF's IsMouseOver property will return false.

---

[*] This list is based on an article by Deepak Kapoor and Nick Kramer entitled "Walking Through Avalon and Windows Forms Interoperability in Code," available at *http://msdn.microsoft.com/library/default.asp?url=/library/en-us/dnlong/html/avalonwinformsinterop.asp* (*http://shrinkster.com/6h4*).

- While the `WindowsFormsHost` has keyboard focus, you won't receive WPF keyboard events and WPF's `IsFocusWithin` property will return false.

- When focus is within the `WindowsFormsHost` and changes to another control inside the `WindowsFormsHost`, you won't receive WPF GotFocus/LostFocus events.

Even with these limitations, the ability to host an existing Windows Forms control in WPF can be a huge time-saver if you've got working code that you'd like to put to immediate use inside of WPF. However, that's only half the story; you may also want to host WPF controls in a Windows Forms host, which is what we'll discuss next.

Hosting a WPF Control in Windows Forms

Hosting a WPF control in Windows Forms is much the same as hosting a Windows Form Control in WPF: we need a host. In WPF, we needed a host that was an element that could fit into WPF but that also provided an HWND for use by the Windows Forms control. In Windows Forms, we need a Windows Forms Control–derived class, so that it can fit into a container's Controls collection. For that, we have the `ElementHost` class, also from the `System.Windows.Forms.Integration` namespace and the `WindowsFormsIntegration` assembly.

The `ElementHost` class derives from `ContainerControl` to enable the hosting of other Windows Forms controls. The element host knows about HWNDs, how to size and paint itself, and how to handle keystrokes and focus. As an example, let's say we've got a form all laid out in the Windows Forms Designer, as shown in Figure B-5.

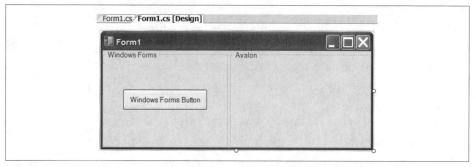

Figure B-5. A Windows Forms Form with space for a WPF button

In Figure B-5, we've got a form with two group boxes, one with a Windows Forms button laid out on the left using the Windows Forms Designer and one blank on the right, all ready for a WPF button to be added at runtime, as shown in Example B-5.

Example B-5. Creating a WPF Button in a Windows Forms application

```
// Form1.cs
...
using System.Windows.Forms.Integration;
```

Example B-5. Creating a WPF Button in a Windows Forms application (continued)

```
namespace HostingAnAvalonControl {
  public partial class Form1 : Form {
    public Form1() {
      InitializeComponent(); // group boxes created in here

      // Create WPF button
      System.Windows.Controls.Button avButton =
        new System.Windows.Controls.Button();
      avButton.Height = wfButton.Height -
        wfButton.Margin.Top - wfButton.Margin.Bottom;
      avButton.Width = wfButton.Width -
        wfButton.Margin.Left - wfButton.Margin.Right;
      avButton.Content = "Avalon Button";
      avButton.Click += avButton_Click;

      // Create a host to hold button and take up entire space
      ElementHost host = new ElementHost();
      host.Dock = DockStyle.Fill;
      host.AddChild(avButton);

      // Add host as single group child
      rightGroup.Controls.Add(host);
    }

    void wfButton_Click(object sender, EventArgs e) {
      System.Windows.Forms.MessageBox.
        Show("Hello from Windows Forms!", "Hello");
    }

    void avButton_Click(object sender, System.Windows.RoutedEventArgs e) {
      System.Windows.MessageBox.
        Show("Hello from Avalon!", "Hello");
    }
  }
}
```

To compile Windows Forms code with WPF added, you'll need to add the WPF assemblies to your project, including at least `WindowsBase`, `PresentationCore`, and `PresentationFramework`. Also, because you're integrating Windows Forms and WPF as before, you'll need to add a reference to the `WindowsFormsIntegration` assembly.

With the appropriate assemblies referenced, Example B-5 creates a WPF `Button` from the `System.Windows.Controls` namespace. However, since there's a `Button` class in the `System.Windows.Forms` namespace, too, you'll have to be explicit when mixing WPF and Windows Forms code. After creating the button, setting its properties, and handling its `Click` event, we create an instance of the `ElementHost` class. Setting the `Dock` property to `DockStyle.Fill` tells Windows Forms to take up the entire client area of the group box with the element host. Then we add the button to the host and the host to the group box, and we're all set to see our WPF button right next to the Windows Forms button, as shown in Figure B-6.

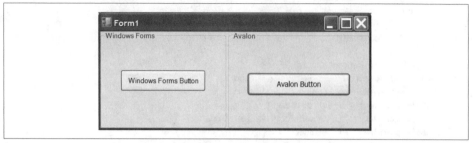

Figure B-6. A WPF control hosted on a Windows Forms Form

Figure B-6 doesn't show much benefit to going to the trouble of hosting a WPF control in a Windows Forms application, but we could update the code to use some of the features that make WPF special, as we do in Example B-6.

Example B-6. Creating a fancier WPF button

```
System.Windows.Controls.Button avButton =
  new System.Windows.Controls.Button( );
avButton.Height = 34;
avButton.Width = 159;
avButton.Content = "Avalon Button";
avButton.RenderTransform =
  new System.Windows.Media.RotateTransform(
    180,
    new System.Windows.Point(17, 79.5));
avButton.Background =
  new System.Windows.Media.LinearGradientBrush(
    System.Windows.Media.Colors.White,
    System.Windows.Media.Colors.Red,
    new System.Windows.Point(0, 0),
    new System.Windows.Point(1, 1));
avButton.Click += avButton_Click;
```

This gives us something a bit fancier, as shown in Figure B-7.

While there is not yet any designer support for hosting WPF elements in a Windows Forms Form, the code-based basics are still the same—i.e., setting properties, calling methods, and handling events.

Hosting WPF in Native HWND Apps

On the other hand, things can get a bit wackier when hosting a managed WPF control in a native Windows application, such as a raw Win32 application or an MFC application. The first barrier to entry is that WPF is managed .NET code, whereas your non–Windows Forms HWND applications are likely written in native C/C++.

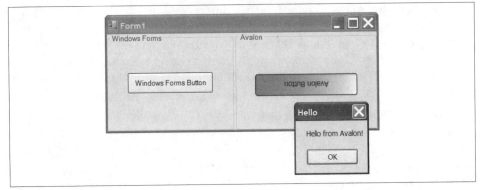

Figure B-7. A WPF button getting jiggy with it

There are various ways to interact programmatically between native and managed code—e.g., Platform/Invoke (a.k.a. P/Invoke) and COM. For example, one way to use a WPF element in a native HWND-based application is to host the WPF element in a custom Windows Forms User Control and use the support in MFC 7.1 for hosting Windows Forms controls.*

However, your smoothest interoperability experience is to use Visual Studio 2005's ability to switch your native C++ application to a managed one. For example, consider an MFC application, such as the simple one shown in Figure B-8.

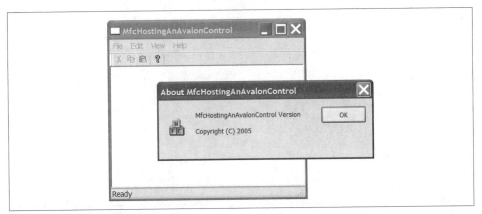

Figure B-8. A managed MFC application

To compile this application as managed code, right-click on the project in the Solution Explorer, choosing Configuration Properties | General, and set the "Common

---

* Hosting a Windows Forms control in an MFC 7.1 application is decribed in "Windows Forms: .NET Framework 1.1 Provides Expanded Namespace, Security, and Language Support for Your Projects," Chris Sells, MSDN Magazine, March 2003, *http://msdn.microsoft.com/msdnmag/issues/03/03/WindowsForms/default. aspx* (*http://shrinkster.com/6if*).

Language Runtime support" option to "Common Language Runtime Support /clr."
Compiling this sample MFC application and running it yields the exact same behavior as Figure B-8 (In fact, Figure B-8 is the managed version—fooled ya...) Once the application is compiled as a managed application, you can reference managed assemblies to bring in ADO.NET, System.XML, Indigo, Windows Forms, and, of course, WPF.

For example, maybe we want the About Box in our simple MFC sample to have some fancy WPF control in it. To start, you're going to need to add the WPF assemblies to your project. The simplest way to do so is to right-click on your MFC project in the Solution Explorer and choose References. This will bring up the project's property pages pre-navigated to the Common Properties | References section, where you can add the WindowsBase, PresentationCore, PresentationFramework, and System assemblies, as shown in Figure B-9.

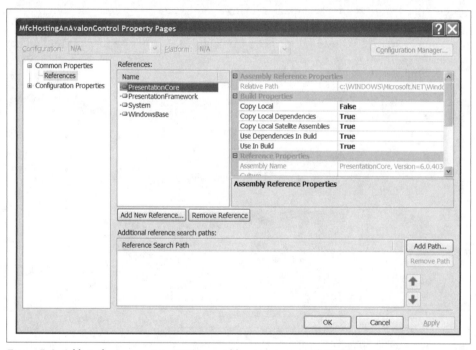

Figure B-9. Adding the appropriate .NET assemblies to interop with WPF

If this were a normal Win32 application, complete with a WinMain function, I'd tell you to add a managed attribute to it so that your main thread was marked as an STA thread, as in Example B-7.

Example B-7. Setting the UI thread to single-threaded mode

```
#include "stdafx.h"
...
[System::STAThreadAttribute]
int APIENTRY _tWinMain(...) { // MFC apps don't have these...
  ...
}
```

The STAThreadAttribute attribute is required on the UI thread for .NET-based UI stacks—i.e., Windows Forms and WPF. However, since MFC applications don't have a custom WinMain (MFC implements the WinMain method for you), that means you need to go another route to mark your entry point as STA-threaded. As of Visual Studio 2005 beta 2, there is no UI to set this, but you can specify the /CLRTHREADATTRIBUTE:STA linker option in your project's properties by setting Configuration Properties | Linker | Command Line | Addition options.

With the appropriate thread settings, we can now create a WPF control host suitable as an HWND child to host our WPF control. The host class is called HwndSource and is part of WPF in the System.Windows namespace. The C++/CLI code in Example B-8 creates a WPF button and hosts it in an instance of HwndSource.

Example B-8. Creating a WPF Button in C++/CLI

```
HwndSource^ CreateAvalonOkButton(
    HWND hwndParent, int x, int y, int width, int height) {
    // Create a fancy WPF OK button
    Button^ avButton = gcnew Button();
    avButton->Content = "OK";
    avButton->Background = ...

    // Host the WPF button in an HwndSource host and return it
    HwndSourceParameters params;
    params.ParentWindow = IntPtr(hwndParent);
    params.WindowStyle = WS_CHILD | WS_VISIBLE;
    params.PositionX = x;
    params.PositionY = y;
    params.Width = width;
    params.Height = height;
    HwndSource^ src = gcnew HwndSource(params);
    src->RootVisual = avButton;
    return src;
}
```

Example B-8 shows a helper function that uses the C++/CLI syntax enabled by the CLR setting we enabled earlier.[*] The helper creates an instance of a WPF button, then creates an instance of the HwndSource and populates the RootVisual property with the button. Using the helper function in the About Box's OnInitDialog method, we replace the native OK button with our managed WPF button, as in Example B-9.

---

[*] For more information about the C++/CLI syntax in VS2005, see the product documentation.

Example B-9. Hosting a WPF Button in an MFC application

```
BOOL CAboutDlg::OnInitDialog() {
  // Get position of the native OK button relative to the About Box
  HWND hwndParent = this->GetSafeHwnd();
  HWND hwndOkButton = ::GetDlgItem(hwndParent, IDOK);
  RECT rect = { 0 };
  ::GetWindowRect(hwndOkButton, &rect);
  // the violence inherent in the system...
  ::MapWindowPoints(0, hwndParent, (POINT*)&rect, 2);

  // Hide the native OK button
  ::ShowWindow(hwndOkButton, SW_HIDE);

  // Create and show the WPF button
  HwndSource^ srcAvButton = CreateAvalonOkButton(
    hwndParent,
    rect.left,
    rect.top,
    rect.right - rect.left,
    rect.bottom - rect.top);
  Button^ avButton = (Button^)srcAvButton->RootVisual;

  // Handle the Click event
  avButton->Click += MAKE_DELEGATE(RoutedEventHandler, okButton_Clicked);

  ::ShowWindow((HWND)srcAvButton->Handle.ToPointer(), SW_SHOW);
  return TRUE;
}

void CAboutDlg::okButton_Clicked(Object^ sender, RoutedEventArgs^ e) {
  EndDialog(IDOK);
}
```

After doing some pedestrian Win32 dialog math to find the location of the native OK button relative to the client area of its parent and hide it, we create our managed WPF button using the helper function and hook up its click event to a member function of the CAboutDlg class that closes the dialog just like our native OK button did.

The click handler is constructed with the MAKE_DELEGATE macro that VC++ provides to help map a native member function to a managed delegate. To make this work, we need to bring in the *msclr\event.h* header file and add a DELEGATE_MAP to our CAboutDlg class declaration, as in Example B-10.

Example B-10. Enabling the MAKE_DELEGATE macro

```
// stdafx.h
...
#include <msclr\event.h>

// MfcHostingAnAvalonControl.cpp
...
class CAboutDlg : public CDialog {
```

Example B-10. Enabling the MAKE_DELEGATE macro (continued)

```
...
public: // VS05b1 requires the delegate map to be public
  BEGIN_DELEGATE_MAP(CAboutDlg)
    EVENT_DELEGATE_ENTRY(okButton_Clicked, Object^, RoutedEventArgs^)
  END_DELEGATE_MAP()
};
```

The result is shown in Figure B-10, although hopefully the look of things will be more refined when WPF 1.0 is released.

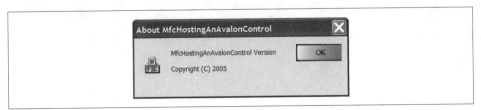

Figure B-10. Hosting a WPF button in a managed MFC application

One final note: while it's also possible to host HWND controls inside of WPF applications, custom HWND controls have largely gone the way of the dodo in favor of ActiveX Controls (and Windows Forms controls and, hopefully, someday soon, WPF controls).

WPF and ActiveX Controls

For hosting ActiveX Controls, WPF relies completely on Windows Forms and its ability to host ActiveX Controls. In other words, hosting ActiveX Controls inside of WPF is a matter of hosting a Windows Forms user control in your WPF form that hosts the ActiveX Control of your dreams.

If you want to go the other way, that is hosting WPF as an ActiveX Control, you can do so by hosting a WPF control on a Windows Forms User Control, as described earlier in this chapter.

WPF and HTML

Unlike ActiveX or Windows Forms Controls, WPF elements cannot be hosted directly on an HTML page—i.e., there's nothing to support something like Example B-11 in HTML.

Example B-11. WPF controls can't be hosted directly in HTML

```
<html>
  <body>
    <h1>Avalon doesn't support anything like this!</h1>
```

Example B-11. WPF controls can't be hosted directly in HTML (continued)

```
    <object
      id="avctrl"
      classid="avctrl.dll#avctrl.MyAvalonControl"
      width="100"
      height="100">
    </object>
  </body>
</html>
```

You can get around this issue again by hosting a WPF control on a custom Windows Forms User control. Or, if you've got a WPF express application as described in Chapter 10, you can host it as a frame like Example B-12.

Example B-12. WPF express applications hosted in an HTML iframe

```
<html>
  <body>
    <h1>Avalon supports this!</h1>
    <iframe src="MyAvalonApp.xapp"></iframe>
  </body>
</html>
```

The downside of this approach is that the WPF application cannot provide any programmatic interface—e.g., properties, methods or events—to the surrounding HTML as an ActiveX Control would.

To go the other way and host HTML inside of WPF is a matter of bringing either the COM or the Windows Forms Web Browser control into your WPF app and feeding it HTML. WPF has no direct support for hosting HTML, but the ease of Windows Forms hosting makes that your best bet.

Asynchronous and Multithreaded Programming in WPF Applications

If you like to write applications that annoy your users, a good way of doing so is to make the user interface stop responding to input from time to time. For extra frustration, you can compound the problem by not giving any visible indication that work might be progressing, leaving the user to wonder whether the application is busy or has simply crashed. Since you'll get this behavior by default if you don't take certain steps to maintain responsiveness, you can stop reading now. Unless, that is, you'd prefer *not* to irritate your users.

Unfortunately, for those of us who try not to aggravate end users, it's all too easy to write an application in such a way that it becomes unresponsive when it performs time-consuming work, such as accessing a server over a network or reading files off a disk. In Windows, all messages regarding user input for a particular window are delivered to the same thread. In general, this is a good thing, because it means your code has to deal with input events only one at a time and does not have to worry about thread safety. The downside is that the application can only respond to input if this thread is available to process it.

Many APIs are *synchronous*—that is, they do not return until they have completed the work you asked them to perform. (Such API's are said to *block*.) If you write a handler for a button's Click event that makes a synchronous API call to retrieve data from a database, that call will not return until the database returns the data. The thread cannot do anything else until that synchronous call returns, so the application will be unable to respond to any other user input for the duration of the call.

Even if you avoid synchronous APIs, you could still cause sluggishness simply through slow code. Code risks being slow if it performs either CPU-intensive or memory-intensive work. Slow CPU-intensive work is fairly uncommon—computers are fast enough these days that you need to find a considerable amount of work for processing to seem anything less than instantaneous, and only a handful of applications do this. However, excessive memory use is much more common, and it can have a drastic effect on speed, particularly once paging to disk occurs. If the OS has to load a page off disk back into memory, the amount of time this takes is long enough to execute millions of instructions. This only has to happen a couple of times before it adds up to a perceptible delay. Whether code is slow due to memory or CPU usage, running slow code on the same thread that handles user input will make the UI unresponsive.

There are two ways of solving this problem. One is to use *asynchronous* APIs. Some parts of the .NET framework offer asynchronous invocation, in which the API call returns immediately without waiting for the work to complete. For example, instead of using the Stream class's blocking Read method, you could call BeginRead. (The stream can call you back to notify you when the read operation completes, at which point you can call EndRead to retrieve the data.) Alternatively, you can use *multithreaded programming*—if you execute code on some thread other than the thread that handles input, it doesn't matter if this other thread executes slow code or calls synchronous APIs, because the input handling thread is free to respond to other user input.

Creating multiple threads in WPF works in exactly the same way as in any other .NET application. This appendix deals only with multi-threading issues specific to WPF applications. For more general information on .NET's multithreading facilities, consult the "Managed Threading" topic in the SDK documentation.

Using asynchronous APIs often results in the use of multiple threads. Although you might not explicitly create any new threads, you may be notified of the completion of some asynchronous operation on a different thread from the one that started the work. So regardless of whether you choose to use asynchronous APIs or multithreading to keep your application responsive, an understanding of WPF's threading model will be necessary.

The WPF Threading Model

Many WPF objects have *thread affinity*, meaning that they belong to a particular thread. Your code must always use a WPF user-interface element on the same thread that created that it. It is illegal to attempt to use any WPF element from any other thread.

If you are familiar with Windows Forms, you will be used to this threading model. If you are familiar with COM, you will recognize this as the Single Threaded Apartment (STA) model.

There are various reasons WPF uses this model. One is simplicity—the model is straightforward and does not introduce any complications for applications that do not need to use multiple threads. This simplicity also makes it fairly straightforward for WPF to detect when you have broken the rules so it can alert you to the problem

---

with an exception. There are also performance benefits—thread affinity avoids the overhead of locking, which is usually required with multithreaded models.

Another important reason for using a single-threaded model is to support interop with Win32, which also has thread-affinity requirements. (It is not quite as strict, in that it is possible to perform many operations from the "wrong" thread. However, such operations are often handled very differently from the same operations performed on the right thread, and there are numerous pitfalls associated with cross-thread window usage.) By adopting a strict thread-affinity model, WPF, Win32, and Windows Forms user-interface elements can be mixed freely within a single application.

DispatcherObject

You might be wondering how you can be sure which types have thread affinity and which don't. While all user-interface elements have this requirement, not every single type you use in a WPF application does. For example, built-in types not specific to WPF, such as Int32, do not care which thread you use them on, as long as you only use them from one thread at a time.

But what about types that are specific to WPF but that are not user-interface elements, such as Brush, Color, or Geometry? How are we to tell which types have thread affinity requirements? The answer is to look at the base class. WPF types with thread affinity derive from the DispatcherObject base class. Brush and Geometry both derive from DispatcherObject, so they can be used only on the thread that created them. Color does not and can therefore be used on a thread different from the one on which it was created.

 The DispatcherObject class defines a few members, all of which are exempt from the thread affinity rule—you can use them from any thread. It is only the functionality added by classes that derive from DispatcherObject that is subject to thread affinity.

DispatcherObject provides a couple of methods that let you check whether you are on the right thread for the object: CheckAccess and VerifyAccess. CheckAccess returns true if you are on the correct thread, false otherwise. VerifyAccess is intended for when you think you are already on the right thread, and it would be indicative of a problem in the program if you were not; it throws an exception if you are on the wrong thread. Example C-1 shows a method that uses VerifyAccess to ensure that it has been called on the right thread.

Example C-1. Use of VerifyAccess

```
public void Frobnicate(FrobLevel fl) {
    // Ensure we're on the UI thread
    VerifyAccess();

    ...
}
```

Many WPF types call VerifyAccess when you use them. They do not do this for every single public API, because such comprehensive checking would impose a significant performance overhead. However, there are checks in enough places that you are unlikely to get very far on the wrong thread before the problem becomes apparent.

If your application causes multiple threads to be created, either through explicit thread creation or implicitly through the use of asynchronous APIs, you should avoid touching any user-interface objects on those threads. If you need to update the user interface as a result of work done on a different thread, you must use the *dispatcher* to get back onto the UI thread.

The Dispatcher

Each thread that creates user-interface objects needs a Dispatcher object. This effectively owns the thread, running a loop that dispatches input messages to the appropriate handlers. (It performs a similar role to a message pump in Win32.) As well as handling input, the dispatcher enables us to get calls directed through to the right thread.

Obtaining a Dispatcher

Recall that all WPF objects with thread affinity derive from the DispatcherObject base class. This class defines a Dispatcher property, which returns the Dispatcher object for the thread the object belongs to.

You can also retrieve the Dispatcher for the current thread by using the Dispatcher. CurrentDispatcher static property.

Getting onto the Right Thread with a Dispatcher

If you need to update the user interface after doing some work on a worker thread, you must make sure that the update is done on the UI thread. The Dispatcher provides methods that let you invoke the code of your choice on the dispatcher's thread.

You can use either Invoke or BeginInvoke. Both of these accept any delegate and an optional list of parameters. They both invoke the delegate's target method on the dispatcher's thread, regardless of which thread you call them from. Invoke does not return until the method has been executed, while BeginInvoke queues the request to invoke the method but returns right away without waiting for the method to run.

Invoke can be easier to understand, because you can be certain of the order in which things happen. However, it can lead to subtle problems—by making a worker thread wait for the UI thread, there is a risk of deadlock. The worker thread may be in possession of locks or other resources that the UI thread is waiting for, and each will wait for the other indefinitely, causing the application to freeze. BeginInvoke avoids this risk but adds the complexity that the order of events is less predictable.

Example C-2 shows the use of the dispatcher's BeginInvoke method. This is a typical way of structuring code that is not running on the UI thread but that needs to do something to the UI. In this case, the code sets the background color of the window.

Example C-2. Using Dispatcher.BeginInvoke

```
partial class MyWindow : Window {
    ...
    public void delegate MyDelegateType();
    private void RunsOnWorkerThread(){

        Color bgColor = CalculateBgColor();
        MyDelegateType methodForUiThread = delegate {
            this.Background = new SolidColorBrush(bgColor);
        };
        this.Dispatcher.BeginInvoke(DispatcherPriority.Normal, methodForUiThread);
    }


    ...
}
```

We're using the C# anonymous delegate syntax here. You don't have to use this syntax—you could just put the code in a separate method. However, anonymous delegates are often particularly convenient in this kind of scenario, because you can use any of the variables that are in scope in the containing method. In this case, we are setting the bgColor variable in the containing method and then using that value in the nested anonymous method that will run on the UI thread. This sharing of lexical scope across two methods makes moving from one thread to another relatively painless.

The first parameter passed to BeginInvoke indicates the priority with which we would like the message to be handled. The Dispatcher does not operate a strict "first in, first out" policy, because some messages need to be handled with higher priority than others. For example, suppose two work items are queued up with the dispatcher, where one is a message representing keyboard input and the other is a timer event that will poll some remote service for status. The remote polling is likely to take a while to complete, so a short hiatus will not be noticed. However, even fairly small delays in processing user input tend to make an application feel unresponsive, so you would normally want the key press to be handled first. The dispatcher therefore handles messages according to their specified priority to allow those that are sensitive to latency, such as input messages, to be handled ahead of less urgent tasks.

The Normal priority level will be suitable for most jobs, but in some cases you may want the work to run as a *background* operation—something that will only run when there is nothing more important to do. For this kind of processing, use either the ApplicationIdle or SystemIdle priority levels. ApplicationIdle will not process the message until the application has nothing else to do. SystemIdle considers activity across the whole machine and processes the message only when a CPU would otherwise be idle.

The second parameter to BeginInvoke is the delegate. The Dispatcher will invoke this at some point in the future on the dispatcher thread. If we had used a delegate type that required parameters to be passed to the target function, we would have used one of the overloads of BeginInvoke that accepts extra parameters, as Example C-3 shows.

Example C-3. Passing parameters with BeginInvoke

```
delegate void UsesColor(Color c);
private void SetBackgroundColor(Color c) {
    this.Background = new SolidColorBrush(c);
}

private void RunsOnWorkerThread( ) {
    UsesColor methodForUiThread = SetBackgroundColor;
    this.Dispatcher.BeginInvoke(DispatcherPriority.Normal, methodForUiThread,
                    Blue);
}
```

Here, we have defined a custom delegate type called UsesColor. It requires its target function to take a single parameter of type Color. The delegate was defined to match the signature of SetBackgroundColor, the method we want to call. This method sets the window background color, so it needs to run on the UI thread. The RunsOnWorkerThread method isn't on the right thread, so it uses the Dispatcher. BeginInvoke method to call SetBackgroundColor on the correct thread.

However, there are a couple of differences between Example C-2 and Example C-3. One is cosmetic—we are no longer using the C# anonymous delegate syntax. The other is that we are now passing an extra parameter to BeginInvoke. You can pass as many extra parameters as you like—one of the BeginInvoke overloads accepts a variable-length argument list. All of these parameters will be passed into the target function on the dispatcher thread.

If you are familiar with the .NET asynchronous pattern, you might be wondering if there is an EndInvoke method. Typically, any call to a BeginXxx method has to be matched with a corresponding EndXxx call. But the Dispatcher does not use the standard asynchronous pattern. BeginInvoke has no corresponding EndInvoke method, nor does it provide a way of passing in a completion callback function to BeginInvoke, as you would expect to see with a normal implementation of the .NET asynchronous pattern. However, it is possible to discover when an operation is executed by using the DispatcherOperation class. This class also supports cancellation, which is not available in the standard asynchronous pattern.

DispatcherOperation

The `Dispatcher.BeginInvoke` method returns a `DispatcherOperation` object. This represents the work item sent to the dispatcher. You can use it to determine the current status of the operation. Its `Status` property will be one of the values from the `DispatcherOperationStatus` enumeration, shown in Table C-1.

Table C-1. DispatcherOperationStatus values

Value	Meaning
Pending	The dispatcher has not yet called the method.
Executing	The method is currently executing on the dispatcher thread.
Completed	The method has finished executing.
Aborted	The operation was aborted.

You will only see the `Aborted` status if you cancel the operation. An operation can be cancelled by calling the `DispatcherOperation.Abort` method. As long as the operation has not already started, this removes it from the dispatcher's queue.

You can wait for the operation to complete by calling the `Wait` method. This blocks the worker thread until the UI thread has executed the method. (This carries the same risk of deadlock as `Invoke`, for the same reasons.) Alternatively you can add a handler to the `Completed` event, which will be raised when the method completes. Unfortunately, this is slightly tricky to use, because it's possible that the operation will already have run by the time you get around to adding the handler. It may be simpler just to write your code in a way that avoids using either of these. Remember that `BeginInvoke` calls the method you tell it to. If you need to do some work after the dispatcher has called your code, just add that to the method, as Example C-4 shows.

Example C-4. Avoiding Wait and Completed

```
MyDelegateType work = delegate {

    DoWorkOnUIThread( );

    DoWhateverWeNeedToDoNowTheMainWorkHasBeenDone( );
};
this.Dispatcher.BeginInvoke(DispatcherPriority.Normal, work);
```

Of course, both of the methods called in Example C-4 will run on the UI thread. If the second method is slow, just use a suitable multithreading or asynchronous invocation mechanism to move it back onto a worker thread.

DispatcherTimer

Applications often create timers in order to perform housekeeping tasks on a regular basis. You could use either of the Timer classes in the .NET class libraries, but both of these would notify you on a thread from the CLR thread pool, meaning you'd have to call Dispatcher.BeginInvoke to get back onto the right thread.

It is simpler to use the WPF-aware DispatchTimer class. This raises timer notifications via the dispatcher, meaning your timer handler will always run on the correct thread automatically. This enables you to do things to the user interface directly from the handler, as Example C-5 shows.

Example C-5. Using a DispatcherTimer

```
partial class MyWindow : Window {

    private DispatcherTimer dt;
    public MyWindow( ) {
        DispatcherTimer dt = new DispatcherTimer( );
        dt.Tick += dt_Tick;
        dt.Interval = TimeSpan.FromSeconds(2);
        dt.Start( );
    }

    void dt_Tick(object sender, EventArgs e) {
        Random r = new Random( );
        byte[] vals = new byte[3];
        r.NextBytes(vals);
        Color c = Color.FromRgb(vals[0], vals[1], vals[2]);
        this.Background = new SolidColorBrush(c);
    }
}
```

By default, the DispatcherTimer uses the Background priority level to deliver notifications. If necessary, you can change this by passing in a value from the DispatcherPriority enumeration when you construct the timer. You can also pass in a Dispatcher. By default it will use the Dispatcher.CurrentDispatcher property to retrieve the dispatcher for the current thread, but you might need to pass the dispatcher explicitly if you are creating the timer from a thread different from the UI thread.

Multiple UI Threads and Dispatchers

It is not strictly necessary for there to be just one UI thread—it is possible for an application to create user-interface objects on several threads. However, all of the elements in any given window must belong to the same thread. So, in practice, you can have at most one UI thread per top-level window.

It is fairly rare to use more than one UI thread. The main reason would be if you need to host a third-party plug-in on a UI thread and the plug-in is unreliable. By using one thread per top-level window, you can minimize the damage should the component freeze—it only takes out one window rather than the whole application.

Each thread that hosts UI objects needs a dispatcher in order for those UI objects to function. In a single-threaded application, you don't need to do anything special to create a dispatcher. The `Application` class creates one for you at startup and shuts it down automatically on exit. However, if you create multiple user-interface threads, you will need to start up and shut down the dispatcher for those manually. Example C-6 shows how to start a dispatcher.

Example C-6. Starting a dispatcher on a new UI thread

```
ThreadStart threadMethod = delegate {

    Window1 w = new Window1();
    w.Show();

    // Won't return until dispatcher shuts down
    System.Windows.Threading.Dispatcher.Run();
};
Thread thread = new Thread(threadMethod);
thread.SetApartmentState(ApartmentState.STA);
thread.Start();
```

The `Dispatcher` for a thread is created automatically the first time an object derived from the `DispatcherObject` base class is created. All WPF classes derive from this base class. So the `Dispatcher` for the new thread will come into existence when the `Window` is created. All we have to do is call the static `Dispatcher.Run` method to ensure that messages are delivered to any UI objects created on the thread. This method will not return until you call `InvokeShutdown` on the dispatcher.

WPF will call `InvokeShutdown` for you on the dispatcher it creates for the application's main thread. However, it is your responsibility to call this method for any other thread on which you call `Dispatcher.Run`. If you fail to do this, your application will continue to run after all the windows are closed.

The `Dispatcher` requires that you set the COM threading model to STA. Although a thread's COM threading model is only used in COM interop scenarios, many system features rely on COM interop under the covers. The `Dispatcher` therefore requires the model to be set even if your application does not use any COM components directly. The call to `SetApartmentState` in Example C-6 ensures that the correct model is used.

BackgroundWorker

The .NET Framework provides a class that can simplify the use of threads in a GUI application. The BackgroundWorker class, which is defined in the System. ComponentModel namespace, makes it easy to move slow work onto a worker thread in order to avoid making the UI unresponsive. It also provides a very simple way of sending progress and completion notifications back to the UI thread. It uses the Dispatcher under the covers, but it provides a wrapper that is simpler to use.

> The BackgroundWorker can be used in both Windows Forms and WPF, despite the fact that these two technologies have different mechanisms to get calls onto the right thread. This works because the BackgroundWorker depends on the AsyncOperationManager. The AsyncOperationManager allows the way in which asynchronous operations are managed to be controlled at the application level. When a WPF application starts up, WPF automatically configures the AsyncOperationManager to ensure that calls are marshaled via the appropriate dispatcher where necessary.

Example C-7 shows the BackgroundWorker class in use. We start by attaching a handler to the DoWork event. This event will be raised on a worker thread. We can do slow work in this event handler without causing the UI to become unresponsive. This example also handles the ProgressChanged and RunWorkerCompleted events. Your code can cause these to be raised to indicate that the work is progressing or has completed. Note that you will not get ProgressChanged events automatically. First, you must enable them by setting the WorkerReportsProgress property to true. Having enabled them, they will only be raised if the DoWork handler calls the ReportProgress method from time to time.

Example C-7. Using a BackgroundWorker

```
partial class MyWindow : Window {

    private BackgroundWorker bw;

    public MyWindow() {
        bw = new BackgroundWorker();
        bw.DoWork += new DoWorkEventHandler(bw_DoWork);
        bw.ProgressChanged += new ProgressChangedEventHandler(bw_ProgressChanged);
        bw.RunWorkerCompleted += new RunWorkerCompletedEventHandler(
                                        bw_RunWorkerCompleted);
        bw.WorkerReportsProgress = true;
        bw.RunWorkerAsync();
    }

    void bw_DoWork(object sender, DoWorkEventArgs e) {

        // Running on a worker thread
```

Example C-7. Using a BackgroundWorker (continued)

```
    for (int i = 0; i < 10; ++i) {
        int percent = i * 10;
        bw.ReportProgress(percent);
        Thread.Sleep(1000);
    }
}

void bw_ProgressChanged(object sender, ProgressChangedEventArgs e) {
    this.Text = "Working: " + e.ProgressPercentage + "%";
}

void bw_RunWorkerCompleted(object sender, RunWorkerCompletedEventArgs e) {
    this.Text = "Finished";
}
```

When we call the RunWorkerAsync method, the BackgroundWorker raises the DoWork event on a worker thread. This means the DoWork handler can take as long as it likes and will not cause the UI to freeze. Of course, it must not do anything to the user interface because it is not on the right thread. However, the ProgressChanged and RunWorkerCompleted events will always be raised on the UI thread, so it is always safe to use UI objects from these.

The RunWorkerCompleted handler is passed a RunWorkerCompletedEventArgs object. If there is a possibility that your DoWork method might throw an exception, you should check the Error property of this object. It will be null if the work completed successfully, and will contain the exception otherwise.

Index

We'd like to hear your suggestions for improving our indexes. Send email to *index@oreilly.com*.

EventTrigger elements, 310
Exclude mode, 253
excusegen.cer, 357
.exe.manifest file, 345
Execute event, 96
explicit data source, 132
express applications, 340, 350–354
    browser hosting, 353–354
    changing locally installed applications
        to, 351
    partial trust, 351
    publishing, 351
        problems with, 353
    versus locally installed applications, 355

F

Figure element, 69, 73
fill period, 299
Fill property, 236
FillBehavior property, 299
FillBehavior.HoldEnd, 299, 300
filtering, 145
FindResource method, 28, 202
FindResources, 203
Floater element, 69, 71
    alignment, 71
FlowDirection property, 76
Focusable property, 93
FontFamily property, 65
FontSize property, 65
FontStretch property, 65
FontStyle property, 65
FontWeight property, 65
FrameworkElement, 272, 322
full trust, 351

G

GDI+, 228
GDI32, 228
Geometry base class, 242
GeometryDrawing, 270
GetValue method, 326
GetValueBase method, 326
global application clock, 292
global applications, 219
globalization versus localization, 220
GlyphRunDrawing, 270
GotFocus event, 93
GotMouseCapture event, 92
GotStylusCapture event, 94

graphics, 33, 225–282
    integration, 225–228
    scaling, 233
Grid panel, 18, 38, 47–60
    column widths and row heights, 49
    consistency across multiple, 56–60
    proportional method, 51
    spanning multiple rows and
        columns, 53–55
Grid.ColumnSpan property, 53, 54
Grid.IsSharedSizeScope property, 59
Grid.RowSpan property, 54
GridLength, 53
GridUnitType enumeration, 53

H

hierarchy, timeline, 289
HorizontalAlignment property, 46, 73, 74
HorizontalAnchor property, 73
HorizontalSlider, 101
HTML, WPF and, 407
HTTP-based applications, 339
HWND applications, hosting WPF
    in, 402–407
HWND, WPF and, 394
Hyperlink element, 13, 66

I

ICollection interface, 390
ICollectionView interface, 138
ICollectionView Sort property, 145
ICollectionView.MovingCurrentToXxx( ), 154
IDataSource, 148, 151
IDataSource interface, 148
ImageBrush, 234, 262, 268
ImageDrawing, 270
images, centered, 266
implicit data source, 128
index syntax, 308
InitializeComponent method, 9
ink events, 94
inline text elements, 66
INotifyCollectionChanged interface, 23, 144
INotifyPropertyChanged, 130
INotifyPropertyChanged event, 124
INotifyPropertyChanged interface, 23, 121,
    130
input gesture, 97
InputBindings property, 97
Int16Animation, 288

About the Authors

Chris Sells is a program manager for the Connected Systems Division. He's written several books, including *Programming Windows Presentation Foundation*, *Windows Forms Programming in C#* (Addison Wesley) and *ATL Internals* (Addison Wesley). In his free time, Chris hosts various conferences and makes a pest of himself on Microsoft internal product team discussion lists. More information about Chris, and his various projects, is available at *http://www.sellsbrothers.com*.

Ian Griffiths is an independent consultant, developer, speaker, and author. He has written books on the Windows Presentation Foundation, Windows Forms, and Visual Studio. He lives in London but can often be found on various developer mailing lists and newsgroups, where a popular sport is to see who can get him to write the longest email in reply to the shortest possible question. More information about what Ian is up to can be found on his blog at *http://www.interact-sw.co.uk/iangblog/*.

Colophon

Our look is the result of reader comments, our own experimentation, and feedback from distribution channels. Distinctive covers complement our distinctive approach to technical topics, breathing personality and life into potentially dry subjects.

The animal on the cover of *Programming Windows Presentation Foundation* is a kudu. Not to be confused with kudzu, a purple-flowered vine indigenous to East Asia, the kudu, native to East Africa, comprises 2 of the 90 species of antelope: Lesser Kudu and Greater Kudu. Both species have coats of a brownish hue, adorned with white stripes. Kudu males are easily distinguished from their distaff counterparts by their twisted horns, whose myriad traditional applications among African cultures include serving as musical instruments, honey receptacles, and ritual symbols of male potency.

Sanders Kleinfeld was the production editor and proofreader for *Programming Windows Presentation Foundation*. Adam Witwer and Claire Cloutier provided quality control. Julie Hawks wrote the index.

Ellie Volckhausen designed the cover of this book, based on a series design by Edie Freedman. The cover image is a 19th-century engraving from the Dover Pictorial Archive. Karen Montgomery produced the cover layout with Adobe InDesign CS using Adobe's ITC Garamond font.

David Futato designed the interior layout. This book was was converted by Keith Fahlgren from Microsoft Word to Adobe FrameMaker 5.5.6. with a format conversion tool created by Erik Ray, Jason McIntosh, Neil Walls, and Mike Sierra that uses Perl and XML technologies. The text font is Linotype Birka; the heading font is Adobe Myriad Condensed; and the code font is LucasFont's TheSans Mono Condensed. The illustrations that appear in the book were produced by Robert Romano, Jessamyn Read, and Lesley Borash using Macromedia FreeHand MX and Adobe Photoshop CS. The tip and warning icons were drawn by Christopher Bing. This colophon was written by Sanders Kleinfeld.

Better than e-books

Buy *Programming Windows Presentation Foundation*
and access the digital edition FREE on Safari for 45 days.

Go to www.oreilly.com/go/safarienabled
and type in coupon code S7JV-6DQK-SJB5-ILKN-EPIK

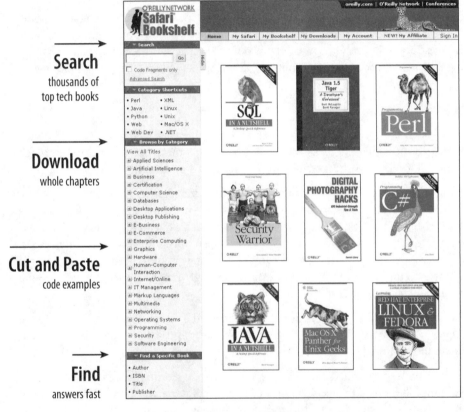